TEACHING WORLD RELIGIONS

Teaching World Religions

A Teachers' Handbook produced by the
Shap Working Party on World Religions in Education

EDITED BY
Clive Erricker
WITH
Alan Brown
Dilip Kadodwala
Mary Hayward
AND
Paul Williams

HEINEMANN
EDUCATIONAL

Teaching World Religions

Heinemann Educational
a division of Heinemann Publishers (Oxford) Ltd
Halley Court, Jordan Hill, Oxford OX2 8EJ

OXFORD   LONDON   EDINBURGH
MADRID   ATHENS   BOLOGNA   PARIS
MELBOURNE   SYDNEY   AUCKLAND   SINGAPORE
TOKYO   IBADAN   NAIROBI   HARARE
GABORONE   PORTSMOUTH NH (USA)

First published 1993

A catalogue record for this book is available from the British Library

ISBN 0 435 30330 9

93 94 95 96 97 10 9 8 7 6 5 4 3 2 1

Designed by Mike Brain
Typeset by Taurus Graphics, Kidlington, Oxon.
Printed and bound by
Thomson Litho Ltd, Scotland

Contents

SECTION THREE:
Further perspectives

SECTION FOUR:
Resources

THE SHAP WORKING PARTY
In 1969 a conference for those interested in the
development of world religions in education was
held near the village of Shap in the Lake District.
Participants came from a variety of religious
backgrounds and represented the full range of
education from primary schools to university. A
working party on World Religions in Education
emerged from this initial conference, taking the
name of Shap from the place where it was formed.

List of contributors

Vida Barnett is a freelance lecturer and writer, and Chair of the Council of Christians and Jews Education Committee. She is also a member of the Shap Working Party.

Margaret Barratt teaches at a primary school in Warwickshire and is helping with the Religious Education and Community Project based at Warwick University.

Andrew Bolton was formerly Head of Religious Education at an upper school in Leicestershire. Currently he is living and working in a Christian community in East Sussex.

Jah Bones is Co-ordinator of the Rastafari Universal Zion Project and a freelance writer.

Alan Brine is County General Inspector for Religious Education, Hampshire.

Lynne Broadbent lectures at Goldsmith's College in London.

Alan Brown is Director of the National Society's RE Centre in Kensington, and Schools Officer (RE) of the Board of Education of the General Synod. He is also a member of the Shap Working Party.

Erica Brown is National Co-ordinator for Religious Education and Special Educational Needs.

Owen Cole is a lecturer, writer and consultant in Religious Education. He teaches at the West Sussex Institute of Higher Education, where he was Head of Religious Studies until 1989. He is a member of the Shap Working Party.

Denise Cush is Senior Lecturer in Religious Education and Religious Studies at Bath College of Higher Education. She is also Chair of the Buddhism Resource Project.

Gavin D'Costa is a lecturer in Theology and Religious Studies at Bristol University.

Alan Ereira is an historian and television producer.

Clive Erricker is a freelance writer and Senior Lecturer in Religious Studies at West Sussex Institute of Higher Education. He is a member of the Shap Working Party.

Jane Erricker lectures in Professional Studies in Education at King Alfred's College, Winchester.

Joe Foster has been a member of the Bahá'í Faith for over 20 years and has served on several national bodies, including the National Spiritual Assembly of the Bahá'ís of the United Kingdom.

Bill Gent is an Advisory Teacher for Religious Education in Redbridge.

John Hammond is a Senior Lecturer in Religious Studies at St Martin's College, Lancaster.

Peter Harvey is a Theravada Buddhist and is Reader in Buddhist Studies at the University of Sunderland.

Diana Hayden teaches at Wigan Sixth Form College.

Mary Hayward is Deputy Director of York RE Centre, University College of Ripon and York St John and a member of the Shap Working Party.

Jim Herrick is the Editor of *New Humanist*.

John Hinnells is Professor of Comparative Religion at Manchester University. He is a member of the Shap Working Party.

Jacqueline Hirst is Senior Lecturer in Religious Studies at Homerton College, Cambridge.

Dilwyn Hunt is Advisory Teacher for Religious Education in Birmingham.

Muhammad Ibrahim is Head of Religious Education in Southgate School, London.

Dilip Kadodwala is Adviser for Religious and

Moral Education in the County of Leicestershire, and is a member of the Shap Working Party.

Sewa Singh Kalsi is a lecturer in Sikhism, Department of Theology and Religious Studies, University of Leeds.

Akram Khan-Cheema was formerly a Senior Education Inspector for Bradford Education Authority. He is now the Principal Consultant for the UK Islamic Education 'WAQF' (Trust).

Sajda Currah was formerly a lecturer in Primary Education at Bradford and Ilkley Community College. She is now a primary school teacher in London. She is also a member of the Shap Working Party.

Kim Knott is a lecturer in the Department of Theology and Religious Studies at the University of Leeds. She is also co-ordinator of the Community Religions Project.

Clive A. Lawton is Senior Assistant Director of Liverpool Education Authority, and a member of the Shap Working Party.

Carrie Mercier has taught in both primary and secondary schools in Britain and recently in the United States. She is now a lecturer in Religious Education at Westminster College, Oxford.

Brian Netto is Deputy Headteacher at Fulham Cross School in London. He was formerly Humanities Inspector in the London Borough of Islington.

John Rankin was formerly Principal Lecturer in Religious Studies at West Sussex Institute of Higher Education, and is a member of the Shap Working Party.

Muhammed Riyami teaches at the Priory School, Portsmouth and is Muslim representative on the Hampshire SACRE.

Piara Singh Sambi was a past president of the Leeds gurdwara and a founder member of the Central Committee of British Sikhs.

Atul Shah was born in Kenya of Jain parents and first came to the United Kingdom in 1980 to start his university degree. In 1986 he started the youth organisation Young Jains. He is also the founder editor of the *Young Jains* newsletter.

Kanwaljit Singh is Inspector for Primary Phase and Multicultural Education in Wandsworth, and a member of the Shap Working Party.

Dennis Starkings is a lecturer in Arts Education at the University of Warwick.

Malcolm Stern is a founding director of Alternatives at St James' Church, Piccadilly, a member of the Monkton Wyld Court Community in Dorset, and is a practising individual and group psychotherapist.

Lilian Weatherley is Diocesan Religious Education Adviser for the Diocese of Winchester.

Paul Williams is Reader in Indo-Tibetan Studies at the University of Bristol, and is a member of the Shap Working Party.

Barbara Wintergill is Professional Officer with responsibility for Religious Education at the National Curriculum Council.

Rashna Writer is a Zoroastrian. She worked as Research Assistant to John Hinnells for a year and the two have collaborated thereafter.

Foreward

There are two things about the Shap Working Party on World Religions in Education which are vital. They are reasons why I feel honoured to be associated with the group over the two or more decades since its birth at the Shap Wells Hotel (a former Stalag for German officers: what a transition!). One reason is that it is genuinely a working party. Its members past and present have done and still do a vast amount to promote its cause, which is the development of teaching on world religions in Britain and elsewhere. The other thing which I admire is that it draws in all levels of education. When I started in the university business there was a lot of snobbery, as though dons should not involve themselves with popularization, still less with secondary and primary teaching, or with other branches of higher education. The Shap Working Party set its face resolutely against this from the very beginning: all branches of education would be drawn together in a communal enterprise; and this rule still holds good. They are essential principles. What is the use of talking about problems in education unless you do something? And of what use is talking about education at all unless you see it as a whole?

The present handbook exhibits these Shap virtues. There are others, too: for instance, the need for a multicultural perspective both in content and in those contributing. We have contributors of differing traditions and from the different branches of education. The introductory material will spell out sufficiently what this handbook hopes to do; it will, I am sure, be useful to teachers – and this is the main criterion of its success.

The handbook also reflects something else which was less evident when the Shap Working Party was founded than it is now: that the world is plural; and that the global city has many sacred and not-so-sacred places. The fact is that young people (and not such young people) are faced with choices in their lives, whatever the gurus and elders say. In a way this is a glory: we are now living in a wonderfully open world civilization. But it is baffling, too, and there are entrenched generational and other conflicts. We need to resolve tensions, while preserving knowledge. We at Shap are concerned with education, and so ultimately with knowledge and empathy. I am sure this handbook will serve those goals. I congratulate the writers, and wish the readers well. We are all in the business of enlightenment.

Ninian Smart
UNIVERSITY OF CALIFORNIA

Introduction

This book aims to promote the teaching of World Religions in Education, which has been the purpose of the Shap Working Party for over 20 years. During that time the 1988 Education Reform Act and the introduction of the National Curriculum have changed the educational climate. This, together with developing plural social landscapes and increasing global interdependency create needs that have to be addressed by today's teachers and by the adults of tomorrow.

We wish to face these issues and to serve Religious Education by the study of the world views of different peoples and of the tensions which they experience. We are also concerned with the nature and development of children's learning. We hope that the handbook will inspire and inform teachers and that the effect will be to challenge, excite and enchant children with the rich visions of life that the different traditions have to offer.

The book is divided into four sections.

Section One provides an overview of the place of World Religions in the curriculum and addresses its relationship with other curriculum areas and important related concerns, such as special needs and spirituality.

The articles in Section Two analyse the methodology of World Religions teaching by addressing the perspectives of six faith traditions most commonly represented in the curriculum: Buddhist, Christian, Hindu, Islamic, Jewish and Sikh; and how they may be taught in the Primary and Secondary age phases. The term 'perspectives' has been chosen to indicate a concern with recognizing the distinctiveness of different world views and the need for teaching methods that enable children to learn in the affective domain, as well as with developing descriptive and analytical skills.

Section Three broadens the scope of World Religions teaching by looking at distinctive world views not usually included in the curriculum, and their particular concerns in relation to contemporary Western society. This includes an article on inter-faith dialogue and one recognizing the Humanist movement's interest in educational issues. We also intend the issues raised to focus the debate between the study of world views and values education.

Section Four provides the teacher with valuable reference material, including annotated bibliographies, access to non-book resources and addresses of religious education centres.

We hope you find this book both valuable and enjoyable.

Clive Erricker

Acknowledgements

We gratefully acknowledge numerous individuals and faith communities for their help, interest and involvement in the project, and Sue Bawden, Julia Jones and Jennifer Hickie for their secretarial assistance.

TEACHING WORLD RELIGIONS

SECTION ONE
World Religions in the curriculum

Introduction

In putting together this section of the new Shap hand-book we have had the following three aims in view:

i it should be of real relevance for teachers and, while it would not approach the pragmatism of the rest of the book, it should identify issues which teachers meet daily;

ii it should cover the range of maintained school education, so that the teacher of the pre-school pupil and the lecturer in a sixth form college would find it equally useful;

iii it should explore the overlapping and often confused areas of 'multi-faith' and 'multicultural' education, for they are not identical, though they may overlap in important areas.

We have tried to highlight some specific areas, like special needs and spirituality, both of which explore the affective in religion and rely on the experience, but often find expression in the framework, of religious belief and behaviour. Elsewhere in the handbook there are other aspects of RE, not covered in the narrative of this section, dealing with the practical application of theories in the context of the classroom.

Dilip Kadodwala
Alan Brown

1 Teaching World Religions in schools: methods and strategies

John Rankin

Introduction: setting objectives

There have been many attempts to define what is meant by religion. I remember Professor Ninian Smart saying of religion: 'Whatever it is, there is a lot of it about!' I will not attempt to tackle the question of definition here, but it is important that teachers should be aware of the complexity of the problem. It was Cantwell-Smith who especially drew attention to the distinction between a religion as it is practised and the ideal presentation of its propositions by adherents.

Sometimes the question is asked: 'What do Christians/Muslims/Hindus believe about . . . ?' The assumption here is that religion will consist in 'beliefs about' various things. In fact, adhering to a religion can be on a spectrum from the most gentle, scarcely conscious, adoption of certain customs to a ferociously conscious and deliberate taking-up of positions and practices. Where people locate themselves on that spectrum is the outcome of a multitude of social influences and conditioning. In homogeneous, religiously conscious societies, some of that conditioning will take place in school as part of the underlying assumptions of the school. In modern Western societies, and in British society in particular, schools also reflect their society, but there is no homogeneous religious assumption. The society reflected is complex, multicultural and open, even if there are pockets of population which appear to have commonly shared religious values.

It must be clear that schools cannot be used as instruments of particular religious conditioning – except in so far as they will help young people to live productively in a plural and complex society. The sole point of this introduction is to say to teachers that they need to decide what they are trying to do in RE. To what extent and in what sense are they engaged in trying to change or develop the existing religious identity of the students in their care? Is it legitimate to have any such intentions? What are the strategic objectives?

Understanding religion

Religion is so much a part of people's lives and has been so much a part of the history of nations that the need to achieve some general understanding of religion in the course of a school curriculum seems self-evident, and yet it is often treated as some optional addition to what really matters! Part of the content of education must include an understanding of religion – and particularly an understanding of how it is communicated. This applies to the whole age range, both primary and secondary levels.

I have already indicated another part of the strategic aim which I think needs to find its place in RE. It must be part of a teacher's function to help equip students to meet the circumstances of living in society and to become good citizens. It follows that the teaching of world religions has to be sympathetic. Part of the strategy is that our own prejudices will be examined and eliminated so far as is possible. At the very least, we will try not to pass on our prejudices to the pupils. It is, of course, logical and important that the RE syllabus should include the study of religions practised in the catchment area of the school and particularly in the context of the lives of the children attending the school. Sometimes this is not achieved, even between Christian denominations, simply because, for instance, children of Roman Catholic parents will attend a different school. The phenomenon of the religious unrest in Northern Ireland should perhaps have alerted us to the need for mutual understanding and respect. However, it is not enough to be aware of the religions practised in one's own immediate neighbourhood. We are all citizens of the world at a time of steadily increasing mobility and communication, and children need to be helped to prepare for life in a world of very diverse religious commitments.

So we are concerned to achieve a sympathetic understanding of religions, including both those which are locally represented and those which have been formative in the lives of people in the history of the world.

Developing perception

There is a further point to be made. Apart from the contention that religions are important existentially and historically, it is probably true that the understanding of religion involves developing certain perceptive faculties which are not totally represented in any other area of experience at school. Some would deny that there is any capacity to be developed different from those to be exercised in the study of poetry or music, for example. Yet these last do not propose in themselves whole frameworks for the interpretation of life. Whatever one's own view, religion represents a very widespread human activity, both at the personal and collective levels, and there is a need to take care that pupils do not lack the 'antennae' to tune into its significance. However difficult to define, part of our aim in RE is to develop capacities of empathy and of response to ideas which may not have a simple propositional content.

It is clear that in the course of pursuing this strategy RE will also be providing pupils with the information which helps them to decide on their own stance in religion. However, care must be taken that this is not the main purpose. The practice of religion remains always, in some sense, 'extra-curricular'. In this matter, schools must preserve their neutrality.

One last word in this section. The requirement for objectivity and sympathetic understanding should not mean that teachers abandon all critical awareness. For example, it would be wrong to encourage children to live in terror of an avenging deity, or to be unconcerned about the fate of others, or to be intolerant etc. There is no way that humane standards developed in our society should be overruled by the need to be sympathetic to any example of religious practice. However, we need, at the same time, to beware of stereotyping. It would, for example, be very foolish to take the Inquisition as the most typical model of Christianity in action!

Methods

Teaching World Religions requires the use of recognized teaching methods as for any other subject. However, some methods seem to correspond more sympathetically than others to the subject matter of religion.

Many years ago, Jerome Bruner divided learning into three 'modes'.[1] These are the 'enactive', the 'iconic' and the 'symbolic'.

Enactive

In the enactive mode, the learner is involved in 'doing'. Bruner's examples were drawn from learning mathematics, and all infant teachers know that, for most children, learning about numbers involves a preliminary physical involvement, an engagement with counters or the classification of like entities. When applied to learning about religions, it implies engaging in some relevant experience. When learning about the mosque or the church or the synagogue, the best method is to arrange a well prepared visit, in which the children's activities are foreseen. One reason why this method is especially appropriate is that visiting a mosque or a church or a synagogue is part of the actual activity of a Muslim or Christian or Jew. Care should be taken not just to bring back observations from the visit, but to experience something which is part of the normal activity in the building. So in the case of a mosque, perhaps the children could experience the sound of the call to prayer, or some reading of passages from the Qur'an. In the church, it would help if, for example, the organ was being played; and in the synagogue, if someone could show one of the scrolls from the ark. If adults were trying to learn about the practice of any of these religions, they would probably arrange to attend when actual religious ceremonies were taking place. That is an 'enactive' mode of learning. When it is not possible to make visits of this sort, teachers should try to re-create some authentic activity within the classroom, even if it is only to cook the appropriate foods for a religious festival.

Iconic

We use the iconic mode when we make graphs and bar charts and all sorts of diagrams. These are used extensively in teaching and, next to the enactive mode, they are most effective. It so happens that the iconic mode is at the centre of most religious expression, and learning to receive concepts in this way improves the understanding of religion. In the case of mathematics, diagrams are used to focus and summarize mathematical concepts. Often in religion icons are used to convey complex ideas which defy other descriptions; icons are often essential features of religions and not simply devices to convey something which could be otherwise expressed. A useful activity, therefore, is the making of models, especially if preceded by discussion on the reasons for each part of them: for example, the advent crown, the Christmas crib or the Easter garden; or the model mosque. In the cases of Islam and Judaism, there is a presumption against the use of images. Nevertheless, the layout of the mosque is significantly iconic, with the Mihrab marking the direction of Makkah. The synagogue has similar iconic features.

Using the iconic mode can also be pursued in the use of drawings or paintings. These can be used either as illustrations shown to the pupils or as part of their own creative activity. In most religions artistic expression is part of the historical experience. In Islam and Judaism there is a general prohibition against using human figures in religious contexts, but artistic creativity flourishes in other ways. In Islam, there is a great heritage of pattern design and calligraphy. In the Christian tradition there is a very rich outpouring of visual art of all kinds. Here, again, there is a degree of conflict between specific traditions, where the more puritan of the Protestant tradition resist the use of outward signs. The Hindu tradition is full of visual representation, and, while aesthetic considerations should not be neglected, it is important to discover the underlying meanings portrayed. Artefacts, too, are often works of art in themselves, but more importantly, they often convey something of the inner essence of a religion.

Under the heading of the iconic mode we should also include the rituals and ceremonies of a religion. Here the enactive and iconic modes meet. If actual participation is not appropriate, at least pupils can be helped to understand the representation taking place – for example, the bread and wine of the Christian Eucharist.

Symbolic

The third of Bruner's modes is the symbolic. By the symbolic mode, Bruner means the use of words. This is not the sense of symbolic most of us are accustomed to use. However, a little reflection shows that it is the most abstract of all the modes. Human beings have developed it to an extremely sophisticated level, in which all ideas and all entities can be translated in the symbolic abstraction of words. Language is the most used of all teaching methods, and even when we are using a different mode it is always accompanied by verbal explanations. We know from experience that 'words alone' are an inefficient mode of learning for the majority of students in school. Truth be told, it is probably inefficient for many adults, too! However, words are important to religions for many reasons.

The main reason is that an essential aspect of all religions is that they should be passed on. Religions do not consider themselves expendable: they are 'for ever'. So the effort is always made to pass on the tradition to succeeding generations. All developed religions have their sacred scriptures, and in three of them – Judaism, Christianity and Islam – there is an especial emphasis on the 'word'. In Judaism, the sacred Torah lies at the heart of all its teaching. In Christianity, Jesus is called the 'Word Incarnate', and the New Testament is endued with special authority. In Islam, the Qur'an is paramount as the 'Word of God'. So teaching with words, and teaching about the sacred words of a religion, chimes in well with the nature of religion as it shows itself.

So it is that these three modes of learning, the enactive, the iconic and the symbolic, not only point to a suitable methodology, but simultaneously reflect modes which are part of the common currency of religion.

Notes

1 Jerome S. Bruner, *Towards a Theory of Instruction*, 1961.

2 Approaching World Religions in the early years of education

Margaret Barratt

It is perhaps amongst those involved in the education of the youngest children that there remains the greatest degree of debate about dealing with World Religions within the schemes for Religious Education. The Education Reform Act and new Agreed Syllabuses now take them firmly into account, but teachers, who are mainly non-specialists, still feel a degree of uncertainty about whether children will be confused by ways of looking at the world quite different from that encountered in their own homes. Experience leads me to affirm that this will not be the case, if teachers keep good practice in mind in approaching this area as they do in approaching others.

Learning 'from' religion

We are unlikely to succeed, if we set out to teach children 'all about Buddhism' this term. Even if we could capture their interest, they would gain very little from such an all-embracing survey. The key lies in the word 'about'. It speaks of knowledge rather than understanding. If we set as our aim, however, to learn something 'from' Buddhism this term, we stand a far greater chance of success. Children's learning, whether 'about' or 'from' is, at the infant stage, a cumulative process, involving a spiral of repeated visits to concepts and material, with understanding gradually increasing and familiarity growing.

Confusion comes when a child is confronted with something alien, to which he or she has no means of approach. If we keep central to our thinking the idea that we must begin where the child is then, gradually, steps taken by widening his or her experience will lead to the new understanding we wish to give to the child. We will be asking him or her to explore one new idea at a time and presenting it in a guise where much of it is not far removed from something he or she recognizes as part of his or her own life. We are then able to keep clear the divide between what is a real part of the world, and what is a purely imaginative story.

From Buddhism, for example, we might take the concept of ahimsa, harmlessness, relating it to the care our children show towards pets. This might lead to questions about attitudes to, and treatment of, other life forms, and to the drawing of parallels. The introduction of a monk's water filter will then be a perfectly understandable thing. Tiny steps can indicate the possibility of sharing ideas with, and learning from, the adherents of a religion of which they possibly knew nothing previously.

Focusing on experiences

The key in early years education is first-hand experience, so we need to begin with whatever that experience is, to explore it, share it and find the points at which it can be broadened into new knowledge. Such new knowledge will be gained most effectively and most naturally by doing and talking, rather than by being told.

This needs to be borne in mind from the stage of planning onwards. The teacher needs to have in mind which Religious Education concepts he or she is hoping to develop, and this will influence the shape of the provision of activities and experience.

The usual context for early years learning is the cross-curricular topic, since young children learn from whole experiences. They don't distinguish subject from subject; they absorb information of many kinds from any experience with which they are presented. It is our task to make such experiences rich and focused.

Visits to places of worship are invaluable as a stimulus to learning, but there is little point in 'doing' the church, mandir or other place of worship without a particular purpose in mind. The purpose will be such as relates strongly to the topic in hand, the centre for the current learning, but also such as will build concepts in the child's religious education. Perhaps one valuable purpose would be to drink in a new atmosphere, a stimulus to awe, or calmness, with the absorption of the senses in stillness. Whilst finding out about 'Sound', such quietness could have impact as a contrast, leading on to an exploration of how sound is used in the setting of a place of worship: the bell at the mandir, the church bells, organ or other instruments, or the adhan or recorded call to prayer used in the mosque. A sound in a silent place is important. The child will experience it and want to know more. As Jake said, 'That bell was like a giant's teacup, so loud the children would even hear it at school. They want everyone to know the church is there, don't they?'

If you are simply looking at buildings, you will be working from a foundation of familiar buildings, and will probably want to look at where this place is like others which the children know, and what is different about it, relating back to solid understanding. Then the senses of children are employed in discovery, and the reasoning in raising questions: 'Why is it different?', 'What goes on there?': and in looking at the clues which the building, often empty when you visit, gives as to the life of the believers. The children will also notice such things as size, colour, materials etc., which have some bearing on RE, but which also link to other subjects.

If you visit the gurdwara during your 'Food' topic, you will build on what the child knows of sharing, through an encounter with the idea of the langar, with its shared meal and the thought that everyone can make a contribution. You will also meet with members of the Sikh religion, who thus cease to be strange and, through empathy, the door is opened to the next step into what is no longer 'the unknown'.

Not every school has the opportunity of variety in the places it can visit, be they places of worship or homes, though most are within walking distance of a church, at least. In this case use can be made of resource centres to give the children hands-on access to artefacts. A selected group of items could be handled in a 'feely bag' making sure that the selection is closely linked by a theme, e.g. items which might be used by a Jewish family celebrating Shabbat.

Wanting children to explore what arti was like in a Hindu home, we presented a magic carpet ride into a classroom, where every area invited us to use one of our senses to explore. There were artefacts to handle, pictures and garlands along with murthi to look at, incense and flowers to smell, bells to ring and tapes of chanting to listen to, and food and spices to taste. When everyone was familiar with everything and all of the comments and questions had been discussed, we assembled a shrine and used the area as a place to talk about things that were precious to us, making clear that such a place, full of precious things, is where a Hindu child might feel close to God.

It would be wrong to involve children in acting out worship without consent on every side, since it would imply an assent to ideas and beliefs not shared by the child. Simulations must be handled with a great deal of sensitivity, taking care that they make no assumptions as to the belief of the child, and that they in no way belittle actions which are full of expressed and symbolic meaning for members of the religion represented. Having said this, they can be very effective as a means of learning if everyone understands that we are 'pretending' and what happens is 'like' what would really happen.

Sharing experiences

On the other hand, celebrations have aspects which can be genuinely shared with believers. Festivals are occasions when such 'sharing' can take place. They require careful preparation if children are to learn as well as have a good time, but preparation is itself part of any celebration. The opportunities for first-hand experience abound. Sukkot normally falls around the same time as Harvest, which most schools recognize. It shares the theme of a God who provides, which links well with topics on food or in the natural world area. What child will not remember building a sukkah? It's like a glorious 'den'. You have to puzzle out what you can make it from (religious rules), and you could sleep under the stars if only you were Jewish and in a warm country (awe and wonder), not to mention the sharing of all sorts of fruit and new dishes (hospitality), with a story too for good measure. In contrast, the children can sense the solemnity of the ceremony with the lulav and etrog, and begin to develop an understanding of what symbolism is all about and the depths which make a festival more than just a party.

A careful choice needs to be made of festivals so that those recognized are relevant to the children's learning. In some schools, believers of any religion may be few in number and, in this case, the choice can be dictated solely by considerations of what experience you wish to open to the children. In schools where there is a representation of children with a variety of religious backgrounds, the choice is more likely to be influenced by the need to celebrate with the children, recognizing and sharing the experience they bring with them. This involves annual repetition in some cases. As teachers we try to include new experiences and activities year by year, but perhaps we need to be aware that the children often long for time-honoured custom. After all, this is a potent part of celebrating a festival in the home. We may learn from what a Ukrainian Catholic mother said recently about making coloured eggs (pysanky) for Easter: 'Every year we do it and I tell them the meaning of what we do. They can't explain it but they love to do it and, by the time they are 10 or so, they understand it all.' Learning is in doing, even though it's often unconscious learning. Children, then, need as many opportunities to share in activities surrounding World Religions as can be reasonably managed – even before they can fully understand.

Exploring the experience of other people

As the first choice, first-hand experience is to be preferred every time, but if you can't do it yourself, talk to someone who has. The first resource you have is a class full of children. Everyone has something to share and, for some, that 'something' will have content related to World Religions. It may be that a child has shared a meal with neighbours, been to a wedding in one religion or another, or attended a birth ceremony. We all puzzled about what the twins' new baby brother would be called when they reported that Grandpa said it must begin with 'He', and couldn't wait until they announced he was to Hemendra. Such unplanned information directed our 'Myself' topic into an investigation of names, what they meant, how we got them and who chose them etc. In that case it led to incidental learning, but by getting to know the children, really listening to their talk and watching their play, we can develop a bank of known resources for future use, from which we can widen into the experience of people of faiths not represented in the class.

It was a simple matter to get permission for Isbar to show us his prayers as part of a topic on 'Pattern' involving Islam. To be told how prayer is performed might well have led to incomprehension expressed in inconstructive ways, but to watch a friend, and to see its importance for him, was a very positive experience for everyone. This included Isbar himself who, as a lone Muslim in the class, had largely denied his background. Children asked questions and attempted to relate his experience with their own experience, raising the issue of other ways of praying and not praying. They also learned to show sensitivity and respect for what was precious in a non-material way.

During a 'Clothes' topic, in another class, Islam was approached through visitors. Hyder had had new clothes for Eid, but the children weren't sure what that was. It was decided that a good idea would be to interview a grown-up who could explain. The children were able to identify some Muslim mums and a dinner lady, and these adults were politely persuaded to act as a panel. The children devised questions in advance and asked them, quite formally on this occasion, finding out not only how local families kept the festival, but also about Muslim dress. Facts were certainly learned, but alongside that came the sense of how it feels to be a Muslim celebrating Eid, something that contact could teach, which mere information would never have achieved. We learned that there's no such thing as 'the Muslims' but that there is a group of people who, as individuals, share the Muslim faith.

The children now see familiar adults as a resource and will quite informally suggest that we could ask a mum or a grandpa when further information is required. Contacts in some areas may not be so easily made, but they can be sought through places of worship or multi/intercultural centres. Now that each LEA has a Standing Advisory Council for Religious Education, one of whose committees represents 'Christian and other denominations which reflect the principal religious traditions of the area', it should be possible to request advice on contacts from this source.

Widening experience through resources

It is not going to be possible to use human resources

on every occasion, and even where people are willing and available, they cannot be constantly present. This points out the need for materials as a second-hand source of learning and a background support to reinforce what children have found out at first-hand.

The best of such materials will be home-produced. There are the photographs taken by teachers and children alike on visits or during past events. Children love to go back over these, whether displayed or mounted into books or albums. They can also be used with future groups as a stimulus to questioning, or to seek information. By seeing children who are familiar to them involved in activities which are not, the children instinctively want to know what is going on. When children are involved in producing such a record for themselves, their discussion revives the experience and often their comments, made in the light of reflection and sometimes recorded by the teacher as scribe, produce an effective text for the book. There are also very good professionally published materials: posters, slides, books and videos. Slides are particularly useful, if of good quality, because the process of showing them is by its nature slow, unlike video, though the same effect can be achieved by freezing frames. By being selective it is possible to avoid flooding children with too much information at once, and there is time to explore the material, allowing each child to relate it to his or her own experience, finding similarities and differences and questioning without a text to get in the way.

With this age group, the most valuable books will be the ones that encourage the child to empathize with a character within the story. By bringing out points at which the experiences and feelings of the character will be similar to those of the children, the authors open up the opportunity for children to 'know' the story child and to want to share in those aspects of his or her life which are new to the reader. This can break down any feeling of this new family with its different lifestyle, beliefs and practices as an exhibit, encouraging acceptance of the unfamiliar and curiosity to try to discover what it would be like to be part of this new world.

Research currently in progress into the nurture of individual children in branches of the major World Religions will lead to more material of this kind. It must be seen as a tool for the teacher to use, involving the children with new ideas (the beginning of the process), aiming to stimulate the curiosity to find out more either by first-hand experience or by further research on the part of the children. It provides a point of comparison with personal experience and hence a trigger to reflection, demanding response. From this starting point, children can employ reading skills to approach reference books, at their own level, to enhance their knowledge; at the earliest stage, it will be through the pictures only. It must always be borne in mind, however, that the learning of facts about World Religions cannot ever be a substitute for Religious Education. If the child is not required to reflect upon what he or she discovers, nor to make a personal response to it in the light of his or her own life-experience, we might just as well be introducing him or her to the porridge ritual in The Three Bears as the point of that story. Knowledge is only the vehicle for the development of understanding. Personal encounter with ideas cannot be avoided if RE is to be effective.

Deepening experience through story and the arts

Another accessible route to the heart of religious traditions can be through the stories, music and works of art of that tradition. Children examining South American ceramic nativity figures were able to absorb from the curves some of the emotional content of the story they represented, as was evidenced when they used clay to shape their own models, gently and thoughtfully forming surfaces and folds as they shared the story with each other.

Pictures can represent a story to children, but they can also tell much more. They are invested with the spiritual and emotional expression of the artist and, in turn, they evoke an emotional response. We do young children a disservice if we underestimate the sources from which they can draw meaning. It may be neither our meaning, nor the intended meaning. It may not be possible for them to articulate it in words: but art's function is not to speak primarily to the logical faculties. One child, taken to look at pictures in stained-glass windows, later drew coloured patterns on a stone floor, but half of the picture consisted of a large cross in juxta-position. Her art provoked thought. Art can be used as a gateway into the symbolism of a religion; dance, too, has this function. Children can be encouraged to puzzle over pictures of Hindu deities, fathoming out a meaning for images which are not familiar, though they are attractive in their colourfulness. It helps sometimes to have engaged with a story as an introduction to a deity such as Ganesh. The picture will then represent a character who is not entirely strange and unknown, and will be seen as a way of finding out more about him. The symbolism can be developed in the children's own paintings, as they try to lay aspects of someone loved by them side by side. Equally, Indian dance movements become a means of expressing the deeper layers of a story. The movements of Natasha's arms and head, as she picked flowers for Prince Rama as part of a dance version of the Divali story, spoke to all who watched, and indicated her understanding of the story. Doing and knowing are brought together once more.

Stories have their own magical hold on the imagination, stirring the child to step outside into a new world. We can prevent this happening simply by interpreting the stories for the children. We can turn them into a formula by explaining that 'a' means 'b', 'c' means 'd'. Our efforts do the children no service. On the other hand, by open questioning, requiring the children to relate the story to themselves, to predict where the story might lead, to raise questions and seek meanings relevant to themselves, we can give children the means of unpacking the story at just those points where it touches their understanding of how life is. One child related the banishment of Rama and Sita to the forest, to the departure of a father on divorce; perhaps that child found hope in the outcome of the story. At least there was an experience to reflect upon. Stories need time for exploration and development in activity, for otherwise the children will know the words and not the story. The chance to re-tell, represent, act out or simply 'play' the story will bring the child nearer to its universal meaning as part of the 'story' of a particular religion than days of careful explanation.

Developing confidence

Children don't usually draw back from new experiences unless those new experiences seem threatening. They are, however, inclined to pick up the 'vibrations' from the adults around them. Teachers need to approach World Religions with confidence, for otherwise their uncertainty may rub off. For many primary teachers the lack of confidence is born of lack of knowledge, since all must teach the subject but few are specialists. Certainly anyone feels happier with material they feel sure of. It is wise, therefore, to begin with a small repertoire of what is firm ground, which will grow amazingly quickly by adding one or two more 'items' each term. It is quality, not quantity, which will achieve most. Good planning will ensure an appropriate choice of material, related quite securely to the topic under consideration, and suitable to develop the RE concepts which have been selected. The involvement of World Religions will widen the scope for fostering appropriate attitudes within the subject and give opportunities for the development of new skills.

The rewards from working with world religions will be measurable in terms of excitement and involvement on the part of the children. This, in turn, will give impetus to further developments. If such initial enthusiasm is generated in the early years, then a firm foundation for Religious Education will have been laid.

3 World Religions in the primary school

Lynne Broadbent

Before embarking upon world religions in the primary school – Buddhism, Hinduism, Islam, Judaism, Sikhism and yes, even Christianity, we should confront three 'existential' questions: What are we doing? How are we doing it? and, most importantly, Why are we doing it?

For nearly 20 years, in an attempt to reflect the changing social situation and in order to meet the needs of the pupils present in our classrooms, syllabuses and teachers alike have adopted a World Religions approach to Religious Education. The approach has given RE a certain 'content credibility', and a methodology which has moved from the study of Christian biblical texts to the exploration of current religious belief and practice, and has helped to refute accusations of confessionalism. But the 'why?' of teaching World Religions in the primary school must be more than a form of mere self-protectionism.

Two focal points

The aims in recent Agreed Syllabuses cite two focal points for Religious Education, one referring to the study of religions, the other to a reflection on human experience.[1]

In the first instance, pupils should acquire knowledge about and understanding of religions through a study of their writings, people, forms and places of worship, festivals and celebrations, and rites and rules. The acquisition of such knowledge is sometimes seen as a means of promoting understanding and tolerance in a multicultural and multi-faith society and certainly the Swann Report[2] acknowledged this pragmatic role for RE. However, RE must provide something more!

The second aspect of Religious Education requires that pupils should be 'enabled to reflect on and respond to human experience', should develop an understanding of their relationships with others in the personal, social, national and international spheres, and should focus also on the natural world, reflecting upon their place within it and their response to it. So there is a personal element to Religious Education, and here we have a link with the phenomena of religions, the writings, the people and the places of worship, for these are the result of a human reflection upon and response to existential questions and divine revelation.

With our two focal points in mind, we have a truly educational model for the teaching of World Religions in the primary school, one which contributes 'to the development of pupils as individuals and members of society', a society which is multi-faith and multicultural, by providing a wealth of material for the exploration of and reflection upon those questions which lie at the heart of human experience.

So, what should we teach? Should we aim to teach each and every world religion by the age of 11? Not only would that seem impossible, but it would be unlikely that such an approach would enable us to fulfil the dual aspects of our aim: there would be an abundance of knowledge, but little time for reflection! Certainly, our planning will include the teaching of Christianity, and Christianity as a world religion. This may mean a reappraisal of our resources so that we include images of baptisms in the River Jordan, as well as at the font; clergy who are black, as well as those who are white – and sometimes even those who are female; and Christians singing and dancing their faith under African skies, as well as those sitting or praying respectably in the village church. And when it comes to Christmas, let us beware of the glittering romanticized images of a blonde-haired, blue-eyed Mother and Child on cards and Advent calendars, and encourage our children to view and discuss African, Asian and Chinese images of the incarnation.[3]

Welcoming ceremonies, special places and a festival: all affect the individual and the community, and all can be explored within Christianity and within Judaism, Islam, Hinduism and Sikhism. In the primary school, World Religions will usually be approached through integrated topics, many of which will be instigated by curriculum areas other than Religious Education. Examples of beliefs and practices from world faiths are naturally included in topics such as 'Sound', 'The Environment', 'Journeys' and 'Water', allowing us not only to learn new information but, through it and along with those who have shaped the religious traditions, to raise questions and reflect upon our own life as a journey, or on our own personal relationship with the environment. If spiritual development is to be promoted through RE, it could begin here!

The inclusion of World Religions can also incorporate the National Curriculum cross-curricular themes and dimensions, suggesting a range of different lifestyles and challenging our stereotypical assumptions. In Judaism, key celebrations such as those of Shabbat and Passover take place in the home with women playing a major role. A topic on 'Homes' which includes reference to Jewish festivals thus lays foundations for discussion of gender issues at a later stage.

Two words of caution here! Firstly, a recent survey of religious education in primary schools[4] indicated that the 'central issues'[5] of RE were not necessarily those included in cross-curricular topics, and that the RE links were often tenuous, the example cited being the inclusion of the story of Jonah in a topic on 'Weather'. This is not only bad RE in that it trivializes the biblical story, but it highlights a second issue, namely the need to respect the integrity and distinctiveness of each individual faith tradition. The significance of 'Journeys' or 'Pilgrimages' is not the same across the faith traditions, within Christianity and Islam for example, and we should not allow differences to be blurred in our desire to include a particular faith tradition within every topic. Each religion must be seen in its own right and not manipulated to fit a 'topical' straightjacket.

Education for all!

How, then, are we to teach World Religions in the primary school? A religious faith is dynamic; its truth-claims confront and challenge adherents in every aspect of their daily lives. To present a purely descriptive model of teaching is, therefore, to misrepresent the nature of religion. To recount the stories of Jesus' birth, without explaining the lighting of Advent candles and Christingles as a way of conveying Jesus as the light of God, is to negate the message of the incarnation for Christians. To light the divas at Divali, tell the story of Rama and Sita, and not address issues of goodness and evil, is to deal in tokenism, not Religious Education. Religion is controversial! To hold an Eid party without considering the discipline of fasting, reading the Qur'an and daily prayer, is to ignore commitment and authority as central issues of belief and practice.

Religion is multi-sensory: it draws upon sound and silence through bell, prayer and song, potent visuals with icons, candles and statues, smells of incense, touch of rosary beads and tastes of bitter herbs. Religion is not just for the bright and the beautiful, the quick and articulate – it engages us all in cognitive and affective learning. An approach to World Religions involves us in a community experience of asking and sharing questions and answers; it involves us in visits to places of worship hitherto unvisited and encounters with people hitherto unmet. And it is these encounters with other human beings who have found 'their' answers to existential questions, and who 'embody' commitment and a sense of worship, which will be remembered long after the words are forgotten.

World Religions in the primary school? Yes, indeed. There can be no programme of 'education for all'[6] without a programme of Religious Education which takes cogniscence of and positively celebrates the religious and cultural diversity of each and every child in our classroom. It is an approach which positively affirms the value of every member of the school and the wider community. But more than this. An approach to World Religions in the primary school can engage us quite naturally in dialogue and reflection upon those questions of meaning and purpose, of relationship and response, which lie at the heart of our humanity and at the heart of religious belief and practice.

Notes

1 *Attainment and Assessment in RE: draft guidelines*, Bedfordshire County Council, 1991.

2 M. Swann, *Education for All: final report of the Committee of Inquiry into the Education of*

Children from Ethnic Minority Groups, Cmnd 9453,
HMSO, London, 1985.

3 *Jesus Worldwide,* poster set, CEM.

4 *Religious Education and Collective Worship in
   Primary Schools,* Culham College Institute, 1992.

5 *Implementing Religious Education 5–16,* CEM, 1992.

6 M. Swann, *op. cit.*

4 An approach to World Religions through beliefs and values in years 10 and 11 in a Leicestershire upper school

Andrew Bolton

The importance of beliefs and values

Our beliefs and values determine our future, what we shall become. We cannot be indifferent about them. At extremes the difference is between becoming a Hitler or a Gandhi or Mother Teresa. Different values hold out different futures for ourselves, our children and other people's children. Pan-Islam holds out a different future from Christendom. Communism has a different vision of utopia from Capitalism.

Religions and ideologies offer packaged value systems, a total way of life, a different pathway in history, an alternative evolution of humanity. It is no wonder religious and ideological wars are fought so ferociously. We have been fighting to determine the future of history.

So many visions of the future. So many contending value systems. So many different possibilities for humanity exist. Yet we have been given only one earth to share, one place to live. Is it possible for us, amidst this pluralism of contending value systems, to find a way forward together? Can RE help pioneer a peaceful future together for our pluralistic world? I believe it can, but to do so effectively some changes in approach are necessary.

One story of the need to change

This story relates to a Leicestershire 14–18 age range upper school which is a comprehensive in a suburb on the edge of multicultural Leicester. It is open to all young people within travelling distance, regardless of gender, religion, race, class, wealth, nationality, ethnic group or ability. It is also a community college, which means it is, in addition,

open to all ages. So it is an institution open to all humans, simply because they are human. We celebrate that fact!

In 1985, after teaching science, working in Japan and then doing an MA in Religion, I became a member of staff at the college. I joined a strong RE department with three full-time RE staff. All students aged 14–16 had two 50-minute periods of RE a week. However, at that time we were out of step with the pluralism of our city and the increasing pluralism of the school. The 'O' level and CSE courses were called Christian Responsibility and dealt with moral issues from just a Christian point of view. The alienation was clearly visible in declining student motivation and increasingly disruptive behaviour over the two-year course. About 66% of the whole year group took an exam, but 34% opted out and were difficult to deal with. Exam results were poor. In 1985, the year I arrived, there were just two students in the whole of the Sixth Form doing 'A' level Religious Studies.

In vivid contrast, the last four years have been a very different story. Students were engaged and classroom relationships generally improved over the two-year GCSE course. For the last two years we have had over 91% opt to take the GCSE qualification. GCSE results have been excellent, although girls tend to do better than boys. For the last three years numbers taking 'A/S' and 'A' level Religious Studies have reached 35–40 students. Exam results at 'A' level have been excellent, with several students over the last four years gaining places at Oxford.

Students are surprised that they enjoy RE. Comments include: 'I feel that RE gives me an insight into other people's ideas and views'; 'It is a lesson which makes me think'; and 'I think I have learned more about myself and what I think about God.' Parents are bemused, and then appreciative. How has this positive change come about?

Developing an approach to World Religions

My first year as an RE teacher in 1985–6 was like doing a probationary year all over again in difficult circumstances. However, I learnt a great deal and began to develop a gut feeling about what we could do to make RE more effective. A number of things started coming together for us.

It seems immoral to teach an RE course from just a Christian perspective. Not to affirm every young person's background and enable them to begin from there in their academic work seemed almost a form of child abuse, and an alienating insult to their family. GCSE enabled us to take the plunge by taking a multi-faith approach. From that very scary and hesitant step we have gone on more radically to affirm students in their home traditions and to enable each one to work academically from that inherited world view.

Developing Belief and Value Modules in the Leicestershire Modular Framework – a mode 3 GCSE

I believe that if RE is to be taken seriously in schools at Key Stage 4 it must have academic credibility. For me that means it must lead to a GCSE. This helps persuade young people and their parents that they are doing something that counts. It is also saying that the exploration of and reflection on beliefs and values should be as academically rigorous as any other part of the curriculum. However, our experience with Religious Studies GCSE highlighted some shortcomings. We needed an alternative.

In 1986 I had the opportunity to help begin developing Belief and Value Modules in the then new Leicestershire Modular Framework. These modules were written so that students could do coursework from the perspective of their home traditions, whether religious or secular. In fact, religious students could work from their particular religious community, i.e. Baptist, Roman Catholic, Seventh Day Adventist, Orthodox Judaism, Reform Judaism, Humanist etc. So instead of many students feeling left out by their religion or world view not being emphasised, every student can potentially be made to feel that their home tradition has value and can be used as a starting point for academic work. The modules also encourage students to examine another tradition in addition to their own, in order to develop a broader perspective. These GCSE modules are the only course I know of that so intentionally enables us to affirm each student's home tradition, academically, in its precise 'denominationalism'.

The modules produced cover many themes, from 'Pilgrimages' to 'Marriage and Divorce'. At least five modules have to be taken for a GCSE course. The ones we are currently using are as follows:

Year 10	Autumn Term	'Religious Meaning Through Stories'
	Spring Term	'Conflict, War and Peace'
	Summer Term	'Worship and Sacred Buildings'
Year 11	Autumn Term	'Marriage and Divorce'
	Spring/Early Summer Term	'Problems of Morality'

Teaching RE through Beliefs and Values Modules

Teacher use of a module is enormously flexible. We have chosen to spend about half our time having teacher-led stimulus lessons on the topic. So, for instance, the module 'Conflict, War and Peace' begins with lessons like the following:

exercises on aggressive, passive and assertive responses to conflict situations;
video on bullying;
a piece of literature on shooting prisoners of war;
a group work exercise on determining rules for a just war (see Figure 1);
a video on Hiroshima and an introduction to nuclear war;
an excerpt from the film *Gandhi*;
a look at culture and violence: the South Fore people of New Guinea and Costa Rica – A Country Without an Army;
a video on the arms trade;
a guided fantasy on emotions of anger, love, sadness and joy.

Figure 1: Students participating in a group activity to come up with rules for a just war.

These introductory lessons are intended to broaden student life experiences and stimulate reflection. Life very much sets the agenda for this introduction, and lesson topics that we know from experience will engage the students are chosen. Discussions and written work for these introductory lessons enable students to explore issues and their own developing beliefs and values.

The second half of our time in a module is much more student directed. Students are given a long list of questions from which they finally choose one to explore in depth. Questions include:

Is it ever right for you to fight?
Are nuclear weapons immoral?
Is religion a force for peace or a force for war?
Did Gandhi and Martin Luther King rediscover what Jesus really meant?

Students can also make up their own questions. With their chosen question students embark on a coursework assignment.

At the heart of each module, and thus each coursework assignment, is a learning process that can be summarized in Figure 2.

Skills in Identifying/Planning, Exploring, Expressing and Evaluating are actually assessed in each module's GCSE coursework assignment. At present the course is 100% coursework assessed, based on five in-depth assignments. The fact that students choose their question and how they go about answering it means that they take ownership of both the assignment and the learning process. It means relevance and thus motivation is maximized from an individual student's point of view. It means, in this RE course, that thinking and research are emphasized more than acquiring knowledge. It means that a GCSE coursework assignment is more like a mini-PhD that merely learning a catalogue of facts about a religion. It means that assessment is based on coursework demonstration of scholarship skills, rather than on merely learning and

1 EXPERIENCING LIFE
Especially in the spiritual and moral dimensions.
Identifying and planning a life question to explore.

4 EVALUATING
Looking back over the process just gone through to see what could be improved next time. Also reviewing what can be applied personally to the student's own life.

2 EXPLORING
Researching to find out more about a life question, including what the student's own religious or secular tradition has to say about it. Look at one other tradition, at least.

3 EXPRESSING
Communicate insights and answers to a life question with careful consideration of evidence before coming to a conclusion.

Figure 2: *The learning process at the heart of each module*

remembering facts for a terminal examination.

I think it is very important that the students learn and practise the process of scholarship. There is a knowledge explosion in what is known and understood about religions and ideologies. It is a waste of time to stress learning facts about religion for some terminal examination: they can be looked up if you have research skills. What is far more important is helping young people learn some effective skills for exploring religious and ideological communities. This potentially opens the door to the possibility of a lifetime of exploration and reflection. Furthermore, the young person is able to direct and control his or her own exploration. It is the very opposite of indoctrination.

Developing resources for student coursework assignments

Developing resources so that students can do their coursework assignment has been very important. The student's own family is one of the first resources available to the student. For students coming from faith backgrounds, their own religious community is also available. The students also have each other to interview or survey.

A lot of hard work by teachers has gone into researching and producing sheets on different religious attitudes to war, capital punishment, marriage, worship etc. However, whilst giving students a start, they are not ideal, in that they are 'secondary' sources of information. Many text books are, unfortunately, also in this category. It has been our goal, wherever possible, to find authentic 'primary' source materials from particular religions and ideologies which students can then use in the classroom. This takes time, but once you begin, you are always on the look-out.

We have recently begun to find and invite people to come and be interviewed by the students themselves. So, for instance, we have had a real pluralism of guests who came to be interviewed by students doing the 'Conflict, War and Peace' module: a local independent Evangelical minister who was willing to defend the 'Just War' theory; the mother of a student in the school, an informed Muslim, on 'Jihad' (she broke many stereotypes and was excellent with students); a colonel, in full army uniform, to explain the army's view (students were surprised to find that he was against nuclear weapons); a person who has a politics degree and is well read on Christian Anabaptism, who came as a committed pacifist.

Letter-writing to religious communities and other organizations is encouraged, so address lists have been produced and made available to students. Our local MP is an excellent correspondent and always answers student letters. He is often controversial but never boring! Here, Citizenship Education overlaps with RE. A young person who finds that he or she can write to and get a reply from an MP on some moral question is empowered to write later as an adult voter.

When we do the 'Worship and Sacred Buildings' module in the Summer Term, the whole module comes to life, as each class actually visits two places of worship. It is not an easy task to arrange these visits for about 330 Year 10 students all in one week, but it is worth it.

In all our resourcing we want to stress the integrity of each religious community or ideological tradition and, wherever possible, let informed and representative 'believers' speak for themselves, either directly or through their own materials.

Developing a student-centred philosophy

In brief, we are attempting to move away from religion-centred RE to student-centred RE. The emphasis in Religious Education swings from Religion to Education. Put another way, using John Hull's wonderful words, RE becomes 'Religion in the service of the child'.[1]

The differences between student-centred RE and religion-centred RE/RS is set out in Table 1. The differences are, in a sense, polarized in order to emphasize some important points.

This student-centred philosophy is one of the most helpful tools to the teaching of World Religions. It enables variety to thrive and affirms each student in his or her inherited world view. It reminds me always to emphasize the worth and integrity of each young person. It enables exploration and development of rigorous skills of scholarship. Its relevance brings partnership and democracy to the classroom. The

Table 1: The difference between student-centred and religion-centred RE/RS

Student-centred RE	Religion-centred RE/RS
The young person is the first consideration.	Religion is the first consideration.
Exploration of meaning, purpose and values beginning from the student's point of view.	Importance of knowing and understanding facts, with some evaluation of them.
Emphasizes thinking.	Emphasizes knowledge.
Process of learning emphasized in syllabus and assessment.	Content emphasized in syllabus and assessment.
Life sets the agenda for the RE curriculum. Students find relevance easy to see.	Religion, generally at second-hand, abstract and generalized, sets the agenda.
Accepts and uses each student's inherited world view, whether religious or secular. Students feel free to go on to explore other world views.	Only one to three major faiths taught.
30 lessons going on in each class (as many as there are students).	One 'official' lesson going on in each class. Many students find their inherited world view devalued by not being included. They and their parents become alienated.
Fosters democracy in the classroom. Emphasis on giving students freedom and responsibility to learn. So the teacher becomes a facilitator of good human relationships and an organizer of student-accessible resources.	Emphasis on teacher teaching. Teacher tied to a content-based syllabus that restricts freedom and which has to be ploughed through for a terminal exam. Can tend to be authoritarian to control resentful students.
Students challenged and enjoy RE because it is relevant. Parents pleasantly surprised.	Students frequently alienated and turned off. Parents not surprised.
RE moves into the heart of the school.	RE/RS marginalized in school.

modular GCSE course we have been following enables us, more than any other course I know, to develop a student-centred approach.

It is very important to stress that a student-centred approach is not at all a soft option for the teacher. It means better organization, a lot of work in resourcing, an increase in the marking load, the developing further of human relationship skills. It means being thorough about teacher self-evaluation. Anonymous feedback from students is sought at least once a term and through a comprehensive end-of-course questionnaire. The teacher is also open to feedback at other times. I want to be continuously open to improving and adapting what I do as a teacher with each class of unique young people. Every time I become over-confident and feel I have it 'sussed' my bubble is burst by students, the like of whom I have never met before! Far more is demanded of a teacher as an academic and as a person in a successful student-centred approach. It is also more demanding on the students. In my experience they find themselves working harder and having more responsibility. The teacher who dictates notes, or who has students copying from a chalk board in preparation for a content-based exam, is operating at a far less demanding and far less skilled level of teaching. His or her students are also operating at a far lower level.

Why work harder and use a student-centred approach? I find great satisfaction in increased student involvement and personal growth. It is satisfying to have a sense of integrity about how young people and their family traditions are respected and honoured. I really enjoy helping young people become better at skills of scholarship. To find a way of enabling mixed ability classes to thrive is a real achievement. Best of all, there are far better relationships in the classroom, and they improve rather than get worse, over the two-year course. It is to this aspect of quality human relationships that I now turn.

Quality human relationships

For really good RE, especially pluralistic RE, quality human relationships in the classroom are needed. At the beginning of the two-year GCSE course, I and some of my colleagues give six lessons that lead to a classroom contract. These lessons can set an ethos, an atmosphere that enables us to begin building quality relationships during the two years. An example of a negotiated classroom contract is given below; only the last point was suggest by the teacher:

Partnership contract
1 Co-operate with each other.
2 Listen to each other (don't speak when someone is talking to the whole class).
3 Help each other.
4 Don't distract people.
5 Be able to say what you think honestly without being put down/laughed at.
6 Don't leave people out.
7 Help each other to be confident.
8 No sarcastic comments.
9 Work towards a GCSE in RE.

What is the effect of quality human relationships and the fostering of student-centred learning? One student wrote this in his self-assessment: 'In RE I have enjoyed the freedom that we were given, which made me more independent and aware. I have achieved a lot in lessons, the main thing I have learnt is that you can learn without the teacher being strict.'

Working with parents

Our approach has been one that clearly wants to affirm the family tradition(s) of each student. However, it is very important to communicate this philosophy at the beginning of the RE course to both students and parents. One way we do this is through a leaflet outlining the course and our philosophy, which we send home and have each parent sign and return with any comments they might have. Parents' evenings are another opportunity to communicate our philosophy of respecting the integrity of each family's world view. We work hard at making sure that lines of communication are open at other times. We have much to learn from parents.

A vision of community

The task of the RE teacher in the classroom is to facilitate a community with the students in all their pluralism and, together, to discuss and explore those values which lead to wholeness of the individual and help us live in peace together. If it is possible for the RE teacher to help students experience genuine community, at least in their RE lessons, then that might become more intentional in the school, in the wider society and in our world.

Thus, it is important that RE teachers in all our schools help students to learn about the beliefs and values of others and to reflect on their own. A student-centred approach helps do this well. It enables pluralism to be celebrated. It enables young people to learn the process of rigorous scholarship. It enables young people to take ownership of the valuing process. It enables young people to discover, in quality human relationships, their own humanity and the humanity of each other.

I used to teach science. For me, teaching RE which uses a World Religions approach is far more important than teaching science. Beliefs and values determine our future, determine how we use science and technology, determine whether we end in nuclear holocaust or create a world where every child and youngster can grow up whole and unafraid. Teaching World Religions, especially through a student-centred approach, can help them and us choose our future. That is why RE is the most important subject in the curriculum.

Note

1   John Hull, *A Gift to the Child: RE in the primary school – a teacher's source book*, Simon and Schuster Education, 1991, page 7.

5   Teaching World Religions in the 16–19 age range

Diana Hayden

'The study of people with opinions by people with opinions'

This is one useful way of thinking about what students in the 16–19 age range are doing when they study religion, especially when the students in question are also studying 'A' levels in their chosen subjects. It emphasizes that the students have a level of intellectual development worthy of respect which should not be patronized (but often seemingly is) by the courses offered to them, and that in studying the views of others they are necessarily reflecting on their own. This lays down the first rule of engagement in the learning process: since having opinions is a shared human activity, fair play, let alone the demands of intellectual integrity, requires that any criticism of the basis of an opinion, and of the freedom to express it or act upon it, must involve self-criticism. The programme of study must, therefore, be very self-conscious.

That self-consciousness begins with the students' understanding of what they are studying and why. Given that there is already some suspicion of the teacher's purpose in teaching, accusations of irrelevance, even of indoctrination, are invited by a course with a hidden agenda. For that reason alone, the aims of the course need to be shared with the students and, where possible, negotiated with them.

This engages them in the learning process and puts into practice another of the rules for dealing with opinions, beliefs and prejudices, which will be followed throughout the course: the rule of respect for the views people hold. If our method of study has no respect for our students' opinions, how can we expect them to treat the views of others as deserving respect?

What our students understand religion to be is also vital. There seems to be a great nonsense in leading students into looking at a particular aspect of a particular religion without knowing what it is they think they are studying, and yet if our subject of study is a religion, or perhaps two religions, then the issue of what religion actually is can be lost in mere description of behaviour and points of view. By focusing on that issue we gain both a framework for the course and a method of study, as the students express what they understand religion to be, and the investigation operates with that point of view in mind.

Inevitably, some points of view will be very negative. Consider the opinion that religion is a belief system opposed by, and largely discredited by, science. Remembering that many post-16 students studying religion will be scientists by curriculum choice, we may expect at least some to articulate or accept this view, providing us with both a subject for study and a resource. To explore it we need to identify some of the particular religious beliefs in question and to challenge the assumptions about what it is the religions are expecting people to believe.

We could begin by demolishing a myth: the myth that religious believers live by faith while others live by knowledge. The place of 'faith' in everyday life is something many students are unlikely to recognize. Some, in fact, can respond aggressively to the suggestion that their behaviour is influenced by beliefs, as if they have been accused of some intellectual crime. To recognize that we are all living as if certain things are true, or valuable, or right, and that in some sense acts of faith litter our day-to-day life, is to raise the status of life-influencing beliefs to the point where their power, if not their truth, is worthy of respect. That is a good starting point for the study of all such beliefs and the ways of living based on them.

Disbelief is also a subject for study

When young people are dismissive of religion, it is both interesting and salutary to ask what it is they are rejecting. To ask what 'god' they do not believe in, to ask why they find the idea of angels ridiculous, or dismiss life after death as fantasy, is often to reveal a level of understanding barely beyond the nursery; they can say the words but have no real grasp of the concepts involved. We are dealing with fundamental religious concepts here, like soul, revelation, heaven and hell, which are easily investigated through many religious traditions. Simplistic understanding of what religious people believe can be found in generalizations like 'Jews and Christians believe that God created the world in six days.' There is a fascination for some in understanding how such beliefs are still possible in today's scientific world, but, in addition, if the assumption is that all Christians and Jews believe this, then we as educators have a great deal of work to do simply to raise the level of awareness about the content of religious belief, let alone its basis and its relationship with the observations and interpretations of science.

A special way of seeing things

A second and generally less well articulated view of religion may be that it is an attitude to or appreciation of life which involves a special way of seeing things or taking things. For example, one person may see nature as the expression of the personality of a creator, while another finds it purely mechanical; and some will find life purposeful and fair, while others find it meaningless and arbitrary.

The emphasiz here is on interpretation rather than observation, and on general attitudes rather than specific beliefs. If we are going to study religion in this sense, then its natural parallels are found in the musical and artistic appreciation of our students, and in their differing senses of humour. All of these involve individual human beings sharing a common experience but each responding to it in a different, and arguably correct, way. To object that looking at religion in this light reduces it to a matter of taste is to trivialize the personal and passionate investment people make in their own way of seeing things, which can be clearly illustrated in the aggression with which the more articulate students defend their own points of view.

By examining what could be termed a religious appreciation of life, the students are exploring the issue of 'truth' in religion, and at the same time the origin and basis of all points of view, including their own. The theory of this may make it sound far beyond the understanding of the majority of students, yet it is an obvious fact of life that different people respond differently to the world around them. For those interested in people, these differences are mysterious and deserving of investigation, and it need be only a relatively small class for us to be able to find in it concrete examples of how, while we all appear to live in the same world, each individual has a unique perspective on it.

With the study slanted in this way the students become the most important resource available to the teacher, as they reflect on their own experience in order to understand the experience of others. If, and it is a very big 'if', the students are able to reflect on their own feelings, including their hopes, fears, sense of inadequacy, motives and inspiration, then they are able to begin to reflect on the feelings of others. The lack of vocabulary, coherence and confidence in expression of feelings often found at this level, however, suggests that our first aim will have to concentrate on equipping the students with the tools necessary for such study.

As well as being inward-looking, the process should enrich the students by adding to their awareness of the kinds of experience human beings have. The kind of subject matter relevant here is very varied. We could centre on some of the seminal religious experiences from which various traditions take inspiration to explore the possibility of spiritual blindness in non-believers. We could be looking at the writings of those who have tried to put their own God-consciousness into words, trying to make sense out of their experience by relating it to our own, while at the same time reflecting on the inadequacy of this as a way of achieving empathy and understanding. It would also be relevant to consider the perspective of a tradition which sees the need to have, hold on to and defend 'our own' point of view, as a source of suffering which we inflict unnecessarily upon ourselves. This can be used to contrast starkly with the conviction of possessing the truth which we find elsewhere, and the sheer urgency of the need to convince others of that truth which others experience.

Religion: a way of living as a way of thinking?

A third approach would consider religion as a way of living rather than a way of thinking. This is the public face of religion, and there is always a danger that, when we examine it, mere description will replace understanding of what it means to be a believer. Many students at this level are quite capable of appreciating that there are different qualities of action, from the purely mechanical to the intensely personal, and many will have participated in religious activity at the purely mechanical level. It is worth remembering that we are often in the position of asking young people to understand that the ritual they have taken part in reluctantly ranks as one of the most important and distinctive activities in the lives of others.

Much religious activity, be it ritual, tradition or ethical conduct, can be seen as imitation of special people. Understanding this gives us a context in which the lives of such special people might be studied, by emphasizing the purpose and value of such work. If we lose sight of this purpose, we could

well lose our way, and our students' interest, in a mass of historical and biographical information which is of only secondary value in understanding religion itself.

The importance of imitating an ideal also provides one context for the study of the authority of scripture or other religious writings. Understanding of the differing beliefs within the same religion about the nature and authority of scripture is necessary for an understanding of the different decisions reached on issues of belief and practice; and if we are to keep our focus on the living religion of believers, then it will be much more important to investigate the decision-making process they go through in order to arrive at their point of view than to be able to list the variety of views which result. Knowing that other people disagree with you is easy. Understanding why they disagree with you, and why you cannot both be right but both of you think you are, is much more difficult and much more worthwhile.

The emphasiz on the value of the individual, and individual opinion, in an approach of this nature requires the course not only to be neutral in matters of religious truth, but also to be almost anarchic in its attitude to authority – with one major exception. While it can allow no assumption to be accepted without challenge, there must be an authoritative method of study, with clearly defined rules, to provide a secure framework in which students can work. There must be an opportunity and an invitation to express a personal point of view, on the understanding that each point of view will be treated and valued in exactly the same way. This means that not only must there be rules of discussion and investigation, but they must be known to those taking part and be seen to be enforced.

In the same way, the students should always be engaged in an activity of which they know the purpose. Given this condition, even the most apparently esoteric aspects of religious studies can be shown to be relevant, and the students can be equipped with the tools needed to pursue an understanding of people with opinions, in whatever context they might meet them.

If objectivity lies in the application of the same method of investigation to every point of view, and of the same criteria for 'truth' to all religious beliefs, then this approach is objective, but it might be more accurate to say that it is interpersonal, and self-consciously so. It never forgets, or allows the students to forget, that opinions are held by people, and that the theoretical study of a point of view which can be described as 'Muslim' or 'Christian' or 'Buddhist' is no substitute for the study of Muslims, Christians or Buddhists, who are people like us. It is also a reminder that while we are studying other people, they are studying us.

6 Religious Education and cross-curricular themes

Brian Netto

The implementation of the National Curriculum, and of other aspects of the Education Reform Act 1988, has further served to marginalize the place of Religious Education in the curriculum.[1] Pressures from right-wing parents' action groups to promote a particular brand of white, 'English' Christianity, and from others who see the role of 'multi-faith' Religious Education primarily as contributing to developing a stable, tolerant and unified nation[2], have tended to polarize discussions on the nature of RE. Its local control through SACREs and Agreed Syllabuses has been used by ministers at the DFE as a convenient means of distancing government from any direct intervention. Out of these tensions, there is evidence that a more considered approach to teaching and learning in Religious Education is emerging, one which shifts the balance from teaching *about* religion to learning *from* religion.

This article will give some ideas about how learning from religion can be enhanced through cross-curricular work. Pupils can be encouraged to learn from religion through the exploration of the spiritual, by reflecting on spiritual teachings and practices[3] – but the article is not directly concerned with this area. Learning from religion will not be concerned simply with enabling pupils to develop positive images of religious traditions, but also with developing critical skills in investigating the contribution of religion to injustice and intolerance in contemporary and past cultures and societies.

Cross-curricular work has come under considerable criticism from different directions, usually on the grounds that it is too often incoherent and unco-ordinated in its planning, that it attempts to embrace too many diverse curriculum areas at the expense of subjects[4], and gives little attention to progression. For example, HMI implicitly criticize cross-curricular topic work[5] and explicitly criticize it in some of their reports.[6] John Hull traces developments in the rhetorics of food metaphor, in the attack on multi-faith Religious Education,[7] which, according to its perpetrators, pollutes and contaminates the originally pure traditions of Christianity, and encourages moral relativism and secularism by concentrating on social and political issues.[8] It is certainly true that much topic work in primary schools, and some modular or integrated courses in secondary schools, needs to be strengthened by having clear learning objectives, and being more sharply focused around key questions and issues.

As an example of such an approach, I will outline possible areas for developing a critical approach within Religious Education to delivering the cross-curricular themes.

It is important to remember that the cross-curricular themes are non-statutory, in that the National Curriculum Council's guidance documents have no statutory force. The National Curriculum does not in itself provide a broad, balanced and relevant curriculum.[9] Alongside the broad areas of economic and industrial understanding, environmental education, health education, citizenship, and careers education and guidance, schools will be building on other areas of the curriculum, such as education in international understanding, development education, political education and media education. There are strong pedagogical arguments for ensuring that coherence is achieved in linking cross-curricular themes, and ensuring that cross-curricular skills (such as information-handling skills, personal and social skills, and oral skills) and cross-curricular dimensions (of personal and social development, and of equal opportunities) permeates the delivering of the themes.

The themes offer opportunities for pupils to investigate aspects of the world not explicit in the statutory orders. They can be characterized as offering pupils opportunities to explore controversial issues, to promote active and participatory styles of teaching and learning, to examine aspects of the real world, to involve important questions of values and beliefs and to promote the acquisition and development of relevant skills for pupils to help them undertake an active and critical role in society. The themes should also aim to expand pupils' learning environments, and to embrace a range of contexts outside the school.

Unlike the imposed programmes of study of the National Curriculum, the flexibility of the content of the cross-curricular themes can help to ensure democratic teaching and learning. This has been described as 'celebrat(ing) negotiation rather than imposition, co-operation and collaboration in preference to competitive individualism; and it prescribes a democratized learning ethos, in place of the established classroom setting, where learning is privatized and knowledge is owned and legitimated by the teacher.'[10]

Columbus 1992: a Key Stage 2–3 theme

I have chosen '1992' as a topical focus for work on Columbus and on the development of the Single European Market. Pupils would be encouraged to look at the presence of Christianity within the Europe of 1492, and to compare this with a contemporary world religions map. Of course, pupils would examine different conceptions of the shape of the world, such as the medieval *mappa mundi*, and the influence of religious beliefs on the colonizing by Europeans of the so-called New World. Pupils would learn that in 1500 the world population was around 400 million, 80 million of whom inhabited the Americas; that by the middle of the 16th century, 80 million had been reduced to 10 million; that in Mexico alone, the population of 25 million was reduced to just 1 million in this time.[11] In addition, pupils could compare a world map of

language distribution, highlighting the extent of English, Spanish, Portuguese, French and Dutch, from the mid-1400s, and could compare this with a language map of the world today. They could investigate what has happened in these 500 years to change the shape of the world (in terms of political boundaries and global power relations), the world population (in terms of indigenous peoples), and the spread of religion (especially Christianity) and language (especially some of the European languages). This Key Stage 2 topic links in closely with the core History Study Unit on 'Explorations and Encounters, 1450 to 1550' (this should ensure that an abrupt and arbitrary end does not occur at 1550, and that this period of history continues to embrace Africa and the Indian sub-continent in the development of Empire). The contrasting studies in the Geography Statutory Orders, of a locality in the UK and a locality in an economically developing country, link in with the History Study Unit, by focusing on the diversity within Christianity found in, say, urban and rural areas of the UK (which could include Northern Ireland), and in a locality in Central or South America or West Africa.

At Key Stage 3, pupils would use the History Study Unit on 'Expansion, Trade and Industry, 1750 to 1990' to explore the economic, political and industrial basis for the expansion and consolidation of the European Empire, in particular the development of class-based systems of religion. The themes of migration, colonialism, expansion and settlement link in with the Human and Place programmes of study in geography.

Alternatively, a focus on the environmental effects on the Brazilian rainforests of deforestation and international debt would enable pupils to investigate the origins and development of the so-called Third World. In RE, pupils could contrast religious structures and practices in First, Second and Third World countries, embracing, for example, Christianity in contemporary USA, Russia or CIS, and in Brazil, Mexico, Peru or Venezuela.

An alternative focus for Key Stage 3 would arise out of one of the optional History Supplementary Units, on Islamic civilizations. This would readily be linked to the core unit on 'Medieval Realms, 1066 to 1500', as a way of contrasting the growth of medicine and the healing arts, and of scientific and technological advance within Islamic countries, compared with the pre-Enlightenment hostility within the European Christian traditions to scientific development.

In studying the growth of Europe, pupils would be introduced to the development of nation states with the collapse of Empire, and to the different means by which European countries developed the conception of the 'Other', represented by black and Third World countries. As the Single European Market becomes a reality, pupils would examine the creation of 'Fortress Europe', comparing this xenophobia with similar episodes in the history of Europe in its relations to other parts of the world. The historical relationship between Christianity and Islam, embracing the Gulf War, would also be the subject of study.

These brief ideas are given in the hope that Religious Education will soon establish itself within the school curriculum in such a way as to be relevant and meaningful to the lives of pupils in a British society which has a plurality of faith.

Notes

1 Most recent HMI reports on the implementation of the National Curriculum paint very bleak pictures of the state of religious education.

2 The social usefulness of RE has been widely celebrated. For example, Chris Arthur suggests that 'a multi-faith approach is better suited to fostering social harmony than any mono-faith alternative.' (C. Arthur, *Biting the Bullet*, St Andrews Press, 1990). This utilitarian argument attempts to build respect and tolerance of religious diversity and plurality, on top of an unjust and unequal society.

In a discussion of anthropology, Claude Levi-Strauss suggests that its traditional object of study, the 'savage' has ' . . . traditionally been provided by the so-called "primitive" peoples . . . That fear (i.e. that of indigenous communities) is that, beneath the semblance of a global ethnography, we seek to portray as a desirable diversity what appears to them as an intolerable inequality.' (quoted in 'The Curse of Columbus', *Race and Class*, January–March 1992).

3 See for example the work of the Religious Experience Research Project, in particular John Hammond *et al.*, *New Methods in RE Teaching: an experiential approach*, Oliver and Boyd, 1990.

4 R. Alexander, J. Rose, C. Woodhead, *Curriculum organisation and classroom practice in Primary Schools – a discussion paper*, DES, 1992, paragraphs 3.2 and 3.4.

5 In, for example, *Aspects of Primary Education: the teaching and learning of history and geography*, DES, 1989.

6 See, for example, *Culloden Primary School*, DES, 1991, paragraphs 17 and 63.

7 John Hull, *Mishmash – RE in Multicultural Britain: a study in metaphor*, Birmingham, 1991.

8 *Mishmash, ibid.*, page 12.

9 See the NCC's circulars and guidance on whole school planning and the delivery of the cross-curricular themes.

10 B. Carrington and B. Troyna (eds.), *Children and controversial issues*, Falmer Press, 1988.

11 *Race and Class, op. cit.*

7 Exploring aspects of World Religions in special school RE and worship

Erica Brown

The concept of special educational needs is a changing one. It was not until 1970 that children with mental handicap were given the right to education. A decade later the 1981 Education Act had a vision of a better world for pupils with special educational needs. It stressed that learning difficulties cover a wide range of educational needs and that the definition of special educational needs is not linked to specific causes and is, therefore, relative to the needs of all children.

The 1988 Education Reform Act appeared to widen horizons for children with special educational needs.

It stated that all pupils share the same rights to a broad and balanced curriculum, including access to the National Curriculum. But the position of Special Schools regarding worship and RE is covered by the Education Act 1983, and not by the Education Reform Act 1988. Paragraph 9 of Schedule 2 Education Act 1983 reads: 'Arrangements shall be made to secure that, so far as practicable, every pupil attending the school will attend religious worship and religious instruction unless his parent has expressed a wish to the contrary, in which case the pupil should be withdrawn from attendance at such worship or instruction in accordance with that wish'.

The clauses of the Education Reform Act 1988 and the Education Act 1983 legislating that collective worship and RE are not obligatory in special schools may have pleased those who argue that religion belongs to mature adult religious communities and therefore has no place in the lives of children with poor cognitive ability. But there are many teachers who argue that gathering together for worship or learning about religion, for example, through signs and symbols, food or dress, provides a framework for a later understanding of many of the experiences which lie at the heart of religion.

The problems facing all teachers who endeavour to help pupils towards an understanding of religion are considerable, but for those working with children who have limited comprehension of their own identity, and confused ideas of the tangible world around them, the task is a daunting one. For it is not until young people have come to terms with themselves that they will be able to build personal relationships with other people, in such terms as love, pity, joy or forgiveness. Neither will they be able to comprehend something of the concept of a personal God.

It is easy to stereotype special children as those who receive and never give. It is even easier if they have no speech, behave strangely and cannot make decisions for themselves. We cannot strip away the illusions which society holds, but if we shut out the chances of exploring a religious dimension to life, we are certainly not offering the kind of broad and balanced curriculum which allows children the chance to further their own religious quest and, ultimately, to be able to put themselves in the shoes of another person.

This article sets out to suggest some active approaches to RE and school worship for children with special educational needs. Whilst it is recognized that worship and RE are not the same thing, and should therefore occupy individual places in the school curriculum, it is also my belief that, where the two are seen as being supported by one another, it is far more likely that children will make a connection between the shared values and attitudes which each sets out to develop.

The theme of light is explored in World Religions, with particular reference to its symbolism in the Jewish, Christian and Hindu traditions. Three examples of worship are included which aim to give pupils the opportunity to link the shared human experience of enjoying a special occasion together with individual patterns of religious belief. All of the activities have been used in the classroom and many will be of value to teachers in mainstream primary schools. Although the assembly examples might be used independently of one another, it is recommended that for the sake of continuity and progression they should be used in the order in which they are described.

Using candles to explore themes of light

Themes of light occur in many religions. Light and darkness are powerful natural forces, and it is not by accident that festivals often take place either at the darkest or the lightest time of seasons.

In the major religions of the world light is representative of:

hope;
new life;
separation;
remembrance;
the triumph of good over evil;
service/dedication;
celebration;
devotion.

In order that pupils increase their understanding of the symbolism of light in worship and practice, it is suggested that teachers use a cross-curricular approach which includes 'hands-on' experience with unlit religious candles.

Christianity

The symbol of light is often used in Catholic, Anglican and Orthodox Churches. Candles are traditionally blessed on Candlemas Day, 2nd February. For Christians, candles are a symbol that Jesus is the Light of the World. Special kinds of candles are used during festivals and celebrations and in daily/weekly worship.

Advent

Advent candles are used during the four weeks of preparation before the festival of Christmas. These are marked and one portion is burnt for each day in Advent. For Christians, the lighting of Advent candles is a symbol of anticipation for the festival of Christmas. Some churches have Advent rings: four candles in a circle of evergreen. One candle is lit each Sunday in Advent. A fifth candle in the centre is lit on Christmas Day.

Paschal (Easter candle)

In some churches an Easter vigil is kept the night before the festival. The building remains in darkness until the Easter fire is kindled. A large Paschal candle is lit from the Easter fire and the light is passed to each member of the congregation so that he or she may light an individual candle.

Symbols on the Paschal candle include:
the Chi-Rho, the first two letters of Christ's name in Greek;
Alpha and Omega, the first and last letters of the Greek alphabet, a symbol that Jesus is the beginning and the end of all things;
the sleeping Roman guards at the tomb of Jesus;
the year in which the candle is to be used;
doves, which represent the Holy Spirit and Peace;
a laurel crown replacing the crown of thorns and representing the Kingship of Jesus;
incense studs representative of suffering.

Baptismal

This is given to a child at baptism with the words: 'Receive this light. This is to show that you have passed from darkness to light'. The candle may be lit each year on the anniversary of the baptism or on the child's birthday.

Votive

In some churches, votive candles are placed by worshippers near a statue of a saint or an icon, in the hope that the saint will continue the prayers of the worshipper after they have left the place of worship. Sometimes a stand holds votive candles, placed there as signs that 'special' prayers have been offered.

Christingle

One of the traditional celebrations of Advent in England is a Christingle service in Church. The children of the congregation are given a candle in an orange, which is decorated with fruit, sweets and a red ribbon. The orange represents the world; the candle represents Jesus, the Light of the World; the red ribbon represents the blood of Jesus; the sticks represent the four seasons; and the fruit represents the fruits of the earth.

An assembly outline
Aims

To help children explore experiences of light and darkness in daily life and secular celebration; and to help children to begin to understand the symbolism of light and darkness in Christian traditions.

Resources

A birthday cake with several candles.

A collection of candles representative of Christian ceremonies and celebrations, displayed attractively and including some of those mentioned above.

Items required to make a Christingle (see below). Matches.

Poem: 'The Christmas Candle' (see below).

A tape of music which is representative of the theme of light/darkness, e.g. Zanfir – Pan pipes; Light of Experience.

A room or hall which can be darkened.

Presentation

Before the pupils arrive, set up the display, lighting one or two of the candles which will not be passed around. Play the tape of music and ask the children to focus their attention on the candle flames.

Light the birthday cake candles and explain that the theme of the assembly is light. Why do we put candles on birthday cakes? Expect the answer: 'To show us how old someone is!' Ask: 'How do candles make you feel?' Explain that just as families at home use birthday candles as a symbol of a special occasion, so does the Christian family in some churches. Introduce the various candles and pass unlit examples around for the children to touch, to smell and to look at closely.

Explain that during Advent Christians sometimes attend a special celebration in church called a Christingle service. Invite a child to the front of the group to help demonstrate how a Christingle is made. Explore the possible symbolism of the various features of the Christingle as they are arranged on the orange.

Darken the room, light the Christingle and ask the children to think about someone who is very special to them as the poem 'The Christmas Candle' is read.

The Christmas Candle

Last night I took a Christmas candle to my room
To watch the curving beauty of the flame against the
    dark,
And I was amazed how light the darkness had
    become.
Could that much light come from one small flame?
And then I blew the candle out
And how dark the darkness seemed.

And I remembered, long ago in a manger
Lay the first Christmas candle:
A new born child
Helpless and small.

Last night I took a Christmas candle to my room
To watch the curving beauty of the flame against the
    dark,
And I was amazed how light the darkness had
    become.
Could that much light come from one small flame?
And then I blew the candle out
And how dark the darkness seemed.

Author unknown.

To make a Christingle

You will need: an orange; a candle; red ribbon; cocktail sticks; raisins and sweets; and pins.

With a knife, make a hole in the top of the orange.

Press the candle into the top of the orange. Thread the fruit and the sweets on to the cocktail sticks and push them into the orange. Put the red ribbon around the orange and hold it on with the pins. Tie the red ribbon in a bow. Light the candle and explain that it is a symbol of the arrival of the Christ child as a Light in the World.

Judaism

Themes of light and darkness are common in Judaism, and candles are used for devotion, celebration and as memorials.

Shabbat

Two candles are lit in Jewish homes on Friday before sunset, the eve of Shabbat. The woman of the house recites a special blessing before they are lit and repeats the words 'Shabbat Shalom' ('a peaceful Shabbat'). The light is a symbol of the goodness and joy of the occasion. The candlesticks are often silver and they may be family heirlooms, passed down from one generation to the next.

Havdalah

The Havdalah candle has several wicks in order to give a lot of light. The name Havdalah means 'separate'. In other words, the Sabbath is unlike the working days of the week. The candle is lit at the Havdalah service which marks the end of Shabbat. Members of the family stretch out their hands towards the candle, a symbol of bringing together the joy and celebration of the occasion.

Hanukiah

A hanukiah is a candlestick with eight or nine branches which is used during Hanukah, the festival of lights. Hanukah is celebrated to remind Jews of the bravery of a small group of people who fought for their faith against a pagan emperor (see below). On the first evening of the festival, as soon as three stars can be seen in the sky, the first candle is lit from the centre servant or shamach candle. An additional candle is kindled each night of the festival. The lighting of the candles is followed by reading the following verse from the prayer book: ' . . . these lights are holy and we are not permitted to make use of them, but only to see them in order to thank your name for the wonders, the victories and the marvellous deeds'.

Memorial

On the anniversary of a death the family of the deceased will often light a memorial candle as a sign of remembrance. The candle burns for 24 hours.

An assembly outline

Aims

To help children explore experiences of light and darkness in daily life; and to help children to begin to understand the symbolism of light and darkness in Judaism.

Resources

A collection of candles representative of Jewish ceremonies and celebrations, displayed attractively and including some of those mentioned above.

A Hanukiah and sufficient candles.

Matches.

Poem: 'Light the Candles' (see below).

Copy of the prayer of blessing recited by the woman of the house.

A room or hall which can be darkened.

A collection of Hanukah greeting cards.

A table set with the following: a clean white cloth; a place setting of fine china; two candlesticks with candles; a goblet; two challot (plaited loaves); and a prayer book which includes the Shabbat service.

Presentation

Before the pupils arrive, set up the display and include other Jewish artefacts if they are readily available.

Ask pupils if they can remember any of the times when special candles are used by Christians. Explain that Jews also use the symbol of light in worship and for special occasions. Invite children to think of the kinds of things which they use to set the table at home for a special occasion. Introduce the theme of Shabbat as a 'special time' and read Exodus 20: 8–12. Comment on the format of the table setting, paying particular attention to the candles.

Ask one child to light the Shabbat candles and explain that the meal cannot begin until the 'mother' of a household has recited a blessing over her family.

Pass around unlit Havdalah candles for children to hold, allowing time for them to trace the plaits with their fingers. Comment that just as Shabbat begins with lighting candles, so it ends the same way, but that the several wicks on the Havdalah candle burn very brightly to remind Jews that the Sabbath is a special day set apart from the other days of the week. Introduce the Hanukiah and retell the story of Hanukah, explaining that it is an eight-day festival which begins with the lighting of candles each evening. Read the poem 'Light the Festive Candles', and demonstrate the sequence of how the Hanukiah is lit each evening throughout the festival.

End the assembly by darkening the room so that it is lit only by the candles and asking each child to break off a small portion from the challot. Ask them to give the bread to the person on his or her right-hand side. Each person must eat the piece of bread given to them before breaking off a piece for the next person and greeting them with the words: 'Shabbat Shalom'.

Hanukah

Hanukah is a Jewish festival of light which occurs in November or December. The festival remembers the victory of Judah the Maccabee over the Syrians, who had forbidden the Jews to worship their God and had put idols in their temple. When the Jews had overcome the Syrians, the first thing they did was to restore the temple. Some people think that this took eight days. The Syrians had stolen the oil which was used to keep the temple lamp burning, and the Jews searched for a long time until they found a very tiny amount – just enough to keep the lamp alight for one day. But a miracle was worked and the lamp stayed alight for eight days. So Jewish people remember the occasion by celebrating Hanukah as an eight-day festival.

Light the Festive Candles

Light the first of eight tonight –
the farthest candle on the right.

Light the first and second, too,
when tomorrow's day is through.

Then light three, and then light four –
every dusk one candle more

Till all eight burn bright and high,
honouring a day gone by

When the Temple was restored,
rescued from the Syrian lord,

And an eight-day feast proclaimed –
The Festival of Lights – well named

To celebrate the joyous day
when we regained the right to pray
to our one God in our own way.[1]

Hinduism

In Hinduism, light is symbolic of the triumph of goodness over evil. During the festival of Divali (a name which means 'cluster of lights'), Divas are placed on window sills and in doorways to welcome Lakshmi, the goddess of wealth and good fortune. Light is used during both private devotion and worship in the temple.

Diva

A diva is a simple earthenware lamp. It is filled with ghee (clarified butter) and the wick is usually made from a piece of folded cotton or cotton wool, which is floated on the oil. Divas are placed on shrines and they also play an important part in worship. In most Hindu homes there is a room or a corner set aside for a shrine. Puja, or worship, will take place here at the start of each day and/or in the evening. Diva lamps are lit as a symbol of God's presence and the smell of incense sticks reminds worshippers that Brahman (God) is present in everything.

An assembly outline

The following outline is suggested for a small group or class gathering.

Aims

To develop an awareness of the events within a community which are significant to its people; to develop an awareness of the diversity of human response to life; to develop an understanding of how religious beliefs and insights are expressed in symbolism; to reflect on the experience of celebration at home, school, and in the wider community; and to acquire an ability to share with others, nurturing attitudes of tolerance and respect.

Resources

A large, circular table cloth.

Indian garlands, Hindu artefacts, Indian musical instruments (finger cymbals, bells, drums), divas, coconuts etc.

Red, yellow and orange tissue paper.

A few small logs or sticks.

Joss sticks and holders.

Coloured streamers.

Indian foods, e.g. samosas, poppadams, sweets (see coconut barfi recipe below), dates.

A tape of Indian music.

Presentation

Put the table cloth in the centre of a fairly large space on the floor. Arrange the coloured tissue paper and the wood in the centre of the cloth to resemble a bonfire. Place the artefacts, the garlands and the unlit divas and joss sticks on the cloth. Light several joss sticks and place around the room. As the children assemble, play Indian music and invite them to sit around the outside edge of the circular cloth.

Give a brief explanation of the display and ask whether anyone can name two objects on the cloth. What are they used for? Do any of the objects remind children of things which are used to celebrate special occasions?

Read a story associated with Holi or tell 'Mrs Lodia Remembers Holi' (see below).

Invite one or two children to discover how the musical instruments are played. Ask what kinds of party foods children enjoy most when they celebrate at home. Name the Indian foods (if they are unfamiliar to the pupils). Pass the food around and sample it.

Play Indian music and move around the circle in a clockwise direction. Some children might like to play finger cymbals or beat drums in time to the rhythm.

Lessen the volume of the music and ask everyone to stand still. Give each pupil a coloured streamer and explain that they are less messy than coloured water! Throw the streamers across the circle and wait for the excitement to settle . . .

Invite everyone to sit down again. Taking care that there is no paper near the divas or the joss sticks, light them. Darken the room and ask each child to reflect on the display as they enjoy the smell and the lights.

Holi

Holi is a two or three day North Indian Hindu festival which marks the turn of the season from winter to spring. It is celebrated in the month of Phalguna in the Hindu calendar (usually March in the Gregorian calendar). The festival takes its name from 'Holaka', a joyful exclamation.

The ways in which Holi is celebrated vary, but it is usually a noisy time, when caste and class barriers are ignored and everyday lifestyles are abandoned. Common themes of Holi are Rag, Rang and Ras, which include the lighting of bonfires and the offering of the first crops of the spring harvest to God; the sharing of food, and the spraying of coloured dyes and powders. In some villages it is believed that the direction of the flames of the bonfires indicates the most fertile land for the following year. As the flames die down, coconuts are roasted and shared and pieces of the hot embers may be carried home to kindle domestic Holi fires. Sometimes dancing takes place around the bonfires, whilst in other areas babies are carried around the fires in a ritual intended to offer protection from harm.

The origins of Holi are obscure, although traditional religious stories are retold, such as those about Lord Krishna. In temples, foods such as nuts and fruits are offered to God, before the celebration begins, with a fast and prayers followed by feasting on dairy products, sweetmeats and vegetarian dishes.

Coconut barfi

225g/9oz sugar
115g/4oz desiccated coconut
8 tablespoons water
60m/2oz milk powder
1 tablespoon pistachio nuts
A few drops of food colour

Method

1 Grease a shallow baking tray.
2 Bring the water to the boil in a non-stick pan. Add the sugar and stir with a wooden spoon until a syrup forms. Bring to the boil and simmer for three minutes, stirring all the time.
3 Add the coconut, milk powder and a few drops of food colouring.
4 Mix thoroughly and place over a very gentle heat until the mixture is very thick.
5 Pour the mixture into the greased tin and scatter the nuts over the top.
6 Allow the barfi to cool and cut into bite-size pieces.

Mrs Lodia remembers Holi

'Holi is my favourite festival. We had a holiday from school on Holi day and the festival lasted one day in Uganda. We'd get together with our friends and mix coloured water, and then we would throw it over each other! Sometimes we'd throw glasses of coloured water. Other times we'd use syringes. We'd wear old clothes and start playing at about two and go on till six. We even threw colours over the headteacher! We used to use a plant that coloured the water orange. After playing Holi we'd shower, put on new clothes and go to the temple. There'd be a bonfire and we'd put coconuts, popcorn and chick peas on it. Later we'd eat some of the roasted coconut as prasad – that's food that's been offered to God. We'd carry small children and babies around the fire. But throwing paint was the best part. When I went to India two years ago I played Holi for the first time for 18 years, since I came to England. Even old people were playing. But it's too cold to do it here!'[2]

(Printed by kind permission of Longman from *Religions through Festivals* by Robert Jackson).

Notes

1 Aileen Fisher, *Walker Book of Poetry for Children*, Walker Books, 1983.
2 Robert Jackson, *Religions through Festivals*, Longman, 1989, page 25.

8 Worship and assemblies

Bill Gent

Introduction

Though many schools have developed homely yet lively patterns of assembly and school worship,[1] the school assembly 'issue' remains problematic. Adding to this a World Religions dimension, then, might seem naïve at best, foolishly dangerous at worst, for have not many within the mainstream religious traditions stirred up dissension and controversy by suggesting or attempting forms of multi-faith worship?

However, this brief article is not espousing multi-faith worship (a term which, like its cousin 'multi-faith RE', needs careful handling anyway) but, rather, a range of imaginative and sensitive ways in which a World Religions dimension can inform and shape school assembly thinking and practice. For, after all, have not many schools already done this in ways which enrich immeasurably the quality of school and community life?

A general approach

One way of introducing or developing a World Religions dimension might be termed a 'general' approach, in that World Religions in general are used to suggest imaginative yet concrete ways of developing school worship. Three examples follow, though others could be formulated.

Even a slight knowledge of world religions suggests that many religious traditions have developed basic statements or affirmations which, as it were, crystallize the beliefs, values and aspirations of the communities which composed and use them. Such statements often feature in worship: they are recited or even prominently written up for worshippers to see, reflect upon and absorb. Schools themselves are communities which have, embedded within them, a range of beliefs, values and aspirations – though the rush of institutional life can make them opaque or invisible. Is assembly, then, a time in which a school's underlying beliefs, values and aspirations can be made more explicit; a time when, as it were, the community – or a significant

grouping within it – stops, reflects and takes stock of itself?

Borrowing the idea from the religious traditions, some schools have chosen to do this by means of a 'school creed', which is either spoken by one person or recited by the group. One example is as follows:

> This is our school.
> Let peace dwell here.
> Let the room be full of contentment.
> Let love abide here:
> Love of one another,
> Love of learning,
> Love of mankind,
> Love of life itself,
> And love of G-d.
> Let us remember
> That, as many hands build a house,
> So, many hearts make a school.[2]

Might such a 'creed' also be written up in a prominent place so that, as part of the school fabric, its spirit might be absorbed?

A further example of the way in which this kind of 'general' approach might be used to suggest imaginative approaches is that of the 'focal point.' When gathering for worship, the adherents of many religious traditions gather in front of a special focal point: the crucifix in Roman Catholicism, the empty cross in Protestant Christianity, the image of the Buddha in some forms of Buddhism, the holy scriptures in Sikhism, and so on. Now these focal points, like the credal statements referred to above, 'remind' (notice the form of this word) the gathered worshippers of the beliefs, values and aspirations which give shape and purpose to their lives – but this time in visual form.

It would clearly be inappropriate for a non-voluntary school to use a religious image as a focal point during its assemblies, for a school, after all, is primarily a learning, rather than a faith community. But this is not to prevent a school (in the spirit of the approach being outlined here) from challenging itself with the question: what visual image could we use in assembly which would effectively symbolize the beliefs, values and aspirations for which our school stands? Thus, what began as a widespread practice in the religions of the world is transformed[3] into educational practice to the benefit of the school community.

Again, an example of an embodiment of this approach might prove useful. A large primary school, in which many assemblies take place in a large central hall, decided to place an 'achievement tree' on the hall's front wall. At the beginning of term, pupils gathering for assembly looked towards the painted outline – trunk, branches and twigs – of a large tree. Its significance soon became apparent. Regularly at the end of assemblies, 'leaves' were presented and public acclaim given to individuals or groups of individuals (and this included teachers as well – for shouldn't assembly be an event involving the whole school community?) who had achieved something 'worthwhile'. As term progressed, the tree began to 'bloom' with green cardboard leaves, each bearing the name of a person or group and a summary of the particular achievement: 'courtesy shown to a visitor', 'thoughtful piece of writing', 'staying late to clear up', and so on. Thus, in a very practical but imaginative way, the school community regularly stopped activity and was encouraged to reflect and take stock of itself. (In the following two terms, the achievement tree was replaced by a night sky with achievement stars and a wall of book shelves with achievement book titles.)

A third example of this kind of general approach is the use of reflection time in school worship. As a broad generalization, it could be said that running through the religious traditions of humankind is the belief that activity is not everything, that activity needs to be balanced with times of inactivity: that 'being' is as important as 'doing'. Many schools, of course, regularly include 'thinking' or 'reflecting' time during school worship, a practice which perhaps has to be institutionalized in order to lose a sense of artificiality. To augment such times of reflection, particularly with groups of older pupils or students, there is a rich body of 'spiritual' material which is not explicitly linked with any particular religion or religious tradition. *The Prophet* by Kahil

Gibran is a well-known example.[4] Another good example is the collection of anecdotes and aphorisms contained in *One Minute Wisdom* by Anthony de Mello. So, for example:

'The disciple asked for a word of wisdom.
Said the master, "Go sit within your
cell and your cell will teach you wisdom."
"But I have no cell. I am no monk."
"Of course you have a cell. Look within." '[5]

A particular approach

If in the approach already outlined there is no direct reference to particular religious traditions as such, this second – the 'particular' – approach does make direct reference to particular religious traditions or elements within them. But how can this be done if school worship must be undenominational?

The answer lies in sensitivity to educational context.[6] The use of prayers from religious traditions might illustrate this point.

Whilst many schools have long lost the habit of including prayers in school assembly, others have not. Indeed, there are many schools which, in the manner of faith gatherings, have maintained an inclusive style of introduction: 'Let us pray . . . .'. But the inclusive mode of introducing prayer is not the only one, and a strong educational argument can be made to support a rather wider style which, whilst maintaining an important place for prayer in school worship, allows for freedom of response.

Take, for example, the well-known prayer of the Christian saint and founder of the Friars Minor, Francis of Assisi, which begins: 'Teach us, good Lord, to serve Thee as Thou deservest. To give and not the count the cost. To toil and not to seek for rest. . . . ' Though some schools would introduce this prayer by using an inclusive form of words, an alternative (contextualized) style would be to begin with a form such as: 'And now, in a moment of quietness, I want to say the words of a centuries-old Christian prayer. Listen to the words carefully. Some of you might like to make the words your own. "Teach us, good Lord . . . ".' Indeed, if the speaker were a Christian, the contextualization might be even stronger, such as: 'And now, in a time of quietness, I want to say a prayer which is often used in the Christian community to which I belong. Listen to the words . . . '. The idea of contextualization can be developed further so as to encapsulate the whole of a school assembly.

The Muslim month of Ramadan is not only a month of fasting but is also a time when the giving of the Holy Qur'an is particularly remembered, some Muslims seeking to read the whole Qur'an during the course of the month. At this time, a teacher at a primary school decided to devote the whole of an assembly to the Qur'an – but in a carefully contextualized manner. The assembly began with the teacher holding up a blue velvet bag[7] and inviting several children to take the bag carefully and to feel and describe the object inside. Having done this, the object was taken out: a wooden Qur'an stand. The teacher said that he had washed his hands before assembly began and then placed a copy of the Qur'an on the stand. After some words about the language of the Qur'an, aided by several Muslim children, a passage of Arabic Qur'anic recitation was played from a cassette tape.[8] The teacher then proceeded to tell the story about how the prophet Muhammad received the first words in the cave of Hira near Makkah at the age of 40. The way in which the story was introduced revealed an instinctive sense of context: 'For Muslims, the Holy Qur'an is a very special book. And the story which they tell about how the first words were given to the Prophet Muhammad is also very special for Muslims. If you were Muslim children, I might tell you the story in the following way . . . '. After the story, the assembly group was invited, during a moment of stillness, to listen to the words of a Muslim prayer, beginning: 'I thank you Lord, for knowing me better than I know myself. And for letting me know myself better than others know me . . . .'[9]

Perhaps the ultimate form of contextualization is when visitors from faith communities are invited to participate in school worship. At the time of year when many Christian communities have traditionally celebrated Harvest, a special school invited two visitors into its annual Harvest assembly. Both visitors – an Orthodox Jewish minister and an Anglican Christian priest – were known to relate well to children. Moreover, they were known to possess that vital 'sense of occasion'

which would prevent them from confusing the school assembly gathering with a synagogue or church congregation. There was a variety of words and activities before the two visitors were introduced. Then, in turn, each visitor was 'interviewed' – asked about why harvest time was important both to themselves and to the communities they served. Thus, the context was set. They were asked to show and describe the objects which they had been invited to bring with them: a Jewish lulav and etrog[10] and Christian Eucharistic vestments. At the end of each contribution, the visitor was asked to say the words of a prayer which was used by their community at harvest time. The gathering was invited to listen and reflect on the words.

A final comment

To include a World Religions dimension in school worship is not, of course, without risk. Particularly in schools and within communities where people's sense of identity is intertwined with 'our Christian heritage', schools would do well to move cautiously and to consider tactical as well as educational issues. Yet, once a school has developed an assembly tradition which incorporates a World Religions dimension, risks and all, there can be no doubt that the gains (social, educational and spiritual) which accrue to both school individuals and community can be enormous. In this, it could be that the school community has gifts of its own to offer the religious traditions.

At the end of the special school assembly referred to above, the Christian priest asked the Jewish minister if he could borrow the lulav and etrog to show to his own church congregation during worship on the following Sunday. Needless to say, the Jewish minister was not only delighted to oblige but also deeply moved by the spirit of the request. In witnessing this interchange, the assembly leader was reminded suddenly that, at the heart of any act of worship (faith- or school-based, corporate or collective), there lies the possibility of new life.

Notes

1 The important distinction between 'assembly' and 'collective worship' is acknowledged

although the range of terms used in this article reflects the realities of school usage.

2 Used in Christchurch Junior School, London Borough of Redbridge. The form 'G-d' is used out of respect for Jews. Quoted by kind permission of the headteacher.

3 'The principal educational responsibility of school assembly is to promote the spiritual and thus to fulfil one of the principal aims of education. It is as religious worship enters into the administrative details of educational provision that its collectivity emerges. Collective worship is the educational transformation of religious worship.' John M. Hull, *British Journal of Religious Education*, Spring 1990, page 67.

4 Kahil Gibran, *The Prophet*, published in various editions, e.g. Pan Books, 1980.

5 Anthony de Mello, *One Minute Wisdom*, Image Books, 1988, page 14.

6 'There is sometimes a place in an act of "broadly Christian" school worship for explicit statements of Christian belief, but if these are "owned by" those who make them, and no assumptions are made that they are commonly held, then they should not undermine the faith of others.' *A Time to Share: a practical guide to worship in Warwickshire schools*, Warwickshire County Council, 1991, page 16.

7 Thus, the use of the 'mystery' or 'feely' bag has a creative role in assembly as well as in RE.

8 The cassette tape which is provided with the *Gift to the Child* primary RE material, Simon & Schuster, 1991, includes Qur'anic recitation.

9 Simply worded prayers from a variety of traditions are to be found in *Book of Prayers*, compiled by Helen Slater, Purnell, 1987. The Muslim prayer quoted above is to be found on page 31.

10 The palm branch held together with myrtle and willow (lulav) and citron fruit (etrog) are associated with the Jewish festival of Sukkot.

9 Spiritual development and the school curriculum

Alan Brown and *Dilip Kadodwala* (editors)

Introduction

Section 1 of the Education Reform Act 1988 requires schools to promote the spiritual development of all pupils. No definition is attached to this requirement; neither is there any indication of how such development should be promoted through the curriculum. The term 'spiritual' was introduced into educational documentation by the 1944 Education Act, where it was used as a broader term than 'religious'.

What is spiritual development?

There is confusion between the terms 'spirit' and 'spirituality'. 'Spirit' refers to an animating principle, common to all people, which makes them distinctively human. 'Spirituality' is a religious term,[1] defined variously by different belief systems. It describes a person's understanding of their origin, identity, purpose and destiny, often in terms of their relationship with God(s). A person's spirituality in this sense invariably has implications for their outlook on life and the way they conduct themselves.

The adjective 'spiritual' derives from both these terms, and may thus be defined in a broadly 'humanistic' way as applying to those aspects of human experience common to all people which are not physical or material, while allowing for those specifically religious interpretations of experience which contribute to a person's spirituality. Both interpretations can be found in HMI publications.

In an educational context, any description of spiritual development must be broad enough to apply to all pupils, regardless of cultural or religious background. Consequently, an exclusively religious definition, which would inevitably be expressed in the language specific to one faith or denomination, would not be appropriate to pupils with no religious commitment. This view is reinforced by the requirement that no part of the curriculum should be 'designed to convert pupils or to urge a particular religion or religious belief on them'.

What is involved in spiritual development?

The following experiences are widely regarded as aspects of spiritual development as described above:

Self-awareness

Awareness of one's identity, of having an inner life in terms of personal thoughts, feelings, temperament, character and needs.

A search to understand what is involved in being human.

Uncertainty

An awareness of one's significance and insignificance in historical and spatial terms, and feelings of awe in the face of eternity and infinity.

A recognition that all knowledge is partial and often temporary, and that new insight begins with doubt and questioning.

Questioning

A search for meaning both at a personal level and in the natural world.

The inclination to reflect upon the ultimate questions[2] of existence which ask 'what does this mean?' as well as 'is this true?'

Valuing

The search for and discernment of values by which to live (e.g. a concern for human rights and justice).

Creativity

The need to express one's innermost thoughts and feelings through various media, frequently involving the use of the imagination and sometimes resulting in works of originality.

These areas of experience are common to most people. What divides the 'religious' from the 'non-religious' are the answers and explanations given to experience, not the experiences themselves.

Why should schools be concerned with developing the spiritual area of learning and experience?

Even if education is seen as primarily a preparation for work, the whole person is employed – not merely a person's cognitive and practical skills. Some

employers regard the personal qualities brought to the workplace as equally important.

If education is regarded as preparation for life in society, it should not ignore the spiritual development of young people, which is a powerful motivator in the making of judgements and the development of attitudes and behaviour.

If spiritual development is concerned with the search for meaning and truth, the development of values, and the reflection on the ultimate questions of life, pupils need the opportunity to discuss these matters in an objective, informed and balanced setting.

How should schools promote spiritual development?

According to the 1988 Education Reform Act, spiritual development is a concern of the whole curriculum. It is implicit in the school's ethos and daily routine. Also, questions relating to spiritual development may arise in any curriculum area. However, not all teachers feel confident in handling these issues, which often require great sensitivity and a degree of specialist knowledge (e.g. if a child is asking what people believe about life after death, or why the world exists).

Questions relating to spiritual development are explicit in all Agreed Syllabuses dating from the 1980s, many of which make spiritual development the focus of RE. RE specialists have the subject knowledge to give a broad spectrum of beliefs, including secular philosophies such as Humanism, and are trained in techniques for handling sensitive issues in the classroom.

All Agreed Syllabuses produced since 1988 include Attainment Targets and Programmes of Study. While no attempt is made to assess spiritual development, Attainment Targets for RE do require a development in abilities related to spiritual development. For example:

Knowledge and understanding of religious beliefs and practice: pupils acquire knowledge of the beliefs of Christianity and other belief systems which relate to the nature of God and of human beings, and the relationship of human beings to the created order.

Application of belief to life: pupils develop an understanding of how people's beliefs influence their values, behaviour and lifestyle, and of how this influence extends to wider societies where one belief system is prevalent historically.

Expression and interpretation: pupils develop their understanding of the various ways in which people have attempted to express their beliefs about life, and develop a language with which to express their own spirituality.

Evaluation: pupils develop an ability to evaluate religious and moral questions by a consideration of what counts as evidence in a religious or moral context, and a consideration of the criteria by which moral and religious judgements are made.

Other important aspects of RE relating to spiritual development are included in Programmes of Study. For example:

Encouraging pupils to respect the right of others to find different interpretations of life and different values from their own.

Giving pupils opportunities for quiet personal reflection.

Encouraging pupils to discuss religious and moral issues in a non-threatening way, and to listen respectfully to others.

Encouraging pupils to raise and discuss questions arising from study in other curriculum areas (e.g. genetic engineering in Key Stage Four science).

Religious Education provides the setting in which the nature and source of the spiritual is most explicitly addressed. This involves raising questions about the meaning of existence, religious experience and the nature of humanity. In the light of the teachings of religious and non-religious belief systems, pupils could be encouraged to engage in informed discussion of the various answers given to these questions.

Notes

1 Some Humanists, although not using the term spirituality, would subscribe to the concept in that they propose theories regarding the origin and destiny of the human spirit.
2 These are usually defined as questions concerning God, the nature of humanity, good and evil, the meaning of life, death and suffering, for example.

10 Islam and the teaching of World Religions

Muhammad Ibrahim

Islam offers a lot for the development of education in this country. Muslims are not here as guests in a foreign land, neither are they here by invitation. The majority of Muslims were born here and an increasing number are from the indigenous population. Islam is a growing part of the British culture and it is here to stay. With this fact in mind it is important to be positive and pragmatic.

First, I shall give a brief Muslim response to the topic based on the Qur'an and the Sunnah (example) of the Prophet Muhammad (SAWS). Then I shall make a personal response as a Muslim teaching RE in a state school. Finally, there is a practical response to teachers with a vision of how Islam does, in fact, offer a good model for RE within a multicultural framework, a model which will fit equally well within other faiths and cultures.

A Muslim response

Islam has often been labelled as the most misunderstood religion in the West: 'To suppose Muhammad was an impostor raises more problems than it solves. Moreover, none of the great figures of history is so poorly appreciated in the West as Muhammad.'[1]

Indeed, the myths about Islam are still being perpetuated. Even in the 1991 film *Robin Hood, the Prince of Thieves*, Islam is portrayed as barbaric. Images are used, such as brutal Turks cutting hands off Christian prisoners. The Moor is portrayed praying Salah (incorrectly, I hasten to add), and repeatedly, the Muslims are spoken of as heathens, despite the fact that a heathen is one who does not believe in one God. Islam, by its theology, is pure monotheism. What would happen should a film portray similar stereotypes about Judaism?

'Antisemitism' would be the cry, and rightly so. Do not Muslims also have a right to ensure that their faith is portrayed with respect? Both the Crusades and the Spanish Inquisition are excellent examples of distortion. Contrary to popular myth, Islam is, in fact, a religion of kindness and compassion and not an ugly form of fascism. Such propaganda needs to stop.

Islam is a religion of no compulsion. The Qur'an says: 'Let there be no compulsion in religion: Truth stands out clear from Error.' (2: 256). Islam is a religion of human rights. Its tenets of compassion existed a long time before the birth of the United Nations. Islam lays down the right for the protection of honour. One group is not allowed to make fun of the other; one must not defame others, insult or back-bite (Qur'an 49: 11–12). Privacy is given esteem, spying is unlawful, and one should not enter another's home without permission. One cannot be imprisoned without having been proven guilty within a proper court. One has the right to appeal against tyranny, the right to freedom of expression, the right to freedom of belief and the right to belong to various parties or organizations (provided they fulfil various conditions which are there for the protection of all). One has the right to the basic necessities of life, and to proper and equal treatment before law. Even the rulers are not above the law (unlike some monarchies!). One also has the right to participate in the affairs of the state.

Islam has a lot to offer within a multicultural environment. Islam is a 'deen': a complete way of life. It expresses itself in social, economic and political as well as religious terms. This, too, is greatly misunderstood. Islam forbids usury (interest). It forbids not just receiving it, but paying it, even recording it. This concept of economics is alien to many, but if one judges the performance of the economy and the economic downfall of any society, then interest is at its heart. The Shari'ah (Islamic Law) is often deemed to be harsh and out-dated, but just as one may see the justice in the forbidding of usury, one can also see the justice of amputation for theft. The Shari'ah is not harsh but kind and compassionate. It is just. I have yet to see someone in Saudi Arabia minus one hand! Indeed, many of the shops there indicate their closure with a draped net, rather than with locked doors protected with steel cages and additional padlocks!

The focus of my attention shall not be the broad dimensions of Islam but, more specifically, education. Education is a major field in itself. Historically, many of the greatest educational thinkers in both the arts and sciences come from Islam. As a faith, Islam encourages a free, open and enquiring mind. One asks, questions and understands before acceptance. Islam is steeped in the tradition of education. Education lies at the heart of the well-being of society. From an early age children are taught that paradise lies at the feet of the mother. The mother is the university to her children. They are taught to love their teachers as much as they love their parents. The key to a strong society is a strong family, and this is achieved through good education. Therefore, it is not surprising to find that the first word revealed of the Qur'an was 'Read' (96: 1)!

Implicit to education is the development of the individual, which seeps through to the well-being of society. This is dependent on the establishment of good moral values. A Muslim will believe that, just as our well-being is dependent upon our parents, so too are we and society dependent on Allah. What better guide can there be than a theocracy? Islam is theocratic. Likewise, just as the gift of freedom involves the criteria of right and wrong, so must it involve freedom of belief. This is why, logically, Islam is a religion of no compulsion. One has the freedom to choose, the freedom of belief. Islam is, therefore, compassionate.

Islam presents itself as an ideal model for multicultural education. It fits neatly within the phenomenological approach to RE. Its greatest strength lies in its objectivity, its freedom of expression: allowing others to have alternative beliefs. This is quite contrary to the image often portrayed through the media. So much so that with careful analysis one can see that many of the positive modern developments in multicultural education have a firm basis in Islam.

A personal approach to teaching RE

The quest for knowledge is of central importance to Muslims. Muhammad (SAWS) said that there are three duties incumbent on all Muslim communities. In order, they are to establish mosques, educate their people and defend themselves. Indeed, Muhammad (SAWS) said that one should go as far as China in the quest for knowledge. Islam encourages a healthy openness to knowledge. Islam also has a clear view with regard to people of different beliefs. Dhimmi is the term which applies to non-Muslims under the protection of Muslims in a Muslim state. The word literally means a 'guarantee' or a 'pledge'. It guarantees the right for non-Muslims to be protected. It is the duty of a Muslim to protect the life, property and honour of a non-Muslim. Unfortunately, several non-Muslim Western writers have brought this concept into disrepute, arguing that it provides Muslims with justification for producing ghetto cultures. Such an opinion is not only prejudiced but damaging, as it fails to recognize that Islam holds the key to a harmonious and successful multicultural society. One needs to have an understanding of freedom: Islam will not accept a multicultural society which will allow all to be 'totally' free. Muhammad (SAWS) warned of the dangers of sexual promiscuity, alcohol abuse etc. The social consequences of such are enormous. It is, therefore, important to recognize that a basic code of conduct has to be imposed on the whole of society, for its whole benefit. A simple analogy is the Highway Code. This contains a series of rules, but such rules liberate, as they help the motorist to travel freely and safely. The Qur'an says: 'Then seest thou any of them left surviving? And Pharaoh, and those before him, and the Cities Overthrown, committed habitual Sin.' (69: 8–9)

Islam has a pure definition of race. The only true demarcating factors are what people believe in – religion – not the colour of skin, nor the country of origin. This presents the Commission for Racial Equality with one of its difficulties. Islam does not place emphasiz on places of origin, colour or status, but on faith. People are classified in accordance with their belief; and leading on from this is culture. Culture is dynamic and constantly changing; and culture is the product of belief. To understand culture and multicultural education, one must have an understanding of belief, of which religion is the principal part. To me, this is one of the most damaging consequences of our 'secular' world: it is the denial of the existence of, or the importance of,

belief. It is like trying to understand the Bible without belief in God. The role of belief and its contribution to human life and understanding has been paramount. The argument that religion is negatively divisive is nonsense. People will divide themselves naturally: girls and boys in a classroom; groups of Hindus, Sikhs or Muslims choosing to live in a particular area etc. Do people have the right to choose to live in a community and to make friends with whom they please? People will naturally group themselves together, and you will find them in places where they feel familiar, comfortable and safe. The basis of this is belief. The promotion of good religious values can be only for the good of society at large. It is, therefore, in the interests of society to recognize the importance of religion as opposed to the devaluing of it. It is worth listening to a natural answer contained in Islam.

Islam has a healthy attitude to faith: it encourages questioning and challenge, and does not rely on dogma. You must use your mind in the search for truth. It is also vital for people living in a multicultural society to have an understanding and tolerance of others. One may not share the same ethical or religious foundations, but it becomes essential for all to learn how to live peacefully. This is all quite a contrast to the crude and harsh notion of the survival of the fittest!

Indeed, many Muslims are themselves ignorant of the purity and aptness of such an approach. With regard to RE, many voice concern. The crusading attitude of some Christians, expecting all children to be given a 'catechismal' diet of Christianity, is bound to scare many away and to throw RE into disrepute. This fear is held by many Muslims who do underrate RE. In many Muslim countries the study of other subjects, like Maths and Physics, is held in high esteem, and should a child fail in these areas they have the view that they can then go and do Qur'anic or Religious Studies instead! This is another example of people putting Mammon before God, so it is not a phenomenon associated only with Christianity!

Likewise, many Muslims do find it difficult to comprehend why and how I can teach multifaith RE. The fundamental flaw lies in the assumption that the teaching and the learning of other faiths is their promotion. State schools are not in the realm of promoting and nurturing a given faith. They are there to educate, to allow the pupils the freedom to learn openly about one another. Nurturing should be firmly in the realm of parents and faith communities. Much of the apathy shown to RE is partly the product of the notion that schools are there to impose belief. The objective, multi-faith approach to RE is, therefore, in tune with Islam; it provides a positive approach which will make a significant contribution to the well-being of society, '. . . and taking advantage of a good education within a strong moral, spiritual and cultural context [is] not only essential to becoming well qualified and to growing up well-balanced, it is also one of the best deterrents against criminality.'[2]

Good RE is easy for practising Muslims because they already have a deep, committed belief. This does help, as it aids enthusiasm. There is already an in-built acceptance of the freedom of belief of others. Muslims recognize that belief is not merely a figment of the imagination, but has a powerful, dynamic influence on the way people behave. A Muslim recognizes that faith is real. I remember teaching in a monocultural comprehensive school. The majority professed to be Christian, but when they were asked if they believed in God, only a minority professed such a belief. This phenomenon is not exclusive to Christian-based cultures, but is shared by all. The problem lies in the insincerity of such commitment. Many do profess to adhere to a given faith, not because they choose to believe, but because it is socially expected. Surely it is good, where possible, for people to try to rationalize what they believe, as this will help them to assess their behaviour and encourage them to respond more appropriately. Islam is a jewel here, as it has a clear code of ethics, but encourages the adherent to understand why and how it works. It brings believers to account for their behaviour, and this helps them to adjust their behaviour accordingly. God is not taboo in Islam; Islam is God-consciousness. Whether one chooses to believe in Islam or not, it does encourage a more honest and healthy appraisal of actions, and this can only be for the good.

The classroom

Having established the position with regard to Islam and education, it is important to translate this practically into the classroom. The principles of Islam centre around pure monotheism, with no elaborate definitions. A Muslim should not compromise. This would present problems when educating Muslim children, especially if they were to be taught issues that are contrary to Islam. The celebration of Christmas, Easter, birthdays and aspects such as the promotion of girl/boy-friend relationships are all wrong to many Muslims, whose natural response would be to withdraw their children. This leads to inevitable difficulties. RE is not always an identifiable part of the curriculum. Hostility can only serve to hinder, whereas it is possible to be positive and to provide something which is educationally valuable, rich and acceptable to all. The initial response by many classroom teachers is one of difficulty. Their fears need to be alleviated. Islam does not forbid the teaching of such areas (like other world faiths etc.), but they need to be taught in a way in which they are not promoted. It is important for people to learn about others, as this will lead to better understanding and co-operation, but it is all too easy on occasions to promote something subconsciously. The basis of good multicultural education is a principle which is in tune with Islam. It is the observation and not the participation principle. Learning about other cultures and forms of behaviour helps one to reflect upon one's own life stance and give greater value and meaning to it. Islam encourages such learning, even more so in a multicultural environment.

The observation principle is straightforward. A child should not take part (i.e. actively participate) in any activity that will contravene his or her principles (tenets of Islam). Children may, however, observe, what others do. This is a learning process. The principle needs careful application, as it will differ depending upon the age of the child. At primary level a child would not have developed sufficiently to be able to evaluate differences, but would still need to be taught that we are different. This is positive, as it reflects reality. A great deal of harm is done to children when we force them to be the same. For example, it is possible to teach about Christmas, but it is wrong to expect all pupils to believe in it. Even if the teacher were to say clearly that this is Christian belief, primary children would still find it difficult to isolate themselves, especially as they, through their child-centred, creative learning, become so involved.

One solution is to select common themes. For Christmas, light, and the passage from good to evil would be a good example. These themes are common to all cultures and faiths. A Jewish child could use Hanukah; a Hindu, Divali; a Muslim, Eid ul Adha (when Ibrahim and Ismail were tempted by Satan) etc. Each child will be able to share a common theme, to have the delight in conveying meaning in what they believe, whilst educating others. This approach is essential for good multicultural education, but it is dependent on good resources. RE needs a higher profile and more training for teachers. Such themes are also cross-curricular and can fulfil various areas of the National Curriculum, so it is possible to build good RE into the curriculum.

At secondary level, the process of observation and non-participation becomes easier. It fits particularly well with the phenomenological or undogmatic approach to RE. The 1971 Schools Council Report defines it as such: 'This sees the aim of religious education as the promotion of understanding. It uses the tools of scholarship in order to enter into an emphatic experience of the faith of individuals and groups. It does not seek to promote any one religious viewpoint but it recognizes that the study of religion must transcend the merely informative . . . '

Remember, Islam is a religion of no compulsion. With the essential groundwork covered, pupils should feel freer to express themselves and feel more comfortable with what they believe, whilst respecting the beliefs and values of others. This will give them greater confidence and prepare them as better citizens for the future.

Conclusion

I do not see it as the intention of Muslims to swamp the UK, to take over, to impose draconian values. This is sheer prejudice. Muslims recognize that this is a multicultural society. They recognize that we all have basic rights and that Islam has a lot to contribute.

The pluralist model as defined: 'with different groups living in their separate communities, and where applicable being educated in a multicultural environment, where pupils will learn to respect and value their own beliefs and those of others,'[3] will be the only one acceptable to Islam in a 'non-Muslim' country. This takes recognition of the true status of religion. It is the only model which is non-racist and complementary to the real society in which we live. Either we continue to promote the myth of this country being 'in the main Christian' and continue to distort the relevance of RE, or we take stock of where we are now and look to the future, and create a system which will be of benefit to us all. This will then serve to provide a fresh insight into the relevance of religion, and will not encourage the further decline of Christianity, but promote a healthy understanding of the vital role which religion can play in the shaping of society. I believe Islam provides the answer.

Notes

1 W. Montgomery Watt, *Mohammad at Mecca*, OUP, 1932.
2 John Patten, *Choice and Diversity*, White Paper, July 1992.
3 Education Reform Act 1988, HMSO.

11 Religious education within a plural society: one person's views and values

Akram Khan-Cheema

The school environment

Most schools may not be able to provide a religious experience, but they can provide an environment within which religious experiences of individuals can be nurtured. In contemporary Britain Humanism or secularization has a significant influence on our social lives. We all have our prejudices and biases, and mine will become evident as you read my views and values within this short contribution. What is important for all educators, not just the teacher, is to understand our own faith or lack of faith in its depth and breadth, and to acknowledge our own prejudices. Without this it will be extremely difficult to understand other faiths and traditions in a positive and meaningful way; it will be difficult to recognize similarities and celebrate strengths and differences.

After nearly 25 years of active participation and genuine collaborative learning within the British education system, and 32 years of a rich if turbulent experience in a culturally diverse society groping its way in and out of a pluralist conspectus, I have to agree with someone much wiser than I, who said that our lives are subject to inner storms far more devastating than those in the physical world around us. What I have always been clear about is that if parents abdicate their responsibility in the home to pass on wisdom and traditions, we should not seek to impose that responsibility on to schools or other professionals. Equally clear in my mind is the fact that it must remain an undeniable right of every child to expect the education system to affirm his or her linguistic and religious heritage. When the educator says it's OK, it becomes legitimate, affirmed. When the school ignores it or errs by omission, it is telling the child that his or her faith and languages other than English are not important. So the school needs to create a climate which allows students permission to affirm their faith; which empowers the learner values and the family, and enriches the school community.

I have observed a fear of other religions amongst many who were raised in exclusivist religious traditions. Fear often leads to hostility and has, as we all know, led to religiously motivated wars. The history of wars creates and perpetuates a cycle of hostility, violence and fear. I have observed a climate of openness to spirituality among a growing number of young people, and an openness to others. Isolation or separateness is a diminishing preference. What has been most disheartening, however, is the fact that many professional colleagues do not appear to take religion, and in particular those who are committed to a faith, seriously. This has often led to a failure of community in schools that reflects the failure of community in society at large. As I have indicated previously, I don't subscribe to the view

that it is the role of the school and the teachers in the state education system to be responsible for religious instruction. That task must be the duty of the parents, the family and the faith community in that order.

Under the present legislation, every maintained school has to provide a basic curriculum which includes provision for Religious Education for all registered pupils alongside the National Curriculum. According to the 1988 Education Reform Act, RE 'shall reflect the fact that the religious traditions in Great Britain are in the main Christian, whilst taking account of the teaching and practices of the other principal religions represented in Great Britain'. RE has equal standing in relation to the core and other foundation subjects within a school's curriculum, but is not subject to nationally prescribed Attainment Targets, Programmes of Study and Assessment Arrangements. Thus RE and collective worship are the only areas of the National Basic Curriculum which are determined within the LEA.

Spiritual development

According to the 1988 Act, the school curriculum will be balanced and broad if it 'promotes the spiritual, moral, cultural, mental and physical development of pupils at the school and of society'.

What does the word 'spiritual' mean, and how will the registered and accredited inspectors (Education (Schools) Act 1992) ensure quality of provision by schools in terms of 'the spiritual, moral, social and cultural development of pupils at those schools'?

The requirement for the governing bodies and the schools, in my view, is to examine the spiritual area of experience and ensure that RE plays a central role in its promotion, as well as ensuring that each area of the curriculum contributes to the spiritual development of pupils. The interpretation of the spiritual dimension is all-encompassing, and the promotion of the development of the spiritual is, therefore, a very wide-ranging and holistic task facing our schools. My observation over the years is that schools do not always realize that they are promoting the spiritual development of their pupils, even though they constantly influence it. They unconsciously pass on the dominant 'spirit' of today, be it materialism or idealism. The implementation of the prescribed National Curriculum and the emphasiz on content which attempts to develop knowledge and skills without attending to the varied spiritual needs and nature of pupils are increasingly becoming prey to the spirit of the age, which is often to do only with consumerism, personal, political and economic exploitation and an impoverishment of what it can mean to be human.

My particular concern is the promotion of spiritual development in the schools of a plural society, where the enormity of their task has proved to be a recipe for inaction, because they cannot agree on what set of values to adopt. This, in turn, has led to an uncritical acceptance of the notion that religious beliefs are somehow inferior to secular ones. Educating for spiritual growth should leave pupils better equipped to meet their own needs, to empathize with the spiritual values and quests of others and not to be discouraged from developing their own spirituality of belief and values. I hope that my own values, steeped in Islamic traditions, don't blind me to those values categorized as secular. I accept that teachers need to be conscious of the fact that not everyone interprets their own life or experience of the world in a religious way; but the evidence I have gathered through my observations in schools is that the rich and substantial contribution to the spiritual development of pupils as religious believers is certainly not at the heart of the National Curriculum, and is often missing from the Agreed Syllabuses of RE.

When RE stops at the stories, festivals, rituals, buildings, places of worship, customs, attire and even fundamental laws, values and beliefs of a chosen few religious communities of a locality, then it becomes an interesting personal and social education of cultures or the 'humanities'. There is nothing wrong with that; but such RE does not lead into the spiritual world of meaning and life. The basis of the development of an appreciation of this inner world must be the pupils' own growth in spiritual self-awareness through an affirmation of their commitment and a deeper exploration of their own faith with security and respect. This should lead them to see what the consequences of commitment are in terms of action and values. I can't help feeling that this only happens when teachers are themselves

on a spiritual journey and, like their pupils, can experience the excitement of discoveries on the way. What is often lacking is the emphasiz given to the faith of the children and young people in our schools, whilst still ensuring that all of them receive an introduction to the breadth of humanity's religious quest. This should take place within the framework of a school policy which offers equal right to the maintenance of their distinctive identities and loyalties of culture, language, religion and custom.

All the areas of the school curriculum, including RE, can and should promote the spiritual development of pupils. This task will need to be even more prominent in the future. Schools need to make this process as conscious and as coherent as possible.

It is through the linguistic area of one's experience that people make sense of their world. Spoken and written languages give shape and voice to the kernel of their perception. The mathematical area of experience should develop abilities to organize, communicate, manipulate, predict and create opportunities for problem-solving and reflective thinking. The scientific area of experience should help to observe, explore and empower pupils to think critically, so that they can identify and distinguish scientific and religious questions. The technological area of experience should ask the pupils to understand human needs and values, and engage in the process of meeting these by new productions of human design and craft. The aesthetic and creative areas of experience should enable pupils to find and create responses to their sensory experiences which tap into their emotional, affective and aesthetic inner selves as they respond to their world in different ways.

Unfortunately the truth about the present level of curriculum content and organization in the vast majority of our schools lies between the ideal described above and that described by the Anti-racist Education Charter (CARE): 'The ideology and politics behind the National Curriculum have neither in orientation or in specific content, taken as its starting point and frame of reference the multi-cultural, multicultural, multilingual and multi-faith composition of British society. The educational needs of working class, black and white children do not inform the Secretary of State's public concern to improve education standards. The Education Reform Act does not acknowledge the existing racial, sex and class inequalities in education'.[1]

If the task of the schools is to promote the religious understanding and appreciation of pupils from all backgrounds by providing opportunities to develop their own skills, knowledge and values in relation to religion and religions, then I fear that the present teaching staff throughout the country is woefully inadequate in realizing this objective without a great deal of personal and professional in-service support and 'coaching'.

As a member of the 'Swann' committee[2] I was on the receiving end of overwhelming evidence which convinced me that the teachers with specialist responsibility for RE were at the forefront of helping schools to create an awareness of an equal and multi-faith society. A cursory examination of the National Curriculum Council's (NCC) publication of the analyses of Standing Advisory Councils on Religious Education (SACRE) reports leads me to believe that RE teachers and their advisory colleagues have only slightly been deflected from their wonderful efforts, in spite of some extremely powerful pressure

groups. It is particularly important that RE teachers get all the support they can from parents, governors and the various faith communities. We must accept that for an enlightened multicultural future we cannot completely separate culture from religion. Some understanding of religions is absolutely vital if we are to seek to provide an appreciation of the different cultures for our future generations. All teachers have a part to play in contributing to the spiritual, moral, cultural and intellectual development of pupils, but ultimately it is the governors and the headteachers who are legally responsible for seeing that RE is delivered and that it is taught well. They must ensure that the school has access to specialist knowledge in RE. They must appoint staff who are suitably qualified, and they must monitor pupils' work to ensure quality throughout the curriculum.

Notes

1 *Multi-cultural Teaching*, vol. 8, no. 2, Spring 1989.
2 M. Swann, *Education for All: Final Report of the Committee of Inquiry into the Education of Children from Ethnic Minority Groups, Cmnd 9453*, HMSO, London, 1985.

12 Learning about World Religions in the basic curriculum

Barbara Wintersgill

For those interested in religious education, the Education Reform Act 1988 introduced two particularly significant changes to the 1944 legislation.

Firstly, Standing Advisory Councils on Religious Education (SACREs) became statutory, with one committee to consist of representatives of 'Christian and other denominations as, in the opinion of the LEA, will appropriately reflect the principal religions in the area'. As a result, most Local Education Authorities (LEAs) now have a SACRE which is representative of both Christian and non-Christian faith communities in the area. In many cases, Humanists are co-opted members. SACRE reports increasingly suggest that representatives of faith groups play an important role in informing SACRE's advice to the LEA and to schools on matters such as

resources and areas of sensitivity in religious traditions.

The second major change relates directly to the curriculum. The Education Reform Act requires any new Agreed Syllabus[1] to reflect not only the fact that the religious traditions of Great Britain are in the main Christian, but also that it will 'reflect appropriately the principal religions of the area'. Subsequent guidance from DES[2] has advised that in order to comply with legislation,[3] an Agreed Syllabus cannot 'exclude from its teaching any of the principal religions represented in Great Britain'.[4]

What is the rationale for these changes? The Act requires the school curriculum to promote the 'spiritual, moral, cultural, mental and physical development of pupils at the school and of society, and to prepare pupils for the responsibilities and experiences of adult life'. Any Agreed Syllabus devised to take account of this injunction could hardly fail to insist that pupils receive some teaching about the major religions represented in the society for which they are being prepared; a society which is increasingly spiritually, morally and culturally diverse. DES Circular 3/89 is more explicit in stating the Government's belief that 'all those concerned with religious education should seek to ensure that it promotes respect, understanding and tolerance for those who adhere to different faiths'.

There is a clear link between the specifications of the Act and subsequent DES guidance. The acquisition of knowledge and understanding of religions clearly contributes to pupils' intellectual development. It is an important part of preparation for life in the world in which they are growing up. But religious education has always been more than 'knowing and understanding'.

The DES letter already mentioned goes on to say of an Agreed Syllabus that it should not 'be confined to information about religions and religious traditions, practices and teaching, but should extend to wider areas of morality'. Few would deny that respect and tolerance, developed through an increased understanding about religions, are essential ingredients in pupils' spiritual, moral and cultural development.

Learning about religions contributes to the growth of knowledge and understanding, respect and tolerance. Recognition of the value of knowledge and understanding of religions extends to the National Curriculum itself. Most explicitly, the statutory requirements for National Curriculum history include optional study units on the Benin (KS2) and Islam (KS3), while also requiring that history be taught throughout with attention to the religious dimension of the past. National Curriculum geography requires pupils to be taught about contrasting societies, both at home and abroad. In practice this will include reference to contrasting religious and cultural differences. In National Curriculum technology, the examples include preparing meals for people of different religious and cultural backgrounds.

Less explicitly, pupils' understanding and appreciation of music, art and dance will be enhanced by an understanding of religious associations with the arts, past and present. A new and exciting view of geometry may be gained from a study of Islamic art, while to many it would be unthinkable to deal with scientific issues such as genetic engineering (KS4) without considering the attendant religious and moral issues from a variety of perspectives, religious and secular.

What pupils learn in Religious Education should not, then, be seen as isolated from the rest of the curriculum. Implicit in all the above examples is the acknowledgement that few areas of learning are left untouched by religious influence. However, what is not always so clear is whether pupils see this connection. It is not always apparent to pupils *why* they are studying 'other people's religions'. Successful teaching about religions is not just a matter of imparting knowledge and developing understanding, but also of ensuring that pupils see the relevance of what they learn in the context of life beyond school.

If knowledge and understanding of religions is integral to pupils' intellectual development, the tolerance and respect for other peoples' views which such study is expected to promote is equally recognized in NCC literature. In March 1990, NCC published *Curriculum Guidance 3 – The Whole Curriculum*. This description of the whole curriculum includes the cross-curricular dimensions and themes which act as binding agents across the curriculum and make a significant contribution to personal and social development. The dimensions include a commitment to providing equal opportunities, and a recognition that preparation for life in a multicultural society is relevant to all pupils. The document acknowledges that 'introducing multicultural perspectives into the curriculum is a way of enriching the education of all our pupils. It gives pupils the opportunity to view the world from different standpoints, helping them to question prejudice and develop open-mindedness'. Many schools would acknowledge that this objective is achieved above all in the teaching of Religious Education, where attention is given to many faith (and secular) perspectives on issues of personal, social and international importance.

Curriculum Guidance 3 identifies five themes

intended to permeate the whole curriculum. They are: economic and industrial understanding, health education, careers education and guidance, environmental education and education for citizenship. Religious Education, like other subjects, is capable of delivering some of these themes in greater depth than others. To select but two, health education and education for citizenship, it is clear that an approach to the issues from a variety of secular and religious perspectives is essential if a balance is to be maintained and open-mindedness encouraged. Sex education, for example (included in health education), while having an important knowledge base, incorporates a wide range of moral and religious perspectives. To be ignorant of how these perspectives are variously expressed within the values of different faith communities would be a disadvantage to anyone following a career in the health, caring or teaching professions. Quite apart from the vocational importance of such knowledge, young people engaged in discussion of sex education issues, including family planning and abortion, need to be aware of the diversity of opinions on such matters if their discussion is to be sensitive to the views of others and properly informed. Health education also covers family life, nutrition and personal hygiene. Any educated person might be expected to understand that these, too, are highly sensitive issues for many religious communities in Britain. For many people, such understanding is not only helpful in the workplace, but in relating to the family next-door.

No less important is the contribution which learning about World Religions can make to education for citizenship which includes understanding about local, regional, national and international relationships. It is difficult to see in this connection how anyone without even an elementary understanding of Christianity, Judaism and Islam could make any valid judgements on issues such as the Salman Rushdie case, the Arab-Israeli conflict or the Gulf War. Equally, some understanding of the Britain's Christian heritage might underpin any study of the law, attitudes towards human rights, public services and voluntary work. Another component of education for citizenship is knowledge and understanding of a plural society with a consideration of its benefits and conflicts. This also would be difficult to achieve in the absence of teaching about religions in Britain.

It is true of course that studying world religions does not automatically increase tolerance, respect and open-mindedness in the young. For this reason, SACREs also have responsibility to advise the LEA on methods of teaching religious education. How religious and secular philosophies are presented to pupils is critical, if the elusive qualities of 'tolerance and respect' are to be developed, and in this context the method of teaching is as important as the content, if not more so. Religious traditions in the hands of an unsympathetic teacher, even if a certain amount of subject knowledge has been acquired, is likely to have quite the reverse effect. Too often, inappropriate teaching methods foster ridicule, disinterestedness and early dismissal of the claims of religions to be taken seriously. SACRE members representing faith communities will have much to contribute on how the beliefs and practices of their communities might most effectively be presented.

Notes

1 This applies only to Agreed Syllabuses adopted after ERA
2 Letter to all CEOs, 18 March 1991
3 Education Reform Act, Section 8 (3)
4 Many Agreed Syllabuses dating from before ERA do include teaching about the major world religions; ERA made this statutory from 1988

SECTION TWO A
Perspectives of faith traditions

Introduction

We are apt to forget sometimes that when we speak of 'religions' we are using a particular model to unite under one banner phenomena which are not always of the same type. Many religions – such as Christianity and Islam – are of such a nature that it would make no sense for an adherent to follow two religions at the same time. But it is possible, for example, to be a Confucian and a Taoist, or both and a Buddhist as well. If this is possible, then what it is to be a Christian or a Muslim is not quite what it is to be a Confucian or a Buddhist, and this is not only a question of their believing different things but, in this context, more a matter of their seeing the world, and religion and its role, in different ways. A common approach to the study of an unfamiliar religion is to begin with the life story of someone identified as the founder, and then go on to the religion's beliefs. We can then 'compare' different religions. The model – the importance of the founder, followed by those tenets, belief in which demarcates adherents from non-adherents – is itself derived from a particular vision of what it is to have a religion, which applies very well in cases such as Christianity but meets severe problems with, for example, Hinduism.

The underlying intention of this section is not to give the basic teachings of the so-called 'six world religions'. These teachings can easily be found elsewhere. Rather, contributors who are themselves members of the faith communities or who work closely with members have been invited to stand back and reflect on their religion's orientation, its perspective, how it sees the world and itself as a religion: in a sense, 'what it is all about'. For example, one religion might stress the centrality of the occurrence of certain events in history, from which springs a particular vision of the world transformed for believers, whereas, for another religion, history may be relatively unimportant, and its vision may come from stressing the ever-present therapeutic possibility of transforming the mind, any mind. Of course, there may be links or similarities on another level. The idea of transformation – in various ways – does seem to emerge as an interesting connection between some religions. But that is a link for the reader to make, and perhaps for another time.

To impose or even suggest to contributors uniformity of approach in indicating aspects of a religion's perspective would be to defeat the purpose of this book. Contributors have responded to an abstract and difficult brief in the way they saw fit. To be able to respond requires not only a deep inside knowledge of a religion but also an ability to stand back, to separate the wood from the trees, and to say what is going on in a way which offers some insight. We hope it is of some value.

Paul Williams

1 On minds and mind-transformation: the Buddhist orientation

Paul Williams

In Oriental countries most Buddhist monks eat meat. Not all, of course, but it often comes as a surprise to non-Buddhists, meeting for the first time those who are thought to be exemplars of compassion, that there are so many monks who will tuck into curried goat with what sometimes seems to vegetarian Westerners to be an indecent relish. 'Is it permissable to eat meat?' I asked a learned and holy Tibetan lama. 'Certainly, although if you are practising meditation on compassion it could be counterproductive.' 'Is it not the case that the one who eats meat bears responsibility for the killing?' The holy man looked astonished. Patiently he explained to me basic Buddhist truths which I should have mastered lives ago. Of course not. The one who eats meat (a) intends to eat, and (b) may or may not intend to eat meat. Meat is, as a matter of fact, what is being eaten. But nowhere in the mental states of our reverend gourmand is there an intention to kill. In fact, in the Tibetan tradition, by the monk reciting suitable formulae over the juicy curry, the goat may actually obtain a more favourable rebirth than would otherwise have been the case. Thus, even while eating meat, our monk can generate compassion and do good towards a creature which was already dead, and dead through no wish of the monk himself.

Our reaction to this reasoning – even those of us who are Western Buddhists – is that it is casuistic. Surely the one who eats meat is a cause for the killing, and is therefore responsible, to at least some degree, not only for consuming a curried goat but also for the actual killing of the goat. Consuming even a meat curry does not on the surface appear to infringe any cardinal Buddhist precepts. But responsibility for killing certainly does.

The centrality of intention

As so often happens when there is an immediate and strong feeling that another group has got it quite wrong, we confront here fundamentally different ways of seeing: ways of seeing which, until they are realized and uncovered, vitiate any attempt at empathetic understanding. We all operate within the world with presuppositions, and layers of further presuppositions within presuppositions. Not everyone sees the world through the same structures of assumptions and concerns that are employed by modern Westerners. Buddhists would be inclined to agree that the one who eats the meat is *a* (remote) cause for the killing of the animal. There is a view found in Buddhist philosophical texts that everything is, in one way or another, a cause of everything else. Any attempt to call a halt to the chain of causal connections could only be arbitrary. What one cannot infer from this, however, is that causality – even causality by a conscious agent – necessarily entails moral responsibility. It simply does not follow, from a traditional Buddhist perspective, that if one is a cause of killing the animal in the sense that one simply eats the animal, one is morally responsible for the killing. A crucial additional factor for significant moral responsibility in this case would have to be the intention to kill, either directly or through an intermediate agent. If our monk does not actually intend the animal to be killed, even though he intends to eat the meat, he is not finally or in any real sense morally responsible for the goat's death.

To transform the mind

Central to Buddhist ethics is intention, but this is just one aspect of a general centrality of the mind in understanding the Buddhist way of seeing things, the Buddhist orientation and perspective. This is of crucial importance; easily said, but the implications of which are not always fully realized. The popular *Dhammapada* begins with '(Good and bad) phenomena have mind as their forerunner, their chief is mind, they are mind-made.' A Western tradition which reaches back to the Pre-Socratics encourages thought in terms of cosmology, physics and ontology, a concern with what is there and how the world is. Of course, these concerns are not lacking in Buddhist thought, but Buddhist traditions have from the beginning shown, in general, greater immediate concern with how things appear to the minds of sentient beings at different stages on a spiritual path to the complete cessation of all forms of greed, hatred and delusion. The image of the Buddha as a doctor, curing sentient beings of the illness of unenlightenment (samsara) is an ancient one within Buddhism. Teachings and tenets of Buddhism can usefully be approached through an appreciation that what may initially appear to a predominantly Western way of thinking as statements about the nature of things may have been intended as mental medicines, prescriptions for transforming the minds of those with very specific existential maladies.

Perhaps there is some value in meeting Buddhism with an awareness of questions like:

i   How is this teaching/practice intended to transform the mind of the practitioner in ways that Buddhists would see as appropriate, i.e. the decreasing of greed, hatred and delusion and the increase of their positive opposites?

ii How would believing and acting in accordance with this transform the mind of the practitioner?

iii Is this a teaching/practice which some/all Buddhist traditions would see as appropriate to all people at all times, or only certain practitioners at certain stages on the path?

With a sensitivity to this perspective, the rituals and doctrines which we encounter cease to be quite what they appeared to be from the outside, and we hesitate before too hasty assimilation with models which we have from other traditions, where the centrality of mind-transformation is not predominant.

Hierarchy and the potential of sentient beings

A corollary of what has been said is the role of hierarchy in understanding the Buddhist orientation. Hierarchy offends against Western presuppositions of equality, an ideological presupposition, even when rarely, if ever actualised. For Buddhists there is a path, and there are those at different stages on this path. Teachings appropriate as mind-transformative for one are by no means necessarily appropriate to another, and there are some who have, through their progress on the path, become beings who are really quite special, almost superhuman. Of course, these people have not attained anything intrinsically

impossible for any other sentient being, since such transformative growth is a matter of the mind and is therefore (at least in theory and in general) possible for anyone who possesses a mind. Nevertheless, what is meaningful as transformative at one stage is not necessarily meaningful at another, and to a Buddhist the appropriate model of understanding for, for example, the Dalai Lama is not the same model as that which is applied to ordinary beings. Once more we immediately feel concern; we immediately notice the dangers; we immediately face a difference in perspective, for which all of us involved in education, in trying gently to generate a sympathetic and empathetic appreciation, need awareness.

Note that the Buddhist refers to 'all sentient beings'. The Buddhist tradition taken as a whole is heterogeneous on the extent of the potential of each sentient being, but while there is a strong tendency to give priority to humanity in terms of present ability to attain enlightenment, the tradition would not see in humanity as such any intrinsic separation from other sentient beings in terms of spiritual potential. There is, indeed, a view found i n certain ancient Mahayana texts that beings fall naturally into certain 'lineages' in terms of their spiritual potential. Some may, as a matter of fact, never become enlightened at all. This is not, however, a view held, as far as I know, by any Buddhist tradition still surviving, and it was anyway nothing to do with humanity as such. Such a view cut across the boundaries of humanity versus non-humanity. There is also a further view that certain beings, by virtue of their present embodiment, cannot in that embodiment become enlightened: beings in the hells, or sometimes it is stated that women fall into this category. But again this is not a matter of potential. Potential is tied to the possession of consciousness, for it is consciousness which can be transformed from a consciousness animated by greed, hatred and delusion into the pure radiant consciousness of enlightenment.[1] Potential is not, for the Buddhist, a matter of humanity. Thus, in Mahayana Buddhism, when the bodhisatta vows to save all beings, it is all sentient beings which are to be saved, even tiny wriggly worms. In terms of the final scope of spiritual practice and care, Mahayana Buddhism gives no privileged status to humanity.

Orthopraxy rather than orthodoxy

The essentially practical concern of Buddhism with a hierarchy of mind-transformation is reflected in the relative importance of orthodoxy and orthopraxy within the Buddhist tradition. As is well known, for a Buddhist one of the worst acts is the promotion of schism. But 'schism' in Buddhism does not mean quite what it tends to mean in religions where faith expressed in a creed predominates. The Buddhist schism – samghabheda, literally 'splitting of the samgha, the community' – is a matter of disagreement concerning monastic rule: in other words a disagreement which, if persevered in, would promote heterogeneous behaviour. A group of monks (or nuns) living together a simple and harmonious life which was designed to offer optimum facilities for inner spiritual growth could not tolerate radically wayward behaviour. The monastic and moral code in Buddhism provides a framework conducive, one way or another, to the spiritual life. The human situation being what it is, this framework is relatively uniform, and common behavioural ideals – orthopraxy – provide, by and large and in general terms, the force which unites the Buddhist world.[2] A simple and a moral life promotes the ideal framework for personal and public happiness and, ultimately, for that mind-transformation which leads to enlightenment.

Buddhism has not tended historically to place any particular premium on orthodoxy, a common doctrine or central belief. Of course this could be overstated. According to Tibetan sources all Buddhist doctrinal systems hold in common what is called the 'four seals': that (i) all produced phenomena are impermanent; (ii) all contaminated phenomena are frustration and suffering (dukkha); (iii) all phenomena lack Self; and (iv) nibbana is peace. This represents a scholastic formulation, refined through centuries of controversy, of the old Buddhist understanding of the way things are: as impermanent, suffering and frustration, and not Self, together with nibbana, peace, as the way out of that existential anguish which comes from the fact that things are this way, combined with our inveterate tendency to try and see them otherwise. Thus a common clarification throughout the Buddhist world of what nibbana

consists is 'seeing things the way they really are', for seeing things this way is the final antidote to greed and hatred, which spring from the root poison of delusion, which is precisely not seeing things the way they really are. But even if one were to accept that, in general terms, these four seals indicate a common Buddhist doctrinal heritage, one would have to acknowledge that in as much as they are common they are vague. When we start to probe more closely what they might mean we run up against that vast range of doctrinal differences, the complexity and heterogeneity of Buddhism which must be realized and appreciated by those who would study the religion and which at the same time make teaching it so very difficult. There is some sort of common orientation to 'the universe and man's place in it' found in Buddhism, but clarification beyond vagueness rapidly involves doctrinal difference. However, there has been a strong tendency within Buddhism, viewing the Buddhist tradition as a whole, to see this doctrinal difference as not, in itself, lamentable. Often it is seen as a rather good thing, for, and this is the point, people are different. Doctrines are medicines, not all people have the same version of the existential illness, and there is no requirement in Buddhism that all hold to the same doctrinal vision, in detail, of how things are. Doctrinal expressions are nothing if they play no role in transforming the mind.

The final truth?

Of course, members of any particular Buddhist doctrinal tradition will be very likely to see its doctrines as expressing (inasmuch as it can be expressed) the final truth – how things really really are – with other approaches capable of being ranked in a hierarchy appropriate to stages on the path and culminating in one's own teaching. This perspective is only natural, and in general for the Buddhist tradition it is not thought to carry with it any imperative that others should adopt one's own teaching. There are many future lives, and it is a Mahayana view that the Buddha taught 84,000 teachings (a number meaning 'a lot'!) out of his skill in adapting the doctrine to the appropriate level and maladies of those who heard him. In this light, the important thing is to adopt and practise the teaching appropriate to one's own level, that which will transform one's own mind to a greater or lesser degree away from greed, hatred and delusion, and cultivate their positive opposites. It would be quite wrong for a doctor always to prescribe the same medicines – an anti-depressant for a cold, for example! At the same time, the movement from one level to another occurs through growth due to inner experience, perhaps in meditation, or – particularly in certain Indian traditions or the dGe lugs (pronounced 'Geluk') Buddhism of Tibet – through critical, analytic reasoning. In dGe lugs thought it is stressed very strongly that the teachings which reflect the final (really real) way of things are those which finally, alone, are shown to be coherent in the light of pure dispassionate logic. Thus difference in doctrine from a Buddhist perspective does not entail persecution or recantation. One practises at one's own level, while at the same time continuing to grow through meditative and perhaps rational probing. Real problems, it is commonly said in Buddhist sources, come only to the person who would grasp a particular doctrine in a dogmatic way, and declare that all others are simply false.

To be honest, not absolutely all Buddhist traditions would see it in quite this way. Even within Mahayana one could point to, say, the Nichiren traditions in Japan which, while accepting that the Buddha adapted his teaching to the level of his hearers, would still be inclined to hold that in our present day and age only one teaching is really appropriate: their own. I have said that it is difficult to find a precise common doctrine across the whole of Buddhism. I have to accept, if only for consistency's sake, that there are exceptions to what I have said. But in general, taking the Buddhist

tradition as a whole throughout history, Buddhism has not put a premium on orthodoxy, and certainly not the same premium it puts on orthopraxy. This, I suggest, reflects and is a result of the centrality of mind-transformation in Buddhist vision and practice, a centrality which gives Buddhism its orientation and which, when appreciated, should contribute towards a transformation in orientation, on the part of those who are not from the Buddhist tradition, towards what they find when they read books on Budhism, meet with Buddhists, or visit Buddhist centres in this country or abroad. Such a reorientation would spring from a general appreciation that not all people and cultures see the world and things within it – particularly their religions – in the same way as do those of us (even to a certain extent those of us who have subsequently become Buddhist) who have been brought up in a culture determined by Christianity and Greek civilization. As such, it seems to me that this would be a Good Thing.

Notes

1 Note that the Buddhist tradition taken as whole refers to a number of different types of enlightenment – the nibbana of arahants, for example, or the full enlightenment of a Buddha. These distinctions are not pertinent at this point.

2 For more on the importance of distinguishing between orthopraxy and orthodoxy, and the understanding of samghabheda with particular reference to what books sometimes, quite mistakenly, term a 'schism' which is said to have produced Mahayana Buddhism, see Paul Williams, *Mahayana Buddhism: the doctrinal foundations*, Routledge, 1989, pages 1–6.

2 How a Christian perceives the world

Alan Brown

Introduction

Anyone brave or foolish enough to try to capture in a few words a comprehensive perspective on 'how Christians see the world' requires sympathy from the readers. This is a view: clearly there will be other Christian views, and many Christians will rightly feel

that their particular perception is missing. What has been attempted, however, is not determined by denominational issues, though they may be relevant from time to time; the article seeks, rather, to explore the fundamental elements in the Christian religion which cause Christians to view the world in a particular way. This leads to the second caveat: not only are Christians a diverse collection of people, but they often reserve their most virulent criticism and condemnation for other Christians, though Christian history is also littered with the oppression of followers of other faiths, notably the Jews. What follows does not deal with this negative aspect, for it can be matched in intent, if not ferocity, by other faiths, but one is not ignorant of the sad dichotomy – or paradox – between Christian belief and occasional practice.

A text

At major sporting events, like the Olympics or the World Cup, somewhere, normally in an eye-catching position, there will be seen a banner with 'John 3:16' written on it. Most Christians read their Bible, and many have a favourite passage, but John 3:16 is a key verse in the Gospel of St John, because it expresses several central beliefs of Christians: 'For God loved the world so much that he gave his only son, so that everyone who believes in him may not die but have eternal life'.[1]

In Christian worship a text of the Bible is often the occasion for the preacher to lead into theological issues, or devotional prayers, or hymn-singing, or dance, but the text itself is important. In this verse Christians are offered several distinct aspects of their faith, which they may interpret in their own way. The verse includes: God, love, the world, giving, the uniqueness of the Son, the closeness of the relationship between Father and Son, belief, eternal life, a caring and intervening God.

To accept Jesus as the son of God, as Saviour and Redeemer, is to recognize that the created universe is an expression of God's creativity and love, and that the birth, life, death and resurrection of Jesus is an ineffable expression of God's love for humanity. In this sense John 3:16 (or other verses in the New Testament) are transforming, for they give a meaning and purpose to life based on faith.

The activity of God

The belief that God was incarnate as Jesus Christ, the Son, to be born, to die and then to rise again, in order to obtain the possibility of eternal life for all humanity, enables Christians to recognize that God is:

(a) interested and involved in creation; (b) concerned for all people who live on earth; and (c) continuing to be present through the activity of the Holy Spirit which was promised by Jesus and, together with the Father and the Son, is one God – the Trinity.

The belief that God continuously intervenes in the activity of the world lies behind much Christian philanthropic work and is one reason, here rather simplified, why Christians feel the need to speak out on social, political, economic and other issues. God cannot be assigned to one part of life, for all aspects of life contain God at the very centre. Christians, of course, may voice different, even opposing, views on the same issues, but the perspective must be that God is in all that has been created.

Traditionally, Christians have tried to capture this activity of God in Trinitarian terms: Father, Son and Holy Spirit. The doctrine is notoriously difficult to formulate accurately – largely, one suspects, because Christians are wishing to affirm something of the nature of God which may not be contained in human language. For the present purpose, it is more helpful to recognize that the Trinitarian formula indicates:

a the personal nature of God and, therefore, the personal relationship that exists between God and creation; and

b that God is not static but is eternally active and creative, and that it is the continuous activity of God which helps Christians see the world as a preparation for eternal life, living in the presence of God. These are important statements but two examples may be useful: (i) there is nothing in the human condition that can be so rewarding, or painful, as human relationships. Poets and songwriters of every land in every generation have expressed the intensity of love, hate, fear and exaltation. So Christians believe the personal relationship they have with God – or with Jesus – reflects the intensity of love. The metaphor of 'Father' and 'Son' has many levels of meaning, but it is a personal relationship which serves as a model of Christians' own relationship with God. (ii) There are 'massive' interventions by God into human affairs. One may be seen as the Passover, the escape of the Israelites from Egypt; another may be the incarnation of God in Jesus, born in Bethlehem. But Christians will always believe that

God intervenes continuously in 'minor' but personal ways: at a death, at a disaster, at a time of celebration, in worship and prayer.

Hence the 'activity of God' reflects the dynamism of God and the dynamic relationship that exists between God and those who believe; or perhaps it is more correct to say 'God and all creation which is recognized, accepted and understood by those who believe.'

Saved from what?

If Christians are saved, from what are they saved? How is their life transformed? Essential to Christian belief, but somewhat unfashionable in current British Christianity, is the sinfulness of humanity. Very few Christians accept the literalist accounts of creation in Genesis 1 and 2 and the story of Adam and Eve in the Garden of Eden; but the vast majority of Christians accept these stories as exhibiting fundamental truths.

The account of Adam and Eve is understood as a fall from grace: a fall whereby the human race lost its privileged position with God because of disobedience – a failure to carry out God's will. As a result, human beings have to face pain, toil and hardship, but, most significantly, a separation from God. This act of disobedience is passed on through humanity and is endemic to the human race. It is called 'original sin'. Each person is born in sin and that sinfulness cannot be avoided. Again, some Christians will not accept original sin as being an essential part of Christian teaching, but it has formed, and continues to form, the teaching of the Church. It is one way of expressing the apparent wilfulness, self-interest and evil of humanity.

It should be mentioned that 'sin' is a theological concept. Christians have prayed about it, written about it, confessed it and suffered for it over two thousand years but each Christian probably has a slightly different understanding of it. Generally it is taken to mean those actions or thoughts which offend against God in some way and therefore separate the believer from the love and grace of God. To pray for repentance in God's name with integrity and honesty is to be forgiven by the grace of God.

Christians believe that the only way to break the circle of sin was for God's son, Jesus Christ, – his only son (remember John 3:16!) – to live on earth, fully human yet fully divine, and, through his death, resurrection and ascension into heaven, to restore to humanity the opportunity to share fully in God's glory. Not only did this sacrificial act demonstrate God's love, but also Jesus' obedience to God's will provided a model of love and obedience for all humanity. The 'sin' of Adam – original sin – was washed clean by the life, death and resurrection of Jesus.

This is rather a long summary, but it is necessary, because from the point of view of Christians, Jesus transformed the world. Jesus' baptism in the River Jordan at the hands of John the Baptist has been accepted by Christians as a symbol of the cleansing of sin, and when Christians are baptized in water, it means they are washed clean from sin. It does not mean the newly baptized person will do no wrong, but it does mean that they have accepted Jesus as Saviour and have entered into a new relationship with God.

It doesn't require much imagination to see how acceptance of Jesus transforms both the Christian and his or her perception of the world. It does not mean that all Christians are 'nice', though many do equate Christianity with politeness. The result can be, however, that Christians recognize the world as inherently sinful and believe that 'Jesus is the Light of the World', so his light has to be taken to all corners of the earth. Christianity is, therefore, a missionary religion (though that is interpreted in many different ways).

Conversion

If Christians want to proclaim the salvation offered in Jesus and the promise of eternal life, then they have to travel the world, speak in the name of Jesus, and bring all people to an acceptance of the Lordship of Christ. That has been the traditional view over the centuries and is probably the majority view within Christianity today. But conversion is more complex than it appears, and there has always been a view in the Church that conversion to Christianity in the classic sense (see below) is not essential to salvation.

Some Christians are able to say exactly when and where they became a Christian. They received an experience, as a result of which they were transformed and their perception of the world in which they live was transformed also. Others have not had such a mind-blowing experience, and their faith has evolved, developed and unfolded in other ways, no less deep or significant. There is some tension between these two groups, though the integrity of both should not be questioned (it often is!).

In order to have a perspective on these powerful experiences the following may be helpful:

a The exemplar of the classic conversion is Saul on the road to Damascus.[2] Here Saul, persecutor of Christians, receives an experience of Jesus and his life is changed so radically that he forsakes his past life, takes the name Paul and becomes the formative figure in the founding of Christianity. His life was changed dramatically at one moment in time.

b (i) In the Acts of the Apostles, Chapter 10, Peter, Jesus' most important disciple, has a vision which reveals that the message of Jesus is for all humanity, and not only for the Jews. Peter appears to have thought Jesus' Messiahship was limited to the Jewish people, but in this passage he is 'converted' because he comes to understand more fully the deep significance of Jesus' life, death and resurrection which is to reach into the Gentile world (c.f. also Acts 15).

(ii) This second 'conversion' example is more controversial, for it involves Jesus himself. In Mark 7:24–30 Jesus is approached by a woman, a Gentile from Phoenicia. She asks for her daughter to be healed, but Jesus' answer appears to suggest that he has come first to the Jews. The woman is not put off, however, and challenges Jesus that all have the right to feed off Jesus' teaching. He agrees and her daughter is healed. This is controversial, because the evangelist uses the story to demonstrate that Jesus, too, needed to have his eyes opened. A deeper awareness of his mission is depicted: that it was also to those who did not share his own, Jewish, religion. Note that in the passage he does not require conversion: he only applauds the woman's answer.

'Conversion' may seem irrelevant to the Christian perception of the world, but if one is introduced to the concept of a loving God, personally concerned with each human being and each community, and one accepts that belief for oneself, then the world changes. Equally, Christians are all sure that they will 'grow in the Lord': that is, that their understanding of God's love and purpose will grow as they continue through life, and that their perception will change too as, in Christian terms, 'God's glory is revealed'.

God's son

Much has already been written about Jesus, for he is central to the Christian religion. Yet Christians respond to him in different ways. For some he is Saviour and Redeemer, for others the great teacher and exemplar; for some he is a friend to whom they talk daily, for others he is the glorified Christ; for some he is the sacrificial victim; for others the risen Christ. In relation to this article, this is indicative of the great paradox: he is fully human yet fully divine; he is in the world but not of the world. His teaching tends to be questioning rather than dogmatic, with responsibility for acceptance placed on the listener – for those who see and understand. The inexpressible God is revealed in the historic but enigmatic figure of Jesus. For Christians, Jesus is unique, he is not one in a line, and he will come again, at the end of the world, to judge. By accepting him as Saviour, Christians believe they have entered God's Kingdom, even though they continue to live on earth. The fear of death is no more; they are secure in the knowledge that when the earthly life is over they will enter into eternal life to be in the presence of God. Consequently funerals, though they are serious and solemn occasions, can also be joyous, for the dead person has entered into God's presence, has been 'called home' as one bishop puts it. There is sadness and grief over the loss of a loved one, but happiness in the knowledge that because of Jesus the dead person now lives eternally.

This is the paradox of Jesus.

The Eucharist

The word 'Eucharist' is here meant to include all the names used for the celebratory meal of bread and wine, i.e. Holy Communion, the Lord's Supper, Mass etc., and it is hoped that no offence will be taken at this shorthand. It is celebrated by nearly all Christians, but notably not by the Religious Society of Friends nor the Salvation Army. It is part of this perspective because, although it is not celebrated by all Christians, the vast majority do hold some form of the Eucharist.

Whenever Christians participate in the Eucharist, they enter into a time warp, for every act is, to some degree, a re-living of Easter. By sharing bread and wine, the sacrificial death and resurrection of Jesus is remembered or participated in and time is transcended. It is one way in which Christians, while living now in the world, participate in 'real' time or 'sacred' time. The term 'parahistorical' could be used to show how Christians bring the past event into the eternal present. The events of Jesus' life help Christians to recognize the temporality of their world. The world is real in so far as a life is to be lived, but it is only the precursor of a future life, where one is eternally with God. So the event of Jesus of Nazareth liberates the Christian from the world of human endeavour to a share in God's Kingdom.

The Eucharist is also a focus for self-sacrifice. In the memorial act there is the recognition that Jesus suffered and died, and that in their lives, too, Christians must be prepared to suffer as a sharing of Jesus' pain.

While Christians transcend time in the Eucharist, they all wish to affirm the historical reality of Jesus. It is essential for Christians that God was incarnate in Jesus of Nazareth. The location of Jesus in a specific place at a specific time gives him a strong cultural identity (hence the interest in the historical Jesus and the Dead Sea Scrolls), but the risen Christ celebrated in the Eucharist is a-cultural, for God cannot be imprisoned within time, place or nation. The truths of Jesus' life, death and resurrection for Christians cannot be limited to any particular interpretation. There does exist a form of Christian xenophobia, of course, but it occurs where the Christian church has allowed itself to become enmeshed in nationalistic attitudes. Christianity is a multicultural religion, Christ is a-cultural, and the truth of Christ is expressed in different ways by different Christian communities depending upon their own cultural traditions and their own perceptions of what Jesus means to them.

Conclusion

So, it appears, to become a Christian is mind-transforming, for the way in which the world and oneself in the world are regarded become fundamentally changed. That change continues for Christians as their faith develops, reflecting the activity of God on earth. Christianity is a religion of faith, and with that faith is love: 'Faith, hope and love, and the greatest of these is love'.[3] This love should reveal itself in action: 'My children, our love should not be just words and talk; it must be true love, which shows itself in action'.[4] Faith, hope and love transform the world and offer, for Christians the promise of eternal life. Love, the greatest of these, is at the centre of the Christian approach to each person, each community and the world at large: '. . . the Father loves you. He loves you because you love me and have believed that I came from God. I did come from the Father, and I came into the world, and now I am leaving the world and going to the Father'.[5]

Notes

1 John 3:16, *Good News Bible*.
2 Acts of the Apostles 9:1–7, *ibid*.
3 I Corinthians 14:13, *ibid*.
4 I John 3:18, *ibid*.
5 John 16:27–28, *ibid*.

3 From diversity to diversity: the unity of Hindu darshan

Dilip Kadodwala

Introduction

Let me invite you to Bobby's restaurant in Leicester, not only because it was one of the reputable places featured in the *Good Food Guide* of 1991–2, but also because it provides a point of departure into some diverse, and often paradoxical, Hindu perspectives on food – and, by extension, into some Hindu traditions.

Allow me to suggest a complete meal in the form of a thali. When the food is served, it is all presented on one large, circular, stainless steel plate. It contains a mix of spicy vegetables, rice, dal and sweetmeats in separate stainless steel bowls. There are also some chappatis and poppadam, an array of chutneys and liquid nourishment in the form of salty or sweet lassi. The food is prepared simply, but with a careful blend of ingredients and spices. It appears, on the surface at least, that there is a clash of tastes: savoury and sweet, all on one plate.

For me, the thali represents the complex diversity found in Hindu traditions, and yet it is all held together by the symbol of the circular plate. The centrality of the thali plate can also be used to indicate the importance of the concept of darshan, through which the divine life is transmitted and through which Hindu life is transformed. As with food, which gives and sustains material life, so it is with darshan, in that it gives spiritual sustenance.

Now let me invite you through the following pages, though not in Bobby's restaurant, to get a flavour of darshan and its transformative capabilities for this pair of Hindu eyes.

What is darshan?

Darshan is sometimes translated as the 'auspicious sight' of the divine, with reference to Brahman, the Supreme Being or Reality. Traditionally, Brahman has been spoken of by Hindus as that without qualities or attributes – nirguna Brahman; and paradoxically also as saguna Brahman, referring to the divine which can be described, because it has qualities and forms, and can be witnessed and experienced in this world as manifestations of the One Brahman.

One way in which such forms are manifested is in the images of deities, such as Shri Krishna or Shri Shiva. So during worship, puja, the worshipper stands in the presence of the deity to see and be seen by the deity. The importance of this experience is neatly summarized by Diana Eck: 'Since, in the Hindu understanding, the deity is present in the image, the visual apprehension of the image is charged with religious meaning. Beholding the image is an act of worship, and through the eyes one gains the blessings of the divine'.[1]

The significance lies in the point that darshan is given by the deity and, in the process of puja, the worshipper is also 'seen'.

The whole process of puja is characterized by dynamism and creativity. This can be illustrated by citing the way my mother (and countless other devout Hindus like her) will talk of worship as 'taking darshan', for example, in the shrine at home. The process begins at 4 am and continues for up to two hours, during which her chosen deities are awakened, bathed, adorned with garlands and honoured with incense, recitals, prayers and offerings. All this is performed in a transformative spirit of selfless sacrifice and devotion: bhakti. As Shri Krishna says to Arjun in the *Bhagavad Gita*: 'Be it a leaf or flower or fruit or water that a zealous soul may offer me with love's devotion (bhakti) that do I (willingly) accept, for it was love (bhakti) that made the offering.'[2]

Darshan, then, in the context of puja means to see and be seen by the deity. However, this meaning can also be extended to 'taking' or 'receiving' darshan in other forms and ways. The divine is not confined to temple and shrine, but can be perceived in nature, sacred places and in holy people, such as sants (saints), sadhus (holy folk) and sannyasins (renouncers). It is not uncommon for villagers in India to flock to take darshan from holy people. The reverence shown towards Mahatma Gandhi illustrates this point well. Also interesting is the fact that Hindus in Britain have increasingly sought darshan from people originating in India who are regarded as being holy. They have been invited to places such as Leicester, Preston and London to address, and be seen by, crowds eager for spiritual sustenance. Notable examples include Shri Morari Bapu, whose tour in Britain in 1991 was described in the newsletter of the National Council of Hindu temples with this comment: 'A summer without Bapu in England would be like a summer without sun'.

The different contexts of India and Britain mean that other factors come into play, not least that of migration and its impact on Hindu communities settled in the British Isles. What is noteworthy is the way in which thousands of Hindus, particularly those born in Britain, gather as a collective body for a variety of purposes, including darshan.

Why darshan?

In the Hindu traditions there are two words which point towards the ultimate purpose of life: moksha and mukti, customarily translated as 'salvation'. They both denote the same thing: the idea of being set free, being liberated or released from rebirth or the cycle of samsara. Simply put, the concept of darshan is ultimately connected with liberation from the weary wheel of existence, from the patterns of time and space. It is to experience, for shorter or longer periods, Ultimate Reality. What might this mean in practice for Hindus, in addition to 'seeing' and 'being seen' by the deity in the context of puja?

Most readers will be familiar with the so-called three paths to moksha: karma marga, the way of works; jnana marga, the way of knowledge; and bhakti marga, the way of devotion. These parts are yet another example of the unity-in-diversity paradox evidenced in Hindu philosophical discourses and religious experiences. For example, the belief that the Supreme Being dwells in the heart of the individual and in the heart of the universe, and the theistic traditions in the Hindu fold would naturally emphasize bhakti, in terms of both means and ends, in the process of realizing the relationship between Brahman and Atman (the individual Self). But this perspective does not exclude other possibilities.

The term darshan also refers to the six Hindu philosophical traditions or schools. Here the term means not the 'seeing' of the deity but the 'seeing' of truth, with reference particularly to the Vedic traditions as exemplified by the rishis or 'seers'. Their visions and discourses are largely articulated in those meditative treatises called the *Upanishads*, which partly form the revealed scriptures in Hindu traditions, and are accepted as such by the six orthodox schools. However, not all of the six schools share or accept a theistic basis in the otherwise shared common goal of seeking moksha. The development of the Vedanta, as an organized system bringing together what are often disjointed articulations in the *Upanishads*, is of interest because of its emphasis on release through knowledge as a means of realizing the unity of Brahman and Atman.

What is the interplay between bhakti and jnana?

The suggestion being made here is that the concept of darshan is inclusive of the ways of devotion and knowledge, though the emphasis of each varies according to particular religious experiences and perspectives. Indeed, it is the fact of such mystical and transformative experiences which gives rise to metaphysical and philosophical analysis.

Ramakrishna, the 19th-century Bengali saint, is a fascinating example of, as it were, the wattle and daub, the devotion and knowledge elements of darshan. He provided testimony to a total devotion to the Supreme Being, conceived of particularly as the goddess Kali, as a result of numerous visionary experiences – 'seeings' of the deity. His sainthood, though, is also in recognition of his ability to slip into a state of samadhi, a state of intense, concentrated contemplation or meditation. Such a state is usually associated with a Yogin, who pursues the long and hard path of Yogic discipline, of intuitive knowledge and perfection, in order to achieve timelessness and liberation, without necessarily having recourse to a deity. What both the Yogin and Ramakrishna do exemplify, however, is the transformative potential and reality of the goal of darshan: to be a jivanmukta – to be released in the midst of life.

Because of darshan . . .

It has already been said that the ultimate purpose of darshan is to be released from the cycle of samsara. There is a danger that this only implies some far-off goal to be achieved in the future, the prize to be won after death. It is not the intention that this should be so. Through the daily act of puja, meditation, sacrifice and love, darshan can offer the vision and experience of the eternal, now. This is what is meant when it is said that to 'see' is to be transformed.

Notes

1 Diana Eck, *Darsan: seeing the Divine Image in India*, Anima Books, Pennsylvania, 1981, page 3.

2 *Bhagavad Gita*, 9.26. Quoted here from R.C. Zaehner, *Hindu Scriptures*, J.M. Dent and Sons, London, 1966, page 288.

4 Islam: an environment of peace and harmony

Alan Brine and *Muhammad Riyami*

What lies at the heart of the Islamic vision of life? The play of meanings contained in the basic word 'Islam' provides the essential perspective from which we intend to interpret this distinctive vision. Although Islam can be translated as 'peace' or 'submission', the words lie uneasily with one another. If we interpret them from a perspective which is Western, peace suggests a positive value with which we can all identify; but submission is more ambiguous. Its negative associations can easily predominate when contrasted with the search for freedom interpreted through a view about the position of women in the Islamic world.

In order to make sense of this tension between 'peace' and 'submission', we need to extend our range of concepts to include the importance of unity and harmony in Muslim experience.

Peace through submission

Al-Hafiz B.A. Masri's essay 'Islamic Concern for Animals' emphasizes that at the heart of the message of the Qur'an is the idea of 'life as one homogeneous organism'. The centre of this organism is the Godhead, Allah, from which all creation derives its existence and meaning. He quotes Rumi:

'Dying from the inorganic, we developed into the
    vegetable kingdom;
Dying from the vegetable, we became men.
Then what fear that death will lower us?
The next transition will make us angels.
From angels we shall rise and become what no mind
    can conceive;
We shall merge in affinity as in the beginning.
Have we not been told, "All of us shall return unto
    him"?'[1]

Everything derives from and returns to God. Achieving the peace which is the goal of Islam depends upon the recognition that harmony stems from the submission of all life to its true origin. To be Muslim is to achieve the state in which one is at peace and harmony through submission to that which truly unifies the created order: Allah.

Muslim forms of expression – almsgiving, prayer, fasting, pilgrimages, law, mystical practice etc. – only make sense from the perspective of the goal of 'peace through submission'.

The underlying unity and harmony

It is valuable to reconsider the use we make of the world 'Muslim'. Most commonly, we find the word used as a noun to identify a person who follows the faith of Islam. But within that tradition, it is common to find the word used as an adjective, to describe a state of being. Hence the natural world, apart from humankind, can be described as 'muslim'; in other words, it exists in a natural state of harmony. It is only the human species which has the unique capacity to undermine and upset the balance of nature. Human beings have the capacity to 'forget'. This notion of 'forgetfulness' is central to Islam. The act of forgetting involves placing something other than God at the centre of life – whether it be family, nation, money or personal success. Hence, the concept of 'Shirk', or attributing a partner to Allah – the inverse of the first element in the basic declaration of faith, the Shahadah: 'There is no God but God'. Islamic art is one of the best expressions of this idea. Much of the art is based on pattern and design, often highly complex. Yet the designs have a basic harmony and structure. The eye may find itself initially bewildered by the complexity, and sense will be made of the images only when the underlying pattern and centre is discovered. So it is with human life. Islam recognizes that all too often our experience is terribly restless and fragmented. There are many different pressures upon us; we are motivated by many competing demands; we are faced with the difficulty of making sense of what seems confused. The goal of Islam is to come to the point where we understand the underlying unity of all experience. If we do not find this we will continue to live with disharmony.

The twin sources of the revelation of the Divine re-emphasize the themes of unity and harmony and the interplay of the environment and humanity. The natural world is a revelation of God, but this is complemented in the Qur'an, the final and complete word of God. The interplay between human understanding and revelation expresses the theme of movement from disharmony to harmony. Both sources of revelation – nature and the Qur'an – share common features. To the confused mind, they appear to be disorganized, repetitive, fragmented and bewildering. S.H. Nasr, in his book *Ideals and Realities of Islam*, has commented: 'Many people, especially non-Muslims, who read the Qur'an for the first time, are struck by what appears as a kind of incoherence from the human point of view'.[2] Nasr goes on to compare the Qur'an with the world of nature: 'The Qur'an is composed of a profusion and intertwining of plant life as seen in a forest, often combined suddenly with the geometry, symmetry and clarity of the mineral kingdom, of a crystal held before light'.[3]

The themes begin to interweave. If the Qur'an and the natural world appear confused and chaotic, the dilemma rests within the human mind. As the mind encounters the Qur'an and the natural world, it finds a multiplicity which echoes its own confusion. Meditation and study of the revelation gradually leads to a discovery of its inner unity as the mind itself comes to its own harmony and peace. What is true of the Qur'an and the world of nature is also true of the world of the community and the individual.

The community

The Muslim community – the Ummah – is an ideal based on a seeming paradox of unity in diversity. The Islamic notion of a universal community which embraces all Muslims appears to defy the 'normal' rules of social life. Ideally it is a community which takes its centre and its sense of meaning from Allah alone. It is a religious/political reality which has no hierarchy, and no priesthood. The cement which holds the community together is not the cult of personality, the rule of law or the democratic ideal. Rather, it is the individual's sense of personal responsibility which binds the community. The community survives and hangs together only if all individuals recognize and perform their obligations to one another, the environment and, ultimately, God – obligations which are embodied in the Muslim

concept of Khalifah.

To the non-Muslim, this notion of community can appear idealistic, even absurd. How can the conflicts and tensions which exist between individuals be harnessed for good without the imposition of some human principle of government, whether it be despotic or democratic? Yet the Islamic perspective encourages the idea that the centre and harmony of the community is real only when each individual understands that it is his or her own personal responsibility. The absence of a priesthood in Islam reflects this understanding of Ummah, the Muslim community. There are no priests – no intermediaries between the individual and God. No-one can take on board another's responsibility. Every individual has to recognize his or her unique responsibility for the community within which he or she places him- or herself.

The sublime expressions of the sense of the peace and harmony which comes from unity in diversity are found in the main patterns of Muslim worship: prayer and pilgrimage. The act of prayer, with its emphasis on the individual facing up to responsibility for his or her actions, is combined with a subtle acknowledgement of the place of the individual within the Ummah. Even when the Muslim prays alone, there is an acknowledgement – in the slight movement of the head at the close of prayer – of the wider Muslim community. If the Muslim prays in a congregation, there is a recognition that no Muslim has any right to a special place within the mosque. Yet, at the moment of prayer, the disparate individuals, who have been standing alone preparing themselves, silently gather to form a community of equals before God, standing shoulder to shoulder.

Similarly, the Hajj, a remarkable expression of unity in diversity, acknowledges no human hierarchy, yet flows with a harmony and sense of peace which expresses for Muslims the distinctiveness of the Ummah as a unique form of communal life.

Centrality of the Qur'an

The Qur'an remains the centre of this picture. The Qur'an embodies the immutable centre of life. Submission to Allah is submission to the Qur'an – the living reality of God in human lives. The concept of individual responsibility extends to the Qur'an. Each Muslim must take personal responsibility for his or her interpretation of the Qur'an. While the guidance of the law schools and Qur'an scholarship exists, it cannot diminish this personal responsibility. Ultimately, it is the individual's own effort which can ensure that the Qur'an's inner meaning is revealed. Nasr again: 'It is man himself who is incoherent and it takes much effort for him to integrate himself with his Centre so that the message of the Divine Book will become clarified for him and reveal to him its inner meaning'.[4]

For the Muslim, once Islam is accepted, the individual is within the community. To place anything other than the Will of Allah at the centre of one's attention is Shirk – the creation of a partner for God. As such, it is the beginning of the loss of harmony and peace both for the individual and for the community.

Islam and the environment

This perspective on life extends into the Muslim's approach to the environment. As the trustees of the creation, humanity must avoid the disharmony created by Shirk. Every action and movement upon the natural world must recognize that the individual cannot act independently but must acknowledge the power of God. Each individual is a Caliph to himself (Khalifah – a trustee of God's creation); each individual has responsibility for his or her action upon the environment. Hence any action which is based purely on personal vanity or personal gain will be destructive of the peace and harmony which are the goals of Islam. The consequence of an acceptance and understanding of this notion of Khalifah is a striving for a balanced, creative use of resources which recognizes each individual's responsibility for the future of the planet. There is no distinction between the religious and the secular activity of an individual's life. Islam is, essentially, a 'way of life' – a striving for peace and harmony in all aspects of

human existence.

The consequences for the Muslim of this approach to the environment are simply expressed in the Muslim Declaration on Nature, produced after the Assisi Conference: 'We are God's stewards and agents on earth . . . His trustees are responsible for maintaining the unity of His creation, the integrity of the earth, its flora and fauna, its wildlife and natural environment.'[5] The garden has been a classic form of Muslim culture which expresses perfectly this sense of stewardship, unity and harmony. In the creation and tending of a garden, the Muslim seeks to flow with the patterns of light, water, colour etc., to ensure that they are enhanced rather than controlled. There is no intention merely to entertain or amuse, to divide the natural elements from their surroundings or to set nature against its own inner pattern and harmony. The purpose of the creation of a garden is to reveal the underlying harmony and unity which exists within the apparent haphazard or chaotic diversity of nature. We need to flow with, and not seek dominion over, the natural world. The symbolism of the garden becomes a central way of expressing the Muslim idea of heaven – an environment of balance, peace and harmony – unity in diversity: 'To the Muslim the idea of unity does not just mean the assertion that there is one God sitting in heaven instead of two or three. . . . Unity is . . . a method of integration, a means of becoming whole and realizing the profound oneness of all existence'.[6]

Notes

1 Al Hafiz BA Masri, *Islamic Concern for Animals*, The Athene Trust, 1987, page (x).
2 S. H. Nasr, *The Ideals and Realities of Islam*, Unwin Hyman, 1985, page 47.
3 *ibid.*, page 48.
4 *ibid.*, page 48.
5 Quoted in J. Rankin, A. Brown and P. Gateshill, *Ethics and Religion*, Longman, 1991, page 100.
6 S.H. Nasr, *op. cit.*, page 29.

5 The Jewish perspective

Clive A. Lawton

Any serious student of Judaism will soon be struck by the sheer quantity of material there is to learn. A tradition that values the written text and interpretations of it, which allows for the possibility of there being 70 correct interpretations of each teaching ('Each word of Torah speaks with 70 tongues'), and has been working the material over for about three thousand years in the light of life experiences in pretty well every country on the globe, is likely to be fairly dense!

Recognizing all that, there is a remarkable sense of relief in accepting that no-one can possibly know it all. What distinguishes the good teacher of Judaism from the not so good is the quality of understanding of the underlying driving forces that make sense of all the bits of ritual, tradition and moral teaching. It is as important to know how Jews are likely to respond to their tradition and why as to know what the tradition is.

So what are these underlying threads? Almost certainly the most important is Torah and its implications, but for reasons I shall explain later I shall leave that till last.

The other fundamental concepts that will help all the information fall into place are: a sense of place, a sense of time and a sense of identity.

A sense of place

Traditionally, Jewish attention is focused on the Temple Mount in Jerusalem. That is the place God chose for the residence of the Shekhina, that peculiarly specific presence of God which is referred to repeatedly in the Bible. It is because the Western Wall is on the border of the Temple Mount that Jews strive to pray there, as near to the Shekhina as possible. (Most Orthodox Jews, at least, do not go on to the Temple Mount itself – now occupied by mosques – because of the prohibition of anyone other than the High Priest to enter the ground of the Holy of Holies; and no one is quite sure where exactly this is.)

Jerusalem as a whole is also of intense significance. Zion, from which Zionism derives its name, is one of the mountains of Jerusalem and, particularly immortalized in the Psalms, it is the focus of Jewish ideals for a city of beauty, peace and holiness.

Then, spreading the ripples further, comes the Land of Israel. The boundaries of that Land are variously defined but, without doubt, the most significant parts are those now generally called 'the West Bank', in Israel, Judea and Samaria. This is the 'Promised Land', the place which, according to the Torah, God gave to the Jewish People as an inheritance in perpetuity. This conviction has confounded geography, history and politics. Regardless of the 'real' situation, Jews have celebrated the agricultural festivals as if they are in Israel (thus Pesach, the spring festival, is celebrated in Australia in the autumn, and Jews in Britain sit out in their open-roofed sukkot in the growing chill of a British October.

Despite their expulsion from the Land or their physical or economic inability to leave the lands in which they found themselves, Jews have aspired to return to the Land. When they have been able, many have gone, despite the frequent local and health dangers inherent in this move. Even today, Jews leave lives in comfortable suburbia in the West, perhaps to shift rocks for a precarious agricultural settlement in the desert.

This connection with the Land also helps explain a host of Jewish practices. Agricultural seasons inform the workings of the Jewish calendar, many aspects of the festivals, and many minor practices. A remarkable closeness to nature's workings has been maintained, despite the urbanization of the majority of Jews over the century. This contrasts strikingly with, for example, the experience of the urban proletariat that emerged out of the industrial revolution in Europe.

However, there is another side to this coin, without which the picture would be perilously incomplete. The idea that God can be anywhere and – as the Sinai experience demonstrated – frequently at His or Her best outside Israel, gives Judaism a remarkable portability. The diaspora experience is an ancient one for Jews. More than 25 centuries ago, Jeremiah was offering the advice to the exiled Jews in Babylon which has informed the attitude of Jews throughout the world: 'Pray for the welfare of the city in which you live, for therein lies your welfare.' This has led to Jews having no difficulty with their aspirations *vis-à-vis* the Promised Land on the one hand and their Land of Adoption on the other. Even the Shekhina turns out to be more portable than we might originally have thought. 'Where two people discuss words of Torah, there dwells the Shekhina,' is a teaching of the rabbis in the Talmud.

Thus, traditionally, Jews live on two intersecting planes. Their place and home and country is wherever they are. They have a religious, let alone a civic, duty to abide by its laws and to further its welfare. At the same time, there is another place, throbbing with the pull of the old ancestral home, with all its dreams and memories. In past centuries this has been much misunderstood. In this age, when half the world seems to be in diaspora, the concept has to be grasped.

A sense of time

Jews also operate at two different rhythms. One is the sweep of history and the other is the here-and-now. This is probably true of most cultures and traditions, but articulating it will help one to understand Judaism better.

The Jews are frequently referred to as a people of history. This doesn't mean that they've been around a long time. It refers to the fact that Jews derive much of their sense of purpose and place by reference to historical events. Thus, the Jewish tradition is about making sense of collective historical experience rather than about exploring personal spiritual experience. Each of the major events is enshrined into the collective memory and explored through study and commemoration or celebration.

The Exodus, for example, is not just an allegory for suffering released by faith; it is a real freedom experience, with political significance and overtones. Similarly, the destruction of the Temple is not just an allegory for the downfall of a people that might lose its way; it is a specific experience of destruction which led to physical exile.

These experiences retain their meaning and significance only by being re-lived on an annual basis. The relevant festival is not a commemoration but rather a re-enactment, so that each Jew makes the experience his or her own. During the course of the year, a Jew experiences the whole of Jewish history at its significant points: annually liberated, wandering in the Wilderness, receiving the Torah, suffering the destruction of the Temple, the Spanish Inquisition, the Holocaust, feeling the relief and joy of the reprieve of Purim or the miraculous victory of Hanukah, mourning through the three weeks of the Roman siege of Jerusalem or the seven weeks of the plague amongst the disciples of Rabbi Akiva.

The meticulous aspect of Judaism delights in the precision and processes of time. A religion which has at its heart the seasons (because of its agricultural concerns), the cycle of the moon (because of its lunar calendar), the week (because of the centrality of Shabbat) and the cycle of the day (because of the original sacrificial system, now transmuted into the daily services) notes the passing of time in a celebratory manner.

History has an even grander sweep. Jews traditionally number their years from the creation of the world, and the High Holydays celebrate its birthday. Jews may well be unique in not numbering their years as if their own existence were the definition of time.

A sense of identity

A third feature that runs like a thread through Jewish reality is the sense of Peoplehood. From their earliest records, the Jews have been nothing if not a family, before they were bound by a coherent belief system. Even after that coherent belief system has started to fragment, following the 19th-century Enlightenment (what a loaded term!), this sense of belonging to a family has bound Jews together who have often had little else in common.

Identity is a complex and ill-defined concept. We come across it in phrases like 'identity crisis' and 'He's taken away my identity.' It is something about one's essential self which transcends the incidental accidents of nationality or class. It is closely allied with ideas of personality, but 'identity' includes one's place in the world and relationship with it.

Jews are preoccupied with Jewish identity. Creating a strong Jewish identity is seen as a fundamental purpose of Jewish education. Maintaining Jewish identity was the deepest challenge to Soviet Jews or other Jews under psychological, as opposed to merely physical, oppression. Working out what Jewish identity is concerns Jews as they face the new phenomena of purely 'secular' Jews (who adhere to none of the Torah-rooted traditions) and different bodies of authority who act upon their asserted right to define Jewish converts and, thus, who is a Jew.

Deep in the Jewish consciousness is the mandate God gave to the Jewish People, to be a 'kingdom of priests and a holy nation'. That is extended by Isaiah's challenge to the Jews to be 'a light to the Gentiles'. This practical role in the world's improvement is further bolstered by rabbinic teachings that God needs the support and help of humanity to complete and perfect the Creation. It might well be due to the concept that the Messianic Age might be brought about by the efforts of individual Jews that has led so many Jews, even those who no longer ostensibly adhere to any such beliefs or teachings, to play such a disproportionate part in the process of reform and progress around the world.

The difficulty that much of the Northern hemisphere, in particular, has had (often including the Jews, who have absorbed the *Weltanschauung* of the Gentiles amongst whom they have lived) in accommodating the Jews within their political and social systems is because religion is seen as a matter of faith, nationality as of geographical or political significance, race (a spurious and unpleasant term) concerning physical appearance and class as relating to power and wealth. Jews fit none of these categories comfortably *qua* Jews. They can be found in all groups under each heading, and yet still they are Jews. The missing concept is Peoplehood. It is an expanded form of family, clan or tribe. A study of political history reveals that the progress of many rulers has only been possible by suppressing the patterns of clan and tribe. This will be large on the political agenda of the southern hemisphere in the near future.

Small wonder, then, that Jewish identity sits problematically in today's political and social schemes. At the same time, an understanding of how Jews have preserved it without compromising their function in the other structures will give invaluable insight into the reality of the Jewish People.

Last but by no means least – Torah

This is the bedrock of all. Even the secular Jew who appears to have no relationship with that which most people would call religion derives his or her historical place from the Torah. What is more, the Torah is much more than the first five books of the Bible. It is a whole body of knowledge and an attitude system. Secular, socialist, anti-religious, Government of Israel, official tourist guides carry the book around with them just to explain what you are seeing and how to look at it.

The Torah has its vast hinterland of traditional interpretation and, without at least having an inkling of what sort of interpretations exist, you will never be able to read the Torah. You'll only ever be reading the beginning of the Old Testament!

Why, then, did I leave it till last?

When studying Judaism, it is hugely important not to end up studying the origins of Christianity only or, worse still, of an odd offshoot of Christianity. Most sincere teachers have no intention of doing such a thing, but often we are susceptible to mind-sets of which we are not even aware. By starting at a distance from the text, the way in which the text is used can be informed by the three concepts discussed above.

To be honest, of course, one could not long consider the concepts above without having to come back to the Torah with its interpretations to make sense of them all. But if one started with the Torah one might be tempted to be guided by Rabbi Hillel. In Roman times, Hillel was challenged to summarize all of Torah as briefly as possible. His response is widely known: 'Do not do to others what you would not have done to yourself.' The response is reassuring for those of us interested in decent relationships between peoples. Nothing too ethnocentric here. That's why some school programmes on Judaism start off with the Ten Commandments.

Hillel's answer foreshadows the debate in the

Talmud between Rabbis Akiva and Ben Azzai about which was the most important line in Torah. Akiva said 'Love your neighbour as yourself.' Ben Azzai said 'These are the generations of Adam . . . . ' Ben Azzai's answer was judged to be the best because Akiva's choice bases moral behaviour on one's own perceptions. Ben Azzai's choice roots human equality in the objective fact of humanity's common ancestry:

we are all created in the image of God. Monotheism and the truth of the Torah are all taken for granted.

Even this little exchange demonstrates why it is so important not to forget the second part of Hillel's answer, which is, perhaps understandably, less frequently quoted: 'The rest is commentary. Go and study it.'

6 Sikhism: perspectives and orientation

Sewa Singh Kalsi

The oneness of God

The central teaching of Sikhism is the oneness of God. All people, irrespective of caste, creed, colour and sex, are regarded as the creation of one God. In order to comprehend the deep meanings inherent within the doctrine of oneness of God, we need to look at the historical context in which Guru Nanak enunciated and developed the message of universal love and truth. Interaction between the Hindu and Muslim traditions was one of the unique experiences for the basis of universalism in the teachings of Guru Nanak. According to tradition, Guru Nanak set out on his teaching mission with the pronouncement that 'There is no Hindu and there is no Muslim.' This declaration clearly points to the unity of all human beings; Guru Nanak was inviting people to engage in the search for that reality which lay beyond sectarian boundaries. He emphasized that the whole of humankind was the family of one God.

One human family

The multi-faith environment in which the Sikh tradition emerged and developed provided unique opportunities for experiencing the true meanings of belonging to one human family. The plural milieu endowed the Sikh community with the gift of tolerance and learning from other religious traditions. It also generated a new climate for translating the message of diversity in God's kingdom into reality, and resulted in creating some unique Sikh institutions. *Adi Granth*, the holy scripture of the Sikhs, is the living testimony of such a divine experience. Alongside the compositions of

the Sikh Gurus, it contains the writings of Muslim and Hindu saints, some of whom belonged to the lowest strata of the Hindu society. Thus, *Adi Granth* not only represents the combined wisdom of a multi-faith society, but also imparts a message of love, unity and equality of human race. It has made an exceptional contribution towards the increasing understanding that all human beings are the creation of one compassionate God.

Diversity: a dynamic and positive force

Another manifestation of the message of the oneness of God is the architecture of Harmandir Sahib (Golden Temple, Amritsar). Its four doors symbolize the omnipresence of God and reject the view that, at the time of prayer, facing towards a particular direction has any significance for comprehending the divine experience. In order to put a seal on this experiment, Guru Arjun Dev invited Mian Mir, a Muslim saint, to lay down the foundation stone of Harmandir Sahib: it is open for everybody irrespective of caste, creed, and sex. Both *Adi Granth* and Harmandir Sahib represent uniquely a most enriching experience in the history of humankind, in which the concept of the diversity of God's kingdom has been celebrated as a key factor for shaping future human relations. In Sikhism, the diversity in God's kingdom is seen as a dynamic and positive force. The true message for all human beings is that all religious traditions are equally valid, as well as capable of enlightening their followers. Sikhism rejects the view that any particular religious tradition has the monopoly on the absolute truth. By belonging to different traditions and standing in different places we can share and broaden one another's vision.

The multi-lingual nature of Indian society made a valuable contribution towards the development of universalism in Sikhism. Linguistic diversity was a valuable tool in the hands of the Sikh Gurus, who employed it most creatively to transmit the message of universal love in their writings. For example, God has been identified by different names, which originated in different religious and linguistic traditions: Allah, Khuda, Kadir and Karim are from Muslim and Arabic traditions, while Bhagwan, Parmatma, Braham and Hari represent Hindu and Sanskrit traditions. These names occur again and again in the compositions of the Sikh Gurus. According to Sikh teachings, all human groups evolved and developed their modes of worship and religious institutions within the context of their social milieu. Whilst a Muslim prayer is called *namaz*, for a Hindu it is *puja*, and a Sikh prayer is called *path-karna/ardas*. In fact, the ultimate aim of each prayer is to ask for the grace of God; only the language and the mode of worship is different in these traditions, and they all lead to the understanding of our common source of existence. Guru Gobind Singh highlighted the essence and universality of religious truth thus: 'Recognise all mankind, whether Muslim or Hindu as one.
The same God is the Creator and Nourisher of all;
Recognise no distinctions among them.
The temple and mosque are the same;
So are the Hindu worship and Muslim prayer.
Human beings are all one.'[1]

It is significant to note that at the culmination of their service, Sikhs all over the world pray for the well-being and prosperity of the whole of humanity.

Social responsibility

Sikh dharma (religious, moral and social commitment) is a world-orientated tradition. In Sikhism the world is perceived as the abode of God and a place in which to practise dharma, which means that all human beings should engage themselves in righteous actions and behaviour in order to create a just social order. Sikhism is a living tradition, and a Sikh is expected to demonstrate his or her dharma through social responsibility. A Sikh is not a passive spectator in this world, but an active participant in the drama of human affairs. Thus, for a Sikh, there is no place for the renunciation of society, celibacy and the pursuit of God in the forest. Guru Nanak denounced the Yogis and praised those who lived in the society and faced the challenge of their social responsibilities. For a Sikh, the life of truthful conduct is more important than the vision of truth alone. Therefore, Sikhs must work hard and earn a living, and must not depend on other people like a parasite. Sikh dharma rejects the doctrine of varnashramadharma (dharma of class/caste and stages of life). Guru Nanak declared that 'Nonsense is the caste and nonsense is the grandeur of name and fame arising from it. All creatures are under the protection of one God.'[2] By introducing the institution of sangat (communal worship) and langar (communal eating), he launched a crusade against the institutionalized inequality built into the social structure of Indian society. The sangat and langar are the means of reinforcing the sense of equality within the human race.

The institution of gurdwara (Sikh temple/place of worship) plays an important role in promoting the ideal of the equality of the human race. Everyone, irrespective of race, colour, creed or sex, is welcome to the gurdwara, and is offered langar and prasad (blessed food) without any distinction. The Sikh children growing up in this country learn the basic lessons in Sikh faith at the gurdwara. Their belief in the diversity and equality of all human beings is confirmed as soon as they participate in the congregation. They begin to appreciate the equality of sexes when their mothers and fathers sit on the same carpet in the gurdwara with other members of the congregation. They also see Sikh women reading the Guru Granth Sahib, as well as taking part in the shabad-kirtan (religious singing). Sikh women receive inspiration from the teachings of Guru Nanak, who rejected the traditional view that women were inherently inferior. The Sikh youngsters receive another lesson of belonging to one human family when they share food in the langar.

Modern means of transportation and communication have brought the people of the world very close to each other, and they are instrumental for creating the sense of belonging to one human family. Sikhs regard the present age of scientific discovery and invention as an essential component of Gian Yug (Age of Knowledge), and a divine gift to humanity. It has endowed the human race with the capacity of creating international institutions such as the UNO etc. These institutions represent the quest to settle disputes through dialogue, the rejection of the path of mass destruction, the determination to end the arms race, and the destruction of nuclear weapons. The whole of humankind is experiencing a new phenomenon of restructuring human relations and institutions all over the world.

For Sikhs in diaspora, the experience of living in multi-faith societies has enriched their lives. They are committed to the notion of multi-faith schools. They will be pleased to see the teaching of all religious traditions as part of a school curriculum, which should aim to educate the young generation in a spirit of tolerance and willingness to learn from other traditions. They reject the idea of separate schools based on religious affiliation, which create a sense of division and discord among people. They not only enjoy being part of the multi-faith environment, but also actively participate in this unique experiment of unfolding the reality of one human family. A few years ago, the Leeds Sikh community organized Sikh Christmas dinners. They invited representatives of all faiths and ethnic groups, e.g. Christians, Jews, Muslims, Hindus and West Indians. On one occasion, the Archbishop of York was their chief guest. For the Sikhs, the experiment of Sikh Christmas dinners was a practical lesson for understanding the meanings of the diversity of God's kingdom. It also generated a new awakening and the sense of belonging to one family engaged in the pursuit of universal reality, called God, by embarking on different paths.

Anniversary of the founding of the Khalsa

Sikhs all over the world are preparing themselves to greet the arrival of the 21st century with confidence and hope for a peaceful future. They are doubly delighted to be preparing to celebrate the 300th anniversary of the founding of the Khalsa (the Sikh Order) in 1699. The founding of the Khalsa represents the unique experiment of rejecting caste divisions and the creation of an organization totally dedicated

to striving for the establishment of a social order based on the principle of equality. Commenting on their vision for 1999 and beyond, Dr Jasbir Singh Ahluwalia, General Secretary of the Guru Gobind Singh Foundation of India, writes that: 'Guru Gobind Singh Foundation has taken a historic decision of setting up of World University of Sikhism in co-operation with other like-minded organizations in India and abroad . . . The Sikhs settled in different parts of the world are today encountering, *qua* distinct groups, challenges of the surrounding faiths and cultures . . . In this context we believe that what is needed is a new centre of research – in a sense a centre of "search" within and without.'[3]

Second-generation Sikhs in Britain

The majority of Sikhs in Britain are either born here or grew up in this country. Their experience of being Sikhs and members of British society is significantly different from that of their parents. Their understanding of the Sikh heritage has developed in the context of a modern, urban-industrialized Britain and away from the Punjab. Although their commitment to their parent's religious tradition may be equally strong, their vision of the Sikh heritage is different from that of the first generation immigrants. There is a growing awareness among second-generation Sikhs of the emergence of caste-based gurdwaras in Britain. Most of the British-born Sikhs can speak Punjabi at a functional, communicative level, and for them it is a second language, mainly used in a domestic situation. They find it difficult to follow the language used at the gurdwaras by the ragis and gianis (religious musicians and preachers), who have been trained in the Punjab. Sikh youngsters are looking for new avenues which will assist them to relate the Sikh tradition to their life situation in this country. Traditional methods of absorbing the meanings of religious tradition are proving most inadequate. There is an urgent need to create religious literature in English and to train bi-lingual ragis and preachers who can interpret Sikhism for the British-born Sikhs, so that they develop the confidence to find their direction and destination in the pursuit of the message of Sikhism – the significance of which needs to be defined against the background of present-day realities.

Conclusion

I have attempted to highlight the significance of the concept of oneness of God in Sikhism. I have further argued that the Sikh community is a vital component of a global human family whose traditions emerged and developed in the context of a rich experience of interaction between Hinduism and Islam. The Sikh Gurus were not concerned with the ultimacy of divisions between Hindus and Muslims, but went beyond these boundaries to foster a religious tradition which was universal in character. Multi-faith Britain is a symbol of hope, as well as a challenge in comprehending the reality of belonging to one human family. By demonstrating that communities can live together despite their diverse religious and cultural traditions, all people can gain mutual understanding concerning the dynamics of the diversity in God's kingdom.

Notes

1 *Dasam Granth*, page 1078.
2 *Guru Granth Sahib*, page 83.
3 *The Sikh Review*, vol. 4110, no. 454, October 1991.

SECTION TWO B
Using the traditions' perspectives in teaching

....

Introduction

The writers in this section have aimed to translate the understanding of a religious orientation into the classroom context. This has not been an easy task, and each writer has employed his or her knowledge and expertise in his or her own way.

Part of the aim has been to engage not only with the perspective of the tradition, but also to work towards an engagement with the pupils' own experience. This demanded that the writers offer teachers ways in which they might initiate an interaction between the world view of a tradition and the concerns of children of different ages. This could not be a precise endeavour, given the span of age-ranges in primary and secondary schooling.

However, the learning strategies and activities offered are intended to stimulate teachers' thinking when they ask children to consider ways in which people from different traditions view the world and to reflect upon their own understanding.

We hope that this will help all of us to recognize the importance of engaging children with the world views of others as an essential educational goal, not only because they will become better informed, but also because their perspectives will be positively challenged and enriched from an early age.

Clive Erricker

1 Tiggy and the Bodhisattva: creating empathy with the Buddhist perspective in the primary classroom

Denise Cush, with the help of *Justine Long*

Why Buddhism?

Although relatively few primary teachers currently include Buddhism in their RE curriculum, the experience of my students and myself is that it can be one of the most helpful traditions to explore in trying to achieve the twin aims of assisting children to understand the nature of religion and aiding the personal development of the child.

There are many features of the Buddhist tradition which make it particularly suitable for primary RE. Buddhism is a practical rather than a doctrinal religion. Like primary educators, it stresses learning through experience. It is not closely tied to one particular culture in this country; Buddhists can be found from many different backgrounds: white middle class families, as well as families whose origins are in Thailand or Tibet. It expands the concept of religion beyond the idea of belief in God. It accepts that there are different ways for different people, and that religious paths should be judged not by their similarity to our own, but by their ability to change people for the better. There is a wealth of stories in Buddhism, many suitable for the youngest children. Finally, the novelty of Buddhism can intrigue both pupils and teachers and revitalize a sometimes neglected area of the curriculum.

Doing justice to the tradition

An exploration of Buddhism that concentrated on festivals, weddings, holy books, beliefs, creation stories, gods and worship might be colourful and interesting, but it could miss the heart of what Buddhism is about: transforming minds through morality, meditation and wisdom. Children can engage with the heart of Buddhism by exploring aspects of experience that reflect central Buddhist concerns such as change, growth and decay, happiness and suffering, and by investigating the purposes of meditational techniques and Buddhist lifestyles. As within the Buddhist tradition, learning should be experiential rather than didactic, and carefully matched to the age, background, interests and experience of the learner. This is the task that faces the teacher who wishes to adapt any of the practical activities that follow for a particular class of children.

Practical ideas for the classroom

What follows is one example of a short unit on Buddhism for junior children based upon one student's work. Justine had only six sessions with a class in an all-white rural school, but managed to convey something of the Buddhist perspective, leaving the children fascinated to know more about Buddhism and be more reflective about their own views and attitudes.

Session one – artefacts

The children were presented with a display of Buddhist artefacts, including Buddha rupas (images), to look at, discuss and ask questions about. This succeeded in uncovering preconceptions and prejudices ('weird'), and in generating interest and a desire to know more. Children can also engage with artefacts by drawing them in a mindful way, after a quiet contemplation or a guided reflection, or expressing their reactions in poetry or prose. They can compare different images of the Buddha and choose their favourite, with reasons. They can discover the meaning of the symbolism in the images after trying to guess it.[1]

Session two – the story

Justine told the class the story of the Buddha, basing her version on that of Jon Snelling.[2] This was taken slowly, with lots of questions, discussion, looking at the pictures etc. This story challenges the belief underlying our current culture that 'development' means increase in material wealth, and that this brings happiness. As well as discussing the story (and it is important for children to know that from a

Buddhist perspective whether the details 'really happened' is an unimportant question), children can sequence pictures of the story, make their own cartoon versions of episodes in it (with respect), dramatize sections, produce a storyboard for a video, choose images for a series of slides, etc.

Session three – metta meditation

Justine undertook a simplified form of metta (loving kindness) meditation with the class. This exercise helps to build up children's self-esteem and concern for others. Children who do not feel comfortable with it can be asked to sit quietly. Buddhists stress that for meditation proper you need an experienced meditation teacher. Sitting in a meditation posture, e.g. upright in a chair with eyes closed, after calming down with concentration on the breathing or the sounds around, you imagine a warm glow of loving kindness like a sun in the region of your heart. You first try to feel this warm, friendly feeling towards yourself, feeling positive about yourself, accepting yourself, and making wishes for yourself: may I be well; may I be happy; may things go well for me. The feelings and the wishes are then extended in turn to a close friend, a 'neutral' person and a person with whom the relationship is not easy. Finally you imagine the warm feeling extending in all directions to fill the classroom, the school, the neighbourhood, the country, the whole universe, and repeat the wish, 'may all beings be happy!'

The children enjoyed this experience, and it led to a general discussion of ways in which we can contribute practically to the happiness of other people. Children can also discuss their feelings about the exercise; some children may not have enjoyed it, and it is important to take the Buddhist perspective: some things work for some people and others for others; don't worry! The exercise can also lead to a discussion of what happiness is and what brings happiness. Children can design 'Happiness is . . .' posters, collect adverts that seem to suggest that their product will bring happiness and give a Buddhist critique of advertising as increasing desire and therefore suffering.

Session four – Avalokiteshvara

The children were fascinated by the poster of the bodhisattva Avalokiteshvara with many heads and

Someone special to me, depicted in the same symbol-language as the bodhisattva Avalokiteshvara. Tiggy gives explanations of her symbols.

thousands of arms and explored the symbolism of the figure. (Posters can be obtained from Tantra[3] and a useful explanation can be found in P. Morgan, *Buddhist Iconography*.) The children then created their own symbolic images of someone very special to them, using the same symbol-language. Thus they were helped both to understand a Buddhist image and to reflect on their own lives. Tiggy's picture of her sister Louise includes her explanations of the symbols.

Session five – the sangha

With the help of pictures, Justine outlined the lifestyle of a Theravada monastic sangha (this is not the only model of the sangha in Buddhism, but an important one). Daily life, diet, the almsround, the precepts, the scriptures and the relationship between the sangha and the laity were touched upon. The purposes behind the practices were always stressed, as the 10 precepts and 227 vinaya rules all have a practical training function. The children then responded by thinking about their own community, and making a list of rules for their school. It was important that children always gave the practical reason behind the rule.

Session six – Wesak

As practical constraints made it impossible for a monk to visit the classroom as planned, Justine concluded her work with a session on the festival of Wesak. The details of the festival were touched upon, but the focus was on seeing whether the children had gained any insight into Buddhism. Their task was to design a Wesak card using symbols which expressed what they thought Buddhism was about. The work that emerged included meditating Buddhas, wise owls, wheels, books, the sun emerging from clouds, trees and flowers and lots of candles – beside the Buddha and lighting up dark houses. They then wanted to send these cards to a Buddhist person with the wish that they would be happy. We concluded that the children had begun to understand the Buddhist perspective, the importance of looking for the meaning behind religious symbols, stories, practices and rules, and had gained insights helpful to their own personal development.

Further ideas

Jataka Tales: stories presented as 'previous lives' of the Buddha, illustrating virtuous ways to live, often through animal characters which appeal to children.[4]

Stupas: children can explore the symbolism of the stupa, trace its development, visit modern stupas, make their own.[5]

Rebirth and Ordination: children may be interested in the life story of Lama Osel, a young Spanish boy (born 1985) who has been recognized as the reincarnation of a Tibetan lama.[6]

Festivals: there are many different festivals in different Buddhist countries.[7] Some colourful ones for the classroom are Hanamatsuri (children can make a garden), Loy Krathong (children can make floating candles) and Hungry Ghosts (have a bonfire of your vanities).

Shrines: Buddhist shrines from different traditions can be set up in the classroom, and the purposes of

Buddhist 'worship' explored.

Suffering: children can collect examples from the news, discuss their own solutions to major problems and compare these with the Buddha's. What three wishes would you make for yourself and the world to change life for the better? Are these selfish? Realizable? How? Write stories illustrating how selfishness leads to suffering.

Change: children can collect their own examples, e.g. baby photos, and try to discover if there is anything that does not change.

Symbols: children can compose their own symbols for central Buddhist concepts such as impermanence, suffering, change, nibbana.

Sacred Places: children can collect pictures of temples from around the world. They can discuss why some people like plain places and others, statues and colour. How do they like their own special places, e.g. bedrooms? Does it matter if some people like images and others do not?

Monks and Nuns: the varieties of monastic lifestyle can be compared. Which monks can watch TV? An imaginary 'day in the life', diary or letter home from the monastery can be composed.[8]

Stories: the Buddha was an excellent teacher and made great use of stories. A favourite is 'the blind men and the elephant'[9], explaining why people see the world differently and suggesting a positive approach to this. A 'feely box' can aid children to share the experience of the blind men.[10]

Elephants: these feature as symbols in Buddhist stories, in festivals and in the Buddha's life. A decorated Asala Perahera procession of elephants can march across the classroom wall.

Clothes: look at monastic 'uniforms' and the reason behind them. Children can explore meanings in their own clothes and other uniforms.

The Wheel of Life: the Tibetan poster can be explored (what do you think is going on?), explained and reproduced.[11]

Refuges: Buddhists declare allegiance by 'taking refuge' in the three treasures of the Buddha, Dhamma and Sangha. Discuss what the three refuges are in the children's life (money? God? Mum? mountains? the dog?) and ask them to invent a ceremony to express their importance.

Daruma Dolls: the low-centre-of-gravity dolls

based on the Zen master Bodhidharma are an excellent illustration of the Buddhist aim of not being too attached to either suffering or happiness. The dolls remain stable and centred when pushed from any side, and the Buddhist realizes the transience of both good luck and bad and tries to maintain 'evenmindedness'.

Flags: look at the modern 'Buddhist flag' and ask the children to design their own.

Badges: collect Buddhist badges, e.g. Tibetan, FWBO, and allow the children to design their own.

Making: malas, prayer wheels, Zen gardens, writing haikus.

Finally . . .

Two stories from the Buddhist tradition to encourage primary teachers to try Buddhism in the classroom.

Why it doesn't matter if you get the facts a bit wrong as long as your aims are in tune with the Buddhist perspective:

'There was once a great famine in Tibet, but one old lady recited a special mantra, and so great was her faith that stones turned into bread. Her clever son, a monk, came to visit and pointed out that actually she was saying the mantra all wrong. She dutifully corrected her prayer to the official wording, but the miracle no longer happened.' (traditional tale).

Why you have to get on with things before you know all the answers:

'There was a man shot by a poisoned arrow who refused to have it pulled out until all his questions had been answered – the wood of the arrow, the type of feather in the flight, the sort of bow that fired it, the

person who shot it . . . that man would die before he found the answers.' (a story from the Buddha).

So, from the Buddhist perspective, you don't have to know everything, but time is short, so have a go and do what you can!

Notes

1 With help from P. Morgan, *Buddhist Iconography*, available from the author at Westminster College, Oxford.

2 J. Snelling, *The Life of the Buddha*, Wayland, 1987. Other useful versions are J. Landaw, *Prince Siddhartha*, Wisdom, 1980 and Association of Buddhist Women, *The Story of the Buddha*, London Buddhist Vihara.

3 Tantra Designs, Gas Ferry Road, Bristol BS1 6UN.

4 Two useful sources of stories are J. Snelling, *Buddhist Stories*, Wayland, 1986 and P. Morgan, *Buddhist Stories*, available from the author.

5 With help from P. Morgan, *Buddhist Iconography*.

6 V. Mackenzie, *Reincarnation*, Bloomsbury, 1988.

7 P. and H. Connolly, *Buddhism through Festivals*, Longman, 1989 and A. Brown (ed.), *Festivals in World Religions*, Longman, 1986.

8 A variety of lifestyles are explored in D. Cush, *Buddhists in Britain Today*, Hodder and Stoughton, 1990.

9 See (4) above.

10 H. Rankin, A. Brown and M. Hayward, *Religious Education Topics for the Primary School*, Longman, 1989.

11 Poster available from Tantra (see 3 above), and explanation in P. Morgan, *Buddhist Iconography*.

2 Primary schools, children and the Christian life-story

Dennis Starkings

This article divides into three sections. The first one tries to show that the quest for a personally significant life-story is not such an unusual thing, and that the Christian (largely biblical) story about the meaning of life is a distinctive fulfilment of that quest. The second section tries to get to grips with practical lesson-planning and teaching. Our aims should be: to heighten pupils' awareness that they possess a

personal life-story full of perceptions and questions about themselves and the world; through this to demonstrate the life-relatedness of the Christian story; and therefore, finally, to leave pupils with an awareness that the larger and broader life-stories of human communities can fulfil the personal quests of individual human persons. Of these three aims, perhaps the last is likely to be least fully articulated in the understanding of primary school pupils – but we shall have worked usefully towards it by means of the other two. The final section illustrates the operation of a method that explores life-experience and the relevance of Christian understandings.

Life-stories

That life is made meaningful by story is not so unusual. Each of us has his or her own personal life-story, into which fictional or imagined possibilities are incorporated – a more or less adequate self-understanding that amounts to an interpreted narrative of our lives. Our parents, aunts and uncles, cousins and friends all have some role in our personally significant story. It is a selective and 'pointed' narrative, of course. It highlights certain events or encounters and discards others as insignificant. The role of the fictional element is interesting. In telling bedtime stories to my own daughter (too many years ago, now) I stumbled by accident on the device of using the names of her friends in sequences of events that were almost entirely fantastic. Neither of us ever confessed to the other that there might be any connection between those names and these real people; but there must have been some reason why 'Lucy and Anthony Stories' were so often in demand. Dangerous stuff, this – and I have to assert that the fictional Lucy and Anthony were never involved in anything but the most ethical and creative of events, though certain traits were borrowed from real life! From time to time there is some experience that leads to a fresh understanding of our personal story; and the urge all the time is towards some larger and more inclusive framework of meaning. Though some stories are discarded or rejected, there are others that we adopt as our own. Or perhaps we adopt aspects or bits and pieces of almost every story with which we become engaged. Anniversary occasions such as birthdays and silver weddings celebrate and affirm the story we tell of ourselves, as do parties to celebrate homecomings and life's achievements.

It seems that Christians understand the world in terms of a much broader and remarkable story. Some of it happened 'behind the scenes of the world' – for example, when Satan reckoned to know better than God and went about the world implicating the rest of humanity in the same mistake. Some of it happened in human history, as when (by the Christian understanding) God himself intervened in human form to remedy the situation through the perfect love, obedience and self-sacrifice of Jesus Christ. That story has yet to be completed. It is an unfinished story in the sense that the Kingdom of God (the whole of creation fully restored in obedience to its creator) represents the destiny available to humankind. That is not all there is to it, of course. The religiously significant history of the Jewish people – recorded in what is for Christians the 'Old Testament' – fills it out in a wealth of story, song, drama and commentary: how things went wrong in the Garden of Eden; how a remnant was rescued by Noah; how Moses led the way to a new commitment and freedom. Such stories and so many others represent the richness of a human experience recorded and shared by the human community.

The 'New Testament' is, of course, a record of that supreme moment of God's new intervention in the world through Jesus Christ – and that growing awareness of it through which the distinctively Christian response took shape. It should not really be so surprising that Christians can be heard to disagree over which parts of the story are historical in the conventional sense, for the story is about ordinary human life understood in the vast perspective of ultimate meanings and purposes, and those ultimate perspectives are represented in narratives no less vivid and detailed than the incidents of plain human history. Was the tomb of Jesus really empty? Did Jesus really ascend bodily into heaven? Perhaps one helpful thing for us to remember (as teachers worried by such apparent problems and anxious not to give offence) is simply this – that whether or not such matters are understood as literal or historical facts, it is their spiritual significance within the whole story that makes them relevant. That Christians know God through Jesus, and know him to be a living reality, is a fact of committed Christian living; and it is this (instantiated with all the particularity of story) that lies at the heart of the Christian world view. We have somehow to communicate the shape and meaning of this overall story – and to teach each bit of it with awareness of its contribution to the whole – if we are to communicate the Christian sense of life. The fact that it can be communicated at varying levels of detail and sophistication brings it within the range of teachers' professional competence, for in every subject of the curriculum there is this same challenge to mediate ideas.

When Christians 'adopt' the Christian Salvation Story as their own, they are adopting what is for them the most satisfactorily inclusive and meaningful framework for the understanding of their own lives. To talk of 'adopting the story as one's own' is perhaps one way to talk of Christian conversion. Prophets, saints and apostles are one's culture-aunts-and-uncles. It is not so surprising to have their stories and pictures about the house and to see them as involved with one's own life and to adapt one's self-understanding in the light of a growing awareness of their significance. If we ask how the Christian story comes to be adopted, it is probably not so often through argument about concepts – as if God were primarily a concept! – as through an inner conviction that this story coheres with one's own life-experience and interprets its significance. Meanings implicit in that wider story-pattern become meanings within one's own life, so that the language of sin and redemption, newness of life, vocation and destiny become natural in this context, even while meaningless to others who stand outside this particular story-frame. Guilt relates to forgiveness; closed and futile turnings in life yield to renewal and a new freedom; and the life one is living has purpose and direction.

If there is any one focus for this consolidation of knowing and believing it is the act of worship. Arguably, all Christian acts of worship honour and celebrate this shared story of the Christian family, so that in participation one makes the story one's own. Many would say this supremely of the Eucharist, otherwise called Mass or Holy Communion. Here, with the bread and wine of the Last Supper as its active focus, is the celebration of Christ's life, death, resurrection and living presence.

Teaching the Christian life-story

These, then, are the elements from which we can construct not only our programme of teaching but also our method. Since the whole process of meaningful story-making needs to be brought to consciousness (pupils are normally hardly aware that they do it), our method needs to highlight the progressive story-making of pupils' own lives, and only on this basis to illuminate the life-relatedness of Christian story. It requires a particular approach to lesson-planning.

First, though the overall scheme of work or sequence of lessons may be long or short (and the range of stories correspondingly ample or limited), it should always embody the teacher's own sense of the human life-experience with which the Christian story or stories may be dealing. To take a fairly accessible example, the story of the Garden of Eden tells of happiness that is spoiled by misplaced ambition, pride and disobedience – though (as a disobedience to the loving purposes of God) it is not quite the same thing as disobeying a teacher, and we should be careful about teaching simple conformity to the teacher's will! Nevertheless the point is that we shall have begun to think about the story's human significance in itself. From this, we shall have begun to gain some clues about elements in the experience of children that they might usefully reflect upon. This experience (rather than the Christian story) will be our practical starting-point in the classroom, orientating the children towards relevant issues that they can eventually apply to the Christian story and so take further in terms of their own reflection.

If lesson-planning starts from our own (but still secret) awareness of the story, our classroom beginning is with the children's own life experience – and we should be prepared for surprises. Preparing to approach the Garden of Eden story, we might ask about how our parents try to keep us from danger – as with the rules of the road, for example – but we can find ourselves talking about all sorts of things they would wish to do and are not allowed to do! If we then ask about happy times and whether they have ever been spoiled, we are likely to get unpredictable responses ranging (say) from a birthday party spoiled by rain to bereavement and other deeply personal experiences of loss. How these can be coped with, our choice of which suggestions to develop and which to pass over more lightly – such decisions can be made only by each of us in the classroom circumstances as we know them. But perhaps enough has been said to suggest the area of personal experiences in which our work initially lies.

A moment will then emerge at which these discussions can usefully turn to the specifically Christian story: a moment at which we think pupils are ready to further their discussion by encountering the story's objective stimulus. It can be managed by their reading or being told the story, or perhaps by discussing a painting of it. How they engage with that story, continue their discussion and enact their understanding in their own work, brings us to opportunities already familiar to the primary class-teacher. We are into the areas of dramatic enactment, artwork and personal writing, for example. When the work is completed, children should have some enhanced awareness of themselves, some sense of liberation through exploration, some sense of having shared in something personally and corporately significant.

An example in action

One of those bookshops that deal in remaindered books had opened temporarily, and one of its large-sized books was a collection of icons from the Orthodox tradition, reproduced in colour. Six illustrations were cut out representing the Virgin Mary and the Child Jesus. They were pasted on to hardboard and sealed with a thin film of PVA. These icons had attracted attention in the context of the approach outlined above. In terms of the Christian story, the icons had, of course, to do with the incarnation of God as the child of Mary. They seemed to represent different states of feeling on the part of the Holy Mother and the Holy Child, and different senses of the relationship between them. As pictures of a mother and child, they connected everyday experience and responses with essential Christian ideas. Some were more obviously affecting and touching. Others emphasized a sort of nobility and restraint. Perhaps there was something common or even universal about the human appeal of these elements of relationship: a broadly human experience of motherhood and childhood. Perhaps the specifically Christian understanding of this unique mother-and-child relationship could be approached from this basic recognition of human responsiveness.

The children (aged 10 or 11 years) were asked to put up their hands if they thought they knew the names of the two people in the pictures. They were asked for the time being to keep those names secret – because we would start from looking at the pictures simply as images of a mother and a child. The first stage was to agree an order from left to right: on the left, those that showed the mother at her most sad and gentle, and on the right, those that showed her as most noble and serene or peaceful. From that point there was considerable discussion of how mothers may have all sorts of feelings about their children: happiness (for example) about new life, and sadness about some of the unhappy things that might have to happen to them in growing up. They were asked to look for those different feelings in the pictures.

When the time felt right, it was explained that these were, in fact, pictures (not photographs!) of Mary and Jesus; and we thought about the way some Christians like to have pictures of people who matter to them, just as we have photos of family and friends at home. Finally, however, there was a connection to be made between this broader experiential approach and the specific meanings of the Christian story. Children were given first a gospel account of the annunciation, and then a gospel account of the crucifixion. Asked at each stage if the gospel account helped them to understand the pictures, they made the appropriate connections. Perhaps the serenity had something to do with her special calling at the annunciation. The apparent maturity of the child Jesus ('He looks like a little old man') was dealt with by giving them the opening words of St John's gospel, spending some time to ensure that they grasped the tremendous idea of the Word of God, present at the creation of the world. Perhaps Mary's sadness had something to do with some awareness that her child would suffer. We established these ideas in conversation. We talked again about the challenge of being a parent: the knowledge that your child will almost certainly have to cope with suffering; the responsibility you have to stand back more and more as your child grows up so that he or she learns to face life; the obligation to prepare your child with the strength to face challenges; the sadness but also the joy of all this. Perhaps we see these things in the face of the Holy Mother – something very special because of the annunciation and the crucifixion, but something that touches everyone in their experience of life.

3 Blind sight – the vision of the seer: sharing a Hindu perspective with primary school children

Jane and *Clive Erricker*

Hinduism is often a difficult tradition for Westerners to grasp. We are presented with myriad images and carefully balanced statements which appear as bemusing contradictions: God is many and one; without and within; with and without form, and so on. The temptation is to leave it alone. The governor of one school I worked in, during the only conversation we ever had about Religious Education, told me he had just come back from India and had come to the conclusion that Hinduism was superstition. 'I don't suppose you will agree with me,' he said. I didn't, but it was difficult for him to appreciate why. This article is, in a way, an attempt to reply to him and the many people involved in education who hold the same view.

To observe and witness may seem to offer evidence that supports one's view, but there is a concept central to Hinduism that explains why it is misleading and simplistic to conclude from this that we actually understand what we are seeing.

The ability to see

Though Hindus are often happy to accept 'Hinduism' as the term for their tradition, it is more correct to start with their own concept of sanatana dharma – the eternal truth. This truth is apprehended only if we have the capacity to do so. This capacity arises through receiving 'darshan': the conferred ability to see truly by eradicating ignorance.

Diana Eck contextualizes this in Hindu worship by saying that 'When Hindus go to the temple, their eyes meet the powerful, eternal gaze of the eyes of God. It is called "darshan", "seeing" the divine image, and it is the single most common and significant element of Hindu worship.'[1]

How do we introduce primary school children to this concept of 'seeing'?

The divine presence

It is important to realize that formal images are not the only objects through which one can encounter the gaze of God. For Hindus, God is everywhere and in everything. All is alive and imbued with the divine presence. Ramakrishna said he recognized Shiva in all he saw. The 15th-century poet Anantdas, speaking of God, said: 'He gave me life and I am his expression now.' Mockerjee, in *Pathway Icons*, explains: 'In India, life, art and religion are one. The process of creating a work of art is also an act of worship, one through which the invisible manifests as the visible, and the artist who "invokes" the image gives form to the formless, seeking to discover the unknown through the known. The act of creation is at the same time a process of self discovery, inspired by a desire to unite the human spirit with the divine. The ultimate goal of life is to discover the divine essence which is a part of all that exists, so that it is no longer the unknown, but becomes an intimate part of living, when the seeker and the object of worship enter into a personal and very special relationship.'[2]

The way to Krishna

Krishna, more than any other God, is the focus of Hindu devotion. Diana Eck illustrates his significance by referring to the importance for pilgrims of visiting Vraj, the land of his exploits and the places associated with him: 'In Vraj, these many places are said to bear the "traces" (cihna) of Krishna, and they bid the pilgrim to constant remembrance of him and his miraculous life . . . The real power of Vraj pilgrimage is in the land of Vraj itself . . . The earth itself is said to be holy here. The "dust of Vraj" (Vraj ki raj) is considered sanctified by the feet of Krishna, and pilgrims touch it reverently to their foreheads.'[3]

The pilgrims are touched and changed by this understanding of what the dust has become and what that environ now is, imbued with mythological significance. It is itself a way to Krishna. Equally, for us all, things become significant once invested with association in this way. This is the beginning of understanding darshan, the art of seeing. From this there emerge live stories, or life-stories, through which we come to understand ourselves by recognizing how we are seen by the one who gazes on us: that is, the one with whom we are in close relation and whose voice we take notice of and internalize. From this we recognize who we are and develop a different sense of selfhood. This is the process of becoming a seer. For the devout Hindu, this investment in becoming is focused on being seen by and recognizing the gaze of God.

In the context of formal worship, we can become aware of the generative processes that enable this relationship. Ritual brings God's presence to mind by focusing the senses with intensity. Bodily actions, in speech and posture, create inner resonances and transform states of consciousness. Thus, to stand before a shrine with a murti of the Lord is to be welcomed into his or her presence and, at the same time, to evoke that presence with offerings, mantra and prostration.

In all this lies the Hindu meaning of the term 'hospitality', which is extended to everyone as a recognition of God's presence within them. Here we can see the connection between going for darshan at the temple or before the home shrine and everyday behaviour expressed, for example, in the namaste greeting, which carries the meaning of 'I bow to the God within you'. Seeing, therefore, involves a transformed perception, from superficial ignorance as to who we are individually and the identities that separate us to an awareness of the wholeness of the Lord's creation, in each expression of which the activity of the Lord can be observed, provided we have eyes to see.

This is an image of Poliaji, made of clay and silver foil, who protects all who pass by. He has a very friendly face.

This is a shrine of Bhairava and the Mother Goddess, with all the objects needed for the rituals that ask for help and advice.

Pathway icons

Images of deity are often local and unknown in the higher pantheon of gods and goddesses, but are important to specific localities, such as villages, occupying their own shrines. Generically, these have been called pathway icons. Two examples are illustrated.

Communication and relationship

Fundamentally, this has to do with communication and relationship and, using these broad categories, we can work analogously with the Hindu experience of darshan. We cannot aim to see God in a Hindu murti (a formal, concentrated image of the deity) but we can attempt two goals: to recognize the power of the concept of darshan; and to enrich our sense of relationship with the world we inhabit, including ourselves.

The following activities offer learning strategies designed to do this. They are not meant to be prescriptive, but to give a sense and structure to the way reflective awareness or the art of seeing can be encouraged with younger children. They are meant to be contextualized within work done on the Hindu tradition that would introduce the gods, the temple, the shrine and the ritual of worship incorporating murtis, mantra and ritual greetings and offerings.

Alternatively, you may wish to select from them and introduce them as best fits the overall topic into which you can introduce the general idea.

The classroom process

Activity one – relationship with a person

I want you to remember a time recently when you really enjoyed yourself or felt fully alive. What were you doing? Who were you with? It may have been a friend, your best friend, your brother or sister or some other relation. Think about what you did together and what you said to each other. Maybe you would like to draw a picture to help you to remember that occasion. Find yourself a partner in the class, someone you feel you can talk to. It doesn't have to be your special friend, but it can be. It can be the person that you were with on that day. Tell your partner all about that day. Try to explain why that time was special and why being with that person helped you to enjoy yourself.

Imagine your ideal friend. What is it about this friend that you like? What do you think this friend would like about you? What do you like about you? You could draw a picture of yourself and write beside your picture all the things that you like about yourself. Then do the same thing with a picture of your best friend.

Activity two – composing a ritual based on remembering a person of whom you are fond or who embodies a particular quality which you admire

This could follow on from the work done in Activity One.

Set up a space. This can be on a chair or small table, or just a space on the floor. In this space put a picture of your person or an object (or a drawing of an object) that you associate with them and which helps you call them to mind. See them as clearly as you can with your mind's eye; concentrate on details of their appearance and their presence. Repeat their name silently to yourself for a few moments. Silently reflect on memories of them. Think of something you would like to say to them, something you would like to give them or a way in which you would like to greet them. Offer this to them in your mind.

Within this activity you may wish to introduce some simple yogic techniques of concentrating on the breath, relaxing the body, visualization, evoking the qualities of well-being and loving-kindness. These traditionally aid concentration.

Activity three – relationship with an animal

Do you have a pet? What kind of animal is your pet? If you do not have one you can imagine the pet you would have if you could. Write a story all about your pet and what you do together. You can draw a picture too. Some people say that pet owners look like their pets. Do you look like yours? Draw a picture of yourself as your pet if you want to. Is your pet's character like yours? In which ways? Write down an imaginary conversation between you and your pet while you are playing together.

Activity four – relationship with a special object or toy

You may wish to bring in an example of a special object that you own. Here is my own example:

I have brought something special to school today to show you. It is something which is special just to me. You could call it my mascot, or even my special toy. It is a small statue of the Hindu god Ganesh. I have owned this statue for 14 years and it has been with me during all the most difficult times of my life, in particular when I was giving birth to my first daughter Katy. Having Ganesh with me, in my hand, has comforted me. I feel that I have a companion who understands me. Have you got a special object or toy? Bring it to school so that you can tell the others about it.

Show your special toy to the class and tell us about it. Remember that other people's special toys are precious to them and must be treated with respect, even if they look strange to you. (My statue of Ganesh is rather strange looking. He has the body of a man and the head of an elephant. But this doesn't matter to me. In fact, it helps me to understand him better.)

Tell us about the occasions when your toy has been a help to you. How was it a help to you?

Activity five – relationship with a natural object

Today we are going for a walk. While we are walking I want you to look for an object that you particularly like. It could be a stone whose shape you like, or a piece of wood. It shouldn't be something that is alive, like a plant or an animal. When you have found it I would like you to think about the character this object has for you. What are its qualities? Is it hard, soft, smooth, jagged or rough? Talk about it with your friends.

Maybe for you this stone is an angry stone or a sad stone. You may wish to paint your object to show what character it has. Which colour should you use for that character? You don't have to paint a face on it. Just paint a design that shows what it is feeling.

Write down a conversation with your object, allowing it to tell you why it is feeling the way that it does. What feelings do you have towards your object? Could you imagine this object ever becoming your special object? Explain why or why not. What do you think makes an object a special one for you?

Conclusion

In all of these activities the aim is to gain a sense of how objects, animals, people and places, in fact all that we come into contact with, become more than what is literally there and enter the metaphorical landscape of our own mind. They shape our sense of personhood. For Hindus, the underlying goal is to appreciate God's presence in everything and their own place and purpose in God's creativity. We can become seers of a different kind, but appreciating the Hindu perspective more readily, by reflecting on our relationships with the world which we inhabit and our own nature in this way.

Notes

1 D. Eck, *Darsan: seeing the Divine Image in India*, Anima Books, Chambersberg, Pennsylvania, 1981, Preface.
2 P. Mockerjee, *Pathway Icons*, Thames and Hudson, London, 1987, Introduction.
3 D. Eck, *op. cit.*, page 50.

4 'What does the word "peace" mean Miss?': teaching Islam in the primary school

Sajda Currah

Peace, harmony and submission

When a pupil asks one the question 'What does the word peace mean Miss?' how does one respond? What do we mean by peace, what do we mean by harmony, or by submission?

These aspects of Islam – peace, harmony and submission – are interrelated, their relationship being that by submitting to the Will of Allah Almighty, a Muslim can attain peace. This peace is achieved at different levels, primarily within oneself: feeling at one with Allah and thereby feeling at one within oneself. Having attained inner peace, one is then more able to establish an atmosphere of peace with those one comes into immediate contact with, be they humans, animals or plants.

An extension to this immediate contact is the relationship one has with the 'wider' environment: an environment which embraces the whole earth and everything which is on the planet. Thus this relationship encompasses all living things, as well as inanimate ones. Ultimately, what these different degrees of peace illustrate to the Muslim is the recognition that everything within us and around us belongs to Allah, and therefore we are accountable to Allah for our every action.

Skills and attitudes

In order to understand these relationships, or at least begin to understand them, pupils need to have some understanding of certain skills and certain attitudes, such as sensitivity, empathy, sympathy – being able to stand in another's shoes and see the world from his or her perspective; having a degree of self-confidence in order to express his or her own views, expressing them from a position of security and within a safe environment and, thereby, enabling others to do the same.

These skills and attitudes, sometimes known as Experiential RE, can be seen as foundations to build upon. They need to be introduced as early as possible, and should then become an integral part of any Religious Education. Before looking at an individual faith in depth with any age range, these basic foundations need to be laid, so that children, through their own experience, begin to recognize an awareness of others and the necessity to be sensitive to others' needs, as well as feeling confident enough to express their own emotions and views in public. This can only be achieved in a secure environment, an environment which allows a child to grow strong. The 'Matrioshka Doll' (identical dolls but of different sizes, which all fit into each other's bodies) is 'a useful visual aid when trying to explain the inner and outer self'.[1] It is also a good activity for children to starting thinking about the 'real me'. Other useful sources for ideas of such a nature are books on shared learning or co-operative learning, illustrating co-operation through games and various activities, and by taking a cross-curricular approach.[2]

Once the teacher feels the class has grasped such fundamentals, work can commence on specific concepts within faith traditions. Starting points will differ and will depend upon how well the teacher knows the children, how much work around the issues to be discussed has been covered beforehand, and in which direction the teacher wishes the class to head. The topic may move into areas which were not planned at all; the primary classroom is not predictable! But the teacher must start from where the children are.

The particular aspect of Islam which this article is addressing is the one of 'an environment of peace and harmony'. This principle is not exclusive to Islam, of course, and this needs to be highlighted to the class. However, it is a very important aspect of Islam and one which merits study and needs to be addressed in the primary classroom.

From the Islamic perspective, such an environment is only fully realized by submission to Allah. As humans tend to lapse in their remembrance of Allah, and in their obligations towards Allah, instead of a state of harmony, discord ensues.

How can such a concept be taught in the classroom – and taught in a manner which allows for personal development of understanding? One method is put forward here, which can be modified and extended to suit individual classes and individual teachers.

If the foundations have been laid, it is easier to begin to look at an environment of peace and harmony in depth. Having decided that one's class is ready for an in-depth analysis, what does one do? A good strategy is to begin with a brainstorm: what images, what thoughts, feelings do the children have about Islam? From the various ideas that children put forward, draw out those directly associated with peace and submission. What do these words mean to a Muslim? As mentioned above, one must start from where the child is. Ultimately we want to look at

these words from the Muslim perspective, but one must begin with situations and experiences with which the child is familiar. Varying degrees of relationship with the environment have been mentioned above. The first relationship is the one with Allah, giving a Muslim inner peace. If the class is comfortable with speaking about inner feelings, then one starts from there.

Me and myself

One of the best starting points is 'me' and 'myself', moving on to 'myself' in the context of a family: those immediate to me and those in the extended family. From there would follow the 'me' in a community setting beyond the family, embracing the school community, and moving on to the wider community, including the town one lives in and ultimately looking at the whole globe. 'The family' or 'the class' are good examples of looking at 'me' as an individual and as a member of a group; a member who conforms to norms, rules set by others or rules one has had a role in making. Good analogies to the human family are families in the animal kingdom and families in the plant world, bringing in the link between us as humans and the ultimate unity we have with the rest of the world in the eyes of Allah. Moreover, a fuller picture can be painted about working co-operatively in a family or community setting by looking at an orchestra.

Activities linked with 'me' can include co-operative work in problem-solving and plenty of discussion in pairs and small groups, ultimately reporting back to the class. Making a class orchestra, is an example of this. Divide it up into the different sections of the orchestra, illustrating how important it is for everyone to work co-operatively, as otherwise there is just a terrible din! The children should be encouraged to make their own instruments, either individually or in pairs, having decided which section of the orchestra they want to be in. Decide how many people are necessary to play the instrument, and then, when everyone has made their instrument, compose a piece of music to play together as a whole orchestra. The class needs to have heard orchestral pieces of work and to appreciate the combined effort of the whole orchestral family.

Why do we have rules? What sort of rules do you

have at home, and why? Who makes the rules? What rules do we have at school in the class, for everyone? Ask the class to make its own rules and state why these rules have been made. What happens when we do not all abide by these rules? Do I always do what I want to do? Sometimes, is it better if I do not do what I want to? Why is it better?

Make posters stating class rules and school rules, going through the whole process of drafting and eventually ending up with a finished product.

Interspersed between activities must be time to reflect and to sit and discuss with friends and others in the class what we have been doing, what new things we have learnt, and whether they have been interesting or useful. Furthermore, did we do our best, and what do we mean by our best? There must also be time to share these feelings and views with the whole class.

Activities should be cross-curricular; this approach in itself illustrates how interdependent learning is, as well as showing how interdependent we are. Co-operation and the value of teamwork can be demonstrated and brought out in PE: the fact that in order for a team to succeed decisions need to be made, decisions which we may not be totally happy with, but agree to for the good of the team. Computer work in pairs; art/craft work, such as drawing and painting in pairs, or creating a piece of sculpture; making stories, writing them together and sharing ideas with others, dramatizing them or presenting them as a possibility for others to use as a piece of drama – all can be used to illustrate interdependency. In Technology, set work for pairs or groups; ask them to design and make something and then explain to the class why and how they made the object. Make family trees, and ask children to bring in photographs from home. They can discuss their families with each other, interview each other about their homes and members of their families or write poems about feelings for the family.

A better environment

Having looked at 'myself', the class can look further afield to their responsibility to others, to fellow humans, as well as to their responsibility for the environment.

This opens a vast array of work which can be done about the environment. Again, one should start from the child's experience. The class needs to look at where they are. In geographical terms, where do they live in relation to school? Make maps of their routes to school, or take the class for a walk to trace their routes to school if they live nearby. Take photographs of their houses; start a collage of the area. What do the children like about their houses? How peaceful is it in the house?

Make maps of the school. How do the children get from the playground to the class? How accessible is the school? How peaceful and harmonious is the environment in school? What would enhance the feeling of peace in school? Who are the people in school who help us, and how can we help them? How can we make school a better environment for us to work and play in?

Then start to look outside the school at the immediate surroundings. How safe is it? What is the role of the lollipop person? Why do we have traffic lights? Look at road safety in general. Ask someone to come in to school and talk about road safety (it could be the local policeman). Are there any animals in the vicinity? What responsibility do we have towards them? Can we find any stories to show how we should behave towards animals?

Do traffic surveys to see how busy the school road is. This can be recorded in the form of graphs; get the class to interpret the graphs and to make different types of graphs. The traffic survey can also be used to see how much pollution there is in the immediate vicinity. Introduce new vocabulary such as 'pollution', 'carbon monoxide', 'environmentally friendly'. Make some music or poems about litter. Start a campaign about keeping the school tidy. Make a collage using litter. Stimulate discussion about our responsibility towards others regarding litter and pollution. How does pollution affect animals, plants, buildings? Write to local newspapers about any issues which the class feels need to be raised regarding the local environment, e.g. if there are inadequate bins in the area, or insufficient road crossings.

Go for a walk: what can we see? How many trees have we in the vicinity? Is it pleasant to have plants and trees around us? Refer to Muslim stories to illustrate our responsibility for the environment.

Refer to Muslim gardens and the use of them in Muslim architecture, e.g. Alhambra in Granada, Spain. Bring plants in and tend them. Grow your own plants so that the class can experience responsibility. Ask children to pay attention to newspapers, local as well as national, and to look out for articles about pollution. Make your own newspapers to highlight issues either in school or outside.

Look at waste: what is waste? what can we do with waste? Is recycling a good thing? Make your own paper. What should be done with industrial waste? The class could make its own stories, based on hadith, about not using any more resources than we need to.

Go further afield and look at 'me' as part of the country. What responsibility have I as a citizen of this country? What responsibilities does my country have to others? Introduce Europe and show the variety of people who live in Europe. Some of these people were originally from elsewhere – where were they from? What kind of environment are they from? Is it easy to go to a new place and feel at peace in that place? What would help people to feel at home? Look at issues of global warming and how our efforts can not only help us but help others as well.

Get the class to interview other members of staff about such issues; find a range of opinions and then get the children to make up their own minds as to what they feel is important for a peaceful world.

At intermittent times see if the children come up with God/Allah at all. Do they feel that Allah has anything to do with the way the world operates? Introduce, in a more explicit manner, the interplay for Muslims between peace and submission and the belief that, ultimately, we are all one homogeneous 'family' with Allah in control. See if the children can draw parallels between what they have been doing and the words 'peace' and 'submission'.

Notes

1 J. Hammond *et al*, *New Methods in Teaching RE*, Oliver & Boyd, 1990, pages 99–101.
2 *Shared Learning*, Development Education Centre, Selly Oak Colleges, Birmingham, 1990; *Co-operation in the Classroom*, Nottinghamshire Education Authority.
3 Hadith taken from Abdul Aziz Kamel, *Islam and the Race Question*, Islamic Book Publishers, 1987.

Further reading

Islamic Foundation story books e.g. *Assalam Aleikum*. The language will have to be modified to suit different age groups. Information on the use of gardens in Muslim architecture can be found in books on Islamic Art. Specific information on Islamic architecture in Spain can be found in books on Moorish and Muslim Spain.

5 'Shabbat Shalom – may you have a peaceful Sabbath': Judaism in the primary classroom

Vida Barnett

How can we help young non-Jewish children value the Sabbath's importance so that it becomes more than 'something other people do', more than a way of engendering respect? How can we make it an experience which stimulates questions relevant to the searcher's own quest for meaning – an exciting, positive point of growth?

Our exploration begins with the youngest children, gradually acquiring depth as we look towards later years in the junior school.

Special days

Initially we need to create an atmosphere of anticipation, excitement and fun – of a 'positive', not a 'negative', day. For Jews, the Sabbath is a special gift of God, welcomed as a very special visitor, a Queen: 'You're not supposed to do any work, which means not writing, riding bikes, etc . . . but . . . it's a great time for meeting people . . . sometimes we play games with the whole family together . . . it's really great.'[1]

Some books for young children emphasize how

preparations for the Sabbath begin each Sunday! Of course, in some classrooms the teacher will have to be very careful when emphasizing family happiness, but there are many other aspects to be explored. *Hurray, Friday's a Short Day*,[2] set in Jerusalem, with attractive illustrations, shows how a five-year-old loves to be involved in the immediate preparations: helping with shopping, buying flowers, giving 'pennies' to help people, tidying up, washing, dressing, laying the table, smelling the cooking, then . . . .

In the classroom, having tidied desks, shelves and window-ledges, we can be very quiet as girls (or teacher) light the Sabbath candles. Joined by the boys (returning from synagogue), we can explore ways of saying 'thank you' for the world around us, for each Sabbath celebrates anew God's gift of the creation. Make up a class poem or song; mount a collage illustrating the excitement and fascination of our world. We need not follow the Jewish pattern: we are extrapolating universal questions, challenges, affirmations, truths.

The Sabbath affirms that people should be good 'stewards' of their world. Increasingly, children can explore environmental, social and political issues in terms of good and bad stewardship; they can participate in a project in their immediate neighbourhood or through a world organization. How far are we or should we be responsible to our world, to other people?

During the meal which follows, zemirot (songs) may be sung:

'My daddy sings the Kiddush prayer
And lifts the cup of wine.
My cup is small, but I don't care –
I'm proud that it is mine.'

Again, children can make up their own songs – as a class, in groups or alone – to a familiar tune, and sing them after returning from lunch, or even in the dining room!

For older children the following activities might be considered:

1 Read Genesis 1–2[3]. Gradually, of course, as they write their own Creation Psalms, teachers may have to face the challenge of disasters etc. Jewish rabbis taught that we need to struggle in decision-making in order to experience full humanity. In a world without hatred there is no love or compassion, without sorrow no joy, without flaws no hopes of anything becoming better. There is good discussion material here.

2 In the *Shabbat Catalogue*, a question and answer dialogue explores the theme of stewardship. 'Why do we light candles?' 'God created light, but we can make light too.' 'Why, after breaking the bread, do you say God brings forth bread from the earth? What about the farmer, miller, baker?' 'We work together with God, as partners.' Very positive, searching, imaginative dialogues can be created by the children.

3 A parallel activity can explore how light banishes darkness, reflecting warmth and happiness. How can we be lights, i.e. good stewards?

4 Gradually children can discuss the claim that the Sabbath is 'The glue that keeps the Jews together': an opportunity to stress the wider family, where nuclear families can be problematic.

5 Others, exploring the 'negative', can discuss whether it is helpful to have strong patterns of saying 'No' in ordinary circumstances, so developing the strength to say 'No' under stress – when taunted and urged to steal etc.

6 Links with themes of Food, Light, Conservation, Responsibility, Who am I? etc. are obvious.

A special place – the synagogue

The wearing of capel and tallit, skull cap and prayer shawl, gives an opportunity to help develop attitudes to difference. Two or three boys may be invited to wear material or paper capels. Of course, the class will laugh. Ask them to think of something they enjoy wearing, then, with closed eyes, imagine walking into the classroom to be greeted by laughter. How would they feel? Of course, it won't 'happen overnight' but gradually many will be helped to understand the courage needed, and the value of being different. The tallit fringes, symbolic of Torah commands – good and bad actions, linked to ideas of justice, relationships etc. – can gradually be discussed and/or illustrated in creative ways. Again, they need not always be strictly 'quoted'; it is the 'spirit' that is important. Some children might enjoy one explanation of why the head may be covered by the large tallit: to form a 'tent', a quiet place, to be with God in prayer.

Older children might:

1 discuss some of the Torah laws, many applicable to an agricultural society. How might they be translated in modern society? Is it helpful to have symbolic reminders that God is looking down upon us (capel), or that certain codes of behaviour are/are not acceptable? What rules of conduct do the class think most important? What would be their 'Ten Commandments'? Symbols also affirm happiness in accepting ethical codes. As the Torah scroll is processed, tallit wearers may touch or point to it with tallit fringes, then put the fringe to the lips, acknowledging remembrance of and love for the message it contains;

2 find links with themes of clothes, symbols, rules etc.

A special book – the Torah

Young children might decide which is their special book. Why is it special? How do they look after it? The Jews have a favourite book which tells them of God, of themselves, of how they should behave etc. They always treat this book very carefully, but especially in the synagogue, where the words are written not in a book but on scrolls. In *Sofer, The Story of a Torah Scroll*[4] Eric Ray describes the special ink and pens used – today, the largest feather (quill) is a bird's wing tip – and the parchment strips from a kosher (permitted) animal, e.g. sheep. The scribe, Sofer, washes and prays before writing. When completed with the strips sewn together, the scroll is longer than a football field. It takes about three years to write. It is 'dressed' in a special cover, kept in a special cupboard or alcove, the ark. When it can no longer be used, it is not destroyed by human hands but left in a room/cupboard/chest or even buried in a simple box in the cemetery, like a loved person. So the Jews show how precious it is. Why is it precious? As a class or in groups children can make their own scrolls and cover, and choose from five or six quotations, exploring their choice. Remember, no illustrations in the text! It tells the Jews what is right and wrong. How do the children learn what is right? Why does it matter how one acts?

Older children might:

1 develop all these activities;

2 discuss why Jews have died rather than give up reading the Torah. The festival of Hanukah points to this: 'We stood there while four of Apelle's men (Syrian Greek oppressors) went into the synagogue, took down the draperies . . . and brought out the seventeen scrolls . . . How well I knew these scrolls . . . I had read them from the time I was able to read. I had pressed my lips to them. With what loving care they had been preserved, each receiving every year a new envelope . . . a moan of anger went up from the people as they were thrown carelessly on a pile of hay . . . Then set on fire.'[5]

3 consider what books are most important to them – and why;

4 make links with story, writing, community, priorities.

A special visit – to the synagogue

Younger children may just like to look and feel, to meet Jewish people as 'ordinary' people, to 'enjoy' the building and contents. Looking at the Torah scrolls, they can show the rabbi (or guide) their scrolls, sing their Sabbath song etc.

Older children might do the following:

1 Take their poems, favourite selected passages or story from scripture, say in three sentences why they feel the passage is important, sing a song composed for Shabbat or synagogue service – perhaps saying why they think these are important; ask the rabbi to robe, read his or her favourite passage or prayer, and say why it is special for him or her. (This would be a creative addition to worksheets and random questions.)

2 If a visit is impossible it can be partially simulated. The children can enter the classroom quietly and sit round three sides, the fourth showing slides (only two or three) of the synagogue interior. They can share their contributions, a Jewish visitor or even the teacher taking the part of the rabbi.

3 Children might gradually design a synagogue – structure, doors, windows, bimah, ark – explaining the design and/or symbolism. Social rooms should be included.

4 Make links with special places, prayer, sacred books and buildings.

A special goodbye – Havdalah

Again the enjoyment of the day should be stressed.

Every Sabbath is like a party day: it is 'The Birthday of Their World'. What will the children remember most? Why? The class might write their own 'goodbye' to accompany candle-light, wine and spices. Jewish boys and girls are encouraged to think immediately of the next Sabbath. The days of the week are numbered: first, second etc., leading to the seventh, the only day with a name: the Sabbath!

Older children might:

1 discuss if such a day would make a difference to their lives;
2 explain, if they also celebrate a special week day, what happens that is important.

During the Primary years, through exploring the Sabbath, children may have developed some understanding of what it means to be human, what it means to accept a faith, which values and attitudes are important. They may have come to see that religion can be enjoyed and is important. Jews – and members of other faiths, races and groups – will no longer be peculiar, but people who have something to teach us all. The children may want to learn more of scriptures, festivals, beliefs, rites of passage etc., so that they may be helped to structure their own lives more meaningfully. Religious experience will then seem worth exploring: 'Judaism is always presented to children not as a chore but as an enjoyable way of life. There's always something that the child can look forward to . . .'[6]

'Shabbat Shalom'

Notes

1 Jean Holm, *Growing up in Judaism*, Longman, 1990, pages 4, 6–7, 9.
2 Yeshara Gold, *Hurray, Friday's a Short Day*, Mesorah Publications, 1986.
3 Ruth Brin, *Shabbat Catalogue*, Ktav, 1978, pages 47, 48.
4 Eric Ray, *Sofer, The Story of a Torah Scroll*, Torah Avra Productions, 1986.
5 Howard Fast, *My Glorious Brothers*, Bonim Books, 1948/1975, page 68.
6 Jean Holm, *op. cit.*

6 Truthful living and the unity of life: Sikhism in the primary classroom

Kanwaljit Singh

'From the Lord's play all living creatures came.
And from the Divine Light the whole creation sprang.
Why then should we divide human creatures into high and low?
The Lord the Maker hath moulded one mass of clay into vessels of diverse shapes.
Free from taint are the vessels of clay since free from taint is the Divine Potter.'[1]

Remembering the unity of life, in all its diversity, is a sacred duty for Sikhs. In honouring this code Sikhs are enjoyed to live in three dimensions:

1 Nam Japna – to remember God.
2 Kirat Karni – to earn one's living by honest means.
3 Vand Chakna – to share one's earnings with less fortunate people.

It follows from this that one does not have to leave the world and live in forests and mountains to commune with God. The Guru asks his Sikhs to lead the life of a family person, with all the responsibilities this entails. It is in relations with others that God is found. The Sikh tradition emphasizes this in many stories accessible to primary school children. The story of Bhai Lalo, who was encountered by Guru Nanak on his travels, is a good example!

When Guru Nanak visited Eminabad he chose to stay with Bhai Lalo, a poor carpenter. One day, Malik Bhago, the local rich man, invited the Guru to his banquet. When the Guru failed to honour the invitation, Malik Bhago got very angry and demanded an explanation from the Guru. Guru Nanak said that he preferred Bhai Lalo's modest food, as it was earned by hard work and honest means, to a rich man's sumptuous feast, that was bought by exploiting poor people.

This story illustrates well the second principle or dimension of Sikh life: Kirat Karni, the importance of earning one's living by honest means. However, this is not just a case of establishing a particular code of conduct for its own sake, or as a matter of social order. Its significance resides first in its effect on the individual soul. The Guru says: 'Dishonesty in business is like the uttering of lies, it causes inner sorrow.'[2]

This strong vision of a just and balanced society is at the heart of the Sikh faith, whether expressed in family relations, in business and work, in politics or in one's relations with oneself. It is guided by the knowledge of truth that comes from God. This is always communicated by the Gurus with the accent on its practical expression, through which a sense of community and self-discovery evolve. Guru Nanak writes: 'Truth is high but higher still is truthful living.'

It is this sense of truthful living, which informs Sikh attitudes and behaviour, that we need to communicate to children in the classroom. The following sections illustrate aspects of Sikh practice that can be worked in order to achieve this. Suggestions for classroom activities are offered to encourage experiential learning, but allowing the teacher to make adaptations of approach according to the age range of the pupils.

The langar

Food is ubiquitously featured in primary school topics, and quite rightly. As we saw above, in the story of Bhai Lalo, sharing a meal is a significant way of showing respect. It is also an important expression of hospitality in Indian culture. Furthermore, it provides an accessible metaphorical link between physical and spiritual nourishment. For these reasons, it is not surprising that one of the most important areas in a gurdwara is the langar. After the service in a gurdwara, everyone joins in to eat langar (food in the common kitchen), which is cooked and served by both men and women. This is to confirm that everyone is equal in the eyes of God and that 'housework' is not a menial job which is only the duty of women. It is also an important communal gathering, indicating solidarity: what is shared is not only food but a sense of belonging together. Preparing and serving food in the langar also illustrates the Sikh Gurus' emphasis on the dignity of labour. Traditionally the langar is also open to

anybody at any time, as an indication of Vand Chakna, which extends beyond the Sikh community.

The following story illustrates the principle behind langar in a way that tests a Sikh's allegiance to it. It is also a useful story for children to consider in order to identify how far they can sympathize with the judgement made by the Guru, and to be aware of the tensions that can arise within a community that seeks always to stand by a particular principle.

The story of Bhai Kanaya

Once the Mughal Emperor attacked Guru Gobind Singh, the 10th Sikh Guru, and in the battle many people on both sides got wounded and some got killed. A group of angry Sikhs brought Bahi Kanaya to the Guru's presence. On enquiring, the Guru was told that Bhai had been caught giving water to the enemy. This action of his was reviving the enemy soldiers to fight again. The Guru asked Bhai Kanaya if there was any truth in these allegations. Bhai Kanaya replied that he had been giving water to all who were injured. He further said that he could not see any difference between friends and foes. They were all, as taught by the Guru himself, God's children and thus members of the same human family. The Guru was pleased with this reply, gave Bhai Kanaya a jar of ointment and asked him to tend to their wounds as well when he gave them water.

A classroom activity

When food is offered it signifies, in the same way as other ritual observances, an offering of friendship, linked with respect and worship. It also facilitates the effect of these intentions with immediacy. At its most intense it is a loving act. Children can reflect on this in the way that at home food is prepared and cooked by their parents, in the way that meals are shared and in the giving of sweets to friends. It is an important means of communication. In the classroom they can decide, with their teacher, what they can prepare and share with each other and how this can be done to best effect. They can also think about inviting a guest and how they might offer and share food with him or her.

The significance of langar can be introduced by considering not so much who needs food as to whom they would like to show friendship, respect and concern. At its most powerful this is often done by making or repairing relationships, which goes beyond simply sharing with friends. Pupils can then consider what they feel able and wish to prepare for another group or guest. Their own experience of a birthday party may provide a framework for this. The importance lies more in deciding whom they wish to invite and why, rather than the particular things they wish to prepare. However, it is helpful to bear in mind that, for Sikhs, langar will be strictly vegetarian, so that no one feels excluded.

The Guru Granth Sahib

Sikhs believe that the highest authority is God, and that his truth is revealed through the teachings of the Sikh Gurus, which are contained in the Guru Granth Sahib. Since the scripture takes the place of the living Guru among the Sikhs, it is treated with the utmost respect and is accorded a similar reverence to that given to the Gurus during their lifetimes. The Guru Granth Sahib contains the authentic writings of the Gurus. It enjoys the full and highest authority and is central to the Sikh way of life, its ceremonies, festivals and code of conduct. This is apparent on a visit to a gurdwara, as it occupies the most revered place, covered in rumala (a covering cloth), rested on cushions on a dais, with a canopy above. A member of the congregation remains in constant attendance and waves a chauri (a traditional fan or whisk) over it, symbolic of its sovereignty and pre-eminence. The worshipper enters the presence of the Guru Granth Sahib without shoes and with head covered, bows and touches the floor with his or her forehead before sitting down. These are the marks of respect to the Guru Granth Sahib through which Sikhs carry out Nam Japna, the remembering of God.

A classroom activity

Producing a class book, and being an author in a writing project that has a real audience, is an important strategy in language work. Introducing the idea of a book as a living source of wisdom and guidance adds an extra dimension and depth to this activity.

In this case, children can individually contribute to a class project to produce a collection of writings: stories, comments and reflections from their own experience, which, when put together, provide a tangible source of things said and events which happened that they consider important when thinking about how to live. The question of where this collection can be kept, how it is to be handled and when it, or parts of it, could be read, can be considered. This will, in turn, introduce children to the function of ritual. This can be related to the Sikh relationship with the Guru Granth Sahib on the one hand and how they treat their own favourite books on the other, giving reference points for making their decisions about their class book. The way in which they establish their relationship with this object can then become part of further discussion, reflection and writing activity. A visitor to the class could be introduced to the importance of the book to the class, which would be analogous to a non-Sikh being introduced to the place of the Guru Granth Sahib in the gurdwara and the Sikh community.

The five Ks and the turban

It will be clear from what we have considered already that Sikhs sought to create a significant impact on the divisions and inequalities they perceived in Indian society. This necessarily brought them criticism and persecution at times. Given this situation, it was the 10th Guru, Gobind Singh, who reminded Sikhs of the need to stand up for their principles and to this end gave them the five symbols known as the five Ks.

The five Ks consist of:

1 Kesh (uncut hair), which is a symbol of saintliness. Male Sikhs cover their hair with a turban and females tie it in a bun or wear it loose.
2 Kangha (a small wooden comb worn in the hair). This signifies cleanliness.
3 Kara (an iron or steel bracelet). This binds the Sikhs to God and reminds them of their duty to do good.
4 Kach (long shorts worn as undergarments). Originally this ensured agility and freedom of movement, but Kach also reminds Sikhs of the need for modesty and sexual purity.
5 Kirpan (a sword), symbolic of God's supreme power but also reminding Sikhs of their duty to defend the weak, the poor and the underprivileged or oppressed.

The significance and possible cost of retaining the

purity of one's principles in the face of persecution is well illustrated by the martyrdom of Guru Teg Bahadur.

The story of Guru Teg Bahadur

Teg Bahadur lived at a time when Hindus in India were being persecuted by the Muslim Emperor Aurangzeb. A group of Hindu priests travelled to see the Guru for his advice. They told him they must either covert to Islam or be persecuted. The Guru replied: 'Tell your tormentors that you will be willing to accept Islam if Guru Teg Bahadur can first be persuaded to do so'. In response to this Teg Bahadur was imprisoned. First they tried to tempt him to accept the Islamic faith. When this did not work, the Emperor said: 'If you are a man of God, you must save yourself by working a miracle.' To try and change his mind, four of his disciples were killed before his eyes. Guru Teg Bahadur was not moved. He understood this to be the will of God; now it was his turn. He was allowed to bathe at a nearby well. Then he was told to sit under a banyan tree on a platform. Crowds of people had gathered to see the execution. The Guru told his executioner: 'When I bow to God at the end of my prayers, behead me.' This is how the Guru died.

A classroom activity

Children develop an idea of dress sense and the importance of image at a very early age. For adults, of course, it is a very firm part of the identity we present to the world. Such images are pervasively present in a host of media representations, from cartoons and comics (consider Batman and Dennis the Menace or Minnie the Minx) through to the faces that stare at us from the covers of magazines on newsagents' shelves.

Young people use dress as a means of identifying with a particular group. Young Sikhs may often experience a great sense of tension in this respect. Introducing the idea of dress and image being related to discipline and conviction bridges the gap between fashion and tradition. Children can be asked what they wear when they are not at school. They could also draw what they wear and bring their clothes, emblems and badges in. Reflecting on why they wear and carry these things and looking at images of others which are contrasting in this way can lead to discussion of what sorts of people they appear to be and what is important to them. In this way, access can be gained to questions about why people look as they do. The relationship between practicality and symbolism can then be explored.

In this context, the wearing of the five Ks and the turban can be understood in greater depth. Creating a tension between obviously contrasting images will not only solicit spontaneous responses from children, but will also reveal the way in which unconscious acceptance of the relationship between image and behaviour is understood. A punk pushing a pram, a vicar hitting someone on the nose and a nun riding a bike are examples. Moving to an understanding of traditional Sikh appearance, we can then relate dress to behavioural expectation in the same way. Children can then work back to their own appearance and the statements they wish to make about themselves in a similar way.

Conclusion

For children and teachers, exploring the Sikh tradition in the manner of this article can have a threefold purpose, which extends to encountering other world views: we understand better the way people in a particular religious group understand themselves; we become more aware of our own sense of identity and commitments; and we develop the skill of looking beyond the image of what we see to an awareness of its significance.

Notes

1 *Guru Granth Sahib*, page 1349.
2 *Ibid.*, page 1062.

7 The dhamma of the mind: teaching Buddhism in the secondary school

Lilian Weatherley

'We are what we think
All that we are arises with our thoughts
With our thoughts we make the world.'
– The Dhammapada

The Buddha saw that when it came to religion people were uncertain as to where the accent should be placed. Humankind had lost its way, its sense of priorities. He saw that the heart of religious teaching had so often been hidden under a 'hotch-potch' of decoration that the reality was being lost. Religion had become like a Christmas tree, with so many decorations that the beauty of the tree itself had been hidden. What Siddhartha taught was a liberation, a freeing from the external trappings.

On the outside, like the visual image of the Christmas tree, people looked healthy enough, but the inner person, like the tree itself, was often being choked of real life. Human beings had an illness of spirit which was much more dangerous and damaging. Symptoms of jealousy, anger, lust, greed, hatred and laziness were hidden by an exterior sense of well-being.

It is not surprising that the Buddha is often regarded as a doctor, and his main teaching of the Four Noble Truths as the prescription and cure, not for an outward sickness but for an inward unhappiness linked to the sickly state of the person's mind, the unsatisfactoriness of human existence, mental anguish, dukkha.

For the Buddha, freedom required mind transformation, the growth into human excellence. The main function of religion was education, the development of the personality. It may be that this was the same message as Jesus', but Buddhists believe that in Christianity the idea of spiritual growth into human excellence is so often blocked by teachings about doctrines.

The challenge for those of us in education is that, for students to comprehend the depth of the Buddha's teaching, they, too, must be able to grasp the idea of mind transformation.

Is there, then, a parallel between our own teaching of Buddhism and that of the Buddha? Are the pupils also likely to undergo some form of 'mind transformation' (no matter how small) in the process, and is this a good or bad thing?

This year I began teaching my Year 10 pupils with this hypothesis, and the results were, in fact, more dramatic than I could have imagined. Having covered the stories surrounding the birth and enlightenment of Siddhartha, I began the dhamma (the teachings of the Buddha), and in particular the Four Noble Truths.

Dukkha – suffering or unsatisfactoriness

The idea that life is unsatisfactory is not at all a difficult concept for the average teenager to explore. We usually begin by looking in the media for examples. This is not a difficult task, and the pupils are quick to bring in newspaper cuttings and other examples. Do the pupils agree that life can be regarded as unsatisfactory? Some do, some do not, and thought-provoking discussions are already beginning to take place:

'I think I agree with the first Noble Truth. I see that there is always suffering and unsatisfactoriness, especially recently with the Gulf War and civil war in Yugoslavia.' – Lavinia Beddard.

The Three Marks of Existence

The Three Marks of Existence are dukkha, anicca and anatta. Having already explored dukkha, we begin to look at anicca (impermanence). I ask the pupils to bring in photographs of themselves at different ages and we discuss the whole idea of change. Are they the same person they were in the pram, or have they moved on? This lesson always causes a great deal of amusement as we look at photographs of ourselves, myself included. I think it is important to join in with this exercise, as it helps to build up a trust within the group.

We then explore other things that change; of course, the list is endless, and the pupils are never short of ideas.

Anatta (selflessness), is probably the hardest concept for the average teenager to comprehend, especially when we spend so much time educating the 'self' aspect of pupils – for example, self-assessment and self-assertiveness. However, I have found that the photographs enable pupils to see themselves changing and this makes the concept of 'no real self' easier to understand. The biologists in the class are always quick to point out that if a body is held under a microscope it is possible to see the cells actively changing from moment to moment.

'Since I have been studying Buddhism it has changed the way I feel about being selfish. I try not to say "I want" or "I need".' – Gemma Crane.

'Since I have been studying Buddhism I've learnt not to be so selfish. I am not important.' – Rebecca Haile.

'I also think about selfishness. Buddhists try not to be selfish. If I become angry or want to be selfish I try to hold back and count to 10.' – Maria Robinson.

Samudaya – suffering comes from desire

'I want' is often the plaintive cry of the teenager, and it is quite easy to explore the reasons for wanting so much. In the materialistic '90s I find this one of the easiest of the Noble Truths to explore. Using a pile of magazines, pupils can soon give me a long list of things that they think they want, from the expensive CD player to the dishiest hunk in Year 11. We can then go on to consider how they might feel if they didn't get what they want and, more importantly, whether or not they would still want the doll's pram or toy train that they so desperately wanted when they were five. It is at this stage, however, that the biggest mind-transformation appears to take place.

'I think wanting things does lead to suffering. If you love someone and they do not love you, you suffer. If you can accept this and just be friends with them it gets better.' – Jennie Blake.

'I have found myself asking questions like "Do I really need a whole new wardrobe, or a hi-fi or a CD?" The monks seem to have fewer possessions in the whole monastery than I have in my bedroom. In the Western world it seems that no matter how poor or rich people are they are always wanting more.' – Elaine Caldwell.

'Buddhism has made me realize how fortunate and well-off we are.' – Jo Thomas.

'I don't want things as much as I did. It might be from growing up, but it could be from studying Buddhism.' – Thelma Crane.

'Buddhism makes me feel very different when I want something.' – David Leighton.

Niroda – rid yourself of desire and craving; rid yourself of suffering

Here we explore the ways in which greed, hatred and ignorance cause suffering in the world today and whether we could ease our own suffering by 'letting go of our desires'.

'I think my views on things have changed. The main things that I have thought about are the Noble Truths, "suffering comes from desire; rid yourself of desire, rid yourself of suffering." The best way to explain this is through someone dying. When a close relation is ill you suffer a lot but because we don't want to let them go we become upset. When my grandmother died I was very upset and didn't know how to cope with her death because I had never had anyone as close as that to me die. After learning how Buddhists handle death by "letting go" I think I will be able to handle death more easily.' – Georgina Hooper.

Magga – the Noble Eightfold Path

The techniques for obtaining human excellence are to be found in the Eightfold Path: behaviour in everyday life that will result in the transformation of the mind. Not surprisingly, the first step on the path to 'enlightenment' is Right Understanding or Viewpoint, to enable the process to begin.

Most pupils had heard of the Ten Commandments and could see a similarity, even though it was necessary to point out that Buddhism does not offer a dogmatic set of rules, but rather guide lines:

Right Understanding
Right Thought
Right Speech
Right Action – including the Precepts
Right Livelihood
Right Effort
Right Mindfulness
Right Concentration

'Learning about the Eightfold Path and the Precepts made me think if only everyone in the world followed this religion how much better the world would be.' –

Amanda Kemish.

'Some of the Eightfold Path has changed my way of thinking but mainly about the environment and animals.' – Clare Heather.

'Before I started Buddhism I would not think twice about harming a small creature.' – Kate Thompson.

'I think that Buddhism in a way has affected the way I think. I try to be nicer. At home I have a cat and sometimes I'm quite cruel to it but recently I've stopped and thought, "What has my cat done that is so wrong that I should harm it?" If I hadn't studied the Eightfold Path I would have carried on being horrible.' – Lynn Challinor.

'Since studying Buddhism I have been saying to myself that spiders have a right to live.' – Sharon Davies.

'I've changed from being sloppy towards the environment to caring about it.' – Sally Murrell.

'I'm a lot more helpful around the house now. I think this is due to some of the principles that I've been learning about in Buddhism.' – Stuart Whatmore.

'Buddhism has taught me that everything on this earth is here for a reason and nothing deserves to be killed by accident.' – Tania Hannan.

'When I'm all het up I try to calm myself down (especially at night when I can't sleep) by meditating or going for a walk to calm my mind. I also try not to say anything that would hurt my friends or insult them (Right Speech) but it's very hard and takes a lot of effort and concentration. I admire the people who follow the Eightfold Path.' – Carly-Jane Blow.

'I think of nibbana when I'm in my room alone and it's peaceful. I can just close my eyes and think of all the peaceful things and let go of all the bad things like hatred, ignorance and greed. I can practise being less selfish towards others.' – Karen Mcgall.

Through beginning to understand Buddhism, the pupils themselves had undergone a far greater mind-transformation than I could ever have suspected. At this point I began to wrestle with my own conscience and question whether or not this was indoctrination. I decided quite definitely that it was not; after all the pupils were not converting to Buddhism. They were, however, now able to evaluate their experience and make informed choices.

'I could not become a Buddhist, but I have come to understand and think about the meaning of life and the Earth. I feel that we are on a journey, a journey in which we will discover "life's meaning".' – Victoria Wooldridge.

'Having studied Buddhism I have come to understand that it is a religion where training of the mind is a key element. I tried keeping the Five Precepts for a day or two, and to be honest it was impossible.' – Natalie Horngray.

'I feel that Chithurst was a good experience for all of us who visited the monastery. As I walked around the gardens I thought to myself, "What would it be like living as a nun?" I came to the conclusion that it would be too peaceful and slow-moving for me. I don't feel that the atmosphere is very stimulating and I would easily become bored. However, for people with patience and the ability to keep all the rules, living at Chithurst must be like living on an idyllic island.' – Katy Dutfield.

Buddhism had simply been the vehicle that had enabled this type of spiritual growth to take place. The pupils had been given the opportunity to reflect in relation to their own experiences. The resulting mind-transformation that had taken place would be equally valuable for Christian, Jewish or secular thinking; indeed, I would now have to re-evaluate my teaching of the other traditions.

I had not ended up with a class of Buddhists, but I now had a class of deep thinking, more caring and less self-centred pupils.

8 Mixers and mystics: teaching Christianity in the secondary classroom

John Hammond

Alan Brown's article (Section Two A: 'How a Christian Perceives the World') sets out distinctive features of the Christian world view in the context of the great shaping beliefs which were articulated during the early centuries of the Christian era. These are Trinity, Incarnation, Salvation, Baptism and

Eucharist. The nature of these beliefs provides a twofold basis for teaching about Christianity: the way of the Mixer and the way of the Mystic.

Firstly, the four beliefs (I'm taking baptism and Eucharist – ritual expressions of belief – as one) are a summons to active involvement in community life. They are a call to put in place on earth the justice and love of heaven. This will involve engaging in all levels of human interaction. Christians are necessarily mixers.

Secondly, these beliefs are a summons to an acceptance of mystery. For though they have been formulated and reflected on down the centuries, their final meaning is elusive. No one fully understands them – not because they are muddled, but because they touch on the infinite and unknowable reality of God. They are a call to let go of clarity and knowledge (the god who is known is a projection, an idol) and stand before the mystery with the acceptance of a small child, or like Moses entering the darkness of the cloud. Believers need to be passive, open, patient. The active, bonding and transformative aspect of the Christian psyche has a necessary counterpart in receptivity, stillness and silence.

Though many Christians are more mixer than mystic, while others, individually or as part of a tradition, will stress mysticism above mixing, the basis of their beliefs implies that all will, in some measure, be both.

Let us look at the four beliefs to see how this is so.

Trinity

Christianity claims that at the heart of all reality stands community, the loving interrelationship of father, son and spirit. The ultimate principle of all things is one God, who is three persons. The breathtaking variety and harmony of the universe is a manifestation of this dynamism of the divine life. Human society should also be in its image and likeness. Human life, for believers in the Trinity, is not about separation and competition between isolated individuals, but about the acknowledging of interdependence and the creation of community. The reality and so ultimate satisfaction and happiness of life exists only in relation with other beings. Trinitarian believers are mixers.

There is a story that St Peter was sitting on the sea shore, pondering the mystery of the Trinity. He was watching a child, who had dug a hole in the sand, repeatedly fill a shell with sea water and run and pour it in the hole. Peter asked what she was doing, and was told that she was emptying the sea into the hole. 'You'll never do that,' said Peter, a fisherman who knew something about the sea. 'I've got more chance of doing that than you have of understanding the Trinity,' said the child, an angelic messenger who knew something about God.

Theologies of the Trinity delineate something of the shape of the mystery and remind us of the size of the sea. But the admission of mystery is not the negation of rationality. It is, rather, that at the extremities of theological endeavour there is a need for silent acceptance. The ultimate source of the thoughtful, decisive actions of the community-building mixer is in the passive stillness of the mystic.

Incarnation

Incarnation is the enfleshment of God. Humankind and all matter is intimately related to the creator in the God-man Jesus. As brothers and sisters of Christ, and so sons and daughters of the Father, Christians see all people as brothers and sisters. Belief in Incarnation implies seeing in humankind and all creation the presence of the divine one. All are holy and of infinite value. The only appropriate response is to love one another as they believe God in Christ loves them.

This is expressed in Jesus' prayer to the Father: 'That they may be one, even as thou, Father art in me, and I in thee, that they also may be one in us, so that the world may believe that thou hast sent me.' (John 17:20). Again, the belief in Incarnation is a call to relationship, to be a mixer.

But how can a man be God? The great Christiological formulations of the early centuries struggled to hold together 'truly God' and 'truly man'. To give up on either was to slip into heresy. God the Father could not suffer. Jesus the Son and the Word of God died on the cross. But Jesus the Son was God. So did God suffer or did Jesus not really die on the cross? Both were unthinkable. The Christiological 'solution' is in distinguishing persons from nature:

not, this time (as with the Trinity), three persons in one divine nature, but two natures – one human and one divine – in one human person. Again the theology, reflecting on the scriptures and tradition, outlines the contours of a mystery which must be approached further through modes of prayer.

In the ancient practice of the Jesus prayer, the continuing mantra-like and meditative recitation of the words 'Jesus Son of God have mercy on us' is the focus of the intention to enter deeper into the mystery of the Incarnation. Again the mixer's active embodiment of Incarnation depends on the receptivity of the mystic.

Salvation

Salvation implies something to be saved from. For Christians this is suffering and death, but more particularly sin. The notion of sin is a puzzling one, because the sinner sins culpably but inevitably. The human condition is said to be both one of freedom and responsibility but also of fallenness and a necessary propensity for evil and failure. Sin is both act and condition.

The incarnation, death and resurrection of Jesus is the way out of this. Salvation is a gift. Remember John 3:16: 'God so loved the world that he gave his only son . . . ' The gift results in a rebirth and in the emergence of a new kind of community, one in which, according to St Paul, all the old divisions will have no place: 'There is neither Jew nor Greek, there is neither slave nor free, there is neither male nor female; for you are all one in Christ Jesus.' (Galatians 3:28).

Salvation is about a new life, freed from the distortions and prejudice based on race, class and gender. Salvation makes possible and calls for a new kind of mixing.

As sin was a puzzle, so is salvation. Does it depend on the gift of the saviour, or on the action of the saved? There has been a long and acrimonious debate among Christians over this. If it is the saviour's gift, what about God-given free will and human responsibility? If it is about human response, why did God need to send his son? And how does a political murder in 1st-century Palestine transform the essence of my life and relationships today? Was it an amazing example of love and heroism on which I can model my life, or have the very structures of

human nature and the entire cosmos somehow been radically transformed? Either way, in the face of injustice and starvation and the endless examples of human cruelty and greed, and the ailing species and life systems of the planet; did it make any difference? This is a hard one for believers: how to maintain belief in the saviour and hope for a transformation of the face of the earth in the face of manifest evil. Again, it is a mystery. It calls for an openness to suffering and an acceptance of one's part in it. It requires sustained reflection on the story of Jesus' death and resurrection and the meanings Christians have given these. There is a need to let go of certainties and uncertainties in order to hold in faith the hope of the English mystic Julian of Norwich: 'That all will be well, and all manner of thing will be well.'

The active transformations of the born-again mixer are rooted in the mystic's acceptance of salvation as gift.

Baptist and Eucharist

Baptism and Eucharist are the ritual expression of the beliefs about salvation. They are a mode of dramatic and bodily participation in the salvation brought by the incarnate God. Baptism is the symbolic burying in the waters to die with Christ and then to rise with him to a new life. The rebirth is into the family of the baptized, the church. The first birth was into the natural family; the second is into the wider horizons of the local and global Christian community.

The Eucharist is an anamnesis, a powerful remembering of the Last Supper and the death and resurrection of Jesus, in such a way that there is a collapse of time between the original events and their memorial. The participants are in some way (interpreted differently by different churches) present to the salvation-bringing events. The reality of their new relationship with Jesus and each other is conveyed in the intimate symbolism of eating and drinking the Eucharistic bread and wine.

Baptism and Eucharist show the believers' new and close relationship with Christ and the community. As members of the body of Christ they see each other's lives in a new light. Their destinies are irrevocably mixed.

The realities of salvation and the new community which the rituals manifest sacramentally are both present and absent. Like the promised Kingdom, they are 'now and not yet'. The Christ is with them but not finally and fully. St Paul spoke of seeing 'through a glass darkly', and the early Christians spoke of their rituals as sacred mysteries. Because they are high points of Christian encounter with the divine, they are mystery, requiring of and bestowing on the participants the stillness and strength of the mystic.

Mystics and mixers in the classroom: three ways of approaching Christianity

By using these two linked categories, the aim is to get a better understanding of Christian beliefs and the experience of Christian life in a way that conveys both the transforming energy and the mysterious and unfinished quality. This will be better grasped if it is connected to the mystery and openness of the pupils' own experience.

Myself as mystic and mixer

A number of exercises would be useful here, but it is important first to unpack the meaning of the terms, perhaps by sorting a series of words around the mystic and mixer poles:

Still, confident, making, accepting, achieving, passive, assertive, growing, receiving, giving, not knowing, busy, knowing, active, waiting, deciding, clear, unclear.

These could be added to, and explored further through body modelling, getting into the appropriate postures and gestures to convey a series of meanings, and then conveying a contrasting set. Pupils could choose and bring or play pieces of music to express aspects of mystic or mixer. Time lines could be used to identify situations in their own history, when they were more mystic or more mixer. Special places which have had a particular memory or association for a pupil can be 'revisited' to see if they relate to the

mystic or mixer. These can be linked to the symbolisms of cave and mountain, and the cave- and mountain-like features evident in the architecture of religious buildings.

Lists of left brain and right brain characteristics can be supplied, and pupils asked to position themselves along the continuum between each pair (see below).

Stilling exercises,[1] the Candle and Wire, and the Wise Person fantasy[2] can provide opportunities for at first silent then shared reflection on the two elements and their relationship in the pupils' own experiences. Stilling exercises could be a useful way to focus on the mysteries in the pupils' own lives. What are the great unknowns, those aspects of relationships with family or friends, or puzzles about themselves or the universe before which they can only ponder and wait?

Or pupils can reflect on their strengths and achievements, those occasions when they were confident and successful, and felt good about what they created for themselves and others. Are there experiences which cannot easily be put into words, but which can, perhaps, be expressed through painting and drawing or captured through music?

The Trina Paulus story, *Hope for the Flowers*,[3] beautifully contrasts, through the life-cycle of caterpillars, the mode of the thrusting, would-be achiever with the transformation wrought by letting go in the darkness of the cocoon.

A source of short, pithy stories relevant to the themes of mixer and mystic are the collections of Anthony de Mello.[4] Working with these stories over time can itself convey something of the nature of the mystic. In the introduction to *The Song of the Bird*, Anthony de Mello writes: 'Read the story again, after you have reflected on it. Create a silence within you and let the story reveal to you its inner depth and meaning. A meaning beyond words and reflections.

Left Brain	Right Brain
Logical – reasons through cause and effect	Intuitive – immediate grasp of whole
Objective – seeking evidence and general principles	Subjective – concerned with feelings and particular meaning
Analytic – dividing up into constituent parts	Holistic – taking something as a totality of elements
Cognitive – rational and dispassionate process	Affective – using emotions and personal feelings
Verbal – words to describe and define	Spatial – using shapes, images and colour
Asks 'how'	Asks 'why'

This will gradually give you a feel for the mystical . . . Theology – the art of telling stories about the Divine. Also the art of listening to these stories. Mysticism – the art of tasting and feeling in your heart the inner meaning of such stories to the point that you are transformed by them.'

Pupils could, on several occasions, place themselves on a continuum between the two poles of mystic and mixer to see whether their emphasis changes or remains constant. This would also reinforce the understanding that, though we might gravitate to one or other end of the spectrum, we all combine elements of both.

Christians as mystics and mixers

A series of Christian figures could be selected for study: potted biographies stressing mixer or mysticism. Some obvious mixers: the bishops Romero, Tutu and Camara; Elizabeth Fry, Mother Teresa and Dorothy Day of the American Catholic Worker Movement. Some obvious mystics: Meister Eckhart, Walter Hilton, Thomas Merton, Hildegard of Bingen, Julian of Norwich and Teresa of Avila.

A further series could be investigated to decide which category best fits Benedict: Francis, Luther, John Wesley, Brother Roger of Taizé. Are they mixing mystics or mystical mixers? What evidence can be found for both characteristics in the first group, in the prayer and meditative life of the mixers, and the activities of the mystics? Where does Jesus belong? What are the examples of his active involvement through his healing, teaching, feeding and supporting? What are the examples of withdrawal, prayer, silence? How should his death and resurrection be seen? Are the acts which Christians see as transforming human life and the whole cosmos those of a mixer or a mystic?

Belief and practice – is Christian belief a call to mixing or mysticism?

This would be an investigation with pupils of the beliefs outlined above: Trinity, Incarnation, Salvation, Baptism and Eucharist.

The study of Doctrine can be a dry business. It is vital that the richness of art and music are included.

Examples from the history of Christian art show the ways in which artists have tried to convey the

mystery of the Incarnation by combining images of the human and the divine in the figure of Jesus; the use of light in Rembrandt's *Nativity* and Georges de la Tour's painting of Jesus in the carpenter's shop, the geometry of Pierro della Francesca's *Baptism* – the circle for heaven, the square for earth; Dürer's *Christ* – using the triangle of the Trinity surmounting the square of humanity; Grünewald's Isenheim altarpiece, where the mutilated figure of the crucified Jesus gives way when the triptych is opened to the blazing, light-filled figure of the risen Christ.

Music can create mood and convey meanings beyond the grasp of words. Music and community singing can bring about a tangible solidarity, in which the singers experience with each other the harmony expressed in the combination of their individual voices. Music fosters mysticism and mixing, often in combination. The resources are enormous: Gregorian chant, Orthodox liturgies, the classical masses and requiems, Pentecostal services, Taizé chants, South African township hymns, peasant masses from Central America, traditional and contemporary British church music, carols. They can be heard and responded to, and the music and words can be related to paintings, the symbolisms of church architecture, and the major beliefs and the festivals which celebrate them.

This investigation of the beliefs would draw on the work of the preceding sections and so bring an awareness of mixer and mystic which is rooted in the pupils' own experience and related to Christian figures of past and present. This would enable them to grasp better the nature of the beliefs and get a deeper understanding of the effect they have on the lives of Christians.

Notes

1 Michael Beasley, *Stilling*, Salisbury Diocesan Board of Education, 1990.
2 John Hammond, David Hay, Jo Moxon, Brian Netto, Kathy Raban, Ginny Straughier and Chris Williams, *New Methods in RE*, Oliver & Boyd, 1990.
3 Trina Paulus, *Hope for the Flowers*, St Paul's Press, 1972.
4 Anthony de Mello, *Song of the Bird*, *The Prayer of the Frog*, *The Heart of the Enlightened*, Collins, Fount Paperbacks, 1982.

9 Learning how to look: teaching Hinduism in the secondary school

Jacqueline Hirst

Introduction: what do you see?

You walk into a Hindu temple in Leicester. What do you see? A garish collection of posters and marble dolls, sending messages of polytheism and idolatry? A colourful array of devotional images and pictures which excite the senses along with the fragrance of incense? Murtis of Lord Krishna and his consort Radha, Hanumanji and others, mediating God's presence to the worshippers? The paraphernalia of worship which may be transcended in the realization of the Supreme Reality within yourself?

Dilip Kadodwala (Section Two A: 'From Diversity to Diversity: the Unity of Hindu Darshan') invites the teacher to consider the concept of darshan and the ways in which this can be linked with inner transformation for a practising Hindu. It is the purpose of this article to ask how these ideas from within a religious tradition can be drawn on in the secondary classroom to fulfil what I take to be the aims of good Religious Education: helping pupils to explore religious traditions, whether their own or others'; to develop their own critical understanding of and sensitivity to the practices, beliefs and values of those whose world they share; helping pupils to explore their own experience, be it religious or secular, and to consider questions of fundamental importance to human beings about their identity and purpose; and enabling pupils to develop ways of understanding how meaning is expressed in religious traditions in verbal and non-verbal ways. I shall suggest that the concept of 'seeing' can be a key to those processes of interpretation which are fundamental to realizing such aims. Allowing pupils to explore the concept of darshan in the course of studying aspects of Hindu traditions may enable them to experience the sort of transformation of viewpoint which is legitimate in educational terms and may give them the flavour of what it might be to experience such transformation within a particular religious context.

If this is to be the case, then teaching must start with what the pupils can already 'see'. This will clearly differ, depending on the cultural mix of the class and the experiences they have been offered at the primary stage, among other factors. Some of the activities I shall include have been described imaginatively by Ken Oldfield for use in the Junior classroom.[1] These methods can also be successfully adapted for students ranging from pupils in Year 3 to teachers on INSET courses! The key is, of course, the level of conceptual understanding which you seek to develop through such methods. Because my experience has largely been with people who have not been familiar with Hindu traditions, I shall work from this starting point, but hope to show that the depth of the material and the ways in which it is handled allow for growth in perception from other starting points, too.

I shall focus on two possible approaches, which might be used cumulatively in secondary courses, at Key Stages 3 and 4 respectively. This work can also be extended into Key Stage 5. Personally, I prefer not to teach in a thematic way, especially at Key Stage 3, believing that the integrity of a tradition is better understood through concentration on features which that tradition itself recognizes as central – darshan in this instance. The material could, however, be adapted to the type of course which raises life issues and draws on different traditions for illustrative material. The idea of transformation is one, for example, which several of the articles in Section Two A share.

The first approach, at Key Stage 3, is that of understanding 'the other'. The second investigates ways in which the understanding and self-understanding of women are fostered in religious traditions and can inspire pupils at Key Stage 4. At Key Stage 5, questions about legitimate interpretations of texts and further social issues may be raised.

Understanding the other: darshan of the deities

In the first approach, the goal is to help pupils understand Hindu devotional pictures and worship involving darshan. In the process, it is hoped to make them aware of their own assumptions and how these colour what they see. Here are three suggestions for introducing the subject. The Martians' view of Christmas[2] is unfailingly successful as an opening gambit – but don't overplay it if the pupils have met it already. Groups of pupils explain the significance of the seasonal rituals as they appear to their 'Martian' eyes. This works well in an all-white or multicultural classroom, and may lead to interesting insights about their understanding of Christmas, quite apart from the point of the game! Another way in is to ask pupils to bring a natural object – say a flower, stone or shell. Get them really to look at it for a few minutes, as they would if they were going to draw it. What happens when they do draw it? What have they actually *seen*? Would they look at it differently if they were going to use it as part of a sculpture? Or if they were classifying it in an environmental science lesson? Or if they were using it as an object to meditate on? A third suggestion is to start straight in with a devotional picture as a puzzle to decode, but with the initial stipulation that such pictures are very special to those whose tradition they come from and hence deserve respect. I usually tell pupils about a Hindu friend of mine who is a lab technician in a city comprehensive. Her delight that the RE department had mounted a display of such devotional posters turned sour when she saw a group of Year 9 pupils laughing at a picture of Hanuman, the monkey god who epitomizes devotion. To her, Hanumanji has had a special place in her daily devotions since the time in her teens when, grieving desperately over the death of her father, she recited the Hanuman Chalisa, and found inner peace as a result.

Understanding devotional pictures

A good subject to start with is Ganesh (or Ganapati), the elephant-headed god. Firstly, it does justice to the place he holds in popular worship. Worship to Ganesh is traditionally offered first: 'Om Ganeshaya namaha' ('Om, greetings to Ganesh'). He is found on wedding invitations as the couple, in the context of their newly joined families, start the householder phase of life. The phrase is written on the walls of new houses while the building is as yet unfinished. It is apt to start with Ganesh. Secondly, Ganesh is so

obviously 'other' to those outside Hindu traditions; yet the symbolism of his trunk and his vehicle, the rat, is quickly appreciated once his role as Lord of Obstacles is understood. It is not only Hindus who pray for help in overcoming the difficulties in their lives, who seek help with new enterprises, who desire blessing on their futures. Nor is it only religious people who share such concerns.

Once pupils have been helped to decode one such picture, they can then be given other pictures to work on in groups. Rather than letting them read in possibly erroneous ideas at the outset, get them to work out the kinds of questions they need to ask to help them really understand what they are looking at. They may then suggest possible answers, progress to researching the pictures for themselves, and then look back critically at their initial assumptions. Useful resources for such research include Hirst and Pandey[3], Killingley[4], Killingley *et al.*[5], Jaffrey[6] and slides and notes from *The Hindu Temple and its Symbols* (Slide Centre, S1525, 1986). Another useful technique is to get one class of pupils to prepare packs on different deities, including illustrations, explanations of symbolism, stories linked with them and festivals celebrating them, which can then become resource materials for other classes to work with. Accuracy and good presentation will then be appreciated by a genuine audience.

It is important that pupils are helped to realize that, for most Hindus, the different gods and goddesses are all expressions of that Supreme Reality which is beyond all description. Demonstrating the ancient Upanishadic example of salt dissolved in water is a graphic way of conveying this.[7]

Understanding puja

Next, an introduction to puja, devotional worship, will help pupils to appreciate the context in which the pictures studied are used. Construction of a classroom shrine may be done by the teacher, by groups of pupils or by Hindu parents and pupils, who might be willing to demonstrate the arati ceremony (offering of light – usually a five-flamed lamp). A discussion as to whether the shrine should be allowed to remain on display in the classroom may allow pupils to show growing sensitivity. If they have been told about the incident involving the picture of Hanuman, they will usually allude to it here to help them debate the issue. If your class is mature enough to handle it, this may be an appropriate point to introduce the idea that many Hindu women will not offer worship while they are menstruating, and may draw a curtain across their home shrine at such times.

If you are not Hindu or do not have a willing Hindu volunteer, it is still important to demonstrate the key features of puja yourself. Care should be taken that the pupils understand that you are not engaged in an act of worship, but in a respectful demonstration of what a Hindu might do. I would therefore remove my shoes and cover my head and take them through the different steps of puja,[8] getting them to look out for actions that express certain key themes: the significance of purity in the place where the deity will reside, that is, in both shrine and worshipper; the treatment of the deity as honoured guest in home and heart; the giving and receiving of offerings. In particular, I would draw their attention to the act of taking darshan, standing or sitting before the deity with hands in the anjali position, looking at the deity and being regarded in turn. I might recount my experience of seeing a young girl take darshan of Radha and Krishna at the Alexandra Palace Festival of India[9] and get the pupils to think of their own experiences of knowing and being known through exchange of glances – a private exercise, not to be divulged to teacher or peers. A useful follow-up to this is the clip from the Exmouth Video, *Aspects of Hinduism*, which shows a woman performing puja at her home shrine. The atmosphere of calm devotion as she takes darshan of the deities is strongly conveyed to pupils who have started to explore the significance of the actions she performs.

Preparing an arati lamp and lighting it in the classroom, and showing how it is moved in worship, is an excellent way to help pupils feel the inner silence which worship may enfold. Any class will be stilled watching the flames flickering as the lamp is circled. Draw their attention to the quality of silence in the room. They are not themselves worshipping nor taking darshan. But the sense of quiet communication may give some small indication of what a worshipper experiences in the presence of God. Here is a poem written by Louise Entock, a Year 11 GCSE pupil, after watching a Bharat Natyam dancer dance the arati to Lord Shiva. She was building on earlier work on puja:

The Indian Dancer
The lamp burns
She appears as if from behind a curtain
So pure as if bathed in milk and honey
With the smell of imaginary incense
The sign of blessing shines,
Her eyes begin to move
Like a chronometer worshipping in time,
The sound so dominating no mind can
Escape it,
The robes of gold.
No eyes can turn away,
Darshan of Shiva in her face
As the lamp burns
With grace and peace dharma is told
And with eyes as powerful as that of Lord
Shiva himself,
So much is understood.

Quite apart from the imagery of the dance and arati themselves, this pupil is communicating an understanding of the power of darshan, both as portrayed by the dancer and as understood by the audience, themselves given the inner eye of Lord Shiva through the dancer's skill.

Understanding ourselves: images of women

Another way of building cumulatively on the Key Stage 3 work above is to develop pupils' ability to 'see' what is conveyed through devotional pictures in terms of images of women. Such work might take place in a general RE or PSE course at Key Stage 4 which was looking at images of self-identity, or at ways in which relationships are understood, or explicitly at feminist issues; or in a deeper specialist study of aspect of Hindu traditions.

Religion and social values: seeing the goddesses

From a wall display of different Hindu goddesses, ask pupils to jot down individually the images of or messages about femaleness which they receive. Give them about five minutes to work on this and prompt their observation if necessary by getting them to look at faces, dress, ornamentation, position relative to male deities, scenes enacted, vehicles and so on. I try to ensure a range of pictures and to order them so that they appear to move from those of submission or even subservience through those of equality to strong images of female power. Examples might include: Draupadi being dragged to the assembly hall but protected by Krishna, Lakshmi massaging Vishnu's feet, Rama and Sita, Radha and Krishna, Santoshi Ma, Shiv Shakti, Ardhanarishvara (Shiva as half male, half female), Amba Ma, Durga, Kali. (These are not unambiguous: Draupadi represents independence of mind and courage as well as purity and virtue; Kali's power is so destructive that the male has to sacrifice himself at her feet to control it, and so forth.)

Once pupils have contributed ideas to the whole class, get them in small groups to choose the four ideas of femaleness that they find most appealing. Very often, independence and power will feature, but so too will responsibility and compassion. In a whole class discussion, get pupils to look at *why* they read certain pictures in certain ways and why certain values are appealing to them. Do they all see them in the same way? Need Hindus all see them in similar ways? How could such pictures be used to strengthen traditional roles of women? What are the advantages of such views? How could such pictures be used to undermine traditional roles and to give inspiration to those who wish to develop new understandings of equality? What are the disadvantages of such views? What about 'spiritualizing' readings of the images? If the Lord is seen as the lover rather than the human husband, is this liberating or a confirmation of social restrictions?

Note that the aim of such a method is *not* to suggest that all Hindu images of women are binding, negative, anti-equality, anti-feminist. It is to stimulate discussion as to how we see and are taught to relate to one another in different ways, and how it is possible to challenge received views, either to find again the importance of their values or to help reshape thinking for the future. No Hindu pupil should feel undermined as the result of such an exercise. No pupil from another tradition should be left with purely negative impressions. All cultural traditions, whatever their key values, have in historical terms subjected women in various ways.

Shaping the future

This opening might be followed up by looking at modern Indian fiction or anthropological studies or women's movements to see how some Hindu women are shaping their future. Some useful resources are given below.[10] Kalpana Bardhan's collection of Bengali short stories[11] shows that in India, as elsewhere, other oppression may go hand in hand with that of women. Work on injustice and human rights could, therefore, also develop from such a start. Since responsibility for others, embodied in one's own dharma, is a key Hindu theme, this will fit well with recent approaches to rights issues which stress that they should not be taught without considering accompanying responsibilities.

After introducing such material at an in-service course for secondary teachers, I was encouraged by the response of a Hindu colleague, who said she felt positively liberated by such an approach to her own tradition, which she now wished to explore further for herself. But does this have anything to do with darshan? In so far as it is to do with new ways of seeing and of possibilities for transformation, yes. In so far as it drives the one who sees to look beyond the social to the spiritual, yes. For, as Dilip Kadodwala shows, darshan is to do with insight into oneself, the nature of the atman (self) and one's relation with the Supreme Reality, understood by Hindus from different darshanas in many profound ways through the centuries. Such an understanding may be developed at Sixth Form level through studying texts like the *Bhagavad Gita* and by using techniques of mental stilling and watchfulness,[12] though with caution.

I hope, then, to have shown that through cumulative courses which build up understanding of others and give opportunities for growing reflection and self-understanding, pupils may come to understand not only key aspects of the concept of darshan within a Hindu context, but, in learning how to look at parts of that rich and varied tradition, may also themselves perhaps learn to see.

Notes

1 Ken Oldfield, 'Teaching Hinduism in the junior school', in R. Jackson and D. Starkings (eds.), *The Junior RE Handbook*, Stanley Thornes, 1990.

2 R. Jackson and D. Killingley, *World Religions in Education: Approaches to Hinduism*, John Murray, 1988, pages 24–5.

3 J. Hirst and G. Pandey, *Growing up in Hinduism*, Longman, 1990.

4 D. and S. Y. Killingley, *Hinduism Iconography Pack*, Grevatt & Grevatt, Newcastle upon Tyne, 1984.

5 D. Killingley *et al.*, *Handbook of Hinduism for Teachers*, Grevatt & Grevatt, Newcastle upon Tyne, 1984.

6 Madhur Jaffrey, *Seasons of Splendour*, Puffin, 1985.

7 Ken Oldfield, *op. cit.*, page 104.

8 J. Hirst and G. Pandey, *op. cit.*, page 16.

9 *Ibid.* pages 8–9.

10 Meena Alexander *et al.*, *The State of Life: an anthology of stories by Indian women*, Kali for Women, New Delhi, 1990.

Lynn Bennett, *Dangerous Wives and Sacred Sisters: social and symbolic roles of high-caste women in Nepal*, Colombia University Press, 1983.

J. S. Hawley and D. M. Wulff (eds.), *The Divine Consort: Radha and the goddesses of India*, Beacon Press, Boston, 1986.

A. Jung, *Unveiling India: a woman's journey*, Penguin, 1987.

Sara S. Mitter, *Dharma's Daughters: contemporary Indian women and Hindu culture*, Rutgers University Press, New Brunswick, NJ, 1991.

11 K. Bardhan (ed.), *Of Women, Outcastes, Peasants and Rebels*, University of California Press, 1990.

12 John Hammond *et al.*, *New Methods in RE Teaching: an experiential approach*, Oliver & Boyd, 1990.

10 Peace, submission, unity and harmony: Islam in the secondary classroom

Dilwyn Hunt

At the heart of the Islamic vision of life are the concepts of peace, submission, unity and harmony. In what practical ways can we help pupils to understand these concepts and thereby help them to find a more profound insight into the faith?

In trying to describe specific classroom situations one has to be cautious. All teachers develop a classroom style and technique personal to themselves. These styles and techniques don't necessarily translate very effectively for other teachers. A word or idea delivered at just the right moment can be like a turn on a kaleidoscope, when the pattern falls into place and the child enjoys a sudden disclosure. But like telling a joke, the timing of that word or idea is critical, and what works for one child with one teacher in one situation might fall flat given another situation or different people.

Nevertheless, we should be able to describe approaches which, all being well, have a reasonable chance of success or which teachers can modify to suit themselves.

The Nature of submission

Let's look at what has already been described as the ambiguous and seemingly negative concept of submission. It is true that for many pupils the word submission conjures up images of weakness, a giving

in, an unthinking and docile acceptance. Yet for Muslims the characteristic attitude of a true believer is one of submission to God. In order for pupils to gain anything like the same vision of Islam which Muslims themselves have, we need to recognize the negative images of the word submission and seek to do something to overcome them.

One method might be to familiarize the pupils with what submission to God really means using examples from the world of nature. A series of slightly comic cards showing animals involved in behaviour foreign to their nature might help. A fish in water is in obedience to its true nature, but a fish trying to survive on dry land isn't. A tiger eating meat is in obedience to its true God-given nature, but a tiger eating a banana isn't. A dog walking on four legs is in submission to God, but a dog that spends all day on its hindlegs is not.

These examples can also be used to help pupils to understand the Islamic concept of peace. The true happiness, contentment or peace of the fish can only come about by returning to the water. A tiger will never enjoy contentment eating bananas; nor will a dog enjoy happiness on this planet walking around all day on its hind legs. Through images such as this, one is trying to help pupils to understand that submission in Islam doesn't mean docility or weakness; it means coming into line with what is natural, true, good and proper. However, when trying to illustrate this in the context of human beings, we find ourselves on more difficult ground.

We recognize that a dog which struggles to walk around all day on its hindlegs is somehow perverse and is not at peace with itself or its true nature. But what would we say about a man who has chosen to take a vow of celibacy and to live in a monastery with other men? Is he also somehow being perverse? Is he also out of line with his true nature? That certainly seems to be the view which many Muslims would take; after all, the Islamic tradition proclaims the life of marriage and family as natural and in line with God's intentions for humankind. The Qur'an also confirms this view when it says: 'And monkhood they initiated; we did not prescribe it for them.' (57:27).

Are there any other images which we can draw upon which illustrate the idea of humans who have abandoned the straight path and so are not in submission to God's will? Teachers are best advised to make their own collection, but there are plenty of examples to draw upon. The solvent-abuser, the prostitute, the perpetrator of violent crime, the lonely pensioner, the abandoned mother, the adulterous husband, the extravagantly greedy, the overtly vain – all provide examples which children can understand of people, or victims of people, who live out lives which Muslims believe are not in accordance with God's intentions.

These images also provide opportunity for pupils to explore the Islamic concepts of peace and shirk. There are people who, in material terms, have been successful; for example, they own portable telephones, leather-bound personal organizers and designer-label clothing; but many of them are preoccupied with work, frequently bad-tempered and are unable to establish lasting relationships. In what sense have such people been successful? Have they achieved peace? Have they sought to fill a vacuum in their life by purchasing a 'look good' image? Have they found a shallow meaning to their existence by devotion to gadgets and expensive adult toys? Are they not really worshippers of false gods? Have they committed shirk – ignored God for the sake of false gods? By raising questions in this way and inviting the pupils to contribute to the discussion, we are not merely encouraging them to

explore at a profound level what Islam is about; we are also encouraging them to reflect more seriously upon their own beliefs and values.

The harmonious universe

How might we encourage pupils to think more deeply about the Islamic claim that the universe is both unified and harmonious? The Islamic tradition tells us that there are obvious signs, or as the Qur'an calls them, ayats, of an intelligence at work which has unified, ordered and harmoniously created things to be as they are. Whenever ideas along these teleological lines are being discussed it is always worthwhile considering whether pupils can profit from being familiarized with John Wisdom's parable of the gardener:[1]

Two explorers come across a clearing in a jungle. In the clearing one explorer points out the existence and beauty of the flowers and announces that a gardener has been tending the plot, while the other notices the overgrown weeds and declares that no such gardener exists. What are obvious signs to one observer do not seem at all obvious to another. The argument is not about the information available, as both explorers agree that there are flowers and that there are weeds. The argument is about how each observer interprets the same data. The parable is a microcosm of a great deal of religious debate, and pupils can certainly respond to and benefit from the insights the story contains.

Another useful way to explore the idea of harmony and unity in the universe is through Islamic art. As has been said earlier, a great deal of Islamic art, based on pattern, does not serve merely to decorate. Rather, it provides the faithful with a reminder that behind what might seem to be an inexplicable maze there is in fact a thought-out and ordered pattern: a pattern which is so coherent and regulated that one couldn't imagine that mere chance or coincidence brought it about. Such patterns, many Muslims would argue, mirror the world we live in – the octagonal structure of a beehive, the hexagonal form of a snow crystal, a flower in full bloom. A collection of such images, put alongside Islamic patterns which closely resemble them, can help pupils to perceive what Muslims mean by an ordered universe in which the hand of God can be seen at work.

A visit to a mosque, or, if that is not practical, the class model of a mosque, can be used to reinforce the

Islamic concepts of unity and harmony. Mosques are usually designed symmetrically. Just as the left hand side of the mosque is balanced by the right hand side, so nature itself seems to be neatly balanced: the summer is balanced by the winter, the day by the night, earth by water, birth by decay. The curves and shapes of mosque domes, towers and arches mirror the curves and shapes of nature: the flower bud, the conifer tree, the leaf. In using such forms the designers were drawing upon what they felt to be the curves and lines of the master designer, God Himself. The creation of a vast dome on a mosque, which seems to support itself without any visible means, serves as a reminder of the miracle and beauty of the sky: 'Among His signs are (the fact) that the sky and earth hold firm at His command.' (30:26).

To help pupils to consider the mosque in this way raises all sorts of important questions. Is this world ordered? Is it in harmony? Did someone or something order it? Did it just come about? Do flowers and trees suggest that there is a God? What do disease and famine suggest? Such questions go much closer to the heart of RE, and encourage pupils to think more seriously about Islam, rather than concerning the pupils with naming and describing mihrabs and mimbars.

Unity in diversity

The concepts of unity, peace and harmony may also be explored with pupils through the physical expressions of Islam. For example, if the Hajj (pilgrimage to Makkah) is 'a remarkable expression of unity in diversity'[2], this idea needs to form a primary focus. An effective way of doing this is by familiarizing pupils with the experiences of those who, while on pilgrimage, have enjoyed the sense of being members of a diverse but unified community.

Abdul Malik Shabbaz, or Malcolm X, as he is better known, wrote a vivid account of his Hajj[3]. Prior to his becoming a Muslim and going on pilgrimage, it would not have been unfair to describe Malcolm X's attitude towards white people as hostile. But while on pilgrimage he declares: 'For the past week, I have been utterly speechless and spellbound by the graciousness I see displayed all around me by people of all colours . . .'. Malcolm X returned from his Hajj with a radically warmer response to all people, black or white, recognizing that all are united as part of God's creation.

Exploring the Hajj may thus become an opportunity to deepen the pupil's understanding of Islam's response to racism and how Islam, both through its teaching and its rituals, can transform people for the good. This also helps pupils to understand the real significance of the Hajj: it is not a catalogue of places to be visited in and around Makkah. It is an experience from which many Muslims return with insights and responses which enrich them for life.

Prayer, fasting and giving similarly all provide fruitful opportunities to examine the central concepts of Islam. But when exploring these rituals teachers need to keep in mind what important lessons can be learnt from them. It is all too easy to become pre-occupied with the minutiae of the external ritual. Approached with thought and care, Islam raises vitally important questions and issues to which pupils can and will respond.

Notes

1 J. Wisdom, *Philosophy and Psychoanalysis*, Blackwell, 1953, pages 154–6.
2 Alan Brine, *Islam: an environment of peace and harmony*, Shap article, page 3.
3 Malcolm X and A. Haley, *The Autobiography of Malcolm X*, Penguin, 1965, page 454.

11 Jews are just like everybody else – but that's not the point! Judaism in the secondary classroom

Clive A. Lawton

The study of Judaism for the non-Jew is not best approached via text, but if you leave off your study without approaching text you will have done the tradition (and the student) a disservice. Torah is the root from which Judaism derives its sustenance and stability; but one would be unlikely to start a course on trees by studying their roots.

Below I will offer some examples of how the teacher might reach the text by approaching the study of Judaism via the three key concepts of space, time and identity.

Studying the Jewish sense of space

There are a number of ways into this topic. One popular field of study at secondary level is the synagogue. Visits to synagogues can be fairly easily arranged in most parts of the country, though you might have to travel a little.

It is obviously good practice to prepare students before going on any trip, so that they know what to look for – but what should that be? I would suggest that, besides looking at the obvious phenomena of the synagogue – the ark, the bimah, the ner tamid and so on – students are prepared to consider the relationship between the temple and the synagogue. In what ways does it function as a replacement, as a reminder, or as something entirely different?

To find out the realities of the temple, you will obviously benefit from quarrying the Tenakh and those parts of the Torah that teach about the portable tabernacle. Students would benefit from speculating on the fact that synagogues are not mentioned at all in the Torah. That discovery alone will loosen them up into understanding, on the one hand, the dislocation of the Jewish people with the destruction of the Temple and, on the other, just how fluid and flexible the Jewish tradition can be.

Another way in is to study the agricultural aspects of the festivals. The three pilgrim festivals of Pesach, Shavuot and Sukkot are all harvest festivals. However, at the time when they take place, it isn't necessarily the harvesting season in Britain. Consideration of how the leap year system works in Judaism, adding a whole extra month periodically to keep Pesach in the spring, and what it feels like to celebrate the autumn harvest on Sukkot as the rain and wind really start to bite, might make the Jews seem a bit odd or out of touch. However, if you put it together with Christmas cards covered with snow (when did we last have a white Christmas?) young people might start to understand something about the process of locating oneself in an idealized world in order to upgrade reality.

A third possibility is to look at the way in which the Shabbat service in England carries a prayer for the British Royal Family and the Government, followed immediately by a prayer for the welfare and peace of the State of Israel. Studying the texts of the prayers is rewarding in itself, but putting it together with, say, the St Patrick's Day parade in New York, which is distinctly Irish, will help young people understand the concept and reality of diaspora.

Another fruitful source of study is to look at progressive Judaism's evolving attitude to Zionism. Originally, it saw Zionism as a destructive throwback to a tribal past which would expose Jews to charges of dual loyalty. Jews, it argued, had grown beyond that. They could now be equally Jewish anywhere and, indeed, one small sign of this severing of links with the ancestral home was the practice of calling their synagogues temples. Thus, they asserted, a temple, for Jews, could be anywhere. It was primitive to hark back to the old one. Much of that has now changed. Progressive Judaism now has an articulate and well developed Zionist movement. A study of their case would be revealing.

Finally, back to Torah. As Moses led the Israelites back to Israel, some of the tribes were so struck by the pleasant land on the east bank of the Jordan, that they decided that they wanted to settle there instead of going through all the bother of settling west of the Jordan. Eventually agreement was reached on how they should proceed. In many ways that agreement has set the pattern on how Jews from outside Israel relate to it. It's worth studying it and considering its implications.

Studying the Jewish sense of time

A consideration of almost any of the festivals will bring students face to face with the way in which Jews do not allow their history to flow away into the past. Again, the pattern is set in the Torah, where Jews are commanded to re-live annually the night of the Exodus. In the classroom, a model seder or baking matzah will give an intensive sense of the way in which Jews turn history into current activity.

Purim offers another opportunity in the classroom – provided you've got tolerant neighbours! A very rapid reading of the Book of Esther with competitive booing at the name of Haman – miss it and lose a point – will bring alive to young people both the critical skill of following text precisely and the way in which Jews still stir themselves at the thought of what nearly happened over two thousand years ago.

A discussion on why Jews number their years from the Creation (don't get too hung up on Darwinism versus biblical fundamentalism – it isn't an issue in Judaism; remember, all texts can be interpreted), rather than from some specific Jewish date like the Exodus or the destruction of the Temple, should draw out valuable insights on how the Jews see the process of history from the Creation to the Messianic Age.

To turn to the more domestic processes of time, students of Judaism should understand how Jewish observance affects the rhythms of a person's life. Reflecting on the festivals, the preparations for them and the possible 'afterglow' might be best encouraged by a mixture of specific study of the practices concerned (clearing out leaven before Pesach, building a sukkah etc.) and reflection on their own experiences of birthdays, Christmas and so on.

More intensively, careful consideration of Shabbat might lead them to reflect on the rhythm of their own lives and that of their families. They could usefully reflect on how observance of Shabbat changes the pattern and activity of the week. How would it change their own lives? Push them to think of the advantages as well as the losses.

Studying the Jewish sense of identity

Recent years have offered a number of revealing, high profile examples of the workings of Jewish identity. The recent struggles of Soviet Jews to emigrate to Israel and the unconditional acceptance and even encouragement by Israel of this mass immigration is unparalleled anywhere in the 20th century. Further, and to put under pressure any outmoded thoughts about race, consider the airlifting of the Jews of Ethiopia – and their own struggle to reach the airlift – deserves study and attention.

A close analysis of the articles in one week's edition of the *Jewish Chronicle* will similarly reveal the wide range of issues that preoccupy Jews and thus reveal the nature of their identity. That analysis demands careful attention. An article about, for example, a Jewish old age home reveals not only the charitable tendencies of the Jewish community and its provision of parallel services to the State, while continuing to pay taxes, but also the plight of the Jewish elderly. Can it be true that there *are* poor Jews? And are there elderly Jews whose children don't cherish them forever in the classic, stereotypical, Jewish family way?

Take a look at the curriculum or examination syllabus for Jewish education. What exactly does one generation try to teach the next in order to equip them to be better, more committed Jews? Studying curricula and syllabi is a very good way for your students to gain an overview of what might be considered essential knowledge and pit their own field of knowledge against it. In this way they can test their own growing collection of information about Judaism and also seek equivalent fields in the general things they have to learn. What, for example, is the British cultural equivalent to learning Hebrew? What about learning Bible stories or studying the specific teachings of the rabbis?

Again, go back to the Torah. Study what the term 'Children of Israel' really means. Find the references to the Jews as 'a kingdom of priests and a holy nation'. Note how those two political words 'kingdom' and 'nation' are put together with metaphysical functions. Discuss what they can possibly mean in today's world. Research ways in which Jews interpret the idea of being a people of God. Look at the ways in which this makes Jews more preoccupied with the details of this world, rather than other-worldly. Jewish mission is fundamentally about improving the world, rather than about changing individual people. At root, this is why Jews could not go along with the interpretation of Jesus of Nazareth's messiahship.

Studying Torah

After some of these oblique approaches, Torah study can be pursued in a more realistic context. Firstly, recognize that Torah legislation is of two different kinds. Some is about relationships between the Jew and God and some is about Jews and their relationships with other people.

Choose two teachings. Perhaps the Ten Commandments will yield up 'Remember Shabbat, to keep it holy. Six days you shall work and on the seventh you shall rest,' and 'Honour your father and your mother that your days may be long upon the land which I promised to give you'. Divide the class into pairs or trios. Then set them the task of identifying all the problems they can find about trying to live out these two teachings. Push them to consider problems of definition as well as practicalities. What do 'holy', 'work' and 'honour' mean? What do you do if your parents give you conflicting instructions? If you're not living in the Land, can you ignore the commandment about honouring parents? And so on.

Then look at some story parts. What is one supposed to learn from the story of Abraham's argument with God about God's intention to destroy Sodom and Gomorrah? Note that the idea of a quorum of 10 for congregational prayer comes from here. Look at the Creation story. What might this teach Jews about animal rights, animal welfare and human responsibility for the environment? Does the story of Noah throw any new light on these topics?

Having looked at some of the text as critically and closely as you can, it is then time to consider its sanctity to Jews. Consider with your students what would be the effect of changing one or two of the words that you have closely discussed to similar but different words. Explore the effects of reading the text in translation. Then explore the force of Hebrew as the original language of the Torah and learn about the processes through which scrolls of Torah and the insides of mezuzot and tephilin in are written.

Conclusion

The rabbis teach, in the text of the Pesach Seder, that one should try to tailor one's teaching to the level, capacity and interest of each individual student. Apparently Plowden didn't think up child-centred education all by herself and foist it on an unsuspecting world, after all. It had been around for a couple of thousand years. The principle is

obviously a wise one and applies for all topics and in all subjects. However, at the risk of stating the obvious, it should be noted that it is a good idea to teach about Bat/Bar Mitzvah to Year 8 children; that it is interesting to explore Jewish teachings on love, sexuality, marriage and divorce to years 10 and upwards; and that at all levels they will never tire of the implications and challenges of 'honour your father and your mother'.

Many young people belong to clans and tribes – football fan clubs, the local scouts or guides, even just 'the gang'. These realities are springboards from which they can leap to an understanding of Jewish identity. Similarly, many young people have a highly developed sense of territory and an almost superstitious commitment to key dates – birthdays, Valentine's Day, Saturday night out and so on.

If young people can be led to understand not that 'Jews are just like everybody else' but that Jews respond to the same issues as everybody else, then your programme will have been successful. Space, time and identity are the media through which all people locate themselves. People relate to those fields by their own responses to the cultural frameworks and assumptions which they inherit. So it is with Jews – with the same diversity as in any other group.

It would be impossible to assess the success of your course by whether or not your students had learnt everything. It is simply not possible. But if they have learnt to recognize the sorts of issues that might be important to Jews, the sorts of responses Jews might have to those issues and where those responses are rooted, then your programme must be counted a success. Indeed, it will have been more successful than many a current attempt to teach those things to Jewish youngsters in a world that neither knows nor cares about the ways in which those Jewish young people are different from their peers.

12 An ideal community: a secondary classroom project introducing Sikhism

Carrie Mercier

A search for an approach

'There is no difference between a temple and a mosque, nor between the prayers of a Hindu or Muslim. Though differences seem to mark and distinguish, all men are in reality the same.' – *The Dasam Granth*.[1]

When I began teaching World Religions I took topics such as 'Sacred Writings' and 'Places of Worship' as my themes. However, I felt uncomfortable with these familiar structures when it came to teaching about Sikhism. My dissatisfaction may have had something to do with the fact that whereas I had learnt about Buddhism, Hinduism, Islam and Judaism through the study of their history and literature, Sikhism I had encountered, not through academic study, but through my friendship with Sikhs.

It appeared to me that the Sikhs I met who were committed to their faith shared some remarkable qualities, and this had influenced my understanding of the Sikh tradition. I was impressed by their openness, generosity and warmth. They welcomed me into their homes, gurdwaras, and circle of friends. They took an active interest in my teaching, setting me up with contacts, supplying me with materials, welcoming classes at the gurdwara, offering hospitality and showing an ongoing commitment to what I was trying to do. But beyond this there was something unique about the friendship I found in the Sikh community. I was acknowledged and respected on equal terms; not as an isolated individual coming from nowhere, but as a person belonging to a community, a tradition and having a life linked with other lives. My background, my family, faith and school community were all taken seriously. These things could have been grounds for finding distance and difference between us, but they were regarded as opportunities for sharing, learning and mutual enrichment.

In introducing my students to Sikhism I wanted them to understand some of the beliefs and commitments that inspired this warmth and openness towards others, and to get an idea of the environment in which it was nurtured. I hoped my students would learn to see Sikhism as a living religion, relevant for life in our society. I wanted them to enlarge their understanding of the terms 'community, equality and respect' and to recognize these as they are expressed in Sikh life and faith.

The ideal community

'The Ideal Community' was a Year 8 project. The first lesson was intended to encourage the students to share their ideas on what they thought would be the ideal society to live in. We began by having a look at newspaper cuttings, images and stories of injustice and inequality in our society. These included examples of cultural conflicts; prejudice and racism; hardship experienced by the elderly and/or those with disabilities; the distance between rich and poor; the alienation of the young; and the growing problems of homelessness and unemployment. The class was divided into small groups and each group was given a selection of newspaper articles to examine and discuss. They were asked to do two things: to identify some of the things in society that they would like to change; and to draw up their ideas about the sort of society they would like to live in.

The students were not unusual in their answers. In general terms they described a society in which they could feel safe and one in which they felt that they belonged. In response to the specific problems that they identified in the news cuttings, they wanted a society where people of different backgrounds would get along together, where everyone could get the education they needed, where everyone had enough to eat and a place to live, where there was no violence, and where the needs of the young, the old and those more challenged than others were catered for. Not all the ideas were 'ideal'. For example, there were one or two who felt that there were people who did not belong in our society. In other words, they felt that a more homogeneous society would lead to greater peace and security, and suggested that different groups would be kept apart – even made to live in different parts of the world. This led to further discussion on whether it would be possible to have a completely homogeneous group, and whether a completely homogeneous group would be an ideal for which to strive. This led to the question: 'Who had tried such an approach and down what path had that led?' The questions and answers were simply put, but the ideas were deep and difficult. For homework each student wrote a poem or a description of what they felt would be an ideal society. There were some interesting ideas:

'I would like to live in a society where everyone felt safe, where everybody felt they belonged and where nobody was left outside because they were black or because they looked different or had a different culture.'

'I think it would be good to live in a society where no one made fun of you if you were different. People should try to understand one another.'

'Sometimes people look down on other people because they are old or poor or not able to do things. I think everyone should respect other people and look after people who need help. Everyone should do some community work.'

'In my ideal society everyone would be treated equally and there would be enough work and houses and food for everybody and no one would be living on the streets in cardboard boxes.'

Finding a model

In the second lesson the students were asked to suggest a way to set up the ideal society. For example, they were asked to consider the idea of a model community or a leader who would bring about change. These options were discussed in class, and it was generally agreed that there were too many risks with a single leader or ruler. Then the students went back into their groups to find answers to the following questions:

If you were to set up a model for the ideal community here in our neighbourhood, how and where would it begin: in a building, with a group of people, with an advertisement? What would be the aims and guidelines for the community? What responsibilities or contributions would you want

from members of the community, e.g. money, help etc.? How could you bring the community together? Who would be in charge and who would run the community? What would be the beliefs of the community?

Once again the groups pooled their ideas. Several of them came up with the suggestion of a community centre which would be both a model and a base from which to work towards the ideal community.

The next step was for the students to design the centre for the ideal community. Practical considerations came to the surface first. The students all felt that the needs of both young and old had to be taken into account, so there would have to be facilities for recreation to suit different ages. There was a general agreement that food and drink should be made available. This raised interesting questions about providing food for different groups of people. The question of alcohol was a difficult one in this respect. Some groups felt that shelter for the homeless and medical services could be provided. Others suggested that educational facilities should be available for the unemployed and evening classes for people to develop their skills and interests. There were suggestions that there should be a place for the community to celebrate special occasions. Some students in each group worked on drawing plans for the community centre, showing the facilities and the general design and layout. Others were concerned with writing a brief to go with the plans. There were questions raised about the need for financial contributions and for the allocation of responsibilities in the community. Some groups introduced the discussion about having aims, guidelines and teachings. This became the next stage in the project.

Beliefs and commitments

The class continued to work in groups. They were asked to draw up a set of beliefs and commitments on which their community would be based and some guidelines and ideas about running the community centre. This was the most difficult area, but the most interesting. The groups were given some trigger questions to think about. For example: Would anyone be regarded as more important than others? Who would do the work to keep the place running? How would such people be chosen to carry out this work? What would people contribute in terms of money or help? How would you help to make people feel they belonged? Would old and young have the same rights and privileges? What rules would there be about behaviour, smoking, noise etc.?

Many of the groups came up with similar beliefs and ideas on which their community would be founded, for example:

everyone is equal, no matter what their age, sex, colour, background, religion or ability;

members should respect each other and accept differences;

everyone who is able should make a contribution, and this could be an offering of their time or skills or money or other resources;

everyone should help keep the centre tidy and safe;

everyone should take a turn at helping to run the activities and facilities, e.g. helping to make coffee, clearing up, locking up etc.;

everyone has the same rights and privileges in the centre unless they deliberately break or misuse things or spoil the enjoyment of others.

Some of the groups suggested a sort of committee of representatives from different sections of the community to make decisions concerning the community and the running of the centre. The idea that young as well as old should be represented was clearly an important issue for the class. There was evidence of a keen sense of injustice and a feeling that the hopes and needs of young people were not taken into account in our society. A few of the students came up with the idea of the need for a community event on a regular basis to bring the community together and to encourage friendship and trust between people. The homework following this session required the students to design a poster that could be put up in the community centre which would set out the beliefs and commitments on which it was based.

Time for a story

The next step was to use the students' ideas about the ideal community to open the way to their encounter with the Sikh community. I wanted to follow this preliminary work with a visit to the local gurdwara. However, I knew that for most of the students the gurdwara would be a very unfamiliar environment, and that they would not immediately see any

connection between what they had been doing and what they were experiencing. I was also concerned that, without some introduction to the Sikh tradition, ignorance and unease might let prejudice rather than openness and curiosity surface. I decided to begin with the story of the life of Guru Nanak and the community he set up. The students had provided nearly all the input so far, and I felt it was time for a shift in gear and a whole class activity. It was time for a story.

We read tales about Guru Nanak's childhood, taken from material given to me by the local Sikh community, written originally for Sikh children. The class discussed the significance of Guru Nanak's links with both the Hindu and Muslim communities. We then read a simple account of Guru Nanak's life and his efforts to set up a community. We discussed the claim that all people were equal and talked about the meaning of Guru Nanak's well known words 'There is neither Hindu nor Muslim'. One or two students were quick to recognize similarities between their own ideas and those behind the setting up of the first Sikh community. We looked at the differences between the beliefs on which Guru Nanak founded his community and the beliefs which the students had drawn up for their ideal communities and how, for example, the belief in One True God who loved and cared for all people would influence the way of life of the community. When we looked at the story of the community set up by Guru Nanak, the students had no background knowledge of the kind of class-ridden society that Sikhism rejected. This needed some explanation, but I wanted to avoid the danger of putting Hinduism in a negative light. Rather than trying to deal with the complexities of the caste system, I explained that the society was not unlike our own, in that there were deep divisions between groups and that it was impossible for some people to feel in any sense that they belonged. The students were able to offer examples of people in a similar position in our own society.

Introducing the Sikh community

In order to bring the story up to date I wanted to introduce the fact that Sikh communities today were running on the same lines as those set up by Guru Nanak and his followers. The idea of a community centre had been important in the class projects on the ideal community. In the case of the Sikh community, the gurdwara was an important focus and often a community centre, as well as a place of worship. I had some slides of Sikh gurdwaras in the Punjab, taken by a friend. These were useful in illustrating the way in which some gurdwaras provided for the medical and educational needs of the wider community, as well as the spiritual and religious needs of their own followers. The students were impressed by the fact that the gurdwaras provided food for all their visitors. For homework the class had to write a brief account of the life of Guru Nanak and say what they thought Guru Nanak meant by words 'There is neither Hindu nor Muslim'.

In the next lesson we turned to look at the Sikh community in a British context. I used sections of the CEM video, *Sikhism through the eyes of Sikh children*, to encourage the students to focus on how the gurdwara served the different people in the community. They were to pay special attention to the ideas of equality and respect. After the video the pupils shared ideas in their groups. Some of the remarks were that:

the needs of young people were catered for;
young people were respected and able to make a contribution in the life of the community on the same level as the adults;
men and women all sat together on the floor for worship;
both sexes could take part in leading the worship;
everyone ate together and took it in turns to help;
there was no priest and no one was more important than anyone else.

It was also pointed out that the Guru Granth Sahib contained the sacred writings of more than one religious tradition. We spent some time talking about the importance of these holy scriptures in the worship of the Sikh community. The students were able to draw some similarities and comparisons between the way the Guru Granth Sahib was at the centre of Sikh worship and the way in which the scriptures were a main focus in other religious traditions. During this lesson the students had a checklist of words to look out for so that we could look up and write down the meaning of new vocabulary at the end of the lesson.

A visit to the neighbourhood gurdwara

The aim of the last section of the project was to work towards an assembly which would be a class presentation on the neighbourhood gurdwara as a model community. We visited the local gurdwara, where we were warmly received, and the students were not disappointed in their expectation of food. We were able to be present when a small group of Sikhs joined in worship at a midday reading of the Guru Granth Sahib. The students received karah parshad along with the worshippers and were then invited to the langar and given cups of tea and biscuits. Although the class did not divide up into groups during the time at the gurdwara, each working group was looking out for different aspects of the life and faith of the Sikh community. This helped to give the students a focus during their visit and it also promoted a variety of questions.

All students were to look for ways in which the teachings of Guru Nanak were expressed in the life of the gurdwara. A number of points came to light: for example, men and women worshipped together and women as well as men could read from the Guru Granth Sahib; there was no priesthood, and the granthi was not seen as higher than others in status; the committee responsible for the running of the gurdwara was elected from the community; the whole community ate together; and every visitor was welcomed, no matter what religion they belonged to. Some students learnt that two Hindu sisters from our own school attended the gurdwara as a place of worship. The students were impressed with the friendliness and generosity of the Sikh community and the way in which the gurdwara was run on voluntary contributions. We took packets of sugar and tea and apples and oranges, but felt that we came away with much more.

The visit to the gurdwara inspired some enthusiastic research. The class worked once again in groups on different aspects of the Sikh faith and community, using text books and a box of resources on Sikhism. Each group had a set of trigger questions from which to start. This work did fall into some of the categories of 'Sacred Writings' and 'Beliefs and Teachings', but I felt that at least the students had encountered the faith as a living community and had been open to the idea that its beliefs and teachings were relevant for life today. The assembly was informative and enhanced the whole school's awareness of Sikhism. Each group from the class presented an account of one aspect of the life and faith of the Sikh community. Readings of students' impressions written after going to the gurdwara indicated that this had been more than a visit to another 'place of worship':

'Everybody made us feel very welcome. We were given food and tea to drink. It was free.'

'The people at the gurdwara were very helpful and they answered all our questions. Then they gave us tea or orange juice and biscuits.'

'Everyone there seemed really pleased to see us and there was no pressure to believe or anything.'

'It was different from visiting a church, it was more like going to someone's home, because they gave you stuff to eat and drink.'

The assembly closed with some questions about how a school, like a gurdwara, could offer an environment where people could learn the meaning of equality and respect and the opportunity for people to work towards a model community.

Notes

1 W. H. McLeod, *Textual Sources for the Study of Sikhism*, Manchester University Press, 1984.

SECTION THREE
Further perspectives

Introduction

In the teaching of World Religions, syllabuses have tended to restrict themselves to the traditions considered in Section Two of this book. We felt there was a need to address a wider variety of world views, and that is one of the aims of this section. However, there are no overriding criteria as to why each particular article was selected. We decided that as broad a variety of perspectives as possible was the first consideration. In this way we hoped that an overall understanding of the contrasting motivations of different world views would become apparent. For example, looking at the differences in character and outlook of the Bahá'í tradition and the Kogi peoples may cause us to reassess our educational perspective.

Behind this concern is a second aim. No world view is static: in so far as it is the expression of a social group, it must address the values of others and respond. This dynamic reflects the vitality of the tradition, and is thrown into high relief in those movements that perceive themselves as minorities in larger social contexts. The articles on Jains, Zoroastrians and Rastafarians reflect this most obviously.

A third aim was to provide an edge between the study of world views and values education. Teaching the former without a concern for the latter can result in a bland diet of information divorced from personal experience. The articles on Humanism and Muslim schools and New Age Spirituality are examples of this interconnection, though all the articles address it in one way or another.

A fourth concern was to illustrate 'transference': the way in which long-established traditions 'variegate' and adapt in new cultural milieus and changing times. Examples of this are the studies of contemporary British Buddhism, varieties of Sikh adherence and Hindu-related new religious movements.

All the authors were asked to address tensions and concerns that exist within the world view they were presenting in relation to contemporary Western society. We hope they enrich your own perspective and generate an appreciation of the importance of the study of world views in education and not just within the confines of RE.

Clive Erricker

1 The Rastafarians: beliefs and practices

Jah Bones

The Rastafarian Movement is not an organization: it is a life-force; what the Rastas call a 'Livity'. This can be taken as a set or series of life-styles that are common to Rastafarians. Although its culture and lifestyle may seem religious, the Rastafarian movement is not a religion in the strict sense of the word. It takes in religion but at the same times goes beyond it; it caters for spiritual, natural and social realities: Rastafarians will discuss anything from religious and spiritual matters to the cinema, popular music and violence. Anything that people do and talk and think about is important to and therefore worth analysing and studying. Rastafarians seek to be 'all-being' and 'all-knowing'; nothing at all should consciously be hidden.

So what is it that characterizes the Rastafarian movement and, further, serves to indicate the ways in which it is different from other religious organizations? Many features of the Rastafarian way of life are quite distinct, while others are less so. The dreadlocks hairstyle, for example, is an obvious feature of the Rastafarian movement. On the other hand, an essential and basic feature such as firmness is not as easily detected. Yet to Rastafarians it is essential to stay unbowed in the face of socio-cultural onslaughts.

From its inception in the early '30s until the present day, the Rastafarians have exhibited a stubborn and tenacious hold on their faith and practices. This is due in part to the profound desire to possess something which is African and Black but which is still universal. In part, it is also due to certain aspects of colonial societies. Now, after 60 years, the Rastafarian movement has developed to a point where it is truly world-wide.

But what do the Rastafarians stand for? What are their chief principles and practices? How do the Rastafarians hope to achieve their objectives and desires?

From the movement's early days, the Rastafarians were interested in the divinity of the Ethiopian Emperor Haile Selassie I; repatriation to Africa; and in justice for the black people who have suffered at the hands of oppressors since the times of the slave trade. Rastafarians look to the philosophy and tenets of the Rt Honourable Marcus Mosiah Garvey (1887–1940), who believed in the return of the African descendants to Africa, their rightful homeland, and who taught self-help and self-awareness, racial pride and advancement as well as preaching self-rule and independence. Garvey formed the Universal Negro Improvement Association (UNIA) in 1912, and the organization had 11 million members by 1922. After 1924, when Garvey was sent to Toombs Prison in Atlanta, Georgia, the UNIA suffered a rapid decline of membership, and by the time he was released and deported to Jamaica in 1977 it was in virtual disarray. Many members of the UNIA came into the Rastafarian movement during the 1930s and 40s. Garvey exhorted an enthusiastic crowd at a meeting in Kingston, Jamaica to look to Africa, where a Black King would be crowned who would reign as God in the form of man. Garvey also urged his believers to see God as black. This message or prophecy was fulfilled on 2 November 1930, when Negus Tafari was crowned as Emperor Haile Selassie I, King of Kings and Lord of Lords, Conquering Lion of the Tribe of Judah and Elect of God.

These events triggered a great interest in the claimed divinity of the Emperor of Ethiopia. People like Leonard Howell, Archibald Dunkley, Robert Hines and Paul Erdington started searching in the Bible for evidence to support Garvey's views, and cited Revelation 5 and 16 as proof that Haile Selassie was, indeed, the Christ returned; the Messiah.

With the experience of slavery in the Americas and with the yearning to return to Africa, the newly emerging Rastafarians saw themselves as modern Israelites, suffering in an alienating diaspora. But the new discovery brought new hope. Emperor Haile Selassie I was the 256th monarch in the Solomonic Dynasty, which ruled Ethiopia for nearly 3,000 years. The King of Kings of Africa is the King of Kings of Israel.

What do Rastafarians stand for?

Rastafarians respect the Bible and accept it as an authoritative book in matters of divinity, theology, history and human behaviour. The Judeo-Christian tradition in religious affairs is accepted by Rastafarians, because it is also the tradition of Ethiopia. Israel (Jacob) and Christ are fundamental to world development and the growth of civilization. This tradition embodies a realization that God is true and living; that God is real, touchable, can be seen and heard. The fact that the Bible humanizes God throughout its readings shows that people think of God as real, alive and personal. This culminates in the man Jesus Christ, who caused a mighty current of controversy to rage about his character, preachings and deeds.

The Rastafarians believe that Christ as a man was God, capital and common, and that Haile Selassie I is his successor, the symbol and personification of freedom. Rastas see Selassie I and Christ as being the same in the spirit, though not in the flesh.

Repatriation to Africa is central to the Rastafarian concept of liberation or freedom. To the Rastas their freedom can only be guaranteed in Africa; where they find the roots of all black people (if not all people). But repatriation is not just a physical thing; it is also spiritual and mental. The return to Africa takes place on two levels. Before one gets to the stage of physical repatriation, one has got to be mentally prepared at least for living in Africa. This really means thinking and talking about Africa a lot, so that one 'becomes' Africa, and Africa is one; the Rastafarian identifies absolutely with Africa. In a social and cultural context, where identity is absolutely vital, Africa is seen as the giver of all things that Rastafarians possess. By seeking to identify fully with Africa, Rastafarians hope to solve the age-old identity problem. Rastafarians genuinely believe that all black people are Africans, regardless of where they were born. To believe otherwise is to believe in an illusion, for Africa is the one and only common denominator. Garvey urged in both speech and writing that Africa is for the Africans – those at home and those abroad.

The identity issue is paramount in the Rastafarian reality. It is also the reason why Rastafarians grow their dreadlocks, an ancient African hairstyle, worn all over Africa by priests in the indigenous religions.

Rastafarians seek to identify with Africa on a cultural level, as well as spiritually and physically. This is necessary because without culture there is no real personality, community or society. If the culture and its values are determined by any form of colonial master, then it is always open to criticism and rejection. This really means struggling against a system of oppressive culture, for with its acceptance freedom is denied.

To Rastas, freedom is itself very highly valued; they feel freer with dreadlocks than without, and identify trimming and shaving with the prison system, the army, police etc. The Rasta wears the dreadlock and beard in order to class him or herself as a Nazirite. The Bible, in Numbers 6, shows that Nazirites obeyed certain cultural laws, some of which were related to hair style, food, dress, beliefs and so forth. These people were ancient Israelites from the area of Nazareth, who grew their locks for seven years, after which they were free to cut them. The Rastafarians see themselves as modern-day Nazirites, but refuse to cut their dreadlocks at all.

Rastafarians love to deal with the things that are pure, organic and natural. This disposition is demonstrated mostly in the area of food and drink, called ital, or natural. Not all Rastas are vegetarians; they believe that people are free, relatively, to choose whatever they need to eat and drink. But the Rastafarians do relate to food and drink on the basis of health and cleanliness. Certain foods are seen as polluted and intrinsically dirty. Alcohol and spirits are not normally permitted. Pork is prohibited because it is held to be totally unclean. Rastafarians also use koli herbs to help to spiritualize themselves. The herbs are also good for health reasons, but they are not a legal plant or compound; thus the Rastafarians run a grave risk of being criminalized on a regular basis because they refuse to stop possessing and using it, as it is not something manufactured by hands but a plant of nature.

Worship for the Rastafarians takes place at the gathering at the Nyahbinghi groundation in order to give thanks and praises. The Nyahbinghi is essentially drumming and chanting, and a Nyahbinghi groundation is held over several hours, mostly at night. In Jamaica, where the Rastas first celebrated with drumming and chanting, the 'binghi' goes on from 7pm to 7am. People are free to dance or 'step' the Nyahbinghi, because the chanting and drumming and dancing serve to drive the participants into a spiritualized experience, triggering off a cleansing process which is felt by all who take part. In Rastafari the church is the people and the gathering, whether indoors or outdoors.

Rasta 'women', or sistrens, are strong in the Rastafarian faith, because they have their own contribution to make. The sistrens' contribution will be specific and unique, for they are mothers. This is a matter of the people (men and women) understanding themselves and knowing exactly how to apply their own specific talents, energies and efforts. The Rastafarian movement is evolving, due to the efforts and thoughts of both brethrens and sistrens. The future for the Rastafarians is bound up with the family; the children of the Rastafarians must be taught to respect their mothers and fathers equally, in order to obtain that necessary balance in the family.

In terms of the Rastafarian community and the wider society, the Rastafarians like to be self-employed. Self-help is highly valued, because it generates autonomy and creativity. The Rastafarians do not like to be bossed around and told what to do. But if it is necessary they will work with others and be prepared to accept a boss. Actually, Rastafarians love to deal with trade and commerce, as in buying and selling goods, either produced by themselves or by others. Farming is very important to the Rastafarians because the land is seen as the basic producer of our food. If you can get to farm your own food, that is the ideal situation, enabling you to grow non-polluted food and therefore to create much better and more wholesome food production.

Rastafari language

In Rastafari language is very important indeed. According to the Rastafarians word, sound and power are the basic sources of speech and meaning. Words are really sounds, and this gives people the power to name things, categorize them and relate to and compare them. The power of words, sounds, also comes through explanation. The explanatory power that is inherent in languages is not properly understood. Language has a key relationship with wisdom, knowledge and understanding. Communication is vital, because it is by speech that we relay our meanings, values, aims and objectives to one another. But if the Rastas are to communicate their values, knowledge and sentiments to others, then it is important that they do so in a language which is their own.

It is widely known that in the West Indies a variety of creole, patois and pigeon languages or dialects is spoken. In Jamaica, where the Rastafarian movement started, there exists an indigenous tongue or dialect called 'patois' or 'patural', and this is what the Rastas are turning into a real language. (Officials in the island would also refer to the dialect as broken African; the Rastafarians call their nascent language 'Afro-lingua'.) The Rastas use the patural as their own, and, moreover, they try to improve on it in order to make it more precise in relation to their level of explanation and communication. Slowly and surely, the Rastafarians are turning the patural into a universal language. With the spread of the Rastafarian faith and movement throughout the world, and also the spread of reggae music, the language of the Rastafarians has become sought-after. It is spoken in response to the need for a manner of speech that best serves the Rastafarian thinking. For example, the Rastas like to use an 'I' sound, and many words are started with the letter 'I'. If, for instance, I wanted to say 'vital', I would remove the 'v', so that the word would become 'Ital'. This is done throughout the entire spectrum of language, so that it becomes a very keen exercise in word search and correction, making the Rasta talk a lively and vigorous speech form.

The Rasta language and reggae music are closely related. Reggae is virtually synonymous with the late Bob Marley who became, in his lifetime, the greatest exponent of the music. In his songs Marley wrote as a Rastafarian by using the method of words, sounds and power and the 'I-talk'.

Nationalism

African nationalism is the political perspective of the Rastafarians. This is bequeathed to the Rastas by the Rt Honourable Marcus Mosiah Garvey and Emperor Haile Sellassie I, and by all black nationalists prior to the establishment of the faith. African nationalism is the springboard for black consciousness and self-help. It is very important to know this because without a philosophical foundation and conception, there would be no positive and direct action. However, by this time the Rastafarian movement has become truly internationalized, having adherents in all the continents. Just a small ratio of Rastas in every nation is sufficient to make the Revolution – the almighty and profound change.

As Rastafari develops, it is slowly but surely changing its original and relatively narrow perspective of African nationalism. African nationalism is now a universal conception, which, if developed wisely and fairly, will serve to liberate many people who are not necessarily African by birth but who are African by outlook, sympathy and empathy; these people, by virtue of commitment and solidarity, class themselves as Rastafarians. Contrary as it might seem, this is happening; but it does not prevent non-Africans (in the biological sense) from developing their own nationalisms. Every woman, man and child must know themselves at root; because every vine and fig tree has to return to its roots. But all roots share the same earth soil.

Peace and love

The 'oneness' that the Rastafarians are seeking springs from a very deep belief in peace and love as the ultimate hope and desire of mankind. Mankind can not live with a perpetual state of war and hate. Peace and love are the only sensible and logical objective that mankind can desire and hope to achieve while living here on earth.

In the Rasta doctrine Jah (God) is one and He is Jah of all. Jah is always good, never bad. Suffering, pain, vice and whatever that can be classed as negative are all a crucial part of the good of life and the divine plan. From the moment that the Spirit took unto itself flesh and became man and woman, it symbolized in a living and real way the start of suffering in human existence or, as the Rastas would say, 'livity'.

How can people of one planet, but so manifestly divided into groups, sections, nations and so forth on the basis of religion, colour, language, land etc., come to be one as Jah Himself? The answer to the question could fill a book, but, to give a short response, it would have to be through peace and love. They are the divine instruments that Jah is using to bring His people together again as they were at the beginning of human 'livity' when differences and divisions were not heard of, when everybody spoke one tongue, ate one food and praised one Jah. Peace and love are the only key to real co-existence. Of course the elimination of poverty, ignorance and greed is very important, and this, when it is achieved, will result in the practice of genuine peace and love. The Rastafarians believe that good will eventually triumph over bad and reign victorious in the Kingdom of Jah Jah in Zion, which is here on earth. Mount Zion, in this time, is not so much a mountain as a higher 'livity' of rightness and goodness here on earth. But to live good and right lives in this world as a rule or a norm is really a mountainous task.

To the Rastafarians, Zion is like Heaven, indicative of the possibility (or even reality) of a higher 'livity'. For since as Jah is the Most I and High, it is He who lives in Zion and Heaven. If you go by the Bible, you will see that, in the history and theology of the Israelites, Zion was a mountain located near or in Jerusalem in the so-called holy land. In the history and theology of Christianity, Heaven is a sphere or an intangible entity which can not be physically attained. However, in the reasonings of Rastafari, they really mean a higher stage of life – and that is all. In this context, 'higher' means wider, longer and expanded in a positive way.

The future

Thus it transpires that the Rastafarian movement draws upon the Bible as a genuine source of authority in relation to divine, spiritual, historical, moral, mental and personal affairs. The movement has come a long way in a relatively short time. Since 1930 we have witnessed a tremendous growth in the Rastafari way of life. The Rastafarians have achieved much respect and recognition, especially considering the merciless persecution that the movement encountered and endured during the first four and a half decades of its formation.

Now, there is a lot of organizing to be done, and for the next three or so decades the Rastafarians will have to attend to the organizational matters that are pressing down on them. It is a matter of utmost urgency that the Rastafarians turn full attention and an abundance of energy to this issue.

Bear in mind at all times that Rastafari is not just a religion. The movement, from its inception, was always multipurpose, and it always refused very strongly to be categorized as another religion. The Rastafarian faith is very strong today, because it knows how to adapt without compromising its basic and substantive values and conduct, beliefs and tenets.

2 Amritdhari, keshdhari, sahajdhari and patit Sikhs

W. Owen Cole and *Piara Singh Sambhi*

The visitor to a gurdwara is often surprised to come across men whose heads are covered with handkerchieves rather than turbans, and who possess short hair and no beards. They are less aware of women who cut their hair because it is hidden by the scarf, or dupatta, which they wear on their heads. However, there are women as well as men who do not observe the traditionally recognized Sikh form. In this article an attempt will be made to explain this situation, and to enable the reader to understand the terms which are used pertaining to these and other Sikhs.

The clean-shaven Sikh

The Sikh religion originated in the Punjab region of India only 500 years ago. It resulted from the preachings of Guru Nanak (1469–1539), the purpose of whose ministry was to bring spiritual liberation to members of all social classes, women as well as men. The Hinduism which he encountered gave little hope to men who did not belong to the twice-born castes, and none at all to women. What began as a movement to bring spiritual enlightenment and liberation to people trapped in religious formalism, or excluded from it, developed into a distinctive religion with particular practices, beliefs and, above all, the outward form for which it is famous today.

During the lifetimes of the Gurus, and since, there have been men and women who followed the teachings given by the Gurus, while remaining Hindus or Muslims. Although it is a fundamental tradition that Guru Nanak and all his successors kept uncut hair, such devotees would not do so. Although Sikhs would say that keeping the full Sikh form became a requirement of Khalsa (the community of the pure) membership from its beginning, in 1699,

nevertheless they would agree that by no means all Sikhs took amrit (sanctified liquid) on that Baisakhi day or in the succeeding months. In fact only a minority of Sikhs do so today.

Another reason for the clean-shaven Sikh has to do with family membership. It is possible to be a Sikh and a Hindu. The notion that one can belong to only religion is more a part of the semitic world than of the Indian. This does not mean that Hindus or Sikhs treat their beliefs and practices lightly. Far from it, as anyone who knows devout members of these religions can testify. It is, however, by no means rare to find extended families which have Sikh and Hindu members, and for marriages to be preferred across religion rather than between castes. In such circumstances it might be deemed wiser to maintain the same forms within the family, instead of some members dressing in the Sikh manner and others as Hindus.

In Britain, the idea developed among Sikhs that the beard and turban were impediments to obtaining employment. Many Sikhs seem to have had their hair cut almost as their first act in landing in the country. Some have not bothered to revert to their original appearance, especially if they have had sons who were or are bullied or ridiculed for wearing long hair with a top knot.

If one asks clean-shaven Sikhs about the various attitudes which they have to the long hair and turban, they will provide the kinds of answers given above, as well as pointing out that it is the moral and spiritual teachings of the Gurus that are important, not outward appearance. There are some Sikhs who remain clean-shaven and do not wear the turban intentionally, to indicate that they do not accept the tradition associated with Guru Gobind Singh as the norm. Moreover, the local Sikh congregation, or sangat, is made up of men and women at various stages of spiritual development. For a variety of reasons, including those mentioned above, one rarely finds total uniformity of appearance.

The Sikh ideal

Despite the variety that may be observed in a gurdwara, it has come to be accepted that the Sikh ideal is for the hair not to be cut, and for men to wear the turban (not to keep the hair tidy, but as a mark of identity). Both these requirements are laid down in the Rehat Maryada, the Sikh Code of Discipline which was promulgated by the SGPC, Shromani Gurdwara Parbandhak Committee, an elected body responsible for gurdwaras in Pubjab, in 1945 after more than a decade of discussions. It gained swift acceptance as an authoritative statement of the Rahit, and is now universally recognized to be the standard guide. It arose from codes of Khalsa conduct (rahits) going back to the days of Guru Gobind Singh, and assumes that the normative Sikh is a member of the Khalsa.

The definition of a Sikh given in the Rahit Maryada is: any person whose faith is in one God, the Ten Gurus and their teaching and the Adi Granth. In addition, he or she must believe in the necessity and importance of amrit (i.e. initiation into Khalsa membership) and must not adhere to any other religion. (As earlier paragraphs show, this injunction is not universally followed.)

Amritdhari

One who has taken amrit pahul, khande di pahul, or khande ka amrit (a number of terms are used in reference to the amrit ceremony) is known as an amritdhari Sikh. Such a person must always keep the five Ks of kesh (uncut hair), kara (steel band worn on the right wrist), kirpan (sword never called a dagger, even if it is only short in length), kangha (comb worn in the hair) and kach (short trousers worn by men and women, often as an undergarment). In rural Pubjab, Sikh men may wear them as shorts when working in the fields. Amritdharis must also adhere to a strict moral and dietary code.

Keshdhari

In a general section entitled *Living according to the Gurus' Teachings*, the Rahit Maryada rules that Sikhs should not cut their children's hair, and may wear any clothing 'provided it includes a turban (for males) and kach'. Such a Sikh is traditionally known as keshdhari. More Sikhs may fall into this category than into the amritdhari group, though it is difficult to distinguish between them quickly. No statistics are kept of Sikhs who have undergone initiation. (Some individual gurdwaras or sant groups may hold records relating to their own conduct of amrit ceremonies. There is nothing in the nature of a central registry of amritdharis.) Evidence which does exist is of an anecdotal nature. The only visible ways of recognizing Khalsa Sikhs may be that they carry a kirpan, though this may be concealed under a shirt, or kameeze, and that men allow the beard to flow, rather than using a net or trimming it. However, these are not reliable tests.

Sahajdhari

The clean-shaven Sikh may be described as a sahajdhari by some Sikhs. Sahajdhari has the literal meaning of one who proceeds in easy stages. The Gurdwaras Act of 1925, amended in 1959, defined sahajdhari as a person who professes the Sikh religion, can recite the Mool Mantra, performs all ceremonies according to Sikh rites, does not smoke, use tobacco or kutha (halal meat) in any form, does not take alcoholic drinks and is not patit (see below).

Although it seems clear that sahajdhari is intended to refer to someone who is progressing towards Khalsa membership, it is common nowadays to find it used, somewhat negatively, to mean a non-Khalsa Sikh.

Patit

This is a term that has no positive connotations attached to it. Such a person is a lapsed Sikh, whose status is symbolized by their abandonment of the kesh. To quote the Delhi Gurdwaras Act, 1971: 'Patit means a Sikh who trims or shaves his beard or hair or who, after taking amrit, commits any one or more of the four kurahts (i.e. shaves the body hair, eats halal meat, commits adultery or uses tobacco).

The Delhi Gurdwaras Act, 1971, also legislated on who could elect members to the Delhi Gurdwara Parbandhak Committee, the body which controls gurdwaras in the Delhi area, and on who could become members. The qualifications of an elector include the provision that no one may be registered as an elector who trims or shaves the kesh; smokes, or takes alcoholic drinks. Qualifications for membership read: 'A person shall not be qualified to be chosen or co-opted as a member of the Committee if such a person is not an amritdhari Sikh; being an amritdhari Sikh, trims or shaves his beard or kesh; takes alcoholic drinks; smokes; is a patit.' It further defines a Sikh as 'A person who believes in one God, follows the teachings of Sri Guru Granth Sahib, the Ten Gurus, the bani of Guru Gobind Singh, takes amrit, and has no faith in any other religion whatsoever.' The increased emphasison the importance of amrit should be noted. It relates to Sikh concern with preserving and stressing the distinctiveness of the Panth (Sikh community) in the context of a growing fear of assimilation into Hinduism.

Gurdwaras outside the areas and types covered by the Gurdwaras Acts of 1925 and 1971 may determine their own rules governing membership, the electoral roll and qualifications for the right to serve on the committee which runs the affairs of the gurdwara. There is no need to go into details here, and no comprehensive study has been undertaken, but it seems that the trend in many British gurdwaras is to restrict rights to keshdhari Sikhs and to bring moral pressure to bear upon sahajdhari Sikhs to adopt the kesh. Many kathas (sermons) in gurdwaras emphasize the keeping of the Sikh form to this minimum extent at least. There seems recently to have been an increase in the number of young Sikhs wearing the turban and keeping kesh as a consequence of such preaching.

The importance of the kesh

Although it may lie slightly outside the remit of this article, it might be helpful to explain why there is such insistence by Sikhs upon the kesh. There are a number of reasons which may be elicited from individual Sikhs, including that of being distinct from Hindus or Muslims. Perhaps the most important underlying reason, however, is that the Gurus stressed that their followers should keep the natural body form with which they were born. Hindus shave the head of a child soon after birth, and when undertaking various vows or performing certain ceremonies. Muslim boys are circumcised. Sikhs reject the necessity or efficacy of any such rites. The Rahit Nama attributed to Chaupa Singh, a servant of the Tenth Guru states succinctly: 'The kesh is the outward symbol of the inward faith of a Sikh.'[1] Other prohibitions are also aimed at preserving this bodily integrity and may be seen as endorsing the teachings of Guru Nanak that spiritually is the product of inner experience and development, not the result of external practices. Guru Nanak kept the kesh to repudiate the spiritual worth of rituals in general: 'Some pick and eat fruits and roots and live in forests. Some roam about wearing ochre robes and are sannyasis. Within them is a great desire for food and clothes . . . Take the Name of God with wholesome heart and mouth. All else is worldly ostentation and the practice of false deeds.'[2]

For the Sikh the question is not why Sikhs keep the kesh. It is why others do not.[3]

Notes

1 W. H. McLeod, *Textual Sources for the Study of Sikhism*, Manchester, 1984, page 75.
2 *Guru Granth Sahib*, page 140.
3 Copies of the Rahit Maryada, often printed as Rehat Maryada, can often be obtained from gurdwaras, but it is also printed as Appendix One in Cole and Sambhi, *The Sikhs, Their Religious Beliefs and Practices*, Routledge, 1989.

Piara Singh Sambhi died on 30 November 1992. The last major joint work of our twenty-two year friendship will be published on October 1993 – *Sikhism and Christianity: A Comparative Study* (Macmillan). – W. Owen Cole

3 Inter-faith dialogue in the global village

Gavin D'Costa

Inter-faith dialogue has existed throughout human history; in fact, the origins of most religions can be seen in part as arising in the context of dialogue (often harsh and critical) with a parent tradition. This is certainly true of Christianity in relation to Judaism, or of early Buddhism in relation to Hinduism. On the other hand, there have been those who behave as if there were no other religions. Henry Fielding's Parson Thwackum would clearly prefer no other Christian denominations: 'When I mention religion, I mean the Christian religion; and not only the Christian religion, but the Protestant religion; and not only the Protestant religion, but the Church of England.' Certainly, much of medieval Western Christendom operated with the assumption that the gospel had been preached to the ends of the earth, and that those who were not Christians were infidel and wilful disbelievers.

Religious pluralism

Today, more than at any other time in history, people are aware of each other. In this respect, inter-faith dialogue is a new phenomenon. The 'global village' is here to stay, with international travel, communications, commerce and warfare. There is more opportunity for information and experience of other religions, both through personal contact and scholarly resources. Statistics for 1991 show that there are some 1.75 billion Christians, nearly a billion Muslims, about 100,000 fewer Hindus, 300,000 Buddhists, and more new religionists than Sikhs and Jews together. Tribal religions account for nearly 100,000. The third biggest grouping is the non-religious, which excludes committed atheists. All I want to highlight from such statistics is that there is simply no getting away from the fact of religious plurality. The question of the relationship between religions is crucial. Faced with global problems regarding the natural and social-political-personal environment, there is often no single sacred canopy under which to shelter. Such a situation is full of both promise and peril. On the one hand, we can applaud

the hopeful and symbolic act of different religious representatives coming together at Assisi in a common witness of mutual concern for peace. On the other hand, there is the tragic witness of irreconcilable conflict, where religions seem to play a major role in perpetuating the situation. This is seen in the Lebanon, Israel and the occupied territories, Northern Ireland, Sri Lanka, the Punjab . . . the list is endless. Of course, the situation is complex, and religion is a single factor, along with many others that contribute to conflict. In this brief chapter I can only deal with a narrow range of topics related to inter-faith dialogue.

Issues in inter-faith dialogue

I shall assume dialogue to be an activity in which at least two persons from different religions take part, which is not explicitly violent, destructive and negating of the other, and where there is a genuine attempt to listen to the other person. Such a definition excludes most of the Crusaders, evangelists who simply preach without discerning the context of their alleged recipient, and other uni-directional activities that take place between two or more religions. I do not want to impose a condition that each religion must respect the rights and claims of others, or that dialogue can only take place when religions drop their missionary claims. In practice, such requirements are highly controversial, are rarely important, and are most often stipulated by Western liberal intellectuals! To define dialogue in any more positive terms will be to prejudice the various dynamics that constitute dialogue in practice. As all dialogue is highly contextual, I should declare before proceeding that I am an Asian Christian working within a British University and professionally and personally committed to inter-faith dialogue (in some narrowly specified modes). This is one reason why I shall use Christianity in dialogue with other religions as a source for my examples.

Doctrines and beliefs

What sorts of issues constitute inter-faith dialogue?

Firstly, one may note dialogue about doctrines and beliefs. Here, dialogue can be about either perceived differences or commonalties. I use 'perceived', as it is often the case that what at first sight seem to be conflicting differences turn out to be otherwise, and similarly with commonalties. Most people have had the experience of meeting someone who professes, for example, not to believe in God. But in conversation it may be discovered that what one person understands 'God' to be is not at all what the disbeliever takes 'God' to be. All that follows must allow for this hermeneutic ambivalence. Let us look at some examples of commonalties and differences regarding belief about God.

Between Jew, Christian and Muslim there may be a common belief in a personal, all-powerful creator-God. There is further commonality in the traditions of worship and praise of such a God and in the attempt to live one's life in community in accordance with the will of God. There is commonality in the way such worship and action forms the social basis of a highly defined community, with various rites of initiation and ritual. All this can be a source for mutual respect and toleration, as well as allowing the traditions to learn much from each other. But there are also major points of difference regarding God which embrace questions of history, theology and philosophy (although these cannot easily be separated). For example, most Jews, Christians and Muslims would agree that Jesus of Nazareth existed and lived and taught in Palestine in the 1st century (Christian calendar). But even at this historical level, there are conflicts, with some Muslim believing that Jesus did not die on the cross – a belief which is central to Christianity and pivotal for theologies of atonement. Here dialogue may centre around verses in the Qur'an and the New Testament regarding Jesus' death. But there is also a wider issue at stake: many Muslims may regard the identification of a human as God (in some way or another) as idolatry, while, curiously, Christians who hold a trinitarian belief also claim to be critical of idolatry. Jews, on the other hand, do accept that Jesus died on the cross, and one Jewish scholar even accepts the resurrection, but without seeing this as vindicating Christian claims regarding Jesus' divinity. Here discussion may centre around Jewish concepts of 'messiah', 'Son

of God', 'son of Man' and so on, and the way in which Jesus did or did not qualify for such titles, and whether such titles would imply divinity. Implicit within such dialogue would be questions of the status of scriptures, methods of interpretation and theological-philosophical presuppositions regarding the nature of divinity. In some forms of dialogue these background issues may be addressed; in others, only the questions in the foreground may be tackled.

It can be argued that discussion of such differences will help each person to understand the other more fully and, in some cases, cause one or other party to re-think central doctrines and beliefs. This encounter is one of the most exciting aspects of inter-faith dialogue. Hence in Christian-Muslim dialogue there have been important clarifications regarding the Trinity, so that some Muslims can see that idolatry is not the central problem. Some Christians have themselves come to abandon the notion of Trinity as indefensible, and have instead taken up categories of 'inspiration', seeing analogies between the status of the Qur'an and the role of Jesus as word/Word of God. Or again, in Christian-Jewish dialogue, some Christians have come to see the Jewishness of Jesus in a new light and have sometimes argued that the divinization of Jesus falsely followed a Greek and not Jewish trajectory. Others, while retaining the divinity of Jesus, have come to appreciate the Jewish objection that Jesus simply did not qualify for messiah status. After all, the world is still in a mess, and far from redeemed. Some Jews have come to regard the claims of incarnation as credible, but stress that Israel is also heir to the covenant of God.

One can immediately see the complexity and open-ended nature of dialogue, even from this cursory look at the three semitic faiths in dialogue. To stay with this 'God' theme, when we look at, say, Christian-Buddhist dialogue, the very issue of God is in question, let alone the incarnation claims of Christianity; while in some forms of Christian-Hindu dialogue the claim that Jesus is an incarnation of God is far from problematic: it is the claim that he was the *only* incarnation of God that causes difficulty. One thing I hope is evident: that commonality and difference exist side by side, and exist at numerous levels of complexity. Any proposal to side-step such central, life-giving beliefs because of the seemingly intractable nature of disagreements is doomed to falter, as it fails to take seriously the religions as they are.

Ethical and social practices

Another level of dialogue can be that regarding ethical and social practices. It would be difficult to distinguish between doctrine and beliefs and ethical and social practices, because most religions hold these two in close and indivisible unity, each continuously shaping the other. But it is worth distinguishing these aspects, for in practice dialogue can operate with a very limited ethical and social agenda, which will not require resolution of doctrinal differences, but will, perhaps, aim at some limited social goal. For example, religious groups have come together to oppose possession of nuclear weapons in Britain, for some within each faith have regarded this as incompatible with its ethical precepts. Other examples can be found regarding legislation over issues like abortion, religious education, freedom of worship and religious adherence. Such coalitions have been formed by the faith traditions in dialogue over a perceived common problem. This co-operation also stems from the conviction that a united front will be politically and socially more effective. Clearly, in such situations, there may still remain substantial ethical and social differences as well as doctrinal differences, but these will not obstruct a limited common goal. It is also the case that working together in dialogue over such issues can often lead adherents of one faith into a deeper appreciation of another, and give access to understanding doctrines and beliefs in a fresh and fruitful manner. For example, while Buddhists may not profess belief in God, some Christians have come to discover the depths and significance of Buddhist reverence for life when working with Buddhists against nuclear weapons. This has caused a reconsideration of the ethical and social significance of anatta (the doctrine of no-self), which has often been seen as nihilistic and ethically fruitless.

However, in the same way that such ethical and social concerns may unite religions in dialogue, they can also be the cause of deep division and criticism between religious persons in dialogue. Two examples will suffice. For some Buddhists, Jains and Hindus, the meat-eating habits of most Western Christians amounts to species genocide. Christians in dialogue with such people (often over very different issues) have been confronted with this implicit critique when it comes to lunch time! And among the meat-eating religions, there are instances where, for example, Christians have accused Muslims of barbaric treatment in the ritual killings of animals.

Another example comes from Christian feminists, who have criticized the oppressive patriarchal structures and ethos of Christianity. In dialogue with others they may find similar structures which they feel duty bound to criticize. Here an interesting ambivalence can be present. Some Jewish writers have warned about the anti-Jewish polemic concealed within certain Christian feminist critiques of Christianity, where Judaism in the time of Jesus is constantly and uncritically portrayed as irredeemably patriarchal in contrast to Jesus' egalitarian outlook. Some Muslim women have criticized the universalizing imperialism of feminist ideology which respects no differences of context and culture – or choice. While it may be appropriate to argue for feminism from a Christian starting point, it might not be from another starting point. Furthermore, some critics have argued that feminism itself arises not from within Christianity but out of a secular ideology which is now firmly embedded in Western Christian intellectual circles. This ambivalence once again indicates the difference between foreground and background when dialogue takes place. Here we have questions of commensurability, translatability and relativism – questions which, in the long run, must also be addressed if any sustained, satisfactory dialogue is to take place.

Under the heading of ethical and social practices one might also group a wide variety of day-to-day problems which occur in modern, pluralist Britain. Mixed marriages pose a host of complex questions regarding dialogue. Is it permissible for a Hindu wife to share Holy Communion with her Christian husband? She may have consented that their children be raised as Christians, and she may actively help in their Christian education at home, and subsequently feel deeply excluded from fellowship with her own family by prohibition from this one act of worship.

Then again, there are questions as to which religion children should follow, and whether it is fair that some groups stipulate themselves as the only answer, regardless of similar claims from the partner's own religion. The issue here is how far one can go in inter-faith dialogue. When does inter-faith dialogue, especially in marriage, inevitably turn into inter-faith prayer and worship? This raises the whole question of dialogue as the sharing of spirituality, and some may class this separately.

These and other problems appear within institutional structures that deal with a religiously pluralist community. For example, a hospital chaplain recounts her dilemma when being asked to bless and pray with a dying Hindu man. And if hospitals have chapels, should they not also provide facilities for other religious groupings? If they do, will it all end up with a barren but otherwise agnostic quiet room, as in Heathrow airport, serving all – and none? Readers of this chapter will be well aware of the myriad problems and opportunities of working with religiously mixed groups in the education system, especially when it comes to assemblies and festival days.

Meta-issues

A third level of dialogue is that of meta-issues. I have alluded to these as background, as opposed to foreground, in the discussion above. Here one deals with what might be termed the conditions for dialogue. Three examples will suffice. Some have argued that if religions are complex and interrelated webs of belief, practice and ritual, all shaping and forming persons within a religious community, then it is facile and distorted to compare isolated similarities and differences, for these operate within a much wider structuring process. It is rather like saying that 'mass' means the same thing to Einstein and to Newton, let alone to a Roman Catholic! Here we have a substantial debate as to the translatability and accessibility of a religion other than one's own.

Then there is the question of cross-religious judgements. I have touched on this regarding feminist criticisms from women within one religion directed at apparently oppressive patriarchal structures in another. Are such cross-religious criticisms simply arrogance and imperialism? Does the alternative simply end in relativism? Such questions require close attention if such a thing as religious dialogue is to be fostered. A third example of a meta-issue would be whether religions must inevitably be supersessionist at their best; that is, that whenever they agree with and acknowledge anything outside themselves they must necessarily recognize it as foreshadowing the truth of their own religion. This is certainly the case historically with Christianity in relation to Judaism, and with Islam in relation to both Judaism and Christianity. The same may be said of Buddhism's relation to Hinduism, and some forms of modern Hinduism's relation with all religions. If one answered that 'Yes, to a limited degree supersessionism is inevitable,' then what are the repercussions and implications for the future of inter-faith dialogue? It is appropriate to finish a chapter on inter-faith dialogue with this unresolved question, for true inter-faith dialogue around the world is itself only just starting.

Conclusion

Dialogue in the modern age has been the source of great inner renewal and transformation amongst religions, as well as a great source of criticism, caution and conflict. It has also been the basis for hope, with religions coming together in a tragically divided, brutal and unjust world. It remains to be said that there is certainly little hope for humans if they cannot speak with one another about what really matters most to them. Perhaps through this dialogue people will begin to understand the 'other' and themselves just a little more. This may be the most that inter-faith dialogue can deliver at the present time – and even this will be a major achievement.

4 The Kogi of Northern Colombia

Alan Ereira

In 1506 the first Spanish ships arrived on the coast of South America. They landed at the foot of a steep mountain on the Caribbean shore, an area now known as the Sierra Nevada de Santa Marta, Colombia. The natives they encountered were highly civilized, with large, well-kept towns and elaborate agriculture. They had orchards, and kept bees.

Over the next hundred years this civilization, which the Spanish called 'Tairona', was destroyed – as were all the other Indian civilizations encountered by Europeans in America. But some of the Tairona people were able to escape by retreating up the mountain, to an area where the Spanish found it difficult to follow. There they remain to this day, living in almost exactly the same way, and clinging to the same beliefs as their ancestors.

The group which has remained most unchanged by the outside world call themselves 'Kogi', a word which also means 'jaguar'. They still live in towns built by the Taironas, under the absolute rule of their ancient priesthood. They probably give us the clearest idea that we can now have of the beliefs and lifestyle of the civilizations of South and Central America at the time of Columbus.

The Kogi believe that they are a different kind of people from us. They explain this by saying that they are our 'elder brothers', and that we are like children in their eyes. They say that, in the beginning, human beings were created to take care of the world, but later a 'Younger Brother' was created who did not understand this, and who lacked the ability to behave responsibly. We Europeans are descendants of the Younger Brother. The world was originally created by the Mother. The Mother was not a person; she was 'memory and possibility', which is all that existed before the universe was created. Their word for this spirit-space, which existed before matter came into being, is 'Aluna'. The Mother is the personality of Aluna. Aluna is mind, spirit, intelligence and life-energy; the Mother is Aluna thinking and acting.

Everything that was created as matter had first to be created as an idea, a possibility, and the Kogi describe the Mother struggling to think about how the world could be made, and how a human being could be formed: 'How does a foot work? How does an eye work? The Mother had to think very hard.' The Mother had to create everything that would ever be possible in her imagination. For that reason, the Kogi are quite unimpressed by our inventions. The Mother made them possible by creating a world in which helicopters, computers and video cameras had already been imagined from the start.

When she had finished the great work of imagining the world, the Mother created the material universe. The Kogi have a number of different ways of explaining all this; their stories are not meant to be taken literally, but are intended to help the listener understand. For example, they might say 'The world was like a flat cloth. Then a corner of it was lifted, and there was a space between the cloth and the cloth. In this space there was everything – trees, birds, mountains, animals.' The cloth being talked about is Aluna, 'memory and possibility'. Memory refers to the past, possibility to the future, so opening a space in the cloth means opening a space between past and future – the present. The material world was created by making the present. Matter exists only in the present; the past and the future are not material.

The Kogi believe that human beings were created last of all, and that their purpose is to help the Mother take care of the material world. Everything in the world was created in Aluna before it could be made real, and Aluna is more than just 'memory and possibility' – it is also the life-force itself. So everything has a place in spirit-space, and everything shares in the life-force. The energy of life is tremendously powerful; the whole universe is charged with it. It is so powerful that it is difficult to hold it in balance and prevent it from running wild, and that is why human beings are needed.

The whole universe is a careful and delicate balance of energy, and everything in it has to be well-balanced (or, in the Kogi way of speaking, 'well-seated' or 'on its bench'). We might best understand it as a garden, in which each plant struggles for its own survival, but which needs a gardener to ensure that the plants are kept in balance and that the garden does not become overgrown and turn back into a wilderness. Human beings were given the responsibility of being the gardeners of the world, to ensure that everything is kept in balance. This means working to ensure that plants and animals have what they need (the Kogi believe that plants are as alive as animals, and that they feel pain), and that rocks and stones are maintained in their proper places (they also believe that the earth itself is capable of pleasure and suffering). The Kogi are farmers, with farms in different areas of the mountain, and they spend their lives walking from farm to farm, carrying seeds and crops from one place to another, ensuring that each part of the mountain is playing its part correctly in relation to the rest. But they also have to maintain this balance in Aluna, the spirit-space. That is the duty of their priests, whom they call Mamas.

Mamas begin life as Moros, babies who are taken (ideally straight after being born) and kept in the dark for nine years. They are cared for day and night, and carefully educated, but they are not allowed to see any light, not even firelight or moonlight. They are kept on a restricted diet of 'pure' foods (all white, and all foods which grew in the area before the Spanish arrived). At nine years old (and in some cases after a much longer period), the Moro is allowed out into the light and sees the world for the first time. Mamas, who were all brought up in this way, are believed to be particularly able to understand and work in the spirit-space of 'Aluna'. At the very least, they are able to put questions to the Mother and understand the answers.

A simple example of a Mama's work would be to look at how pottery is made. When a man wants to make some pottery jars (for cooking in, and as storage vessels), he has to seek permission from a Mama. Making pottery involves violating the earth – taking some earth out of the ground, shaping it, baking it and using it. The earth gives life to plants and animals; it is one of the forms of the Mother, and it is as alive as the potter. So the Mama must first see whether the potter will be permitted to do this work. He does this by divination. He takes a small bowl, made from a gourd, and fills it with water. (Water is also alive; in fact, the Kogi often refer to Aluna as 'the sea', and the life-force as 'water'.) He then takes a hollow Tairona bead, made of coloured stone, and throws it into the bowl. A pattern of bubbles rises to the surface, and from the bubbles he hears the answer – 'the water speaks to him'. If the potter is to be allowed to work, he is then told that he must live apart from his wife for a month, under the supervision of the Mama. He must meditate for the whole month on the meaning of his work, and keep asking permission mentally from the Mother while he gathers his clay, prepares it and works it. He must also make small offerings – leaves, pebbles, pieces of cotton – which are taken from different places on the mountain and placed in the earth or under the clay as the Mama dictates, advised by the bubbles in his divining-bowl. All the time he works, the Mama will be fasting and working in Aluna, standing over him and concentrating on harmonizing the work in the spirit-world. At the end of the month, if the work has been done correctly, the potter is allowed to return to his wife, having made jars which are points of good balance in the universe; food kept in them will remain fresh, meals cooked in them will ensure good health and the world will have been made more harmonious.

The golden objects which the Tairona used to make (and which the Spanish were particularly keen to take and melt down) were also points of good balance, made with a similar reverence. Gold had a particular significance, because it does not decay; being an immortal, unchanging substance in the changing, mortal world, it was a bridge between the mortal material world and the immortal world of Aluna. Gold was the life-energy in concrete form.

The Kogi base all their lives on teachings which they say were given by the Mother when human beings were first created. They are proud of maintaining these teachings, and living in the way they were first taught in the beginning. But the Younger Brother, they say, never listened, right from the start. The Younger Brother was created some time after the original people, and lacked the capacity to concentrate; one of the Kogi terms for us is 'multi-coloured people', people with butterfly minds. The Kogi themselves dress in plain white tunics and baggy white trousers, woven from their own cotton.

They explain that because the Younger Brother did not listen to the Mother's teaching, he was a threat to the balance of life on the mountain. Since the mountain is the Heart of the World, and the harmony and well-being of all creation depends on it, he had to be sent away. 'He would dig at the earth, tear at the Mother.' So he was given knowledge of machines, and sent away to the other side of the sea. Eventually, however, he returned. The Kogi talk about the coming of Columbus as 'his return'.

The Kogi do not use writing; they believe that humans can only learn from person-to-person teaching, and that writing is mainly a system we use for creating legal documents to enable one person to 'prove' that they 'own' something; the Kogi believe that the idea of ownership is a European invention. Because they have no writing, they have no written records, but they have passed on detailed and accurate accounts of the Spanish conquest from generation to generation. They still find it deeply shocking and terrible; the Younger Brother came to take away everything they used, and to live on their lands. The Tairona were hunted down with dogs and guns, and slaughtered. Many of those who survived the attacks died of starvation and thirst, as the elaborate structure of Tairona civilization was destroyed.

The Kogi are convinced that the Younger Brother is moving steadily towards the final conquest of their mountain, and that when his machines eventually invade the Heart of the World, the Mother will die. In the early years of this century two sides of this triangular mountain were largely deforested, mostly for cattle ranching and banana farming; in the last 20 years many new settlers have moved on to the lower slopes of the third side, and the Kogi have retreated to the higher slopes. At the same time, they have observed a steady decline in rainfall and rise in temperature, which convinces them that their prophecy is coming true.

Younger Brother thinks
'Yes! Here I am! I know much about the universe!'
But this knowing is learning to destroy the world,
to destroy everything,
all humanity.

It is the mountains which make the waters, the rivers
and the clouds.

If the trees are felled they will not produce any more
water.

They have taken the clouds from the mountain top.
They have sold the clouds.

Younger Brother, stop doing it. You have already
taken so much. We need water to live.
Without water we die of thirst. We need water to
live.
The Mother told us how to live properly, and how to
think well.
We are still here and we have not forgotten anything.

The earth is decaying, it is losing its strength, because
they have taken away
much petrol, coal, many minerals.

The Mother is suffering.
They have broken her teeth
and taken out her eyes and ears.
She vomits,
she has diarrhoea,
she is ill.

If we cut off our arms, we can't work,
if we cut off out tongue, we can't speak,
if we cut off our legs, we can't walk.
That's how it is with the Mother.
The Mother is suffering.
She has no-one.

In 1990, the Kogi broke their deliberate, 400-year isolation to send this message to the world. They are convinced that they can no longer successfully maintain the harmony of nature in the face of the scale of our destruction of the environment. They have no doubt whatever that they understand what is happening, because they have no doubt that they understand the true relationship between human beings and the life of the universe. They regard us with sad horror, baffled by our failure to perceive the delicacy of nature and by our apparent belief that we can tear what we want from the world without injuring it. They have not grasped that we believe the earth itself to be dead and inanimate; it would be an inconceivable and monstrous idea to them.

The Kogi have seen nothing to indicate that their own understanding is deficient. They live longer than we do (once they have survived the dangers of childhood, the Kogi expect to reach the age of 90); their animals are remarkably free of parasites, and their crops appear to grow well. They know that on land which under modern farming methods can barely support 30,000 people, their ancestors grew enough to feed 10 times that number. Although there is a large modern city at the base of their mountain, no Kogi has chosen to live there; they see it as wretched, violent and barbaric.

Now they are waiting to see whether we can change our behaviour, or whether the world will die. They wish, in the meantime, to remain as isolated as possible, and to have no visitors from the outside world.

5 Bahá'í social teachings in the context of contemporary society

Joe Foster

The Bahá'í Faith was founded in Persia by Bahá'u'lláh, 'The Glory of God' (1817–92). In 1992, with a total of approximately 6 million Bahá'ís in over 200 countries, Bahá'í is said to be the world's fastest growing religion (over 1.5 million enrolled during the past six years) and, according to the *Encyclopaedia Brittanica*, already has a geographical spread second only to Christianity. Its 165 national bodies comprise the Bahá'í International Community.

The role of the individual Bahá'í

In a rapidly changing world where traditional values are being questioned, young people in particular have great difficulty knowing where to turn for moral and spiritual guidance. The Bahá'í Faith has written guidance on a wide range of subjects for new followers, to enable the gradual transition from 'novice' to a 'deepened' Bahá'í: 'When a person becomes a Bahá'í, he gives up the past only in the sense that he is part of this new and living Faith of God, and must seek to pattern himself, in act and thought, along the lines laid down by Bahá'úlláh. The fact that he is by origin a Jew or a Christian, a black man or a white man, is not important any more, but . . . lends colour and charm to the Bahá'í community in that it demonstrates unity in diversity.'[1]

Although the Bahá'í teachings cover the main issues of individual life, in many cases individuals must make up their own minds in the light of prayer, consultation and conscience. 'Abdu'l-Bahá, eldest son of Bahá'u'lláh, has said: 'He is a true Bahá'í who strives by day and night to progress along the path of human endeavour, whose cherished desire is so to live and act as to enrich and illumine the world; whose source of inspiration is the essence of Divine Perfection, whose aim in life is to conduct himself so as to be the cause of infinite progress. Only when he attains unto such perfect gifts can it be said of him that he is a Bahá'í.'

Shoghi Effendi, who succeeded his grandfather 'Abdu'l-Bahá as head of the Faith on the latter's death in 1921, said in answer to a question from an individual believer: 'The primary reason for anyone becoming a Bahá'í must of course be because he has come to believe that the doctrines, the teachings and the Order of Bahá'u'lláh are the correct thing for this stage in the world's evolution. The Bahá'ís themselves as a body have one great advantage: they are sincerely convinced Bahá'u'lláh is right; they have a plan, and they are trying to follow it. But to pretend they are perfect, that the Bahá'ís of the future will not be a hundred times more mature, better balanced, more exemplary in their conduct, would be foolish.'[2]

Bahá'í laws

The laws of Bahá'u'lláh are contained in the Kitáb-i-Aqdas (the 'Most Holy Book'), which is currently being translated into English. Shoghi Effendi has said, in a letter to a National Spiritual Assembly: ' . . . the Laws revealed by Bahá'u'lláh in the Aqdas are, whenever practicable and not in direct conflict with the Civil Laws of the land, absolutely binding on every believer or Bahá'í institution whether in the East or the West. Certain laws, such as fasting, obligatory prayers, the consent of parents before marriage, avoidance of alcoholic drinks, monogamy, should be regarded by all believers as universally and vitally applicable at the present time. Others have been formulated in anticipation of a state of society destined to emerge from the chaotic conditions that prevail today . . . What has not been formulated in the Aqdas, in addition to matters of detail and of secondary importance arising out of the application of the laws already formulated by Bahá'u'lláh, will have to be enacted by the Universal House of Justice. This body can supplement but never invalidate or modify in the least degree what has already been formulated by Bahá'u'lláh, nor has the Guardian any right whatsoever to lessen the binding effect, much less to abrogate the provisions of so fundamental and sacred a Book.'[3]

Tensions within the movement

It is precisely because the main purpose of the Bahá'í Faith is to unite Arab and Jew, black and white, Protestant and Catholic, men and women, rich and poor that the mechanism needed to carry out these changes is provided in the Writings.

Bahá'ís from all backgrounds of religious persuasion, social class and political leanings are brought together at meetings, Feasts, Holy Days and Spiritual Assembly Meetings to pray, to read the Writings, to consult and to decide about collective actions. Bringing people of such diverse opinions together would create tensions in normal circumstances in everyday life. However, Bahá'u'lláh has given guidance by these words: 'Take ye counsel together in all matters, inasmuch as consultation is the lamp of guidance which leadeth the way, and is the bestower of understanding.'[4] The importance of Bahá'í consultation is reiterated in the words of 'Abdu'l-Bahá: 'The principle of consultation is one of the most fundamental elements of the divine edifice.'[5]

The tensions which exist within the Faith are usually about what it means to the individual to be a Bahá'í. The elected international governing body of the Faith, the Universal House of Justice, has written about this matter as follows: 'The process by which a new believer reaches this state of acceptance varies according to his individual capacity. In some societies, for example, most believers must go through all sorts of intellectual processes and re-orientation of their thinking before coming to this

acceptance. In a primitive society the new believer may reach this stage of conviction quite easily and directly. The stage of conviction is the important thing and not the method by which he arrives at this conviction.'[6]

There are also tensions that come from Bahá'ís working out, individually and collectively, what principles like 'equality of opportunity for men and women' and 'unity in diversity' actually mean, bearing in mind the differeing and often limited experience and ways of thinking that Bahá'ís bring into the movement when they declare their faith in Bahá'u'lláh. It must be remembered that most Bahá'ís are either converts or second-generation believers brought up in present-day society. The Bahá'ís are in the transition between simply advocating such principles and actually putting them into practice, and recognize that it is essentially a dialectical process.

Living in two worlds

The understanding of the process of change may be essential for the growth and development of the Bahá'í community. So diverse are the followers in various parts of the world that people are at different stages in working through this process, and their outcomes will often be different – but all are valid.

Bahá'ís see a twofold process at work. On the one hand, they see a breakdown of the old order whereby cherished institutions are being dismantled, long-held ideals of morality are being challenged, wide areas of our freedom are continually disappearing, the gulf between rich and poor is ever widening and the forces of law and order are being eroded. On the other hand, Bahá'ís believe that through Bahá'u'lláh's teachings mankind has entered a new era which cannot be compared with any past era. We are making a completely fresh start, which is irreversible. Hence the tension and frenetic activity in which Bahá'ís find themselves involved. They are living in two worlds.

'A new life,' Bahá'u'lláh proclaims, 'is, in this age, stirring within all the peoples of the earth; and yet none hath discovered its cause, or perceived its motive.'[7] Bahá'ís themselves are only just beginning to become aware of the tremendous responsibility which they have, both individually and collectively, in the organic growth and gradual unfolding of this new world civilization. Bahá'u'lláh says: 'All men have been created to carry forward an ever-advancing civilisation.'[8]

World unity: the goal

'Unification of the whole of mankind is the hall-mark of the stage which human society is now approaching. Unity of family, of tribe, of city-state and of nation have been successfully attempted and fully established. World unity is the goal towards which a harassed humanity is striving. Nation-building has come to an end. The anarchy inherent in state sovereignty is moving towards a climax. A world growing to maturity must abandon this fetish, recognize the oneness and wholeness of human relationships, and establish, once and for all, the machinery that can best realize this fundamental principle of its life.

'The unity of the human race, as envisaged by Bahá'u'lláh, implies the establishment of a world commonwealth in which all nations, creeds and classes are closely and permanently united, and in which the autonomy of its state members and the personal freedom and initiative of the individuals that compose them are definitely and completely safeguarded. This commonwealth must, as far as we can visualize it, consist of a world legislature, whose members will, as the trustees of the whole of mankind, ultimately control the entire resources of all the component nations, and will enact such laws as shall be required to regulate the life, satisfy the needs and adjust the relationships of all races and peoples. A world executive, backed by an international Force, will carry out the decisions arrived at, and apply the laws enacted by this world legislature, and will safeguard the organic unity of the whole commonwealth. A world tribunal will adjudicate and deliver its compulsory and final verdict in all and any disputes that may arise between the various elements constituting this universal system.

'A mechanism of world inter-communication will be devised, embracing the whole planet, freed from national hindrances and restrictions, and functioning with marvellous swiftness and perfect regularity. A world metropolis will act as the nerve centre of a world civilization, the focus towards which the unifying forces of life will converge, and from which its energizing influences will radiate. A world language will either be invented or chosen from among the existing languages, and will be taught in the schools of all the federated nations as an auxiliary to their mother tongue. A world script, a world literature, a uniform and universal system of currency, of weights and measures, will simplify and facilitate intercourse and understanding among the nations and races of mankind. In such a world society, science and religion, the two most potent forces in human life, will be reconciled, will co-operate, and will develop harmoniously. The press will, under such a system, while giving full scope to the expression of the diversified views and convictions of mankind, cease to be mischievously manipulated by vested interests, whether private or public, and will be liberated from the influence of contending governments and peoples. The economic resources of the world will be organized, its sources of raw materials will be tapped and fully utilized, its markets will be co-ordinated and developed, and the distribution of its products will be equitably regulated.

'National rivalries, hatreds and intrigues will cease, and racial animosity and prejudice will be replaced by racial amity, understanding and co-operation. The causes of religious strife will be permanently removed, economic barriers and restrictions will be completely abolished, and the inordinate distinction between classes will be obliterated. Destitution, on the one hand, and gross accumulation of ownership, on the other, will disappear. The enormous energy dissipated and wasted on war, whether economic or political, will be consecrated to such ends as will extend the range of human inventions and technical development, to the increase of the productivity of mankind, to the extermination of disease, to the extension of scientific research, to raising the standard of physical health, to the sharpening and refinement of the human brain, to the exploitation of the unused and unsuspected resources of the planet, to the prolongation of human life, and to the furtherance of any other agency that can stimulate the intellectual, the moral and the spiritual life of the entire human race.

'A world federal system, ruling the whole earth

and exercising unchallengeable authority over its unimaginably vast resources, blending and embodying the ideals of both East and the West, liberated from the curse of war and its miseries, and bent on the exploitation of all the available sources of energy on the surface of the planet, a system in which Force is made the servant of Justice, whose life is sustained by its universal recognition of one God and by its allegiance to one common Revelation – such is the goal towards which humanity, impelled by the unifying forces of life, is moving.

'Who can doubt that such a consummation – the coming of age of the human race – must signalize, in its turn, the inauguration of a world civilization such as no mortal eye hath ever beheld or human mind conceived? Who is it that can imagine the lofty standard which such a civilization, as it unfolds itself, is destined to attain? Who can measure the heights to which human intelligence, liberated from its shackles, will soar? Who can visualize the realms which the human spirit, vitalized by the outpouring light of Bahá'u'lláh, shining in the plenitude of its glory, will discover?'[9]

Social teaching for a new age

Bahá'ís have been given guidance on many aspects of the new age which mankind is entering. Below are listed three subjects of current concern.

Politics

'Though loyal to their respective governments, though profoundly interested in anything that affects their security and welfare, though anxious to share in whatever promotes their best interests, the Faith with which the followers of Bahá'u'lláh stand identified is one which they firmly believe God has raised high above the storms, the divisions and controversies of the political arena. Their Faith they conceive to be essentially non-political, supra-national in character, rigidly non-partisan, entirely dissociated from nationalistic ambitions, pursuits and purposes. Such a Faith knows no division of class or of party. It subordinates, without hesitation or equivocation, every particularistic interest, be it personal, regional or national, to the paramount interests of humanity, firmly convinced that in a world of interdependent peoples and nations the advantage of the part is best

to be reached by the advantage of the whole, and that no abiding benefit can be conferred upon the component parts if the general interests of the entity itself are ignored or neglected.'[10]

Disarmament

'Banning nuclear weapons, prohibiting the use of poison gases or outlawing germ warfare will not remove the root causes of war. However important such practical measures obviously are as elements of the peace process, they are in themselves too superficial to exert enduring influence. Peoples are ingenious enough to invent yet other forms of warfare, and to use food, raw materials, finance, industrial power, ideology, and terrorism to subvert one another in an endless quest for supremacy and dominion. Nor can the present massive dislocation in the affairs of humanity be resolved through the settlement of specific conflicts or disagreements among nations. A genuine universal framework must be adopted.'[11]

Religious discrimination: incitement to hatred

Also of particular concern is the question of religious discrimination and incitement to hatred of a religious group. Bahá'ís in many countries have been subjected to both discrimination and hatred, particularly in the birthplace of their Faith. From the time of its birth in the middle of the last century to the present, Bahá'ís in Iran have been persecuted, killed, outlawed, imprisoned without legal cause, made the public victims of abuse, calumny and every conceivable form of discrimination, yet they have remained firm in the Faith, acting as good, responsible citizens. The response of the Bahá'ís to this opposition has been strict obedience to the law, proper appeals for redress and a reliance on the efforts of their fellow believers outside Iran to take their case through recognized legal channels in international fora.

Conclusion

A new vision must be brought to mankind, a deeper understanding of the essential nature of man and the world, while at the same time creating a closer living relationship to the divine.

Those who are engaged in planning for social projects are recognizing that change in one area often has repercussions in other areas, hence the need to think in terms of the whole. Bahá'ís are conscious that although there is clearly much that is progressive and fruitful in many organizations, they all have aims and objectives which, when measured on a global scale, are narrow in concept. These objectives can only be ultimately achieved if they are viewed in a broader perspective and brought together in a unified and fully comprehensive plan for the whole world. I believe that this is done by the Bahá'í Faith.

Notes

1 From a letter written on behalf of the Guardian of the Bahá'í Faith to an individual believer, 12 March 1949, *Bahá'í News*, 251, January 1952, page 2.

2 Shoghi Effendi, from a letter written on behalf of the Guardian to an individual believer, 5 July 1947, *Teaching Work Among the Masses*, page 2.

3 From a letter written on behalf of Shoghi Effendi to the National Spiritual Assembly of the United States, 11 August 1935, *Principles of Bahá'í Administration*, Bahá'í Publishing Trust, 1976, Fourth Edition, pages 6–7.

4 Universal House of Justice, *The Heaven of Divine Wisdom*, Bahá'í Publishing Trust, Oakham, 1978, page 3.

5 Universal House of Justice, *Consultation*, Bahá'í Publishing Trust, Wilmette, 1980.

6 National Spiritual Assembly of the Bahá'ís of India, *Lights of Guidance*, Bahá'í Publishing Trust, New Delhi, 1983, page 56.

7 Shoghi Effendi, *The World Order of Bahá'u'lláh*, Bahá'í Publishing Trust, Wilmette, 1965, page 202.

8 Shoghi Effendi trs., *Gleanings from the Writings of Bahá'u'lláh*, Bahá'í Publishing Trust, 1949, page 214.

9 Shoghi Effendi, 1965, pages 202–6.

10 Shoghi Effendi, 1965, pages 198–9.

11 Universal House of Justice, *The Promise of World Peace,* statement given on 24 October 1985, page 11.

6 The theology of liberation a generation on

John Hammond

In 1971 the Peruvian theologian Gustavo Gutierrez published his *Theology of Liberation*. He spoke there of its purpose as 'an attempt at reflection based on the gospel and the experiences of men and women committed to the process of liberation in the exploited and oppressed land of Latin America.'

All Christian theology is essentially about reflection on the experience of the Christian community in the light of the gospel. What was distinctive and increasingly contentious about liberation theology was the concrete and particular nature of the reflection: how the gospel can liberate from this exploitation and this oppression, experienced here and now; liberation not just from the ancient universals of sin and death, but from the 'structural sin' of feudal land tenure and a capitalist economy, and from death from malnutrition or at the hands of death squads.

Commitment to liberation required a choice, a 'preferential option for the poor', and so a stand against oppression and the oppressors – that is, against those who benefit from and maintain the structures of injustice. These are the rich and powerful, many among them staunch supporters and faithful sons and daughters of the church. It was unavoidable that a theology that would liberate the poor would also provide religious support for a class struggle and split the Latin American church. The consequent opposition came from both church and state.

This distinctively Third World theology is associated with a group of (European-trained) theologians[1], whose thinking took shape in a series of conferences in the mid-'60s which sought to give a Latin American face to the renewal of the second Vatican Council; but its base is much broader than academic theology. It is inspired and sustained (and also constrained) by two other elements: the base communities (CEBs) and the Latin American Episcopal Council (CELAM). It was at the meeting of CELAM at Medellin in 1968 that bishops formulated the 'preferential option for the poor' and provided a new identity for Catholicism in Latin America. The Medellin Council questioned traditional hierarchical patterns and offered encouragement to the popular church movement, particularly to those lay people who gathered in the base communities to pray and interpret the scriptures in the context of their own lives.

The theologians saw their work as providing practical assistance to these communities, helping them to read the Bible with an awareness of their own situation of dependency and exploitation. True evangelization would be not the proclamation of doctrine, but the prophetic critique of the social order.

Opposition

The growing opposition to Liberation Theology surfaced in the Synod of 1974. Certain 'unacceptable forms' were listed:

1 The acceptance of Marxist social analysis, which (it was thought) would involve adopting Marxist ideology.
2 The refusal to allow reconciliation between social classes and the 'demonizing' of certain groups.
3 The over-politicization and concretization of revelation.
4 Turning revelation into an instrument of revolution by making a class option.

There are two main elements in the critique: first, the association with Marxist social science. It cannot, say the critics, be split off from its atheistic and materialist world view. If you employ one you will be contaminated by the other; second, the truths of revelation cannot be cashed out in particular concrete classes or groups. Religion cannot be reduced to politics. Both these strands continue in official pronouncements critical of certain aspects of Liberation Theology.

At the opening session of the 1979 CELAM conference at Puebla, the Pope warned against the politicization of Christ and the Kingdom of God. Yet he also showed his support by speaking out against the violation of human rights in Latin America. Similarly, the Father General of the Jesuits, Pedro Arrupe, warned that Marxist analysis implies an anthropology and view of human history which is incompatible with the Christian vision. He then went on to denounce capitalist social analysis as unchristian also.

This pattern of criticism, allied with a measure of support, is also evident in the response from the

Vatican's Congregation for the Doctrine of the Faith. The 'Instruction on certain aspects of Liberation Theology' of 1984 concentrates solely on what it sees as the negative features; but a second, much longer, document of 1986 describes Liberation Theology as making an important contribution to the process of integrating more fully the social teaching of the Roman Catholic Church with its theology of God and salvation. It speaks of the movement's positive contribution, giving it the credit for uniting the political economy with the 'economy' of salvation.

Though some theologians have been targets of continuing intervention by Rome (Leonardo Boff has recently resigned his priesthood and membership of the Franciscan order after years of conflict with the 'cruel and merciless' doctrinal power), the movement as a whole has not suffered blanket condemnation. Rather, it has steadily gained in influence, resulting in a profound impact at all levels of the Latin American Catholic Church, shifting it away from the traditional alliance with the elites and turning it toward the urban masses, indigenous peoples and other oppressed groups. It has inspired and permeated emergent theologies across the Third World, particularly in South Africa, India and the Philippines, and has made Christians in the rich north increasingly uncomfortable about the nature of their economic relationship with the people of the southern hemisphere.

The role of Marxism

What of the Marxist influence? Commentators argue that this has been overstated or used by opponents to discredit the movement.[2] Gutierriez, in his 1984 essay, *Theology and the Social Sciences*, claims that there was no attempt to create dialogue with Marxism, but rather that the meeting was between theology and the social sciences, Marxism among others. He insists that theology is neither dependent on nor uncritical of the tools of the social sciences: 'An economically based, determinist view of class struggle is completely alien to liberation theology . . . There is no question of indentifying a preferential option for the poor with an ideology or specific political programme that would serve as a framework for reinterpreting the gospel or the task of the church.'[3]

The roots of Liberation Theology are in the scriptures, particularly the writings of prophets and the life of Jesus, who is sent to bring the good news to the poor. However, the practical outworking is through a critique of capitalism and the building of socialist organizations. In the light of the collapse of communism and what is seen to be the discrediting of Marxist social theory, should not Liberation Theology shift its allegiance to capitalism as the economic system which can most efficiently, through its market mechanism, supply the needs of the greatest number? Michael Novak in the United States and Brian Griffiths in Britain[4] are among a number of writers who argue for the intrinsic compatibility of Christianity and capitalism.

The preferential option for the poor appears to make this change of political camps impossible. According to Charles Davis, 'Capitalism requires the acceptance of systemic or structural injustice in the name of economic success and individual freedom.'[5] The systematized competition of capitalism, which rewards with goods and services the strivings of the privileged and able, necessarily creates losers: the poor. To be on the side of the poor is to be in opposition to the mechanisms which make and keep them poor. But it is not just material inequality that its critics see as endemic to capitalism. Davis argues that is of the nature of capitalism to erode the essential humanity of the majority: 'The essential question is whether a social order is just in which the majority of people have no share in the ownership of the means of production and are compelled for their livelihood to sell their labour as a commodity in the market. The socialist case is that such a social order is a routinized disorder, violating the dignity, freedom, solidarity and essential equality of human beings.'[6] Capitalism, it is argued, is at best flawed; at worst it creates the extremes of mass poverty and minority affluence, and the military force to keep them in place, that have become familiar throughout much of Latin America.

Changing focus

In his letter explaining his resignation from the priesthood, Leonardo Boff wrote: 'There are moments in a person's life when, in order to be faithful to himself, he must change.'[7] The changes in Liberation Theology over the last two decades have been subtle but no less radical.

The original exclusive focus on political economy as the source of oppression has broadened out to include issues of gender, race and ethnic diversity. The concern for the liberation of humankind is being extended to all creation with the knowledge of the intimate links that prevail between humans and other beings, and that the same systems of oppression threaten all life forms.

Today, for the first time since the 7th century, most Christians are not Europeans. By the middle of the next century Christianity will have its centre of gravity in the southern hemisphere.[8] Every major denomination except the Orthodox will have its heartland there. Typically, Christians of the next century will be young and poor. Christians in the north will have to come to terms with the fact that they are members of a church which is not only for the poor, but is also the church of the poor. It is likely that in its theology, liturgy, organization and political awareness, this church will be extensively shaped by Liberation Theology.

Notes

1 For example, Rubem Alves, Hugo Assman, Clodovis Boff, Leonado Boff, José Bonino, Ernesto Cardenal, Gustavo Gutierrez, Juan Luis Segundo, Jon Sobrino.

2 Arthur F. McGovern, *Liberation Theology and its Critics*, Orbis, 1989.

3 Gustavo Guttierez, *The Truth Shall Make You Free*, Orbis, 1984.

4 Michael Novak, *The Spirit of Democratic Capitalism*, Simon and Schuster, 1982; Brian Griffiths, *Christianity in the Marketplace*, Hodder and Soughton, 1982.

5 Charles Davis, *What Remains of Socialism as Moral and Religious Ideal?* Paper delivered to the conference on Religion and the Resurgence of Capitalism, Lancaster University, July 1991.

6 *Ibid.*, pages 16–17.

7 *The Tablet*, 11 July 1992.

8 John Taylor, 'The Future of Christianity', in John McManners (ed.), *Oxford Illustrated History of Christianity*, 1989, page 635.

7 Contemporary British Buddhism

Peter Harvey

There has been an informed British interest in Buddhism since the late 19th century, and a Buddhist Society was formed in London as early as 1907. Progress at first was gradual: a vihara (monastery) for Sinhalese monks existed from 1928 to 1939; another was established in 1954; and a Thai monastery was set up in 1966. From the late '60s, Buddhism started to put down firm roots, as seen by a more widespread commitment to Buddhist practice, as opposed to a still mostly intellectual interest, and by the development of a social dimension, with the establishment of an indigenous sangha (monastic Order) and many Buddhist centres. The way for such developments was prepared by scholarly and popular works on Buddhism, literature influenced by Buddhist themes, dissatisfaction with aspects of Western religion and values, 'hippie' interest in things 'Eastern', ease of international travel, and the presence of Asian teachers, e.g. the Tibetan refugee lamas.

Buddhists in the UK are predominantly indigenous Britons, the largest actively Buddhist immigrant community being the 6,000 or so Indian Ambedkar (ex-untouchable) Buddhists of the Birmingham area. Most British Buddhists find their way into the tradition through an interest in meditation, along with some acquaintance with Buddhist ideas. In Asia, people are born into a Buddhist culture, and meet its devotional, ethical and doctrinal sides first. They may never go beyond this, though the practice of meditation by the laity has been increasing in the 20th century. For Western Buddhists, experience of the benefits of meditation tends to prepare the way for appreciation of ethical and devotional aspects of practice, and a deeper exploration of Buddhist teachings.

British forms of Buddhism

The strongest British Buddhist traditions are Theravada, Zen, Tibetan, and a syncretistic group known as the Friends of the Western Buddhist Order. The 1991 *Buddhist Directory* for the UK indicated the presence of a number of forms of Buddhism:[1]

	Monastery/Temples	Centres	Society/Groups	Total
Theravada	9	6	34	49
Zen	2	3	38	43
Tibetan	4	21	12	37
FWBO	0	19	18	37
Shingon	1	0	0	1
Pure Land	0	0	2	2
Vietnamese	1	0	0	1
Korean	1	0	0	1
Non-specific	0	5	21	26
Total	18	54	125	197

Most of these are in England, though increasingly they are developing in Wales, Scotland, and, most recently, in Northern Ireland. The Buddhist Society (founded 1924), which is located in London, acts as a forum, especially through the pages of the *Middle Way*. It offers classes in Theravada, Tibetan and Zen traditions, and has an annual summer school. Those interested in Buddhism are likely to be exposed to several traditions, and adherents of these interact to a fair extent: probably more so in Asia, due the wider geographical dispersal there. Besides the listings above, there is also a Buddhist prison chaplaincy organization, a Buddhist hospice project, a Buddhist animal rights group, the Network of Engaged Buddhists (concerned with peace, ecology, and the persecution of Buddhists abroad), the Buddhism, Psychology and Psychiatry Group and the Scientific Buddhism Association. All of these were established in the 1980s. The growth of Buddhist monasteries and meditation centres has helped stimulate something of a revival in Christian meditation, and Christian monks and nuns sometimes learn techniques from Buddhists. There are probably between 10,000 and 100,000 non-Asian Buddhists in Britain.

The growth of British Buddhism

In 1954 William Purfhurst travelled to Thailand to

ordain, becoming Ven. Kapilavaddho.[2] In 1956 he returned to England and founded the English Sangha Trust, whose aim was to establish an indigenous sangha of the Theravadin tradition. In the following year he disrobed due to bad health, but his disciple Ven. Paññavaddho continued the work of teaching vipassana (insight) meditation; however, there was not much success in recruiting or retaining new monks. A Thai-trained Canadian monk, Ananda Bodhi, founded the Hampstead Buddhist vihara in 1962, under the auspices of the English Sangha Trust. Two years later, an invitation to his Thai teacher to visit England led to the establishment of a Thai vihara in London, which opened in 1966. Ananda Bodhi moved on to found the Johnstone House Meditation Centre in Eskdalemuir, Dumfriesshire, and Kapilavaddho re-ordained and returned as incumbent of the Hampstead vihara. By 1969 there were four monks at the vihara, and there were regular meditation classes. In 1970, however, Kapilavaddho disrobed, dying in 1971. The other monks also disrobed, largely due to a wish not to be confused with somewhat disreputable robe-clad guru-figures who were then in evidence in England. They continued Buddhist activities, however, and this led to the establishment of two vipassana meditation centres.

In 1977 the well-known Thai meditation teacher Ajahn Chah visited the Hampstead vihara, at the request of the English Sangha Trust. His pupil, the American monk Ajahn Sumedho, stayed on and organized the introduction of a sangha of Western monks, trained in the forest tradition of Thailand. This soon moved to Chithurst House, West Sussex, a near-derelict country house until renovated by the monks and lay helpers. A nearby 108-acre forest forms an integral part of the monastic settlement.[3] Branch monasteries were then opened in Northumberland (1981) and Devon (1984). In 1985, the Amaravati Buddhist Centre was opened near Hemel Hempstead, becoming the largest monastery of the group. It includes a training centre for nuns, and also runs lay-related activities from meditation-retreats to weeks for family activities. By 1988, this sangha had 63 members, including monks, ten-precept nuns, and postulants. They live a simple life, emphasizing vinaya (monastic discipline),

meditation and non-attachment in daily activities. For lay people, they offer weekend and ten-day introductions to meditation, emphasizing vipassana practice, and have regular teaching contacts with groups throughout the country. Senior monks travel to related monasteries recently established in Australia, New Zealand, Italy and Switzerland and to a group in South Africa.

The Samatha Trust, a lay-led organization of the Theravadin tradition, was set up in 1973 by pupils of a Thai meditation teacher, Nai Boonman. It specializes in the teaching of breathing-based samatha (Calm) meditation, with classes in ten towns and cities, a meditation centre in Manchester and a national meditation centre in rural Wales. Besides meditation, activities include Pali chanting and Sutta and Abhidhamma classes.

The International Meditation Centre in Heddington, Wiltshire, was founded in 1979 to provide a facility to teach Vipassana meditation, and follows the teaching and example of Sayagyi U Ba Khin, founder of the International Meditation Centre in Rangoon, Burma. There are regular courses which begin with four formalities, recited in Pali by the participants: taking the Three Refuges and Five or Eight Precepts; surrendering to the Buddha; and making a formal request to be taught the dharma. The first four days are devoted to the practice of mindfulness of breathing to develop calm, and this is then used as a basis for the development of insight-wisdom through Vipassana. Other Theravada-inspired groups offer Vipassana shorn of devotional accompaniments.

All four schools of the Tibetan tradition are established, with the Kagyu and Geluk being strongest. In 1967 Ananda Bodhi invited Chogyam Trungpa and another lama to teach at Johnstone House. This led to its transformation into Kagyu Samye-Ling Tibetan Centre, which works to pass on not only Buddhist teachings and practices, but also Tibetan arts, crafts and skills. Its workshops and Tibetan art school have also been used to build an impressive new temple. There are also plans for a small college. In 1991 the centre bought a bleak Scottish island as a place for long retreats.

The main Geluk centre is the Manjushri Institute, in Ulverston, on the edges of the Lake District. This was set up in 1976 by pupils of Lama Thubten Yeshe

Rinpoche. When Lama Thubten died, a two-year-old boy, the son of a couple running a Buddhist Centre in Spain, was recognized as his reincarnation. The key function of the Institute is to act as a College for the study and preservation of the Geluk tradition. Besides a few Tibetan Lamas and a number of Western monks and nuns, 50 or more lay people live in the community. The Institute also spawned Wisdom Publications, a rapidly growing Buddhist publishing house.

While Rinzai Zen is strong in the Buddhist Society, Throssel Hole Priory, near Hexham, Northumberland is a key Soto Zen centre. This was founded in 1972 as a branch monastery of Shasta Abbey, California. Throssel Hole acts as a training monastery for Western monks and nuns (also called 'monks', for egalitarian reasons), and a retreat centre for intensive meditation: not, of course as a retreat from life, but as an opportunity to face and understand it. Throssel Hole's resident monks and lay visitors live a life emphasizing discipline, tidiness, meditation and hard work. The monks visit various groups, conduct weddings and funerals, and ordain people as lay Buddhists. They also conduct a lay ministry programme.

The Friends of the Western Buddhist Order is a lay movement of mostly Mahayana influence, and has a very Western emphasiz.[4] It has a strong social dimension, and more working class members than most Buddhist groups. It was founded in 1967 by Ven. Sangharakshita, an English monk with experience of the Southern, Northern and Eastern traditions. The movement consists of a network of four types of organizations: urban centres, offering meditation classes, retreats, and talks for the public; local groups; co-operatives, in which members work on a team basis with an emphasis on ethical livelihood, which helps the personal development of the individual; and communities where many members live, often having a 'common purse'. The movement has spread from Britain to continental Europe, and to New Zealand, Australia, the USA, Canada, Malaysia, Sri Lanka and India, where it does educational, medical and spiritual work among the ex-untouchable Ambedkar Buddhists.

The Nichiren Shoshu (Soka-gakkai), a faith-oriented Japanese lay-led movement, entered Britain in the 1980s; by the end of 1986 it claimed 3,000 followers and was growing rapidly, partly based on its promise of worldly success and peace of mind.[5] Like its parent body in Japan, it has little contact with other Buddhist groups. Besides its national headquarters, it has five regional centres and over a hundred small groups meeting in people's houses. Its adherents include a number of well-known people from the worlds of creative arts and public relations.

Monks and nuns of the Nipponzan Myohoji Order, a small sub-sect of the Nichiren school, dedicated to working for world peace, have also been very active. A few monks of the order first arrived in Britain in the late '70s and became involved in marches for the Campaign for Nuclear Disarmament. They then moved on to building stupas, or 'peace pagodas'. Over 60 have been built in Japan, including those at Hiroshima and Nagasaki, two in India, and one in Sri Lanka. In 1980 the first consecrated stupa in the West was opened at Milton Keynes. The London stupa in Battersea Park, beside the Thames, is 110 feet high and contains relics from Nepal, Burma, Sri Lanka and Japan. The sect also hopes to build pagodas in Moscow and opposite the United Nations building in New York. In recent years the monks have built a temple near Willen lake, Milton Keynes.

Diversity and integration

The different forms of British Buddhism, while from diverse Asian roots, all share the need to work out an accommodation with Western culture. In this, the Forest Sangha under Ajahn Sumedho and the FWBO perhaps lie at the two ends of a spectrum.

The Forest Sangha

The Forest Sangha has sought to introduce a mostly traditional monastic life-style, with no deliberate attempt to adapt to Western conditions. Ajahn Sumedho holds that: 'If one trims the tradition down before planting the seed, one often severs or slightens the whole spirit.'[6] To those who criticize the importation of 'Asian' customs, such as Pali chanting, he replies that only dogmatically clinging to traditions for their own sake should be avoided. Rather than dogmatically rejecting traditions and conventions, he prefers the middle way of using them skillfully. This could be characterized as a non-dogmatic pragmatic traditionalism. Teachings at the

Forest Sangha are fairly traditional, though 're-birth' is seen primarily as something to be observed in changing states of mind during this life. As regards life after death, a somewhat agnostic attitude is conveyed.

The Forest Sangha continues the monastic traditions of the forest monasteries of Thailand. The monks wear orange-brown robes (slightly adapted for a colder climate), have shaven heads (as do the nuns), and eat only one meal a day, before noon. A form of two-year adult postulancy has been developed for Westerners, so that when they ordain as monks, following 227 precepts, they are less likely to break key precepts and so be expelled from the sangha. Male postulants are known as Anagarikas ('Homeless Ones'), follow eight precepts (including celibacy and not eating after noon), have shaven heads and wear white. The ordination line for full nuns (Bhikkhunis, following 311 precepts) died out in Theravada lands, and the only existing Asian model is the eight- or ten-precept nun. This issue of the revival of the Bhikkhuni Order is a live one, for example, among nuns in Sri Lanka. Doing this, however, will require ordination by Mahayana Bhikkhunis, whose ordination line and vinaya comes up to Theravadin standards. Nuns of the Chinese tradition in America are a possible source of such ordination. In 1988, twelve Theravadin nuns, mainly Asian, received such ordination in America; but Ajahn Sumedho does not seem to wish his nuns to seek such ordination until it has come to be accepted as valid by the Thai sangha. At present, women may become Anagarikas, eight-precept postulants, then brown-robed ten-precept nuns (Dasasilanti). A set of training rules is also being evolved for them, partly based on the vinaya of the monks and full Bhikkhunis, so that they actually follow over 100 precepts.

The Forest Sangha has successfully introduced the close lay-monastic relationship of Thailand, and is supported by lay donations, both from Asian communities in Britain and Thailand and from indigenous Britons. A periodic alms-round has even been instituted in Newcastle-upon-Tyne, in an area where a number of Buddhists live. Another traditional practice is that of 'going dhutanga'; wandering on foot on long journeys, supported by alms, and sleeping under large umbrellas (tents are used in Britain). The longest such journey, so far, has been a twelve-week walk from Sussex to Northumberland, via various Buddhist centres and lay-Buddhists' homes: 800 miles in all.[7] The monk was accompanied by a lay supporter to cook the occasional meal and carry a little money. The journey of the two through rain, mud, heat and midges produced a generous and good-hearted response from those they met, even from some complete strangers.

The FWBO

The FWBO emphatically seeks to develop a Western form of Buddhism, and has criticized other Buddhist groups for importing what it sees as extraneous cultural accretions along with 'essential' Buddhism. It selects practices and teachings by the criterion of their contribution to the development of 'the individual', on which it puts much stress. Paradoxically, while being syncretistic, it has less dealings with other Buddhist groups than the more traditional schools. It is also the most antipathetic to certain features of Western culture, such as what it sees as 'pseudo Liberalism'. Unlike other Buddhist groups, it is also very critical of Christianity, which it sees as both limited and harmful, an 'enemy' blocking the way to a healthy society. On the other hand, it has much admiration for the English mystic William Blake.

The FWBO is centred on the Western Buddhist Order, which had 400 members worldwide in 1990. Other members are either 'Friends', who are supporters in regular contact with Centres etc, or 'Mitras' (Sanskrit for 'friends'), who have some initial commitment to the Buddha, dharma and sangha. The 'sangha' is taken to mean the WBO plus Sangharakshita, the FWBO's one monk. WBO members follow ten precepts (which are in fact like the usual five lay precepts – undertakings to avoid harm to living beings, theft, sensual misconduct, lying and intoxication – but without reference to drink), take a Sanskrit name, and are united by their commitment to the Buddha, dharma and Order. A male Order member is known as a dharmacari (dharma-farer) and a female as a dharmacarini. Great stress is laid on the value of spiritual community among members. These live in communities (mostly single sex), alone or with their families. The FWBO is very critical of the nuclear family, however, seeing it as a claustrophobic social institution which restricts the growth of the individual. The Western idea of an 'alternative society' has also been influential, so that the WBO is seen as the nucleus of a 'new society', in which the values of human growth are paramount. The emphasis is on the movement being an economically self-sufficient society-unto-itself. The economic base is provided by 'right livelihood' co-operatives such as vegetarian restaurants, wholefood shops, building teams, an arts centre and a printing press.

Along with selected Buddhist practices, including chanting in English, Sanskrit and Pali, the FWBO members also practise yoga, t'ai chi and karate to develop the physical side of their being. In its teachings, the FWBO emphasizes the 'higher evolution' of the individual.

Traditional Buddhism, of all schools, ultimately aims to transcend I-ness and ego-attachment. As a crucial preliminary to this, the development of self-reliance and the purification and development of character are also important. The FWBO, however, only seems interested in a version of this preliminary process. The 'individual' is to break free of previous conditioning and become more aware, positive and 'emotionally radiant'. This ideal is influenced by ideas of certain western philosophers: Kierkegaard's notion of the 'individual' and Nietzsche's romantic ideal of the heroic 'superman'.

Between two extremes

If the Forest Sangha is a case of seeking to introduce and gently adapt a tradition, the FWBO is a case of developing a tradition using elements drawn from various Asian and Western cultures. In between these two poles come for example, the Tibetans, who have the urgent task of transmitting a threatened Asian tradition to Western consciousness.

8 Humanism and Islamic schools

Jim Herrick

Secular Humanism

Secular humanism is an approach to life – a life-stance, some would say – which is based on the premise that humankind must live in a universe

Notes

1 *The Buddhist Directory*, Fifth Edition, The Buddhist Society, 58 Eccleston Square, London SW1V 1PH, 1991. This gives addresses and basic details of centres and groups etc. The Buddhist Society's jounrnal, *The Middle Way*, is also a good mirror of the ongoing variety of British Buddhist life. A fairly comprehensive, if flawed, survey is Ian Oliver, *Buddhism in Britain*, Rider, 1979 (now out of print). A good selection of interviews with Buddhists is contained in Denise Cush, *Buddhists in Britain Today*, Hodder and Stoughton, 1990.

2 For Kapilavaddho's life, see Richard Randall (as Kapilavaddho called himself after disrobing), *Life as a Siamese Monk*, Aukana Publishing, 1990.

3 For information on the establishment of Chithurst monastery, see Ajahn Sumedho, *Cittaviveka*, 1983: available free from Amaravati Buddhist Centre, Great Gaddesden, Hemel Hempstead, Herts HP1 3BZ. *The Forest Sangha Newsletter* can also be obtained from this address.

4 For information on the FWBO, see Dharmacari Subhuti, *Buddhism for Today: a portrait of a new Buddhist movement*, Element Books, 1983. See also their magazine, *Golden Drum*: available from Windhorse Publications, 136 Renfield Street, Glasgow G2 3AU.

5 R. Causton, *Nichiren Shoshu Buddhism*, Rider, 1988. The national centre of Nichiren Shsohu UK is at 1, The Green, Richmond, Surrey TW9 1PL.

6 'Ajahn Sumedho Interviewed', in *Middle Way*, vol. 58, no. 4, February 1984, page 41.

7 For an account of this journey, see Bhikkhu Amaro, *Tudong – The Long Road North*, 1984: available free from Amaravati Buddhist Centre.

where there is no deity and no afterlife. We must therefore take responsibility for our own lives and those of the community in which we live. Moral tenets are reached through secular principles, such as the golden mean: 'Do unto others as you wish they would do unto you.' There is no worship of man or woman; on the contrary, in a vast and impersonal universe we may be puny, insignificant blobs of life. There is a sense of awe in the face of the beauties of nature (a sunset, a waterfall) or the wonders of art (a Beethoven string quartet, a Renaissance portrait). There is full and rich emotion in human relationships. Reason is valued as a means of resolving problems and disputes, and the scientific method is considered an important means of finding out about the universe. We favour an open, democratic society, in which as many people as possible play a full part. However, humanists do not believe in Utopia, but rather in goals towards which imperfect humans can strive.

The humanist tradition predates Christianity, and is to be found in ancient Sanskrit texts and in the ideas of some thinkers in ancient Greece. The Renaissance emphasis on the classics and the humanities led to a greater focus on the purely human; the 18th-century Enlightenment was expressed by rationalists such as Voltaire, Diderot and Condorcet; and John Stuart Mill, in the 19th century, and Bertrand Russell and Julian Huxley, in the 20th century, are exemplary modern humanists.

There are four national humanist organizations in the UK: the National Secular Society, which is the most critical of religion; the Rationalist Press Association, which is primarily a publishing organization; the South Place Ethical Society, which concentrates on the examination of ethical principles in relation to the current world; and the British Humanist Association, which is particularly interested in humanist ceremonies and promoting fair education about life-stances in schools. None of the organizations has a clear written code of attitudes to all issues. In all organizations there will be disagreement between individuals, which should be resolved, not by reference to any received truths, but by examination of facts and arguments, by discussion, and possibly by vote at Annual General Meetings or similar events.

Demand for Muslim schools

The questions of Religious Education and separate religious schools have exercised humanists for most of the century. A new slant is being given to the arguments by the demand from Muslims for separate, voluntary-aided, Muslim schools. At the time I write, an Islamic primary school in north London is putting its case for voluntary-aided status before the High Court, having been turned down in 1990 by the then Secretary of State, John MacGregor. The Muslim Parliament, in the White Paper, *Muslim Education in Britain* (March 1992), has called for denominational Muslim schools, and makes long-term proposals for nursery schools run by Islamic housewives, a system of supplementary mosque schools, local Muslim colleges and, eventually, an Islamic Open University.[1] The Labour Party in the last election moved in the direction of accepting state funding of Muslim Schools.

What is the humanist attitude to all this? There is not full agreement and even individuals feel divided about the issue. Humanists try to base their arguments on facts and evidence, not prejudgement. We recognize that it is necessary to go beyond the stereotypes of Muslim behaviour which have arisen in Britain and the Western world. I think it is fair to say that humanists are not, on the whole, better informed than the rest of the general public about the nature and traditions of Islam. The Rushdie affair with its images of book-burning and persecution, and the activities in Lebanon, Afghanistan and Sarajevo of what are perceived as fundamentalist Muslim groups, have reinforced stereotypes. We do have an awareness of the great Muslim cultural tradition in art, poetry and mathematics; no one who has seen the Taj Mahal, or investigated the Muslim influence in Spain, can deny the existence of a great culture. However, there is ignorance of Muslim beliefs, of what the Qur'an actually says, and of the life of Muhammad.

We should aim for dialogue and understanding, which is why the British Humanist Association invited Hesham El-Assawy from the Islamic Society for the Promotion of Religious Tolerance to speak to its Annual Conference in 1991. The humanist attitude to Islam and Islamic schools must be based on two cardinal principles of humanism: justice and tolerance. But how far can tolerance and understanding extend in the face of the persecution of Rushdie, or the demand for separate Muslim schools which create a Muslim ethos?

The Rushdie case is an interesting parallel to Muslim schools, as far as the humanist position is concerned. Most humanists defend freedom of speech for Rushdie, and some admire *Satanic Verses* as a literary masterpiece. Muslims have called for an extension of the law of blasphemy to cover religions other than Christianity. This is a just demand: why should Christianity be given special protection not given to other religions? The humanist answer is to abolish the law of blasphemy, so that equality between religions is achieved. Similarly, most humanists would argue for an abolition of all voluntary aided religious schools, rather than creating others.

The two approaches to religion and schools are seen in the humanist attitude towards RE and morning assemblies. Some feel that there should be no religion in schools at all; that this should be the province of the home and the place of worship. Others argue that RE should be 'objective, fair and balanced', that it should cover all religions and similar life-stances, such as humanism; that it should teach about religion, not how to be religious, and that morning assemblies should look at the world and moral behaviour from a multicultural and sometimes secular viewpoint. For this reason, humanists – along with minority religions – have been angered by recent changes to the law which insist that RE and Morning Worship should be 'predominantly Christian'. Humanists believe that moral education should be distinct from religious education, with personal and social education providing opportunities for youngsters to empathize with others.

Abolition of Government support for religious schools

The division in humanist attitude to RE is also reflected in the attitude to voluntary aided schools. The justice of the Muslim case is difficult to refute, and the remarks of Cardinal Basil Hume in opposing the case for Muslim schools, while defending the existing religious voluntary aided schools, seem thoroughly hypocritical.[2]

Some humanists, rather than supporting Muslim schools, oppose all religious voluntary aided schools

as a just solution to the situation. The National Secular Society, in a recent press release, called on 'all political parties, teachers' unions, educationists, responsible religious leaders, communicators, and members of the general public . . . to support the transfer of any redundant church schools to the appropriate LEA.' In a later press release, the NSS President, Barbara Smoker, said: 'We favour an educational system in which children learn to live together in a pluralist society and learn about all kinds of religious as well as political views in a genuinely educational context.' She continued: 'We oppose voluntary aided Muslim schools, just as we have always opposed the recognition of Christianity and Judaism in state schools.' Muslims may say, with some justification, that this is not a realiztic argument: there is no sign of the denominational school system being dismantled, so the humanist case is purely hypothetical. However, humanists do, on the whole, prefer a diminution of the system rather than an expansion.

Opposition to Muslim schools

It is worth considering why humanists might oppose Muslim schools. Primarily, the objection is that they will create racially separated schools, which might well hinder the development of a harmonious pluralist society. Racial tensions tend to worsen when the different groups see themselves as part of a strongly identified group, rather than as a part of society as a whole. Muslim schools would presumably follow the National Curriculum; but in creating a Muslim ethos, would they provide skills which would enable youngsters to develop so that they could be employed and be able to integrate into society? According to a spokesman for the Iqra Trust, which works with local authorities and teachers to provide information about the Muslim way of life: 'We cannot see anything in the National Curriculum that could not be taught from an Islamic point of view.'[3] What is the Islamic point of view on evolution, on political democracy, on women's rights? On the other hand, Muslims can argue that, in the existing educational system, Muslims may be underachieving because of low expectations from teachers.

The position of women is another matter which

worries many humanists. The likelihood is that there would be single sex schools, and that girls would be prepared for a life at home rather than in the community. Against this it must be said that there are women of intellect and force emerging within the Muslim culture. Fadia Faqir, who was brought up a Muslim, has criticized Muslim attitudes to women, and called for change: 'Combating the misogyny of already existing Islam might lead to the liberation of Muslim women and the establishment of a more egalitarian Islamic society.'[4]

A further argument against Muslim schools is that there is evidence that Muslim parents do not want them: they prefer their children to gain an education that equips them to deal with a modern secular society. Daphne Gould, a former head teacher of a school where 90 per cent of the pupils were Muslim, has said: 'The majority of parents do not want separate schools. They value education, and they were always worried that if they were in separate schools they would not necessarily be able to enjoy that education . . . '[5].

Finally, some critics ask whether Muslim schools would breed intolerance towards other religions and groups in society. How tolerant would Muslims be towards a minority of Christians or humanists in a primarily Muslim school?

Many of the humanist fears about Muslim schools may be quite unjustified, and we must look at the case and talk to Muslims involved. Humanists are, on balance, swayed by the arguments against Muslim schools, although there must remain the primary matter of justice and equality for Muslims.

The humanist ideal – in schools and in society – is a plural community, where people with different beliefs can tolerate and even be enriched by the variety. As Shelley put it, in a pamphlet addressing Lord Ellenborough after a case involving free speech: 'The time is rapidly approaching, I hope, that you, my Lord, may live to behold its arrival, when the Mahometan, the Jew, the Christian, the Deist, and the Atheist will live together in one community, equally sharing the benefits which arise from its association, and united in the bonds of brotherly love.'[6] Nearly two centuries later, his plea (with the addition of 'sisterly') remains a valid objective.

Notes

1 *Observer*, 19 March 1992.
2 *Times Educational Supplement*, 3 April 1992.
3 *Observer*, 19 March 1992.
4 *New Statesman & Society*, 14 February 1992.
5 *Observer*, 19 May 1992.
6 Letter to Lord Ellenborough, 1812.

9 Being a religious minority in contemporary Britain: the Zoroastrian experience

John Hinnells and *Rashna Writer*

The question of recognition

One problem for many religious minorities is external recognition of what they are. This problem is particularly acute for the smaller minority groups. Anyone who claims to be a Zoroastrian generally meets a blank stare. If people do not recognize what you are, how do you identify yourself?

The typical Zoroastrian sees him- or herself as part of the world's oldest prophetic religion; as part of the foundation of the great Persian Empire which ruled the world from Cyrus the Great in the 6th century BCE to the rise of Islam in the 7th century CE; as one of a stalwart few, ruthlessly persecuted by Muslim rulers in their Iranian homeland; as part of a community

which included the great educators, industrialists and politicians of 19th-century India; and as part of the oldest Asian community in Britain. In 1992 Zoroastrians emphasized the fact that their community provided the first three Indians to become MPs at Westminster (the first being Dadabhoy Naoroji in 1892, who campaigned for such issues as votes for women, universal old age pensions, limiting the working day to eight hours, the abolition of the House of Lords, and justice for India and Ireland).

Outsiders commonly mistake Zoroastrians from Iran either for Arabs or for Iranians (and therefore associate them with Islamic militancy, a cruel irony in the light of their history). The Indian Zoroastrians are descendants of those who migrated eastwards in the 10th century CE in search of religious freedom, and are known as 'the Persians', or Parsis; but in present-day Britain they are often given what is to them the offensive label 'Pakis'. The other external image, held by the slightly more informed, is that they are the descendants of the Magi, said in Matthew's gospel to have visited the infant Jesus. 'Magi' is the plural for the singular 'magus', the correct term for a Zoroastrian priest. (Their identification with kings is a much later Christian legend.) From the Zoroastrian perspective, a priest is a man of moral and spiritual righteousness, a wise and holy man. School Christmas plays often stereotype 'the wise men' as subservient, subordinate, bowing the knee before, or inferior to, the infant Jesus, or as astrologers.

The Zoroastrians in Britain

Who are the British Zoroastrians, when did they come, why and what are their problems, and what are the tensions and dynamics of the community?

The first Zoroastrian to come to Britain arrived in the 17th century; a number came in the mid-19th century in search of education (mainly in law and medicine at the universities of Edinburgh and London) and of trade (mainly textiles in London and Manchester). The Zoroastrian Association was formed in 1861 in London. It grew after World War II, with an influx of doctors, and again with the migration from the New Commonwealth in the 1960s and 1970s.

The Zoroastrians are based mainly in London but have a formal group in Manchester and informal groups in Leicester, the North-East and Birmingham. There are about 5,000 members, typically middle class professionals; most (72%) have a university degree; they almost always have small families (rarely more than two children); most have migrated from India, and some come from Pakistan, East Africa (mostly Kenya and Zanzibar) or Iran (mostly after the fall of the Shah and the rise to power of Ayotollah Khomeini). This has created some tensions, in that the different countries of origin have produced different patterns of life, emphases of belief etc. The biggest difference now is between Iranian Zoroastrians and the émigré Indian Parsis. The

former speak Farsi, eat Middle Eastern food and have assumptions regarding religion not unlike some of those in Islam, e.g. that religious authority lies with the words of the prophet revealed in the holy book; priests are often associated with the later corruption of the pure teaching of the prophet, and complex temple rituals may be thought to obscure the route to God. India-based Parsis, however, speak Gujarati or English, eat Indian food and have more Indian-style religious assumptions: that a priest is a man of holiness and a spiritual guide; that rituals involve powerful forces which assist the soul on its heavenly path; and that purity is a necessary condition for spirituality.

Internal community dynamics

The migrants' countries of origin have an effect on how they settle in a new environment; thus Parsis who have migrated from rural Gujarat are typically more traditional, speak in Gujarati and 'acculturate' less than those who have migrated from cosmopolitan Bombay. The word 'acculturation' needs comment. There is no common pattern associated with this phenomenon. Not only do various people acculturate in different ways; individuals acculturate differently in different parts of their lives, e.g. they may think in English but follow traditional attitudes to marriage. The language in which people think affects their pattern of acculturation (e.g. preservation of religious beliefs), although what language individuals think in can vary according to the people they are with (e.g. school friends or grandparents) or what they are talking about (e.g. business or death).

Another obvious dynamic or tension is that between generations. The outsider's caricature of migrants from the sub-continent is that the older generation is more traditional, while the youngsters drift from the religion and the third generation assimilates. Our research suggests that this is a gross oversimplification. In so far as there is a pattern, we suggest rather that those who came to Britain in the 1960s tended to be the more upwardly mobile, Westernized, liberal individuals, and it is among them that there are often symptoms of acculturation. More recent arrivals, especially those from East Africa and Pakistan, tend to be more traditional (though in slightly different ways); the women tend to be more traditional than the men (especially regarding issues relating to the family, such as intermarriage); the very highly educated (especially science post-graduates) tend to acculturate more than the business men. Although there are some ways in which the second generation have acculturated, there are signs that the third generation may swing back to the traditions they feel their parents have 'thrown overboard'. Currently, among the British Zoroastrian youth, there is quite a revival of interest in their heritage. In so far as there is a 'life cycle' of Zoroastrians, what seems to be typical is that, until children leave home at 18 or so, they follow the religion of their parents; at university (a far higher percentage of Zoroastrians than white Anglo-Saxons go there, in excess of 60%) they commonly leave their religion behind; and when they approach marriage, traditional ties are often revived, and these ties are consolidated when they have children.

External relations

Relations with those 'outside' the community raise a whole different set of issues . In a survey of Zoroastrians in India, Africa, Britain, America/ Canada, Australia, and Hong Kong, the authors found that more Zoroastrians in Britain than anywhere else in the world thought they faced frequent racial discrimination. Despite the popular image, most did not think they found this among the police, but rather in schools: especially from peers, but also from teachers and the structure of the school curriculum (the next most common sources were employment and housing). Generally the reaction to perceived racial discrimination was a tendency to withdraw more into the community and to reaffirm identity. Relatively few thought that they would acculturate to avoid prejudice. Their overwhelming impression of the majority white Anglo-Saxon population was one of moral laxity, especially with regard to sex and family responsibility; 100% of elders questioned said they would not like their children to grow up like the white Anglo-Saxons. The other 'British' characteristics commonly referred to were 'coldness', 'unfriendliness' and 'distance'.

However such a small minority may perceive the majority population, they obviously mix more frequently with them than with their co-religionists. They cannot, therefore, live in isolation. What are the effects of interaction? One obvious effect is intermarriage. Typically, Zoroastrian parents regret such a step and, indeed, most of the youth questioned preferred to have a Zoroastrian spouse, if a suitable partner could be found. The reasons are many. Historically Parsis may have been affected by the caste system. Iranian Zoroastrians also oppose intermarriage because they do not want to see any weakening of their distinctive 'Iranian-ness' (there is a very strong sense of their being the original Iranians and Islam being a later, 'foreign' Arabic conquest). In addition, there is a strong belief that intermarriage brings a clash of cultures, a weakening of sense of religious identity among the offspring and a loss of family ties. Because of the greater numbers and resources of Christians, there is a fear that intermarriage will mean the loss of the next generation from the community.

Another common problem is what to do about non-Zoroastrians attending ceremonies. One group considers that they should be encouraged because it will help deepen appreciation of the 'goodness' of the Zoroastrian religion and thereby aid recognition of the community (many find that because few have heard of Zoroastrians they are assumed to be members of a 'weird, new cult'). However, Zoroastrianism has a strong tradition of ritual purity. Fundamentally their belief is that God created the world perfect, all that is conducive to suffering, misery, disease and death – e.g. dirt, rust and tarnish – or anything leaving the good living body – such as breath, spittle or blood – are dead matter, and are therefore locations where the destructive work of evil is powerfully present. The pure life is one lived apart from evil in both the spiritual and the material world. Non-Zoroastrians, naturally, do not follow these codes and are, therefore, ritually impure (although that is not to question their goodness). Hence non-Zoroastrians should not be present in the prayer room, for impurity should not be brought into the presence of the holy. But the issue is more complex than this. If any small minority allows 'outsiders' to be 'spectators' at their worship, then being 'stared' at changes the atmosphere. It produces a 'zoo effect'. Further, as one 16-year-old Zoroastrian informant put it: 'Every day of the week I am in a multicultural environment at school. I want one place where I can go and be myself.'

Diaspora religion

A diaspora religion, be it Jewish or Zoroastrian, must necessarily differ from that in 'the old country'. There is not the same support network of consecrated temples, full-time priests or access to community centres. The religion has to meet different needs; for example, in Zoroastrian communities in Iran or India, the religion is 'caught not taught'. People grow up into the tradition, and it is not something they have to justify or articulate. The well intentioned teacher or friend asking a Zoroastrian (or a Zoroastrian child asking his or her parent) 'What is the Zoroastrian teaching on . . . ?' is calling for an explanation or rationalization which the individual may not be in a position to give. The practice of worship changes. In temples in 'the old country', worship is commonly seen as a pilgrimage conducted alone, and in purity, to stand before the flame of the sacred fire, the 'symbol of He who is pure, undefiled light', the living, formless icon of the source of heat and life (Zoroastrians have often in the past been referred to as 'fire worshippers', a deeply offensive term). Such permanently burning temple fires are not available in the West, where the need is for the community to come together as a group, so that congregational worship, not typical of the ancient tradition, has gained ground (through the development of a traditional rite known as the 'jashan'). It also, of course, accords with the main perception of worship in the Western world.

There are numerous other ways in which religion is affected. Perhaps the most common is that Zoroastrian children rarely wear the badges of the faith with which they are invested at initiation, namely the sacred shirt and cord (the sudreh is like a white vest, the kusti a long cord, tied around the waist to the accompaniment of prayers). The reason for not wearing them is most commonly the mockery of other children when they are changing for PE or 'games' at school. Religious problems can cause severe personal distress. The traditional Zoroastrian funeral involves exposing the corpse in a 'Tower of Silence' (or daxma), a practice accompanied by long

and solemn rites requiring the resources of a fully consecrated pure temple. Such funerals cannot take place in Britain, so the faithful have to evolve a rationale for a funeral that they believe to be wrong (e.g. cremation, where the impurity of the corpse pollutes the pure flame of the fire; or burial, which pollutes the good earth created by God). The natural grief felt at bereavement is compounded by the sense of not being able to do the 'right' thing for the soul of the deceased. This grief is made yet worse by the gross insensitivity of the Western press in the way these practices are reported, which in the eyes of Zoroastrians holds them up to ridicule, both before the public and before their own children. From the Zoroastrian point of view, the rite of exposing the dead is swift (they argue that the vultures take 20 minutes to do what worms take eight years to do after burial); hygienic, with no rotting bodies left, hence ecologically sound; natural, since, as we eat birds and animals in life, it is natural to feed them at death; economic with land (no vast cemeteries); and socially significant, for the rich and poor are treated alike, with no scope for lavish expenditure on ornate monuments (Zoroastrians have always, instead, given to charity in memory of the deceased).

There is currently in Britain a vast 'race relations' industry, but few books consider the specifically religious dimension of 'ethnic relations'. This is a serious omission, for our research strongly indicates that people are more 'religious' after they have migrated than they were back 'in the old country', and that for the youth born here, religion can often be a marker of identity, a link with one's roots. The transmission of that tradition is not easy in an environment perceived as at least different, if not alien; as 'unfriendly', if not 'immoral'. How minority groups maintain their identity is, therefore, at once a crucial and complex matter.

An international comparison

There are interesting comparisons between the different processes of preservation of tradition in different countries – for example, between England, America and Canada. This is not the place for a detailed analysis, and therefore generalizations are essential, some of which merit qualification or elaboration. Broadly speaking, Britain tends to be seen by Zoroastrians as a secular country, and they fear lest their offspring are distanced from religion. However, they also fear the 'covert' indoctrination which can come through RE. They rarely withdraw their children from lessons because they do not want to be thought unco-operative, and because it may weaken the interest of the young in matters religious. In infant schools it is, in any case, practically impossible to withdraw from religion, not least at the time of the Christmas play. Christmas also presents other problems. Should they decline to celebrate it, and give presents, because it is a Christian festival? Or would that make them seem mean in comparison to the parents of their Christian counterparts?

America generally presents a different range of problems. There, religion has a high profile in society, though excluded from school. Evangelism concerns Zoroastrians for two reasons: (a) tele-evangelism (and the antics of many of the preachers) makes the parents fear that the young will think all religion is like that, and will be put off altogether; and (b) the local but well resourced evangelical groups pose threats of conversion through the attraction of teaching materials, youth centres and religious facilities, in contrast to those of such a small, disparate group. A yet greater perceived danger is the threat of the 'American melting pot'. Official American policy has now changed, but the image has remained of a culture where all individual features are 'melted down' to produce one conglomerate 'American'. Zoroastrians have always been loyal subjects in whichever country they have lived be it Hong Kong, Australia or Pakistan, and so they wish to be in America. However, they also want to preserve their Zoroastrian identity. The way they have sought to counter the threat of the 'melting pot' is to evolve the most developed RE programme and network of youth groups of any Zoroastrian community in the world. There are 18 formal Zoroastrian Associations in America and Canada, with an over-arching organization, the Federation of Zoroastrian Associations of North America (FEZANA), to try and pool the resources of the different groups. The problems vary in different centres, e.g. between Chicago and Houston, Texas,

but by working together they hope the Associations can overcome their diverse problems.

The situation in Canada is slightly different. Racial prejudice, at least before the 1960s, was strong. The government has, however, realized that with its declining population (due to a falling birthrate), it is going to have to attract migrants to develop industries and resources. To this end, migrants have to be harmoniously settled; hence there is a high profile multicultural programme, with funding, which encourages groups to preserve their identity. In Toronto, for example, the Zoroastrians were given a substantial grant by the State Authorities to develop their own centre. 'Canadian-ness' is not, therefore, typically seen as a threat to being a Zoroastrian, and in our study we found more Zoroastrians in Canada willing to assert that they are Canadians than we did Zoroastrians in the States willing to say that they are American. There are countless other differences: different types of people tend to be drawn to different countries, e.g. the States tends to attract high-flying scientists (in New York and Chicago 92% of Zoroastrians have been to university), and this has inevitable consequences for the internal dynamics of the community. It also has an impact on the community in 'the old country', because many of its potential leaders, especially the able young males, are migrating, leaving a social imbalance back in India.

Conclusion

The concluding point has to be the vital importance of religion within small diaspora communities: religion understood not simply as a set of beliefs, or even (ritual) practices, but rather the total culture, value system and ideals. Knowledge of other cultures is woefully lacking in British society, and without knowledge there is inevitable prejudice. The problem is far greater for members of the smaller minorities, because the ignorance is greater, and there is no powerful international force or oil-rich state to help them as there is, for example, in the case of Islam. Schools tend to look just at the big groups, leaving the smaller ones to struggle ever more with the problem of how to help their young preserve their identity.

10 The world views of Hindu-related new religious movements

Kim Knott

In the last edition of the Shap Handbook, World Religions in Education, I discussed some aspects of the diversity of Hinduism in Britain in an examination of four new Hindu movements: Transcendental Meditation (TM), the Hare Krishna Movement, the Sathya Sai Baba Fellowship and the Swaminarayan Movement. As I explained, the first two of these had come to prominence in Britain in the late 1960s and early 1970s on a wave of interest in new and alternative spiritual movements, particularly those related to Hinduism. The other two had become popular through the efforts of Indian and East African Hindus who migrated to Britain in roughly the same period. However, despite the conditions of the arrival and original membership of these movements, two of them proved to be able to broaden the base of their following. Whilst TM remained a meditation movement catering almost exclusively for the needs of Westerners, and the Swaminarayan Movement remained focused on its natural constituency, the Gujarati Hindu population, the other two attracted both young white adherents and those with ethnic origins in the Indian sub-continent.

The Sathya Sai Baba Fellowship in Britain has comprised, to a substantial degree, birthright Hindus from South India and Gujarat. However, a number of Westerners have become involved in the movement and have made visits to India: they, like their fellow Hindus, have been attracted by the charisma of Sathya Sai Baba himself, a guru from Andhra Pradesh. The Hare Krishna Movement, a bhakti sect focusing on the worship of Krishna, has taken most of its full-time committed membership from the youth of white America and Europe, but has been supported strongly in Britain by vaishnava Hindus (followers primarily of Krishna or Rama) of Indian and East African origin.

As I indicated briefly in the previous article, the beliefs and practices of these four groups, as well as their strategies for attracting followers, are causal in determining their ethnic composition. What I wish to do here is not to repeat the descriptive account I gave there, but to examine one perspective of the self-understanding of each of the four groups: that is, their attitude to the world. This may seem rather general, and I will shortly be more specific. I wish to suggest, however, that their stance on this helps to attract or discourage potential followers.

One sociological perspective on the world views of new religious movements

In his book, *The Elementary Forms of the New Religious Life*, Roy Wallis sought to organize such movements according to the way in which they chose to orient themselves to the social world. He devised a threefold typology along the following lines: 'A new movement may embrace (the) world, affirming its normatively approved goals and values; it may reject that world, denigrating those things held dear within it; or it may remain as far as possible indifferent to the world in terms of its religious practice, accommodating to it otherwise, and exhibiting only mild acquiescence to, or disapprobation of, the ways of the world.'[1]

Relating his work to the purposes of this account, he categorised TM as a 'world-affirming movement', one which saw people as the possessors of enormous personal potential and which presented itself as having the means to unlock this for them. As such, it was seen as being an individualistic movement, focusing not on correct belief but on responsibility for personal perfection. It was happy to utilize the structures and processes of the world to explain the movement and its practices, and to bring about its ends.

According to this view, then, TM was not in tension, but rather in tune with the contemporary social world. The Hare Krishna Movement differed radically in being a 'world-rejecting movement', one which saw the present material world as a departure from that prescribed by God. It anticipated radical religious and social transformation through conversion and a consequent communal separation of the faithful from the doomed. Unlike TM, in which individuals were said to be free to take or leave as many of the teachings and practices as they wanted, the Hare Krishna Movement was held to be authoritarian, demanding the total subordination of the individual to the leadership and community. Wallis' third type, the less clearly drawn 'world-accommodating movement', in which a separation between religious and social interests implied an indifference to the social world, I shall mention no further as it does not concern us here.

Wallis does not mention either the Swaminarayan Movement or the Sathya Sai Baba Fellowship. If I were to attempt to fit these groups into his typology I would tentatively place the former in the 'world-rejecting category, and the latter in the 'world-affirming' category. Objections could be raised to this, or indeed to Wallis' original classification. His idea of attempting to illuminate similarities and differences between groups on the basis of their orientation to the social world was interesting, but rested on his understanding, as an external sociological observer, of their perceived attitudes and practices. He reflected hardly at all on their theologies or the rootedness of these in the Hindu religious traditions. I do not mean to criticize Wallis here; his task was of a different order to my own.

The world views of new Hindu movements

If we look at what these movements teach their followers about the world rather than how we, as outsiders, might perceive their public face, a rather different picture emerges. I shall begin with TM.

The public presentation of TM, as Wallis noted, accords with a positive view of the social world. The movement has used a medical model to explain its meditative technology, scientific tests to affirm its efficacy, and modern quantum physics to legitimize its world view. Since the late '70s, it has developed a bureaucratic structure covering aspects such as health, education and local administration (with a World Government, Ministries and City Parliaments). What is more, it engaged with contemporary national politics in 1992 by entering the election campaign as 'The Natural Law Party'.[2] The manifesto made clear some of the party's teachings (which I am taking to be akin to those of

the TM movement). Of central interest is its view of the 'Unified Field Theory of Natural Law'. The Unified Field is pure consciousness or intelligence and is non-different to the individual's own 'self-referral consciousness', his or her own Self. Education in meditation enables the development of knowledge of one's Self. In accordance with Natural Law, policies leading to the free market, pollution-free agriculture, full employment and the elimination of the need for contemporary forms of law and order are suggested. Although the party's policies are idealistic, they show a willingness to present the teachings in terms of contemporary social norms and expectations. Few non-English terms are mentioned in their account.

It is the philosophy of Shankara's advaita vedanta, however, with its equation of brahman, the Absolute, and atman, the individual Self, which lies at the heart of this orientation.[3] In this sense, it does not so much affirm the world as we know it as require a rethinking of both its foundation and our understanding of it. A distinction is drawn between 'man-made law' and Natural Law. It is only by means of the latter – 'the intelligence of Nature with its infinite organizing power' – that government can work properly. Then 'heaven on earth' awaits, but this is a bliss of a different order from that inherent in conventional understandings of the phrase.

If TM's affirmation of the social and physical world needs to be qualified by reference to its philosophical roots, does the same apply to the apparent rejection of the world by the Hare Krishna Movement?

Unlike TM, which is a monistic movement, Hare Krishna is theistic and sees a separation between the soul of the individual and Krishna, though recognizing them to be of the same spiritual nature.[4] The ultimate goal of devotees is to serve Krishna, thus being in constant relationship with Him.

While the material world and human body are seen as impermanent but attractive, and thus potentially ensnaring, they provide the context in which correctly motivated souls may seek self-realization. They are neutral, and can be used for good or evil ends, in knowledge or ignorance. Relations with other people are also of this nature. They can provide a means for the devotee of service to God through sankirtana, devotional outreach (which can take many forms including congregational chanting, distributing literature, spreading Krishna consciousness through classes etc.).

As Wallis noted, the Hare Krishna Movement, in offering an idealistic, alternative social world comprising like-minded seekers, encouraged the development of separate communities. Sociologically, however, this has been balanced by attempts at outreach for the purpose of the transformation of individuals and institutions.

Both Hare Krishna and TM attempt to transform the social world in accordance with their own philosophical perspectives. Both, to a greater or lesser extent, communicate with outsiders while maintaining separate esoteric enclaves. Both teach of the problems of material existence, maya, and offer a means of liberation from it.

Transformation, of both the individual and the world, is central to these and the other two groups, the Swaminarayan Movement and the Sathya Sai Baba Fellowship. The first of these, though focusing primarily on Lord Swaminarayan rather than Krishna as the supreme form of God or purushottam, has similarities with the Hare Krishna Movement.[5] While encouraging lay participation and service, it provides an ascetic path for the fully committed (in some branches for men alone; in others for both sexes). It sees the contemporary social world as materialistic and misdirected, though providing a challenge for those on the path to liberation. The ultimate goal of these souls is akshar, the eternal and highest abode, but the greatest achievement in this life is seva, service to God. Often, this service takes the form of outreach, and the Cultural Festival of India, held in 1985 in London, was an excellent example.

One important difference between these two movements, however, concerns their potential constituencies. Hare Krishna, though rooted in Bengali vaishnavism, appeals deliberately to an ethnically diverse population, while the Swaminarayan Movement is not universal in its outreach, but caters specifically for Gujaratis in India and abroad. This is essentially a cultural, rather than a philosophical difference. Both movements, however, appeal to those desiring a comprehensive spiritual world view based on a personal God and opposed to the contemporary material view available in the West. In this sense, they could be said to be 'world-rejecting'. However, neither wholly eschews the social world; both engage with it and see it as offering the potential for individual improvement and communal transformation.

The Sathya Sai Baba Fellowship has more in common with TM in this regard. Adherence to it is highly informal and, apart from those who reside for long periods with the leader himself, there are no full-time members or ascetics. Sathya Sai Baba is said to be 'a social deity' whose followers are not required to 'become enemies of the world'.[6] At first sight, he affirms the world. This is not the full story, however, as the distinctive feature of this world view is the miraculous power of Sathya Sai Baba himself, his ability to transform the lives of his devotees, to heal, to alter what we take to be normal reality. He sees himself as an avatar of Shiva (who does not normally manifest in this way), but, unlike the central figures in the other movements, does not locate himself formally in relation to one or other of the vedanta traditions. Nevertheless, his world view has more in common with advaita vedanta, despite the presence in it of the divine figure of Sathya Sai Baba himself. He, his devotees and the world all share in a divine benevolence which gives significance to every action and object to those with the vision to see and understand it.

As with TM, although there is no obvious hostility to the world in its social or physical forms, it is not all it seems. It is of a different order from that experienced by an uninitiated consciousness. Those who accept the all-embracing benevolence of Sathya Sai Baba, like those with knowledge of the Unified Field in TM, will understand the true nature of reality. However, in addition to those who become drawn in deeply to the world views of these two movements, there are those followers who do not necessarily wish to change their lives radically, but who are interested in exploring their spirituality either through meditation or a relationship with a guru. It is certainly possible to append this exploration to established forms of behaviour and belief in a way that is difficult in the other two movements.

It is important not to overstate this difference, however. Each of these groups has grown and changed since the early '70s, when they first became established here. Each now offers greater or lesser participation and fast and slow routes to self-realization. In addition, as we have seen, all are eager to bring about some kind of transformation of the individual and of social institutions. This process, in all cases, but to differing degrees, involves engaging with the world outside the movement. The style and perception of this engagement differs, however, according to the fundamental principles of each movement. The Hare Krishna and Swaminarayan Movements, which see perfection in a personal deity and impermanence and illusion in the material realm, wish to make sacred the latter by rooting it in service to God. This makes them develop parallel organizations and activities where they can be in the company of like-minded souls, into which outsiders can be drawn and through which they will be changed. Although the Sathya Sai Baba Fellowship is also focused on a divine figure, like TM, it sees transformation lying in the acquisition of an altered perspective on nature rather than in the development of an alternative society.

The world views of these movements – particularly their stance on the nature of ultimate reality and its relationship to the individual soul or atman – inform their attitudes to the social world. In Wallis' terms, they either reject or affirm it, though, as I hope I have shown, this rather crudely describes their engagement with it. Rather, they all seek, in differing ways, its transformation.

Notes

1 Roy Wallis, *The Elementary Forms of the New Religious Life*, Routledge, London, 1984, page 4.
2 The manifesto of the Natural Law Party appeared in a number of daily newspapers. The quotations here are from the *Guardian*, 20 March 1992, page 14.
3 The Maharishi Mahesh Yogi, the founder of TM, was initiated into the advaitin tradition of Shankara.
4 This movement is located spiritually in the advaitin tradition of Madhva, though some commentators have noted the similarity of its philosophy to that of Ramanuja.
5 This movement is located in the vishishtadvaitin tradition of Ramanuja.
6 Lawrence Babb, *Receptive Encounters: three modern styles in the Hindu tradition*, University of California Press, Berkeley, 1986, page 201.

11 Jainism in the modern world

Atul K. Shah

This article has benefited greatly from the comments of the late Kenneth Oldfield.

Jainism is an independent Indian religion dating back thousands of years. Of its 24 prophets, the latest, Lord Mahavira, was born around 600 BCE. Jain philosophy has many similarities with other Indian religions such as Hinduism and Buddhism. For example, all these religions believe in reincarnation and the role of karma, or deeds, in improving one's own happiness. All focus on self-purification, where salvation arises within oneself, through one's own actions. The one unique aspect of Jainism is its strong emphasis on non-violence (ahimsa) towards all living beings. Jains are strict vegetarians, and the monks do not eat root vegetables, owing to the violence involved in digging them from the earth. Mental violence such as hate, anger or jealousy are also strongly discouraged. The Jain principle of aparigraha, or non-acquisition, states that happiness cannot be obtained through material possessions, and that individuals should limit their possessions to their needs. Brahma charya prescribes that Jains should limit sexual activity to procreation and not indulge in it for purposes of pleasure or desire. Such behaviour is the root of unhappiness. Tapas, or penance, places importance on a simple diet, and fasting is also commonly practised by Jains, sometimes for several days. Greed for material comforts or wealth creation is also strongly discouraged through the principle of asteya, or non-stealing. In summary, Jainism is a strict philosophy which emphasizes individual self-discipline and careful conduct.

Jain scriptures

The basic Jain literature consists of some 60 scriptures covering various aspects such as logic, mathematics, botany, cosmology, karma theory (reincarnation) and Jain principles. An eminent French scholar, Louis Renou, wrote: 'Based on profoundly Indian elements, the Jain tradition is at the same time a highly original creation, containing very ancient material, more ancient than that of Buddhism and yet highly refined and elaborated.'[1] For example the Acharanga Sutra (500 BCE) has this to say about plants:

As our body is born, plants are born
As we grow, so plants grow
As we have reason (mind), so plants have reason
As our body is damaged when cut, so a plant is
    damaged when cut
As we need food, so plants need food
As we are mortal, so plants are mortal
As we have ups and downs, so plants have ups and
    downs
As we have some irregularities (in our life), so plants
    have some irregularities

Knowledge and study have a very important role in Jain philosophy, and Jain monks are considered to be amongst the most learned men in the world. They have to memorize many scriptures as part of their initial training, and write books and give lectures on a regular basis. Poetry and literature are central to Jain scholarship.

The following Jain sutra (Iriya Vahiya) is a good example of the depth and emphasis on non-violence (ahimsa) in Jainism:

With good wishes, O Lord, I wish to retract from this
    path,
I wish to retract from sins
While going to and fro
Whatever types of lives I might have destroyed
While walking
While attacking
While crushing
On dews
In ant holes

In water
In clay
In cobwebs
While cleaning or brushing
Whatever types of lives I might have destroyed
Those with one sense
Those with two senses
Those with three senses
Those with four senses
Those with five senses
I might have kicked them, rolled them, touched
    them, scared them, displaced them, separated
    them from their own kinds, or killed them
In connection of all these things
May my sins or faults be destroyed

The significant volumes of Jain scriptures written in the ancient languages of Prakrit and Ardha-Maghdi are little known in the West, although some attempts are being made to translate them into English. The Western Jain communities have discussed the need to establish a chair of Jainism at prestigious universities such as Harvard or Oxford, but the funds for doing so are, as yet, unavailable. There is still little Western interest in Eastern scholarship, and this does not help the awareness of and research into Jainism.

Jain society

The total world population of Jains is no greater than 10 million. Of these, the majority live in India. There are some 30,000 Jains in the United Kingdom, and a similar number in the United States and East Africa. There are Jains in the Far East and in Australia, as well. By trade, most Jains are either businessmen or professionals such as accountants, doctors, pharmacists or lawyers. There is a historic reason for this: owing to their faith, they have kept away from violent trades such as the meat industry or the army.

In the United Kingdom, a large proportion of young Jains are professionals – accountancy being the most popular, as dealing with numbers is relatively non-violent. Other professions include pharmacy, medicine and law. Many Jains are also in business, focusing on retail and wholesale of textiles, food and household items, but refraining from meat or related businesses. There are also a few banks owned by Jains, and insurance broking and financial services are popular areas of work.

Contradictions within Jainism

At one time, Jainism was a major Indian religion. Evidence of this can be seen from the hundreds of beautiful Jain temples in various parts of India. Some, like the Dilwara temples at Mount Abu in Rajasthan, are regarded by many as true 'wonders of the world'. There are a few different sects in Jainism, although the central philosophy remains the same, and in recent years there have been calls for unity, with some success achieved through the actions of Jains living outside India. However, many of the differences remain, and are unhealthy for such a small religious community. In addition, the strict adherence to ancient monastic vows and their restrictions on foreign travel has meant that the global awareness of this ancient and scientific philosophy has remained negligible. In stark contrast, Buddhists have travelled all over the world to spread their message. In recent years, a few Jain monks have broken the restrictions on travel, and are residing in New York. The Terapanthi order, under Acharya Tulsi, regularly sends trained samans and samanis (travelling monks and nuns) abroad. Jain scholars and teachers, trained by monks, are also sent abroad to give lectures to the Jain communities, reminding them of their rich philosophy and heritage.

From the earlier glimpse of Jain ethics, one gets the impression of a very strict and austere religion. In the modern world, however, these principles are really being tested. For example, many Jains live in the West, where non-vegetarian diets are the norm and material comforts are regarded as an important goal in life. Even in India, these tensions are apparent as the society tries to emulate the West. Jainism is not institutionalized, and it has no enforcement mechanism for observing the Jain code of conduct. It is up to individuals themselves to practise the philosophy. As a result, there has been some erosion of values and ethics amongst the Jain community, especially outside India.

Generating awareness and interest amongst young Jains

In the last 20 years, there has been a significant rise in Western interest in nature and the environment, as well as in ethical values. This has led to a revival in interest in Jainism amongst the younger Jains educated in the West, to whom the scientific basis of Jainism has become a source of great pride. For example, some 2,500 years ago, the Jain scriptures stated that plants have life. Jains have always believed that all life is sacred and that we must endeavour not to destroy it in our actions. This fact is slowly beginning to be accepted in the West, and there is now a growing interest in a vegetarian diet as a truly environment friendly and healthy way of living. The first Jain animal sanctuary outside India has been started in Sussex by the London Jain Community. The Jains were the eighth faith to participate in the World Wildlife Fund's project on religions and the environment, and made a 'Jain Declaration on Nature' at Buckingham Palace in July 1990.

In the United Kingdom, an innovative youth organization under the title of 'Young Jains' is making some impact among younger Jains growing up in a foreign country. Its approach is to address Jain issues from a scientific and questioning perspective, and it has recently completed a bold project on 'Experiments with Jainism', where young people undertook to practise each Jain principle in turn in their own life, without interrupting their daily routines.

Experiments with Jainism

Young people in the West often question the practice of Jain principles. For example, why is it that, if Jainism prescribes ahimsa (non violence), Jains often breach the principle by getting angry? Some feel that it is probably an outdated principle, not relevant to modern life. 'Young Jains' launched an experiment on ahimsa, where participants were asked to refrain from any form of physical or mental violence for a whole week, irrespective of whether or not it was necessary. They should not interrupt their everyday lifestyle, but should be fully aware of this principle for one week, and try their best to observe it. Some suggestions were given, e.g. Gandhiji tried to control his anger by observing a vow of silence for a certain period each day, and we suggested this to the participants. They were all asked to keep detailed notes of their experiences and feelings, and at the end of the seven days, participants had to complete a questionnaire and a meeting was organized to discuss individual experiences. It was found at this meeting that ahimsa was, indeed, a powerful principle relevant to modern society. However, society was weak in observing the principle. The experiment opened people's eyes to observing an ethical code, and some found it a rewarding experience. It made them aware of their own inner strengths and weaknesses, and the power of our ancient Jain principles.

Several other experiments were conducted, on asteya (non-stealing), satya (truth), tapas (penance/fasting), and aparigraha (non-acquisition). On the aparigraha experiment, participants were asked to make a list of all that they possessed and break it down into need, comfort and luxury categories. Next, they had to minimize the use of all material possessions for one week. For example, instead of a car, they had to use public transport. Assuming there was no radio or television, they could only read or say their prayers in their spare time. As there was no washing machine, all clothes had to be washed by hand for one week. At the end of the week, participants had a sense of relief and had, at the same time, learnt a great deal about how little they needed to lead a happy and fulfilling life.

Through the experiments, an attempt was made to translate Jain principles into modern life in a scientific manner. Much was gained, and a sincere interest in understanding Jain principles and philosophy was created amongst young people. The results of this project have been published in a booklet, *Experiments with Jainism*, available from 199 Kenton Lane, Harrow, Middlesex HA3 8TL. Young Jains also invite other non-Jain speakers who practise spiritual principles in Western life to talk about their experiences. For example, Dr Jean Dreze, a researcher at the London School of Economics and an active campaigner for non-violence and peace, spoke about his own experiences and how he became motivated to live a very modest and simple life. Such an open-minded approach to the promotion of Jainism has been refreshing for Western-educated youngsters and has drawn them closer to their own heritage of Jainism.

A Jain world view?

In his famous best-seller *A Brief History of Time*, the eminent physicist Stephen Hawking concludes: ' . . .

if the universe is completely self-contained, with no singularities or boundaries, and completely described by a unified theory, that has profound implications for God as Creator.'[2] Jains have their own complex theory of the universe, which is intimately connected with the concepts of time and space. They do not believe in God as Creator of the universe. In Jain philosophy, the universe has no beginning and no end: it is eternal and everlasting.

Rarely do Jains campaign to uphold their beliefs outside their community. One exception in the United Kingdom is Mr Nitin Mehta, who has organized large vegetarian rallies (at London's Hyde Park) to promote the vegetarian cause. This passivity in local and global issues has some links with the Jain philosophy, which can be interpreted as introvert. However, Jains in the West are slowly taking an interest in promoting and upholding their values outside their own community. Many Jains believe strongly that their religion has a very important message for resolving global problems. For example, the non-vegetarian diet has strong links with environmental exploitation, a fact which scientists are reluctantly beginning to accept.

The problems faced by Jains are not that different from those faced by any of the other major religions such as Islam, Christianity and Judaism. How do we live as part of a multicultural society and yet hold on to our old values and beliefs? How can we prevent ourselves from being dominated by greed, hatred, violence, materialism and other values of modern society, and counter them with religious values like love, compassion and dignity?

As Jains, we remain optimistic that our family and community values will survive and become a source of inner strength. Young people will take an active interest in our culture and heritage and have a positive influence on society through their own ethical values and approach to life. We believe that ancient religions can be translated into modern life if the issues are tackled with care and genuine commitment.

Notes

1 P.S. Jaini, *The Jaina Path of Purification*, University of California, Berkeley, 1977.
2 Stephen Hawking, *A Brief History of Time*, Bantam Press, 1988, page 174.

12 The New Age/alternative spirituality

Malcolm Stern

In the last half of the 20th century, a wide-ranging network of centres, communities, writings, therapies, exhibitions, specialist shops, and an ever-expanding base of individuals – healers, philosophers, scientists, artists and teachers (in the broad sense of the word) – have sprung up worldwide under the very loose umbrella of the 'New Age Movement'.

Before exploring the movement as a whole and understanding its significance, it is important to define what is commonly meant by the term 'New Age'. Here are quotes from two writers: David Spangler, one of the main inspirers behind the Findhorn Community in Scotland, and Bishop Stephen Verney. Bishop Verney, in the foreword of his book *Into the New Age*, states: 'There can be little doubt that we stand on the edge of a new epoch. Old patterns of behaviour are breaking up, and by the end of the 20th century our way of life will be very different. Anyone who dares to think and to feel at such a time must be looking towards the future with a mixture of terror and hope. I believe that we could enter the new age for good rather than for ill through the discovery of interdependence. We are more earthy and more heavenly than we have dared to admit.'[1] David Spangler writes in his introduction to the book *Revelation – The Birth of a New Age:* 'We live in a strange time. We are either afraid of the transcendental, the mystical, the sublime within ourselves and within our world, denying its existence or importance in the scheme of things; or we swing to the other extreme, becoming too irrational, too mystical, too given to the pursuit of elusive occult powers and knowledge, yearning for some messiah to supernaturally deal with our problems. Between these extremes, however, revelation is taking place in many areas of human endeavour. A new consciousness of reality, a new image of humanity and the universe is taking shape in our midst.'[2]

The need for a New Age is obvious. To those with eyes to see, this society which we have created is clearly breaking down. Even the environment which sustains us is frighteningly unstable, thanks to humankind's greed and exploitation. If we carry on blindly in the same ways, very soon the air will be unfit to breathe, the water too polluted to drink, the sun too dangerous to expose ourselves to and the animal kingdom decimated in the name of expansion. We humans lack integrity. Our governments lie and we accept it. We lie to our children. We tell 'white lies' effortlessly, and shade the truth as it suits us. The patriarchal society dishonours not just women, but the feminine values of tenderness, receptivity, integrity and caring. These values are the parts of the human psyche, which are repressed and stunted and therefore missing in our basic societal structures. We have to transform ourselves and society, if we are to survive.

When I first became interested in the philosophy and lifestyle of the New Age movement in the mid-1970s, I thought, like many others, that we were on the verge of an unprecedented era in the history of 'love, light and peace'. Today, still many are attracted to the movement naïvely believing that in the twinkling of an eye the world will be magically transformed. I have come to see that it is only through a process of evolution that the New Age can be ushered in. Evolution is, by its very nature, a gradual unfolding; and those values of love of humanity, light of spiritual consciousness, peace of mind and peace among nations are, indeed, the highest of goals and a necessary way forward. However, in order to achieve external change of such magnitude, we need to be prepared to make internal changes of equal magnitude.

What I believe we are witnessing is the breakdown of a decaying culture and the birth pangs of that which will take its place. Our dream or vision is of a world that works for all – where none go hungry; where violence, greed and wars are part of the history of less enlightened times; where the earth and all its inhabitants are honoured and respected. As with any birth, the struggle of the old to survive is savage and desperate, but as Werner Erhard, the founder of EST (an organization specializing in intensive weekend self-development courses) says: 'Nothing is so powerful as an idea whose time has come.'

In the introduction to *The New Age Almanac,* our understanding of this phenomenon – the New Age – is deepened: 'An attempt to understand the New Age movement easily can be frustrated by the movement's diversity. It has no single leader, no central organization, no firm agenda, and no group of official spokespersons. It is, in other words, a genuine social movement – dispersed into hundreds of individual efforts and organizations, fast-paced, complex and extremely malleable. While a product of the occult-psychic-metaphysical movements which preceded it, New Age concepts have in turn permeated the entire metaphysical field and have moved beyond it to include the vast domain of alternative medical systems – in particular the holistic health movement – and even political concerns. The surge of activity within the self-help and green movements in the US and worldwide are only two of the more obvious manifestations of New Age ideology transformed into action.'[3]

Marilyn Ferguson, in her book *The Aquarian Conspiracy,* indicates that by the year 2000, 25 per cent of Americans will be a part of the New Age movement in some way or another.

In Britain the largest New Age forum is 'Alternatives' at St James' Church in Piccadilly, London. Alternatives is dedicated to the exploration of ideas which provide creative spiritual alternatives to currently accepted Western thought. It supports the freedom of each individual to choose their own path of personal and spiritual growth.

St James' Church itself is an extraordinary phenomenon. In 1980 Donald Reeves became its rector and published a ten-year plan for the development of the church. This included the seven lamps he wished to see lit: a Health and Healing Ministry, a Political forum (Dunamis), a Music Ministry, Christian Faith and Practice, a Visitors' Ministry, a forum for the Arts and a New Age ministry (which has evolved into Alternatives). This beautiful Wren Church can hold 900 people and on Monday nights, when the Alternatives lecture series takes place, between 100 and 900 people gather to explore the numerous facets of the New Age. In this respect Alternatives provides a shop window for the New Age. It is very rare to see a speaker read out a lecture. The audience is intelligent and inquiring and has come to expect a high standard of both presentation and integrity. Most speakers find a way to create an experience of what they are communicating, thus making it possible for the audience to grasp the ideas at a level of personal understanding which doesn't require blind acceptance.

As a way of exploring the parameters of the New Age movement, here is a list of some of the speakers and topics that have been addressed as Alternatives:

Healing, death and dying

Elizabeth Kubler-Ross, the world-famous authority on death and dying, helped in her presentation to remove some of the taboos associated with her specialist field. In a society where death is hidden and unseemly, her stories are a breath of fresh air.

Meditation and the grace of guru

Ram Dass (former Harvard Psychology Professor, Richard Alpert) demonstrated with humour and compassion the absurd way that we perceive the very nature of reality. His journey into awareness, initially as a legitimate LSD experimenter and subsequently in the service of his guru in India, makes for compulsive listening.

Radical aliveness

Dr Richard Moss helped the audience to experience what he calls 'radical aliveness,' a means of living more fully in the present moment.

Creation-centred spirituality

Matthew Fox, a Roman Catholic priest, author of many books and the founder of Creation-Centred Spirituality, was censured by the Vatican for his outspoken questioning of much of orthodoxy, especially the concept of 'original sin'. He rejects the traditional 'fall and redemption' theology, in which humans are born fallen and corrupt into a world that is fallen and corrupt. He speaks instead of 'original blessing' and calls for a new, mystical tradition which celebrates and reveres the whole of creation.

Wicca and the goddess tradition

Starhawk helped initiate an understanding of the Goddess tradition, which is the impetus behind the emergence of the feminine. She is also a member of Matthew Fox's staff.

Kabbalah

Warren Kenton, (Z'ev Ben Shimon Halevi) has made the Kabbalah, the Tree of Life in the Jewish mystic tradition, accessible, and has demonstrated that system as a map for the spiritual journey.

Green issues

Jonathan Porritt, Satish Kumar (editor of *Resurgence*), veteran anti-nuclear campaigner Dr Helen Caldecott and Greenpeace Director Pete Wilkinson are some of the speakers who have addressed the Green issue.

A new role model for men

Robert Bly, the American author and philosopher, helped blaze a trail for men's groups which are now springing up countrywide. Many 'New Age Men', in their search for femine values, have surrendered their maleness in the process. Bly's use of myths and fairy tales, together with his innate wisdom, provide a credible map of the male psychological and spiritual journey – territory which has remained poorly charted, with a lack of role models.

Creative arts

Lex Van Someren, a Norwegian clown, presented an extraordinary evening on 'The Sacred Art of Clowning', showing that wisdom is about play, fantasy, humour and wonder. By removing our masks of personality, for a while, we can find the sacred place of wonder that the child occupies in all of us.

Psychotherapy and the human potential movement

R D Laing, John Grinder (NLP), Lady Diana Whitmore (psychosynthesis), Ursula Faussett (gestalt), Anne Dickson (sexuality and assertiveness), John Heron (co-counselling) and Eva Chapman (enlightenment intensives) are some of the psychotherapists who have shared their experience and techniques.

Buddhism

Thich Nhat Hanh, the Vietnamese Buddhist monk nominated by Dr Martin Luther King for the Nobel Peace Prize in the '60s (for his championing of non-violent opposition to the Vietnam War) has touched our audiences deeply with his gentleness and wisdom in teaching Buddhist philosophy and values.

Christianity and the New Age

Father Bede Griffiths, now in his 80s, provides an important bridge between Christianity and the New Age, and Sir George Trevelyan, also an octagenarian, has presented an inspiring vision of humanity's future.

Music

Music plays an important role, and evenings have featured musicians striving to capture the magic of the heart, such as Stairway (whose Keyboard player and Percussionist Jim McCarty was a founder member of Yardbirds) and ex-Eurythmics flautist Tim Wheater.

Diversity and immaturity

In the variety of these presenters I have tried to illustrate the rich diversity of the New Age movement. It is also important to mention its immaturity. Like the 'quacks' of the Wild West, who sold cure-alls in dollar bottles, there are plenty of confidence tricksters who sense an abundance of gullible souls, ripe for the plucking. There are also those who seek power and sexual rewards, and ego-centred teachings abound. There tends to be a sloppiness about agreements between 'New Agers', in the belief that each party's spiritual nature will prevail. Some adherents are so spiritually minded that they are of no earthly use. However, overall, the New Age continues to represent hope for the future.

There are no criteria for 'membership'; the process of joining this invisible, leaderless network is self-selection. Evolution is the magnet which is attracting myriad souls who are prepared to swim upstream, be tested, refined and disciplined to challenge internally the status quo, in order to make the changes necessary for humanity's survival.

Nowhere, in my experience, is there a more powerful or inspirational vision of the New Age and all it represents than in Christopher Fry's magnificent 'A Sleep of Prisoners', and I close this article with an extract from that:

'The human heart can go the lengths of God.
Dark and cold we may be, but this is no Winter now.
The frozen misery of centuries cracks, breaks, begins
   to move.
The thunder is the thunder of the floes.
Before the flood the upstarts spring.
Thank God our time is now, when wrong comes up
   to meet us
everywhere, never to leave us till we take the longest
   stride
of soul man ever took.

Affairs are now soul-size.
The enterprise is exploration into God.
Where are you making for?
It takes so many thousand years to wake,
but will you wake – for pity's sake?'[4]

Notes

1 Stephen Verney, *Into the New Age*, Fontana, 1976.
2 David Spangler, *Revelation – The Birth of a New Age*, Findhorn, 1976.
3 J. Gordon Melton, Jerome Clark and Adian Kelly, *The New Age Almanac*, Visible Ink Press, 1991.
4 Christopher Fry, 'A Sleep of Prisoners', OUP, 1951.

SECTION FOUR
Resources

Introduction

Resourcing' can signal many things: perhaps, simply, adequate funding; or good books and artefacts; a wide range of audio-visual materials; computer programmes; radio and television broadcasts; direct experience through visits, and contact with faith communities. In the years since the first Shap Handbook (1972), the range and quality of such resources has increased and improved hugely – even if RE teachers have not always had 'purchasing power'!

But 'resourcing RE' may also refer to the key resource – teachers. The selection of resources provided here is intended as a tool for them – to provide, for example, starting points in moving into unfamiliar areas, or an *aide memoire* to an area in which one has worked before. None of the lists provided here is exhaustive, but most items in each (teachers') list of books would quickly lead the user to further sources of information. Whilst necessarily selective, each list has attempted to provide a balanced diet. A brief descriptive comment accompanies each entry.

The bibliographies

These relate particularly to Sections One and Two (A and B) of this book. Many people have advised and played a part in the compilation of the bibliographies.

Buddhism, Christianity, Hinduism, Islam, Judaism, and Sikhism are each covered by a bibliography for the teacher and one 'for the classroom'. The compilers of, or contributors to, the former have shaped their own contributions as they considered appropriate to the tradition. No attempt has been made, therefore, to impose common categories. These lists provide for some in-depth reading for deepening personal understanding, and list books which might also be used by those involved in 'A' level teaching.

The bibliographies for the classroom focus as far as possible on fairly recent material (post ERA in many, but not all, cases). Each book is provided with a key stage reference, which should be understood as relating to the years/ages suggested in National Curriculum documentation (and utilized in many Agreed Syllabuses since 1988).

Bibliographies relating to religious traditions are preceded by a list of recent books on the theory and practice of Religious Education. A key feature which emerges from this list is the number of recent books available to support RE teaching in Key Stages 1 and 2.

A selection of books relating to the movements described in Section Three is included under the heading 'Further Perspectives'.

Non-book resources

This important area is covered by the provision of a selective and annotated address list. It should be noted that all the addresses provided relate to producers and suppliers operating on a commercial basis. This is an address list for teachers, not for students who want to write away for information, e.g. for projects. We recommend therefore that contact is made through the teacher, and advise enclosing a s.a.e.! Every attempt has been made to ensure that the information is correct but details may be subject to change.

Access to resources

Religious Education Centres can provide the opportunity to see, and often to try out, resources before purchase. The Federation of National and Regional RE Centres may be able to put you in touch with a centre in your area; its five 'national' centres are listed here. Each of these carries a large resource base, is professionally staffed, runs courses and welcomes visitors and enquiries.

Mary Hayward

Acknowledgements

The following have all given generous help and advice in the compilation of the bibliographies: Denise Cush, Paul Williams (Buddhism); Peter Doble, Trevor Shannon (Christianity); Robert Jackson, Dermott Killingley, Eleanor Nesbitt, Frank Whaling (Hinduism) and Jacqueline Hirst (Women's Issues); Vida Barnett, Dilwyn Hunt (Islam); Owen Cole, Eleanor Nesbitt (Sikhism).

Bibliographies

I Religious Education: theory and practice

Arthur, C., *Biting the Bullet*, St Andrew Press, 1990. ISBN 0 7152 0635 4
Subtitled 'Some personal reflections on Religious Education', this book is a series of essays which reflects on present 'orthodoxies' in RE and argues for the subject's importance as an area in which 'live' issues of social, personal and spiritual importance are examined.

Bastide, D. (ed.), *Good Practice in Primary Religious Education, 4–11*, Falmer Press, 1992. ISBN 1 85000 639 3
Collection of essays on key subjects, e.g. artefacts, story, planning in RE, the role of the RE consultant, from contributors who are all practitioners in the field of primary RE – in schools, training institutions or the advisory service.

Brown, A. S., *Religious Education and the Pupil with Learning Difficulties*, OUP, 1987. ISBN 0 521 33720 8
Practical guidance which looks realistically at the problems faced by non-specialist RE teachers and children with learning difficulties in mixed ability classes.

Cole, W. O. and Evans-Lowndes, J., *Religious Education in the Primary Curriculum*, RMEP, 1991. ISBN 0 900274 32 8
A book of teaching strategies and practical activities which takes seriously the issues which confront teachers and students in handling RE in the primary school, e.g. questions of commitment, of RE's purposes, of curriculum planning.

Copley, T. *et al.*, *Forms of Assessment in Religious Education*, FARE Project, University of Exeter, 1991. ISBN 0 9518041 0 3
Final report of a school-based project – FARE – in the University of Exeter, which looked at attainment and the assessment process in RE.

Grimmitt, M., *Religious Education and Human Development*, McCrimmons, 1987. ISBN 0 85597 401 X
The first part of this book offers a detailed consideration of the part Religious Education might play in the process of human development. The author offers critical reflections on much contemporary theory and practice in RE and suggests a way forward through a re-shaping of the RE curriculum into the 'Adolescent Life-World Curriculum' and the 'Religious Life-World Curriculum'. The practical outworkings of this two-fold approach are illustrated through over 100 curriculum units, drawing on five religions and aimed at young people aged 11–16.

Grimmitt, M., Grove, J., Hull, J. and Spencer, L., *A Gift to the Child: Religious Education in the Primary School (Teachers' Source Book)*, Simon & Schuster, 1991. ISBN 0 7501 0128 8
The 'Gift to the Child' Project offers a distinctive approach and strategy for explicit religious education at KS 1–2. Focusing on seven specific 'religious items', e.g. an artefact, a story, practice, the source book offers 28 detailed lesson plans and support materials for the teacher. 'A Gift to the Child' also provides 14 full-colour story picture books for children and an audio cassette which complements the books.

Hammond, J., Hay, D. *et al.*, *New Methods in RE Teaching: An Experiential Approach*, Oliver & Boyd, 1990. ISBN 0 05 004303 X
A book which has prompted much discussion and which has its roots in a concern for the spiritual dimension of religion. The contributors offer a rationale for their approach and methodology, and a range of tried and tested activities. The book arose from work which the Religious Experience Research Project undertook with teachers.

Jackson, R. and Starkings, D., *The Junior RE Handbook*, Stanley Thorne (Publisher) Ltd, 1990. ISBN 1 871402 31 X
A clear introductory handbook in five sections: Principles and Planning, Guides to Religions, Teaching about Religions, Religious Education and the Arts, and Methods and Issues: which considers, e.g. Special Needs and RE, Inset in RE and Collective Worship.

Kincaid, M., *Learning in RE*, Hodder & Stoughton, 1991. ISBN 0 340 55779 6

An exploration of effective learning and teaching in RE. Topics include recent developments in RE, the organization of learning, personal development, moral education, evaluation, assessment and planning. Stress throughout on young people developing skills.

King, U. (ed.), *Turning Points in Religious Studies*, T. & T. Clark, 1990. ISBN 0 567 09564 9
Not actually a book about RE – although many of its chapters have a bearing on what happens in RE, and two pay attention to RE and Collective Worship. The book should be of particular interest to RE specialists in secondary schools who would like an overview of developments in Religious Studies, which might be shared with students considering taking a Religious Studies Course in Higher Education.

Rankin, J., Brown, A. and Hayward, M., *Religious Education Topics for the Primary School*, Longman, 1989. ISBN 0 582 00334 2
Forty-two topics arranged in three age phases (5–7; 7–9; 9–11) and drawn from Buddhism, Christianity, Hinduism, Islam, Judaism and Sikhism. Each topic spread offers aims, information, approaches, activities and resources.

Rankin, J., Brown, A. and Hayward. M., *Religious Education across the Curriculum*, Longman, 1991. ISBN 0 582 06052 4
Companion volume to *RE Topics for the Primary School*, suggesting contributions RE might make to 21 popular cross-curricular topics and indicating aims, approaches, activities and resources.

Read, G., Rudge, J. and Howarth, B., *How do I teach RE?*, MGP, 1986. ISBN 0 86158 894 0. New edition: Stanley Thornes (Publishers) Ltd, 1992. ISBN 0 7487 1470 7
Represents the underlying philosophy and approach of the Westhill Project RE, 5–16. This book explores RE as a school subject and shows how its aims can be translated into classroom practice, and offers guidelines on syllabus planning and curriculum development. The revised edition incorporates new thinking in relation to attainment and assessment.

Religious Education: A Local Curriculum Framework, National Curriculum Council, 1991.

ISBN 1 8726276 59 6
Slim A4 booklet, offering guidance on planning and structuring the RE curriculum. Might be used as a basis for discussing RE in school, or by statutory conferences setting out to prepare the agreed syllabus.

Religious Education in Europe, Inter-European Commission on Church and School, 1990.
The definitive book on RE in Europe has yet to be written. This booklet simply provides a brief introduction to the requirements concerning RE and indicates whose responsibility it is and who may teach it in 13 European countries. New edition available in 1993.

Rudge, J., *Assessing Recording and Reporting RE: a handbook for teachers*, The Regional RE Centre (Midlands), 1991. ISBN 0 9502706 6 0
This is the outcome of a project sponsored by 33 Local Education Authorities, and follows on from an earlier publication, *Attainment in RE*. The handbook offers a framework for thinking about and developing assessment procedures, and is a tool for teachers' own creative use in their own location rather than a blueprint.

Watson, B., *Education and Belief*, Basil Blackwell, 1987. ISBN 0 631 15208 3
Calling for recognition that all education has to do with values, this essay first considers the relation of belief and education and then moves to set out the author's understanding of religious education and its practice. While there is much here from which to dissent, the author marks out areas for proper concern and suggests at least one side of the case; this is a book with which to hold an argument, so it earns a place in this list.

II Books about a number of religions

Books for teachers

Brown, A. (ed.) for Shap, *Festivals in World Religions*, Longman, 1986. ISBN 0 582 36196 6
Still the only book which provides such a broad overview of calendars and festivals. Festivals included are Bahá'í, Buddhist, Chinese, Christian, Hindu, Jaina, Japanese, Jewish, Muslim, Sikh and Zoroastrian (Parsi). National and secular events are also considered.

Eliade, M. (ed.), *The Encyclopedia of Religion*, Macmillan and Free Press, 1987. ISBN 0 02 909480 1 (set) 0 02 909890 4 (vol. 16, Index)
A 15-volume encyclopedia, plus index (vol. 16), with contributions from leading scholars across the world. Teachers may find this useful for 'A' level teaching and personal reference. Obviously this is to be sought out in a library – probably in a college or university.

Smart, N., *The World's Religions*, CUP, 1989. ISBN 0 521 34005 5 (Hbk); CUP, 1992. No ISBN (Pbk)
Written for the general public and for students who wish to learn about the world's world views. Religions are analysed in terms of seven dimensions, art being added to Smart's earlier six dimensions. Religions are considered in a historical context and viewed in relation to periods of formation and re-formation. Attention is also given to secular world views.

Sutherland, S., Houlden, L., Clarke., P and Hardy, F. (eds), *The World's Religions*, Routledge, 1988. ISBN 0 415 00324 5
A reference book just short of a thousand pages and falling into six parts: Religion and the Study of Religion; Judaism and Christianity; Islam; The Religions of Asia; Traditional Religions; and New Religious Movements. (It has subsequently been published in 1991 in four paperback volumes.) Whilst the selection and balance of material in some sections has been criticized – only one out of 12 essays in 'Judaism and Christianity' is about Judaism! – the focus on a religious tradition's development in different parts of the world offers much interest. Islam, for example, is presented in 10 contexts – from contemporary Europe to China.

Whaling, F. (ed.), *Religion in Today's World*, Clark, 1987. ISBN 0 567 09452 9
Subtitled 'The Religious Situation of the World from 1945 to the present Day', this collection of essays brings together contributions from a group of leading world scholars. They address 'religiousness' and religions in the present, but also cults and religion, secular world views, spirituality and the significance of the study of religion.

World Scripture: *A Comparative Anthology of Sacred Texts*, Paragon House, New York, 1991. ISBN 0 89226 129 3
This is the result of a mammoth project involving 27 eminent scholars from all parts of the world. Its purpose is 'to celebrate and honour the richness and universality of religious truth contained in the world's great scriptures' and 'to demonstrate that there exists a variety of spiritual common ground'. In doing so, however, the editors have not fallen into the trap of implying that all religions teach the same thing.

There are five parts divided into 21 chapters. The sections cover: Ultimate Reality and the Purpose of Human Existence; Evil, Sin and the Human Fall; Salvation and the Saviour; the Religious Life; Providence, Society and the Kingdom of Heaven. Although 'Human Fall' is used in the title of Part Two, Buddhist, Sikh and other views of the natural condition of human beings are included: what is distinctive about a tradition is not obscured. Christianity, Islam, Buddhism, Hinduism, and Chinese religions are most prominently featured but there are many passages from the Mishnah and Talmud, Native American traditions, the Guru Granth Sahib, and Japanese, Jain, African, Baha"ı´ and Zoroastrian religions. Scientology, Latter Day Saints, Christian Science and Theosophy are also represented.

Users are helped by an introductory essay which surveys each of the religions covered by the anthology; by an index of sources, and by a subject index which makes cross referencing easy. In a 914 page volume this is important!

World Scripture will be a useful resource for teachers and students who want to follow through particular themes in sacred writings; it could also be a useful resource for collective worship in school.

Books for the classroom

Bennett, O., *Exploring Religion*, Bell & Hyman Ltd, 1984.
People ISBN 0 7135 2331 X
Buildings ISBN 0 7135 2330 1
Worship ISBN 0 7135 2328 X
Writings ISBN 0 7135 1503 1
Festivals ISBN 0 7135 1500 7
Signs and Symbols ISBN 0 7135 2329 8
Teacher's Guide ISBN 0 7135 2458 8
A series which has proved very popular and is still available and used. Christianity and two other faiths are drawn on in each book. Appropriate for years 6 and 7. KS 2–3.

Brown, A., Rankin, J. and Wood, A., *Religions*, Longman, 1988. ISBN 0 582 22341 5
A GCSE study course which offers a wealth of carefully presented information on six religions; colour and black and white illustrations of a good quality. Non-specialist teachers at all stages will also find this a useful book. KS 4 – GCSE.

Cole, W. O. (ed.), *Five World Faiths*, Cassell, 1991. ISBN 0 304 32478 7
A reprint of an earlier volume – *Comparative Religions* (1982) – distinctive in that each faith is represented in a chapter written by a member of the faith community. KS 4 and above.

Cole, W. O. (ed.), *Moral Issues in Six Religions*, Heinemann Educational, 1991. ISBN 0 435 30299 X
Written by practising members of the religions, indicating something of religious responses to contemporary social and moral issues – family, peace and conflict, humankind and nature, work, wealth and leisure, evil and suffering, the individual in society, and social ideals. Each religion is handled separately to allow for its distinctiveness. KS 4 – GCSE.

Cole, W. O. and Morgan, P., *Six Religions in the Twentieth Century*, Hutton/Stanley Thornes, 1984. ISBN 0 7175 1290 8
Thematic and popular secondary school text. KS 4 – GCSE.

Curtis, P. and Smith, C., *Thinking about Living*, Folens, 1990. ISBN 1 85276093 1 (Resource Book. 1 85276094 X)
Curtis, P., *Thinking about Religion*, Folens, 1990. ISBN 1 85276095 8 (Resource Book. 1 85276096 6)
Curtis, P., *Thinking things through*, Folens, 1982. ISBN 1 85276097 4 (Resource Book. 1 85276098 2)
These three books comprise 'Folens Religious Education' Course; photocopiable resource materials are available to accompany each of the books. *Thinking about Religion* offers a thematic approach and draws on six religions; themes include God, suffering, belonging, worship, celebration and holy books. 'Implicit' foundations for these are explored in the first book, whilst explicit and implicit are brought together in Book Three. Colour illustrations and black and white and line drawings.

Fageant, J. and Mercier, C., *Skills in Religious Studies 1*, Heinemann Educational, 1988. ISBN 0 435 30200 0
Skills in Religious Studies 2, Heinemann Educational, 1989. ISBN 0 435 30201 9
Skills in Religious Studies 3, Heinemann Educational, 1990. ISBN 0 435 30202 7
A course designed to introduce young people to six religions and to provide a basis for exam work. Presented in self-contained double page spreads, with alternate spreads in full colour. Volume One has an (implicit) thematic structure with a focus on festivals and pilgrimage. Volumes Two and Three are approached via each religion, with approaches to belief and worship and to rites of passage respectively. KS 3.

Hanlon, D., *Themes in World Religions*, two vols., OUP, 1988.
Two large loose-leaf files, each providing 58 photocopiable masters. Volume One focuses on three themes: development, places of worship and festivals; whilst the second volume explores pilgrimage, symbols and holy books. Each theme is looked at across six religions. KS 2 (selected sheets) 3–4–GCSE.

Johnson, C., (ed.), *Praying Their Faith*, CEM, 1992. ISBN 1 851000 0451 8
Drawing on six religions, this 40-page booklet introduces a selection of prayers which, it is hoped, will enhance students' and teachers' insights into these traditions and helpfully supplement textbooks used in school. Teacher resource for KS 3–4.

Rankin, J., Brown, A. and Gateshill, P., *Ethics and Religions*, Longman, 1991. ISBN 0 582 03307 1
Five issues are explored from the perspective of six world religions: Buddhism, Christianity, Hinduism, Islam, Judaism and Sikhism. The issues with which the book is concerned are marriage and the family, abortion and medical ethics, the natural world, peace and conflict, and capital punishment. The intention is that students should work towards discovering what they themselves think about these issues. KS 4 – GCSE.

III Books relating to six religions

Buddhism

Books for teachers

General

Bechert, H. and Gombrich, R. (ed.), *The World of Buddhism*, Thames and Hudson, 1984. ISBN 0 500 25089 8
A lavishly illustrated and readable survey by some of the world's leading scholars.

Harvey, P., *An Introduction to Buddhism: teachings, history and practices*, CUP, 1990. ISBN 0 521 31333 3 (Pbk)

Lamotte, E. (trans. S. Webb-Boin), *History of Indian Buddhism: from the origins to the Saka era*, Institut Orientaliste, Université Catholique de Louvain, 1988. ISBN 90 6831 100 X
The most important and influential academic survey of early Buddhist doctrinal and cultural history.

Paul, D.Y., *Women in Buddhism: images of the feminine in Mahayana tradition*, University of California Press, 1985. ISBN 0 520 05445 8
Translations of source materials with introductory comments.

Snelling, J., *The Buddhist Handbook*, Rider, 1987. ISBN 0 7126 1554 7
This book covers the main schools of Buddhism and their basic teachings and practices.

Source books

Conze, E., *Buddhist Scriptures*, Penguin, 1959 (many reprints). ISBN 0 14 044088 7
Idiosyncratic at times, but a reasonably reliable source book.

Conze, E., Horner, I. B., Snellgrove, D. and Waley, A., *Buddhist Texts through the Ages*, Harper and Row, 1964.

Beyer, S., *The Buddhist Experience: sources and interpretations*, Dickenson, 1974. ISBN 0 8221 0127 0

Introductory Surveys

Rahula, W., *What the Buddha Taught*, Wisdom Books, 1985.

A recent reprint of a standard introduction to Buddhism. This book and many others on Buddhism (not only their own) can be obtained from Wisdom Publications, 402 Hoe Street, London E17 9AA. They also publish an excellent catalogue.

Saddhatissa, H., *The Buddha's Way*, Allen and Unwin, 1985. ISBN 0 04 294071 0
A very reliable, easy introduction to the Buddhist perspective, written by a well-known Theravadin monk.

The life of the Buddha

Carrithers, M., *The Buddha*, OUP, 1983. ISBN 0 19 287590 6
An excellent, academically respectable yet readable account of what we know of the Buddha and his teaching.

Theravada

Carrithers, M., *The Forest Monks of Sri Lanka: an anthropological and historical survey*, OUP, 1983.
A study of the forest meditation tradition among Theravada monks. Useful for teachers at upper secondary level.

Chah, Ajahn, *Bodhinyana: teachings of Ajahn Chah*, The Sangha of Bung Wai Forest Monastery, 1982.
The teachings of one of the most influential Thai meditation masters can be obtained free of charge together with other works by Ajahn Chah and his disciples from Amaravati Buddhist Centre, Great Gaddesden, Hemel Hempstead, Herts. HP1 3BZ.

Collins, S., *Selfless Persons: imagery and thought in Theravada Buddhism*, CUP, 1982. ISBN 0 521 24081 6
A sophisticated and philosophically aware study of the no-Self teachings, and allied issues.

Gombrich, R., *Buddhist Precept and Practice: Traditional Buddhism in the rural highlands of Ceylon*, OUP, 1971. Recently reprinted by Motilal Banarsidass, Delhi. A witty and important study of Theravada Buddhism as it is actually practised, and how this relates to Buddhist doctrinal teachings.

Gombrich, R., *Theravada Buddhism: a social history from ancient Benares to modern Colombo*, Routledge, 1988. ISBN 0 7102 1319 0

Mahayana

General:
Williams, P., *Mahayana Buddhism: the doctrinal foundations*, Routledge, 1989. ISBN 0 415 02537 0
A survey stressing the variety and heterogeneity of Mahayana Buddhist doctrine.

Indo-Tibetan:
Snellgrove, D., *Indo-Tibetan Buddhism: Indian Buddhists and their Tibetan successors*, two vols., Shambhala, 1989. ISBN 0 87773 311 2
An up-to-date and well-written – if controversial – and readable historical study.

Cozort, D., *Highest Yoga Tantra*, Snow Lion, 1986. ISBN 0 937938 32 7
The best introduction to what Tantric Buddhism – the esoteric Buddhism associated particularly with Tibet – is all about. Written from inside the contemporary Tibetan perspective.

Chinese:
Ch'en, K., *Buddhism in China: a historical survey*, Princeton University Press, 1964.
Dated, but still of some value as a general survey.

Luk, C., *Empty Cloud: the autobiography of the Chinese Zen master Xu Yun*, Element Books, 1988. ISBN 1 85230 031 0
A fascinating, absorbing account of the life of a Chinese Ch'an (Zen) monk, who purportedly lived to be 120 and died in 1959, having lived through one of the most turbulent periods in Chinese history.

Weinstein, S., *Buddhism under the T'ang*, CUP, 1987. ISBN 0 521 25585 6 (Hbk)
A scholarly and interesting study of Buddhism during an important era in Chinese thought (618–907 CE).

Japanese:
Bloom, A., *Shinran's Gospel of Pure Grace*, University of Arizona Press, 1965. ISBN 0 8165 0405 9
By far the most accessible and influential introduction in English to the history and 'theology' of Japanese Pure Land Buddhism, the Buddhism of faith and gratitude to Amitabha Buddha, with its parallels to and contrasts with Christian theologies.

Dumoulin, H. (trans. J. W. Heisig and Paul Knitter) *Zen Buddhism: a history*, two vols., Macmillan, 1988.

ISBN 0 02 908270 6 (vol. 1)
The first volume treats India and China, the second volume, Japan, tracing the history of Zen Buddhism, well-known for its austere meditation and its influence on the arts in East Asia.

Matsunaga, D. and Matsunaga, A., *Foundations of Japanese Buddhism*, two vols, Buddhist Books International, 1974/6.

Montgomery, D. B., *Fire in the Lotus: the dynamic Buddhism of Nichiren*, Mandala, 1991. ISBN 1 85274 091 4
Nichiren Buddhism, with various sub-schools, is a tradition very popular in contemporary Japan. With its often vigorous advocacy of the spiritual and material virtues of chanting the name of a Mahayana scripture – the Lotus Sutra – it has stimulated considerable interest and has many converts in the West. A sympathetic and readable study.

Statler, O., *Japanese Pilgrimage*, Picador, 1984. ISBN 0 330 28375 8
A wonderful and readable picture of Japanese religious life, centred on a pilgrimage associated with Kobo Daishi (Kukai, 774–835), the founder of the Japanese tradition of Shingon Buddhism. Highly recommended for an account of the spirit of Japan.

Note: Perhaps this is the point to mention books by Christmas Humphreys. These are easily available, but not reliable as studies of Buddhism, although they may be interesting as examples of a particular type of Western appropriation of Buddhism, influenced heavily by Humphreys' early espousal of Theosophy.

Buddhism

Books for the classroom

Association of Buddhist Women in the UK, *The Story of the Buddha*, available from London Buddhist Vihara, 5 Heathfield Gardens, London W4 4JU.
Well illustrated and inexpensive publication which arose from the need for a book to read to children in the West and for children to read for themselves. KS 2–3.

Bancroft, A., *The Buddhist World*, Macdonald, 1984. ISBN 0 356 07524 9 (Hbk); Simon & Schuster, 1992. (Pbk)

Attractive information book with many excellent colour photographs which portray Buddhism in different cultural contexts. KS 2–3.

Bancroft, A., *Festivals of the Buddha*, RMEP, 1984. ISBN 0 08 030611 X
One of the Living Festivals series. The festivals are approached here through following the celebrations of Malee and her family in Thailand. KS 2–3.

Cush, D., *Buddhists in Britain Today*, Hodder & Stoughton, 1990. ISBN 0 340 51948 7
An attempt to give an authentic picture of Buddhism in the UK. This is approached by means of interviews with 10 practising Buddhists from the variety of traditions represented in this country. Questions and suggestions for further work, a bibliography and useful addresses are also provided. KS 4–GCSE and above.

Cush, D., *A Student's Approach to Buddhism*, Hodder & Stoughton, 1993.
A general introduction directed at 'A' level and first year degree students. KS 4–GCSE and above.

Connolly, P. and H., *Buddhism*, Stanley Thornes, 1992. ISBN 1 871402 07 7
A GCSE text covering: the early scriptures and life of the Buddha; history and development of Buddhism; Buddhist teachings, festivals and ceremonies; and Buddhism throughout the world. Black and white pictures and line drawings illustrate the book. Suitable for average to above average students. KS 4–GCSE.

Connolly, P. and H., *Religions through Festivals: Buddhism*, Longman, 1989. ISBN 0 582 31789 4
An introduction to Buddhism – and its festivals – which tries to convey something of the diversity of this tradition as it has taken root in different cultural contexts. KS 3.

Hunt, D., *Leaders of Religion: the Buddha*, Oliver & Boyd, 1987. ISBN 0 05 004135 5
Lower secondary book designed to promote active learning. KS 3.

Landaw, J. and Brooke, J., *Prince Siddhartha*, Wisdom, 1980. ISBN 0 86171 016 9
Finely illustrated version of the Buddha's life, written with children in mind. KS 2–3.

Morgan, P. M., *Buddhist Iconography; Buddhist Stories*, available from the author at Westminster College, Oxford.
Two booklets providing useful information and insights for teachers coming 'new' to Buddhism, especially those working with younger children. The first offers line drawings and notes about Buddha, rupas, stupas, the wheel of life and other symbols. The second offers a broad collection, including Jataka stories, the story of Avolokitesvara (Chenresig), and information about Pu-Tai, the laughing Maitreya Buddha, whose image is very common in shops in the West.

Morgan, P. M., *Buddhism*, Batsford, 1987. ISBN 0 7134 5203 X

Morgan, P. M., *Being a Buddhist*, Batsford, 1989. ISBN 0 7134 6015 6
The first of these books is a dictionary offering explanations of many key terms in Buddhism. The second offers extracts from a wide variety of written sources to convey what it means to be Buddhist. KS 3–4.

Naylor, D. and Smith, A., *The Buddha: a journey*, Macmillan, 1987. ISBN 0 333 41595 7
A presentation of the life of the Buddha which tries to foster active involvement of the students: many suggestions of things to do and to think about. Offers a clear introduction to the Four Noble Truths. KS 3–4.

Penney, S., *Buddhism*, Heinemann Educational, 1989. ISBN 0 435 30303 1
One of the Discovering Religions series for less able secondary school students; usable illustrations and activities for a range of ages and abilities. KS 3.

Samarasekara, D. U., *I am a Buddhist*, Franklin Watts, 1986. ISBN 0 86313 261 8
A picture book which focuses around the life of Udeni, a 10-year-old girl from a Sri Lankan family who live in Britain. One of the My Belief series. KS 2.

Snelling, J., *Buddhism*, Wayland, 1986. ISBN 0 85078 722 X
An introductory book describing the ceremonies, customs and festivals of Buddhism, along with the principles taught by the Buddha. Good colour photographs throughout. KS 2–3.

Snelling, J., *Buddhist Festivals*, Wayland, 1985.
ISBN 0 85078 572 3
A short 'information' book which attempts to provide sufficient information about Buddhism to place festivals in context, and which approaches the festivals 'geographically', looking at Thailand, Sri Lanka, Tibet and Japan. Illustrated with colour photographs. KS 2–3.

Snelling, J., *Buddhist Stories*, Wayland, 1986.
ISBN 0 85078 864 1
Retelling by a Buddhist of six classic stories from the Jataka Tales, illustrated in the style of traditional Buddhist art. 'Jataka' means 'birth story' and each story recalls an incident in one of the previous lives of the Buddha. KS 1–2.

Snelling, J., *The Life of the Buddha*, Wayland, 1987.
ISBN 0 85078 903 6
A retelling of selected episodes from the life of the Buddha. Illustrated by Carol Barker, as is the previous book. KS 1–2.

Weatherley, L., *Themes in Religion: Buddhism*, Longman, 1992. ISBN 0 582 02965 1
A lively accessible introduction to Buddhism. Suitable for a mixed ability GCSE group. Focuses on beliefs, scriptures, meditation and worship, pilgrimage, values and everyday living.

Wood, J., *Buddhist*, Franklin Watts, 1988.
ISBN 0 86313 674 5
Attractive colour pictures, many from *I am a Buddhist* (see above), and a simple, large type text for young readers. KS 1.

Christianity

Books for teachers

Though bibliographies for Christianity are immense, it is difficult to find readable, introductory material which views the tradition from an objective standpoint. The following selection is necessarily limited, but the bibliographies within the following books will also offer further guidance.

Surveys

Banks, R. *et al.*, *The Quiet Revolution*, Lion, 1985/1989.
ISBN 0 7324 0028 7

A readable survey of the way things are in the Christian world today, this book, written from an evangelical perspective, highlights Christianity as a global faith wrestling with modernity. There are useful sections on Africa and Latin America; that on Eastern Europe has been overtaken by events.

Barrett, D. B., *World Christian Encyclopaedia*, OUP, 1982. ISBN 0 19 572435 6 (Hbk)
Expensive, large and exactly what its title says it is, here is a factual statement of the variety, size, growth, distribution and relations of the churches in the Christian families.

McKenzie, P., *The Christians*, SPCK, 1988.
ISBN 0 281 04297 7
This is an 'adaptation' of a German source; the diversity of practices and beliefs within the Christian tradition is related not to historical development but to phenomena and concepts.

Smart, N., *The Phenomenon of Christianity*, Collins, 1979. ISBN 0 00 215115 4 (Hbk)
Smart treats the Christian tradition sympathetically and objectively, noting both its great diversity as people live out their interpretations of the tradition in differing cultural and ecclesiastical contexts, and the ways in which those interpretations are expressed and transmitted.

Jesus and the New Testament

The bibliographies of this area are huge. What follows offers an introduction to some of the major questions which have concerned Christians in the past fifty years or so, and to some of the current issues and perspectives.

Court, J. and K., *The New Testament World*, CUP, 1990.
ISBN 0 521 34007 1 (Hbk)
This has the advantage of having been jointly written by an academic and a teacher. A survey of the world in which the New Testament emerged, the book introduces the people, ideas, thought and literature of the New Testament itself.

Houlden, J. L., *Jesus: a question of identity*, SPCK, 1992.
ISBN 0 281 04573 9
Lucid, searching exploration of the present state of the Jesus question: what can be known of him, and

what is to be made of the range of beliefs about him? Readable introduction to the evolution to the present of Christian thinking about Jesus.

Theissen, G., *The Shadow of the Galilean*, SCM, 1987. ISBN 0 334 01512 X
Scholarly, novel-like attempt to develop a modern 'life of Jesus' taking account of his social, political and religious context. The distinctive feature of this 'life' is that at no point does Jesus appear; his person and deeds are the subject of others' words and acts, in which his shadow is a discernible reality. Each chapter ends with a letter by the author to an academic colleague offering a scholarly defence of the chapter's contents, discussing whether or not this attempt at a 'life' of Jesus is academically justifiable.

Tuckett, C. M., *Reading the New Testament*, SPCK, 1987. ISBN 0 281 04259 4
A systematic and usable survey of the tools – such as Form and Redaction Criticism – commonly used by students of the New Testament, this book is an excellent introduction to an often misunderstood world.

Vermes, G., *Jesus and the World of Judaism*, SCM, 1983. ISBN 0 334 02094 8
A Jewish perspective on a Jewish Jesus by an acknowledged authority.

Worship and calendar

Metford, J. C. J., *The Christian Year*, Thames & Hudson, 1991. ISBN 0 500 11021 2 (Hbk)
A painstaking attempt to set out the shape of the Christian calendar and how it came to be the way it is.

Wainwright, G., *Doxology*, Epworth, 1980. ISBN 0 7162 0384 7
A magisterial introduction to Christian worshipping as the vehicle of Christian credal development. Big and demanding, it is realistic, full of insight and learning, and a treasury of the variety of Christian belief and practice.

World perspective and history

This section suggests some introductory historical material.

Allan, J. D., *The Evangelicals*, Paternoster, 1989. ISBN 0 85364 499 3

'Evangelical' can be a slippery word. In this survey of the Evangelical Movement, the World Evangelical Fellowship has offered an account of the political and religious influence of this Christian perspective as it developed historically. The volume contains contributions by a number of evangelicals, such as Billy Graham and John Stott.

Board, D. M. (ed.), *A Way of Life: being Catholic today*, Collins, 1982. ISBN 0 00 599705 4 (Hbk)
Although 10 years old, this popular survey of the life of the Roman Catholic community in Britain offers a self-understanding of a major Christian tradition. Its format is threefold: a news review of an area of the church's life (e.g. 'the church serves' or 'the church learns') is followed by a reflective account of the principles involved in that area, and the section ends with information about the organizations or structures within the church which support activity in that area.

Boff, L. and C., *Introducing Liberation Theology*, Burns & Oates, 1987. ISBN 0 86012 156 9
A simple, authoritative introduction to a significant development in the Christian presence in Latin America by two of the movement's creative thinkers and actors.

Broun, J., *Conscience and Captivity*, Ethics and Public Policy Center, 1988. ISBN 0 89633 130 X
Although the map, political relations and hopes of Eastern Europe continue to change, there is still much in this book which explores and explains the religious scene up to its date of publication. While the text is principally concerned with the Christian tradition, there is also much here about Islam's position in the countries presented. A factual survey of tensions between political institutions and religious communities.

Chadwick, H. and Evans, G. R., *Atlas of the Christian Church*, Macmillan, 1987. ISBN 0 333 44157 5 (Hbk)
Particularly notable for its illustrations, this coffee-table book offers the Christian tradition's history, spread, practice and belief in one volume.

Hastings, A., *A History of English Christianity 1920–1990*, SCM, 1991. ISBN 0 334 02496 X
This account rapidly became a classic, largely

because it sensitively gets inside so many traditions and so many issues. It is essential reading for anyone who wants to understand the present situation of churches in Britain.

Herrin, J., *The Formation of Christendom*, Fontana, 1989. ISBN 0 00 686182 2
A very readable account of the period between the fall of Rome and the coronation of Charlemagne, this book indicates something of the indebtedness of the West to the Arabs and to Byzantium, as well as to the synods of the 4th century. The 'Dark Ages' are illuminated here.

Parratt, J. (ed.), *A Reader in African Christian Theology*, SPCK, 1987. ISBN 0 281 04308 6
A selection of 12 essays by African theologians and Christian leaders, this volume offers insight into the richness and diversity of the Christian tradition on a continent where its growth and vitality are notable.

Ware, T., *The Orthodox Church*, Penguin, 1963. ISBN 0 14 020592 6
Something of a classic now: a treatment of the Orthodox tradition, its history, beliefs and practices.

Visual expression

Dillenberger, J., *Style and Content in Christian Art*, SCM, 1986. ISBN 0 334 02344 0
This is a useful essay on the processes of representing Christian concerns in a concrete form, which raises, *inter alia*, questions about what is Christian and what is art.

Moore, P., *Christianity*, Ward Lock, 1982. ISBN 0 7062 4125 8
This remains the best short introduction to the ways in which Christians have expressed and transmitted their 'experience through dress, dance, drama, music, language, writing, painting, sculpture, the places where they worship and the objects used in their ceremonies'.

Scharper, P. and S., *The Gospel in Art by the Peasants of Solentiname*, Orbis Books, 1984. ISBN 0 88344 382 1 (Hbk); Gill & Macmillan, 1984. ISBN 0 7171 1333 7 (Hbk)
Sixty-eight pages of double-page spreads, each of which comprises both a vigorous painting by one of this Nicaraguan base community, expressing his or her understanding of the gospel lection for the day in the idiom of the present, and an associated excerpt of the kind of dialogue about the reading which has come to take the place of a homily within their liturgy. The book makes an excellent introduction to Liberation Theology seen from within, as a way of being Christian rather than thinking or talking about it.

Takenaka, M., *Christian Art in Asia*, Kyo Bun Kwan, 1975. (Hbk)
These visuals firmly root Christian tradition in a non-Western cultural setting and show how vigorously it is being interpreted. The book's introductory essay raises questions about what might be meant by 'Christian' art; its arrangement is loosely thematic: Creation and Promise; Incarnation; Ministry; Suffering and Victory; Discipleship in the World.

Wessels, A., *Images of Jesus*, SCM, 1990. ISBN 0 334 00697 X
Concerned primarily with conceptual (before visual) images, this is an excellent introduction to the variety of Christologies to be found in Christian traditions. Attentive to historical roots and political dimensions in imaging Jesus, the author introduces his readers to, e.g. Black and Liberation Theologies; to Jewish and Muslim perspectives; to Hindu and Buddhist connections. The book's bibliography is useful.

Values and issues

Where Christianity meets the world it encounters questions – about political issues, about the presence of other great religious traditions, about its own claims of truth. Some of these encounters are discussed in the books in this section.

Cragg, K., *The Christ and the Faiths*, SPCK, 1986. ISBN 0 281 04240 3
An authoritative, sometimes demanding discussion of Christian encounter with others in the religious world by an expert practitioner of dialogue.

Forrester, D. B., *Theology and Politics*, Blackwell, 1988. ISBN 0 631 15283 0
A readable introduction to the history and present state of uneasy relations between Christians and political power. It includes a discussion of Liberation Theologies.

Gill, R., *Christian Ethics in Secular Worlds*, Clark, 1991.
ISBN 0 567 29198 7
A sensitive introduction to what is presently
happening in Christian ethics, this little book is
rooted in real issues. Gill treats questions relating to
the environment and to society.

Gosling, D., *A New Earth*, CCBI, 1992.
ISBN 0 85169 222 2
An excellent introduction to current Christian
thinking about the environment and human relations
with it. The author, professionally and personally
involved in ecological issues, both surveys
ecumenical Christian teaching in this area and
develops a viewpoint in which questions of justice
and peace are seen to be interdependent with the
integrity of creation.

Hampson, D., *Theology and Feminism*, Blackwell, 1990.
ISBN 0 631 14944 9
Sharply focusing questions about the relation of
women and Christianity, this book argues that,
because Christianity is neither true nor moral, it is
ideologically loaded against women and is
incompatible with women's proper religious
aspirations. New, post-Christian ways of talking
about God are essential. The author urges a position
in which women's equality with men is seen as an
ethical issue.

Jones, R. G., *Groundwork of Christian Ethics*, Epworth,
1984. ISBN 0 7162 0399 5
Sets out clearly and systematically issues in the
methodology of Christian moral decision-making: a
good introduction.

Morley, D., *The Sensitive Scientist*, SCM, 1978.
ISBN 0 334 01386 0
A fascinating series of ethical studies by a
distinguished multi-disciplinary working group
including scientists, ethicists and theologians. The
working group developed from an approach by the
Royal Society to the British Council of Churches
seeking discussions on ethical issues raised by the
practice of the sciences; medical, genetic and
environmental questions are among the issues
discussed. Although now dated, this volume offers
insights and methods that remain relevant to present
concerns.

Peacocke, A., *Theology for a Scientific Age*, Blackwell,
1990. ISBN 0 631 15426 4 (Hbk)
Written by an ordained academic scientist, this book
explores ways in which Christians may speak of God
in an age whose framework of understanding the
world differs from that in which classical doctrines
were framed.

Polkinghorne, J., *Science and Creation: the search for
understanding*, SPCK, 1988. ISBN 0 281 04344 2
An academic physicist and priest, Polkinghorne
writes an introduction to the discussion of the
relation of scientific and theological thought-forms in
the question of 'creation'.

Christianity

Books for the classroom

Bennett, O., *Colin's Baptism*, Hamish Hamilton, 1986.
ISBN 0 241 11846 8
Picture book with explanatory text which documents
a family's preparation for their baby's baptism and
the ceremony (Anglican) itself. KS 2.

Brown, A., *The Christian World*, Macdonald, 1984.
ISBN 0 356 07523 0; Simon & Schuster, 1992. (Pbk)
An information book providing a cameo of
Christianity; powerful visuals picking up the
tradition's dimensions. KS 2–3.

Brown, A. and Perkins, J., *Christianity*, Batsford, 1988.
ISBN 0 7134 5319 2
From the series Dictionaries of World Religions, this
volume offers a series of cross-referenced articles,
which will prove a helpful resource at GCSE level.
Usefully indexed and offering a helpful bibliography.
KS 3–4.

The Chichester Project, Lutterworth/Clark:
1 Rankin, J., *Christian Worship*, 1982.
   ISBN 0 7188 2499 7
2 Brown, A., *Christian Communities*, 1982.
   ISBN 0 7188 2455 5
3 Erricker, C., *Christian Experience*, 1982.
   ISBN 0 7188 2497 0
4 Shannon, T., *Jesus*, 1982. ISBN 0 7188 2498 9
5 Curtis, P., *Exploring the Bible*, 1984.
   ISBN 0 7188 2575 6

6 Curtis, P., *The Christians' Book*, 1984.
ISBN 0 7188 2576 4

7 Shannon, T., *Christmas and Easter*, 1984.
ISBN 0 7188 2577 2

8 Erricker, C., *Christian Ethics*, 1984.
ISBN 0 7188 2578 0

9 Rankin, J., *The Eucharist*, 1985. ISBN 0 7188 2607 8

Curtis, P., *Christianity*, Lutterworth, 1986.
ISBN 0 7188 2633 7
Books One–Nine are intended for use at KS 3–4; the unnumbered volume was written with upper juniors in mind. Each book, in A4 format, comprises a mixture of source material, visual and written, and varied activities. There are plenty of good black and white pictures – but the absence of colour is a pity. The books are not intended as a scheme – each stands in its own right – but together they attempt to give a 'rounded' picture of the Christian tradition. There is an associated book for teachers: Erricker, C. (ed.), *Teaching Christianity*, Lutterworth, 1987, ISBN 0 7188 2634 5, a collection of essays relating in part to the themes of the student books, but also addressing a wide range of related issues, e.g. Commitment and the RE Teacher, Classroom Practice, Visits.

Cole, W. O., *Christianity*, Stanley Thornes, 1989.
ISBN 1 871402 08 5
A GCSE text in the World Religions series. Distinctive in that it includes chapters on areas not always given attention in texts on Christianity: Anti-Semitism, Racism and Apartheid, Peace, War and Liberation Theology, Christianity among the Religions. KS 4–GCSE.

Courtie, B. and Johnson, M., *Christianity Explored*, Lion, 1990. ISBN 0 7459 1800 X
Written specifically for students preparing for GCSE, this volume emphasizes the place of the Bible in Christian tradition. Fifty-eight units in 224 pages explore Christian belief and practice in relation to traditions about Jesus and the developing church. There are also sections on the creed and people whose views were held to be heretical. A typical unit is substantially the offering of information through a variety of source materials linked to a 'follow-up' box containing questions. KS 4.

Cush, D. *et al.*, *Christians in Britain Today*, Hodder & Stoughton, 1991. ISBN 0 340 51947 9
Through a series of interviews with named people, the authors draw a picture of the present variety of Christian practice, experience and belief in Britain. KS 3–4.

Davey, C., *John Wesley and the Methodists*, Marshall, Morgan & Scott, 1985. ISBN 0 551 01290 0
Large format information book with colour and black and white illustrations introducing the beginnings of Methodism for children in the middle years. KS 2–3.

Hammond, J. and Jacob, M., *Christian Belief and Practice*, Oliver & Boyd, 1990. ISBN 0 05 004312 9
Some pressing issues (e.g. peace and war; work and wealth; humankind and nature; marriage and the family) are studied in the light of central Christian convictions as they are expressed in the Eucharist. A feature of this book is its attention to the Christian tradition in Latin America and in Africa. KS 4.

Holm, J. and Ridley, R., *Growing up in Christianity*, Longman, 1990. ISBN 0 582 00283 4
One of the Cambridge Project books, with interesting text which uses first-hand experience to convey the significance of practice and belief. Good colour photographs and a genuine attempt to draw on the cultural diversity of the Christian tradition. KS 2–3.

Hughes, R. O., *Christianity*, Longman, 1991.
ISBN 0 582 02970 8
Colour and black and white illustrations which draw on Christianity in many cultural contexts, and a lively text with assignments suggest this will be a very accessible book for GCSE. One of the series Themes in Religion. KS 4–GCSE.

Jenkins, J., *Christianity*, Heinemann Educational, 1989. ISBN 0 435 30312 0
This volume in the Examining Religions series is designed to support work towards GCSE, and covers the roots, growth and present diversity of Christianity. Written so as to support either thematic or systematic study, the book's units seek to engage a student with source material, verbal and visual. KS 4.

Jenkins, J., *Contemporary Moral Issues*, Heinemann Educational, new edition, 1992. ISBN 0 435 30317 1
A large-format book in the Examining Religions

series, in three parts: personal issues, social issues, global issues. It offers 93 distinct units, looking at issues from a Christian perspective and from non-religious standpoints, especially that of Humanism. Double-page spreads offer stimulus material and ways for a student to engage with the topic. Teachers using the volume will need to ensure that students appreciate that Christian moral perspectives can be more complex and subtle than those sketched here, but the selection of topics is useful. KS 4.

Lealman, B., *Christian Buildings*, CEM, 1990. ISBN 1 85100 009 7
A booklet intended to stimulate interest in Christian buildings (not just churches), their uses and the people who use them. Shows the variety of Christian architecture, from the Canadian Arctic to Australasia. A poster pack of six A3 posters is available to accompany the booklet. KS 4–GCSE.

Living Festivals Series:

Ewens, A., *Advent*, RMEP, 1987. ISBN 0 08 034372 4

Mayled, J., *Christian Festivals*, RMEP, 1988. ISBN 0 08 035099 2
Teacher's Handbook of photocopiable masters and brief notes to use alongside student texts in the series. KS 2–3–4.

Sampson, F., *Ascensiontide and Pentecost*, RMEP, 1986. ISBN 0 08 031775 8
Earlier books in this Living Festivals series looked at Christmas, at Shrove Tuesday, Ash Wednesday and Lent, at Holy Week and Easter. Short books outlining what is remembered: key aspects of the celebration, symbols and the meaning of the festivals. KS 2–3–4.

Martin, N., *Old Testament Stories*, Wayland, 1986. ISBN 0 85078 862 5; *The Life of Jesus*, Wayland, 1986. ISBN 0 85078 865 X; *The Lives of the Saints*, Wayland, 1986. ISBN 0 85078 885 4
Three selections of stories that Christians tell; from Wayland's Religious Stories series. Less successful than the series' presentation of those from other traditions, especially in the illustrations, but usable.

Morton, S. A., *Encounters: a sketchbook of world Christianity*, CEM, 1992. ISBN 1 85100 047 X
A handbook of more than 80 examples of Christianity

in action from over 50 countries, biased towards the Third World. Considers encounters with other faiths and cultures, politics, conflict, human need and the environment. KS 4-Teacher Resource.

My Belief Series:

Killingray, M. J., *I am an Anglican*, Franklin Watts, 1986. ISBN 0 7175 1069 7

Roussou, M., *I am a Greek Orthodox*, Franklin Watts, 1985. ISBN 0 86313 259 6

Pettenuzzo, B. and Fairclough, C., *I am a Pentecostal*, Franklin Watts, 1986. ISBN 0 86313 428 9
I am a Roman Catholic, Franklin Watts, 1985. ISBN 0 86313 258 8
Established series, in which each book looks at a particular religious tradition through the eyes of a young child. Good illustrations and simple explanatory text. KS 2.

Read, G., Rudge, J. and Howarth, R. B., *Christianity*, Mary Glasgow, 1986. ISBN 0 86158 895 9
This teacher's manual, part of The Westhill Project, RE 5–16, sets out the series' understanding of the Christian tradition in three broad sections: Christian beliefs; Christian spirituality; and Christian practices related to family life, personal life, community life and public life. Christianity is treated as a World Religion in an open way and the manual ends with a suggested teaching scheme on Christianity for KS 1–4.

Read, G., Rudge, J. and Howarth, R. B., *Christians*, Mary Glasgow, 1987.
1. 0 86158 694 8, KS 1
2. 0 86158 695 6, KS 2
3. 0 86158 696 4, KS 3
4. 0 86158 697 2, KS 4
Part of The Westhill Project, RE 5–16, these four volumes offer a systematic progression throughout four key stages towards an understanding of the Christian tradition. The volumes are accompanied by a photopack (0 86158 896 7) of 20 pictures and notes. The course is closely related to an underlying 'map' of religious education which allows an 'open' approach. KS 1–4.

Rye, J., *The Story of the Christians*, CUP, 1986. ISBN 0 521 31748 7

An information book to survey the growth and diversity of the Christian church. Simple illustrations. KS 2–3.

Self, D., *Stories from the Christian World*, Macdonald, 1986. ISBN 0 356 11508 9
Nineteen stories ranging from St Aidan to Harriet Tubman, St Francis to Samuel Adjai Crowther, Thomas More to Corrie Ten Boom. KS 2.

Thomas, R. and Stutchbury, J., *The Pope and the Vatican*, Macmillan Australia, 1986.
ISBN 0 333 43017 4
Focusing on Pope John Paul II, this slim simple volume of 30 pages uses its illustrations, photographs and text to introduce young readers to the Pope and the Vatican. KS 2.

Vaughan, J., *Easter in Greece*, Macmillan, 1988.
ISBN 0 333 46975 5
Picture book with simple text which focuses on the celebration of the festival in a Greek community. KS 1–2 (lower end of age range).

Windsor, G. and Hughes, J., Exploring Christianity series, Heinemann Educational, 1990:
Jesus and the Birth of the Church. ISBN 0 435 30270 1;
Worship and Festivals. ISBN 0 435 30273 6;
The Bible and Christian Belief. ISBN 0 435 30271 X;
Christian Life, Personal and Social Issues.
ISBN 0 435 30272 8
The series was designed for the lower secondary school. Each volume comprises double-page spreads, alternating between black and white and colour presentation; they are in large format and seek to promote active learning. The variety of the Christian present and the tradition's roots are both explored. KS 3.

What the Churches Say on Moral and Social Issues, CEM, 1991. ISBN 1 85100 042 9
A pack of materials produced by seven major churches, concerning the ways in which they arrive at agreed statements and what they have said on six issues: relationships and the family; medical ethics; law and order; prejudice and discrimination; environment and world development; peace and war. KS 4 and above.

Wintersgill, B., *Christianity: a living faith*, Macmillan, 1989. ISBN 0 333 37644 7

Written with the demands of GCSE in mind, this volume stresses both a wide picture of Christianity and an activity-based approach to learning. The belief dimension is explored as a thread emerging in each chapter and interlocked with each facet of the tradition. It offers suggestions for coursework. KS 4.

Wood, A., *Being a Christian*, BFSS National RE Centre, 1990. ISBN 1 872012 03 5
This slim volume of 64 pages, whose author draws attention to the beliefs of the Jewish community, is an attempt to get inside another faith and let it speak for itself. The result is an interesting collection of source material illuminating many aspects of Christian community, practice and faith. Suggestions for engagement with the text are offered at the close of each section. KS 3–4.

Hinduism

Books for teachers
General

Basham, A. L., *The Sacred Cow*, Rider, 1990.
ISBN 0 7126 3946 2
An account of the origins and development of classical brahmin tradition, posthumously edited from unpublished papers. Covers some of the same ground as Zaehner's *Hinduism* (OUP, 1962) and Brockington's *The Sacred Thread*, as well as Basham's great work, *The Wonder that was India*. The latter has frequently been published in paperback since its first publication (1954). It is long (568 pages) but fine on Indian culture, history and society, as well as religion.

Biardeau, M., *Hinduism: the anthropology of a civilisation*, OUP, 1989. ISBN 0 19 562409 2
This book brings together the diversity of Hindu themes in a unity of treatment.

Brockington, J., *The Sacred Thread: Hinduism in its continuity and diversity*, EUP, 1981.
ISBN 0 85224 393 6
A comprehensive and scholarly treatment which is reasonably cheap. This is a clear, balanced survey of Hindu tradition from prehistoric to modern times. It is illustrated with black and white photographs and supported by a very useful bibliography. Amid the

great diversity, Brockington traces a continuity of philosophical emphasis. Particularly helpful background for teachers in upper secondary.

Dumont, L., *Homo Hierarchicus: the caste system and its implications,* University of Chicago Press, 1981 (revised edition). ISBN 0 226 16963 4
The influential and epoch-making scholarly analysis of the Hindu caste system seen within the Hindu world view.

Hopkins, T. J., *The Hindu Religious Tradition,* Dickenson, 1971. Library of Congress, 74 158118
A very good historical introduction to the Hindu tradition.

Source books

de Bary, W. T., *Sources of Indian Tradition,* two vols, Columbia University Press, 1958. ISBN 0 231 08600 8 and 0 231 08601 6
Still the best single source book, including fine background comments.

O'Flaherty, W. D., *Hindu Myths: a sourcebook translated from the Sanskrit,* Penguin, 1975.
ISBN 0 14 044306 1
A fine scholar gives a comprehensive and insightful account of the main Hindu myths in their textual background. Again, most useful for teachers of upper secondary classes. Includes Hindu texts from five languages – but mainly Sanskrit – accessible in readable English, amply annotated. Ritual is a major theme, but philosophy, narrative and doctrinal texts are included.

Panikkar, R., *The Vedic Experience: an anthology of the Vedas for modern man,* Dartman Longman & Todd, 1977. ISBN 0 232 51438 0 (Hbk)
A thematic collection of Vedic texts, aimed at contemporary understanding and a possible contemporary celebration. Long.

Ramanujan, A. K., *Speaking of Siva,* Penguin, 1973. ISBN 0 14 044220 7
Devotional Poems of the Virashaiva or Lingayat sect, translated from the Kannada language by a poet and scholar.

Zaehner, R. C., *Hindu Scriptures,* Dent, 1966 and various reprints. ISBN 0 460 01944 9
A fine selection of the classical scriptures.

Zaehner, R. C., *The Bhagavad Gita with a Commentary Based on the Original Sources,* OUP, 1969 (Pbk 1973). ISBN 0 19 501666 1
Probably the best book written by a scholar on a scripture from outside the tradition. Influenced by the author's own ideas, but a great help in approaching this important text.

Art and aesthetics

Eck, D. L., *Banaras: the City of Light,* Routledge, 1983. ISBN 0 7102 0236 9
A sensitive insight into Banaras, the premier Hindu holy city, which gets inside the Hindu view of what Banaras means.

Eck, D. L., *Darsan: seeing the divine image in India,* Anima, 1981. ISBN 0 89012 042 0
A superb 79-page insight into Hindu aesthetics.

Kramisch, S., *The Art of India: traditions of Indian sculpture, painting and architecture,* Phaidon, 1965. BNB ref.: B65–18762
A well illustrated account of Indian Art.

Michell, G., *The Hindu Temple: an introduction to its meaning and forms,* Harper & Row, 1977.
ISBN 0 236 40088 6
Singles out the Hindu temple for special treatment and does it in a straightforward and helpful way.

Stutley, M., *An Illustrated Dictionary of Hindu Iconography,* Routledge, 1985.
ISBN 0 7100 9294 6 (Hbk)
The headwords are Sanskrit terms for the various mythological figures, animals, plants, gestures, ornaments etc., used in classical Hindu art. A glossary enables you to find the entry you want. Clear descriptions, illustrated with line drawings.

Zimmer, H. R., *Myths and Symbols in Indian Art and Civilisation,* Princeton University Press, 1945 (Hbk); Bollingen, 1972. ISBN 0 691 01778 6 (Pbk)
The classical account by a great scholar of India and of myth, edited by another great scholar and interpreter of myth and symbol (Joseph Campbell).

Themes

Babb, L. A., *The Divine Hierarchy: popular Hinduism in Central India,* Columbia University Press, 1975.

ISBN 0 231 03882 8
An anthropologist's observations and interpretations of Hindu practice, which show how some of the important all-India concepts are understood in a particular region.

Ions, V., *Indian Mythology*, Paul Hamlyn, 1967; Newnes, 1983 (revised edition).
ISBN 0 600 34285 9 (Hbk)
An illustrated survey of main Hindu mythological themes.

Jackson, R. and Killingley, D., *Moral Issues in the Hindu Tradition*, Trentham Books, 1991.
ISBN 0 948080 50 7
A useful book for teachers who are using GCSE syllabuses in Religious Studies and for students taking higher education courses that ask for some knowledge of Hindu ethics. There is material here on the family and marriage, peace, conflict and minority rights, humankind and nature: material not so readily accessible elsewhere.

Killingley, D. (ed.), *Hindu Ritual and Society*, Grevatt & Grevatt, 1991. ISBN 0 947722 06 8
Three essays on caste, marriage rituals and death rituals. If you already know something about Hindu ritual and social norms, this will help you to understand the complexities involved in putting them into practice.

Kinsley, D., *Hindu Goddesses: visions of the divine feminine in Hindu religious tradition*, University of California Press, 1986. ISBN 0 520 05393 1
A clear insight into the theme of the goddess in the Hindu tradition.

Kinsley D., *The Sword and the Flute: Kali and Krishna*, University of California Press, 1975.
ISBN 0 520 02675 6
Another clear insight into two main Hindu themes: the goddess Kali and the Lord Krishna.

Lott, E., *Vedantic Approaches to God*, Macmillan, 1980.
ISBN 0 333 27109 2
Helpful introduction to the three main Vedantic schools which are central for Hindu thought.

Narayan, R. K., *Gods, Demons and Others*, Macmillan/Heinemann, 1965. ISBN 0 434 49600 6
A retelling by an Indian author of the outstanding Indian myths and their function in the Indian village setting. Narayan's retelling of these popular stories from the epics is a lively continuation of a timeless tradition. Recommended for teachers of all age groups!

Whaling, F., *The Rise of the Religious Significance of Rama*, Motilal Banarsidass, 1980.
The main account of the religious significance of the Hindu Lord Rama, and the Ramayana.

Hindus in the UK

Bowen, D. F., (ed.), *Hinduism in England*, Bradford College, 1981.
Seven essays on the Hindu tradition in different parts of England, the first attempt to survey the English situation.

Burghart, R. (ed.), *Hinduism in Great Britain*, Tavistock, 1987. ISBN 0 422 60910 2
An anthology of papers on various aspects of the Hindu scene in Britain, including chapters on 'Sectarian' movements, as well as studies based in particular locations in the UK. There is also an analysis of changing conceptions of Hinduism in the RE literature.

Modern Hinduism

Knott, K., *My Sweet Lord: the Hare Krishna movement*, Aquarian Press, 1986. ISBN 0 85030 432 6
An interesting account of an important recent movement of Hindu origin which attracts converts in the West. Includes useful explanations of its relations with the Hindu tradition.

Radhakrishnan, S., *The Hindu View of Life*, Unwin, 1960. ISBN 04 294045 1
Classic 1927 lectures giving a modern Hindu insight into the philosophical essence of the Hindu tradition through Vedanta eyes.

Richards, G., *A Sourcebook of Modern Hinduism*, Curzon Press, 1985. ISBN 0 7007 0173 7
A valuable resource on the main Hindu reformers from Ram Mohun Roy to recent times.

Handbooks relating to teaching Hinduism

Jackson, R. and Killingley, D., *Approaches to Hinduism*,

John Murray, 1988. ISBN 0 7195 4362 2
This was written specifically for teachers and combines an introduction to the tradition with detailed guides to books for teachers and pupils and audio-visual suggestions for teaching at all age phases. The book points out the dangers of thinking in terms of an entity called 'Hinduism'. Instead, the loosely knit Hindu tradition is illustrated with case studies of Hindus from different parts of India and in the diaspora (including England). Each case study illustrates a theme (e.g. family, society, sects and movements, life cycle rituals) and is followed by a more general discussion and then teaching ideas.

Killingley, D. (ed.), *A Handbook of Hinduism for Teachers*, Grevatt & Grevatt, 1984. ISBN 0 9507918 6 5
Written by a team of teachers and others, with advice on classroom approaches. The primary section aims to give a feel for Hindu culture, using play and story. The secondary section has more factual detail, but with emphasis on what the tradition means for Hindus. Line drawings.

Postscript

In addition to the books listed above the following titles relating mainly to women's issues are suggested in relation to chapter 9 in section 2.

Alexander, Meena *et al.*, *The Slate of Life: an anthology of stories by Indian women*, Kali for Women, New Delhi, 1990.

Bardhan, K. (ed.), *Of Women, Outcastes, Peasants and Rebels*, University of California Press, 1990.

Bennett, L., *Dangerous Wives and Sacred Sisters: social and symbolic roles of high-caste women in Nepal*, Columbia University Press, 1983.

Gatwood, L., *Devi and the Spouse Goddess: women, sexuality and marriages in India*, Riverdale, Maryland, 1985.

Hawley, J. S. and Wulff, D. M. (eds.), *The Divine Consort: Radha and the goddesses of India*, Beacon Press, Boston, 1986.

Holmstrom, Lakshmi (ed.), *The Inner Courtyard: stories by Indian women*, Virago, 1990.

Jung, A., *Unveiling India: a woman's journey*, Penguin, 1987.

Leslie, J. (ed.), *Roles and Rituals of Hindu Women*, Pinter Publishers, London, 1991.

Liddle, J. and Joshi, R., *Daughters of Independence: gender, caste and class in India*, Zed Books, London, 1986.

Mitter, S., *Dharma's Daughters: contemporary Indian women and Hindu culture*, Rutgers University Press, New Brunswick, 1991.

Narayana Rao, Velcheru, 'A Ramayana of their own: Women's oral tradition in Telegu', in Paula Richman (ed.), *Many Ramayanas: the diversity of a narrative tradition in South Asia*, University of California Press, 1991.

Hinduism

Books for the classroom

Note: story material is listed separately here in view of the many collections that are available.

Aggarwal, M. and Fairclough, C., *I am a Hindu*, Franklin Watts, 1984. ISBN 0 86313 168 9
One of the titles in the popular My Belief series. Hinduism through the eyes of a young child, portrayed in colour photographs with a simple text and background information. KS 2.

Bahree, P., *Hinduism – an Illustrated Dictionary*, Batsford, 1984. ISBN 0 7134 3654 9
Clear, short articles, a useful resource book for secondary students. KS 3–4.

Bahree, P., *The Hindu World*, Macdonald, 1989. ISBN 0 356 07521 4 (Hbk); Simon & Schuster, 1992 (Pbk).
Lucid introduction to many facets of Hinduism; its excellent illustrations and photographs provide a 'text' in their own right and offer much to explore with children. KS 2–3.

Bennett, O., *Holi: Hindu festival of spring*, Hamish Hamilton, 1987. ISBN 0 241 11986 3
Children in a school in Coventry are shown preparing for and celebrating Holi. Colour photographs and a clear direct text which looks at the festival's story and also its celebration in home and mandir. KS 2.

Cole, W. O., *Meeting Hinduism*, Longman, 1987.

ISBN 0 582 22385 7
An introduction to Hinduism, drawing on India and Britain, and focusing on key areas, e.g. Hindu villages, caste, family life, scriptures. Black and white illustrations – overtaken by more imaginative illustration and colour in more recent Longman publications. KS 4.

Deshpande, C., *Divali*, A & C Black, 1985/1987. ISBN 0 7136 2643 7
An account of a class (in which there are a number of Hindu children) discovering Divali. Excellent colour photographs, clear direct text, and a source of ideas for teachers. *My Class at Divali* (Franklin Watts, 1986) follows a similar line, but portrays all white children. KS 1–2 (lower end).

Hirst, J. with Pandey, G., *Growing up in Hinduism*, Longman, 1990. ISBN 0 582 00285 0
From 'The Cambridge Project'. This series offers a young person's view of what it means to be a member of a world faith and to grow up in a religious family. This is an informative and attractive introduction to Hinduism drawing on Hindu practice and experience in Britain, as well as recognizing Indian roots. KS 2–3.

Jackson, R., *Religions through Festivals: Hinduism*, Longman, 1989. ISBN 0 582 31788 6
An approach to Hinduism by way of its festivals, this book uses pictures and Hindus speaking to foster understanding of the tradition. Its value lies also in the range of festivals covered – Navaratri, Ganesha Chaturthi, Janmashtami and Pongal, for example. KS 3.

Jackson, R. and Nesbitt, E., *Listening to Hindus*, Unwin Hyman, 1990. ISBN 0 04 448121 7
As its title suggests, this book helps the reader to encounter the experience of Hindus living out their beliefs – largely in Britain in the present. Illustrations are used in the text, as are extracts of Hindus speaking – the reader is invited to engage with them. KS 3–4.

Kanitkar, V. P. (Hemant), *Hinduism*, Stanley Thornes & Hulton, 1989. ISBN 1 871402 09 3
A very thorough overview of Hinduism for GCSE students, written out of the author's experience of the tradition in India and in Britain. The book is written in two parts – 'The Living Faith' and 'Historical Perspective' – and offers both a more detailed and broader coverage of Hinduism than most GCSE texts. Some GCSE candidates will find it difficult and it is likely to be of use to A level students and to teachers. KS 4 and above.

Kanitkar, V. P. (Hemant), *Indian Food and Drink*, Wayland, 1986. ISBN 0 85078 897 8
A resource book which will be of interest not just for the information it gives on the religious aspects of food, but also for its notes on regional variations in diet and its nutritional comments. KS 2–3.

Mercier, S. C., *Hinduism*, Longman, 1991. ISBN 0 582 02968 6
From the Themes in Religion series. Material is arranged around the themes of worship, beliefs and concepts, rites of passage, celebrations and pilgrimage, whilst a final section on values considers how Hindus respond to the contemporary world. Good quality illustrations. KS 4–GCSE.

Mitchell, P., *Dance of Shiva*, Hamish Hamilton, 1989. ISBN 0 241 12550 2
From The Way We Live series, this is an introduction to the Bharata Nayam tradition of dance, provided through the experience of two girls and their dance lessons. Excellent colour photographs throughout. KS 2.

Oldfield, K., *Hindu Gods and Goddesses*, CEM, 1987. ISBN 1 85100 035 6
Straightforward and accessible introduction. KS 3–4 –Teacher Reference.

Shanson, L. and Chowdry, A., *Journey with the Gods*, Mantra, 1987. ISBN 0 94679 80 4
The story of two children, awoken by the light of a magical moon, who embark on an adventure with gods and heroes from Indian mythology: Shiva and Parvati, Ganesh, Ram and Sita, Hanuman and Krishna are all encountered. A colourfully illustrated book. KS 2.

Suthren Hirst, J., *The Story of the Hindus*, OUP, 1989. ISBN 0 521 26261 8
A clear and straightforward introduction to Hinduism accessible to children in the middle years. KS 2–3.

Wood, J., *Our Culture: Hindu*, Franklin Watts, 1988.
Picture book with simple text introducing aspects of
Hindu life for young children. Many of the pictures
appeared first in *I am a Hindu* (see above). KS 1.

Collections of stories

Chatterjee, D., *The Elephant-Headed God and other
Hindu Tales*, Lutterworth, 1989. ISBN 0 7188 2786 4
Twelve stories from Hindu Mythology. KS 2–3.

Dalal-Clayton, D., *The Adventures of Young Krishna:
the blue god of India*, Lutterworth, 1991.
ISBN 0 7188 2839 9 (Hbk)
A collection of stories about Krishna which focus
particularly on his birth and childhood in Vrindaban.
KS 2–3.

Gavin, J., *Stories from the Hindu World*, Macdonald,
1986. ISBN 0 356 11509 7 (Hbk)
Twelve popular stories, simply told and illustrated
with brief explanatory notes for the teacher. KS 2.

Husain, S., *Demons, Gods and Holy Men from Indian
Myths and Legends*, Peter Lowe, 1987.
ISBN 0 85654 050 1 (Hbk)
A collection of 40 stories from all parts of the sub-
continent, including India, Pakistan and Bangladesh.
The book is illustrated with 18 large full colour
paintings in traditional Indian style, supplemented by
line drawings. It offers an index to people and places
in the stories. Includes material from the Mahabharata
and the Ramayana, as well as stories about Shiva.
Useful source for teachers. KS 3–4 and above.

Jaffrey, M., *Seasons of Splendour*, Puffin Books, 1987.
ISBN 0 14 031854 2
Tales, myths and legends of India organized in such a
way as to be linked with the author's personal
experiences of India, its festivals and her own
childhood. Richly illustrated by Michael Freeman. A
book for all ages, but likely to be used at the stages
indicated. KS 1–2–3.

Singh, R., *The Indian Storybook*, Heinemann, 1984.
ISBN 0 434 96330 5
Eight stories recalled by Rani Singh and told in a
style for which she has become known. The stories
include some not so frequently found in other
collections. KS 2.

Singh R. and J., *The Amazing Adventures of Hanuman*,
BBC Books, 1988. ISBN 0 563 21425 2
The story of Hanuman, including his part in rescuing
Sita, well told and with clear colourful illustrations.
KS 1 and KS 2.

Thompson, B., *The Story of Prince Rama*, Viking
Kestrel, 1980. ISBN 0 670 80117 8 (Hbk)
A telling of the story of Rama, beginning with his
childhood. This book is special on account of its
colourful illustrations, many of them coming from a
300-year-old Rajput manuscript from north-west
India, now in the British Library. From KS 2 – all ages.

Islam

Books for teachers
General

Ahmad, K., *Islam: its meaning and message*, Islamic
Council of Europe, 1976.
Fourteen writers from many parts of the Muslim
world speak of beliefs, values, social principles,
cultural aspects and contemporary problems; of
Muhammad, the Qur'an, social justice, women,
politics and present-day crises and challenges.

Danner, V., *The Islamic Tradition*, Amity House, New
York, 1988. ISBN 0 916349 16 0
An introduction to Islam for the general reader which
tries to convey something of the experience of being
Muslim and the tensions the tradition faces in the
contemporary world.

Khabani, R., *Letter to Christendom*, Virago, 1989.
ISBN 1 85381 119 X
A personal memoir of growing up as a Muslim,
offering an insight into Muslim identity and heritage
through the eyes of one woman. An insightful piece
of writing prompted by the experience of Western
prejudice towards Muslims.

Lewis, B. (ed.), *The World of Islam*, Thames and
Hudson, 1976, ISBN 0 500 25046 4 (Hbk); 1992.
ISBN 0 500 27624 2 (Pbk)
Encyclopaedic volume which introduces Islam,
primarily through its rich culture and attempts to
explore its achievements. Prepared originally to
coincide with the World of Islam Festival in 1976.

Nasr, S. H., *Ideals and Realities of Islam*, Allen and Unwin, 1966. ISBN 0 04 297034 2
An introduction to key aspects of Islam which attempts to convey something of the 'innerness' of Muslim practice and experience. There have also been various paperback editions of this volume – evidence of its continuing popularity.

Rahman, F., *Islam*, University of Chicago Press, 1979. ISBN 0 226 70281 2
An attempt to introduce the general development of Islam throughout the approximately 14 centuries of its existence. The author aims at description but recognizes that as a Muslim there is also an interpretative element in what he writes. Useful introductory chapters, e.g. on the Shari'a, on theological and philosophical movements in the early centuries of Islam, and on sectarian developments.

Rippin, A., *Muslims: their religious beliefs and practices: vol. 1: The Formative Period*, Routledge, 1990. ISBN 0 415 04519 3
Contribution to an established series, which attempts a scholarly analysis of Islam. Considers structural elements in the formation of Islam, the emergence of Islamic Identity, and 'alternative visions' of such identity (Shi'ism, Sufism). The book is intended to redress a perceived absence of critical thought in many textbooks on Islam. Such an approach will inevitably be at odds with Muslim self-understanding and thus highlights the perennial tensions raised by 'Western' analyses of Islam.

Robinson, F., *Atlas of the Muslim World since 1500*, Phaidon, 1982. ISBN 0 7148 2200 0
Coffee-table book introducing the global significance of Muslim history and Muslim society. Part One deals with revelation and Muslim history, looking at this from 622 to the present century. Part Two, headed 'To be a Muslim', considers religious life, arts of Islam, society and the modern world. Good illustrations throughout – many in colour.

Qur'an and Hadith

There are many interpretations of the Qur'an available in English. *The Meaning of the Glorious Qur'an* (M Pickthall) has often been recommended and remains available in different editions. Among acceptable and accessible interpretations Yusuf Ali's is widely available in the UK in a number of editions, some with introductory essays and commentary.

A number of books offer passages from the Qur'an arranged thematically. Among these the following are readily available, the first having enjoyed a wide circulation:

Irving, A., *The Qur'an: basic teachings*, Islamic Foundation, 1979. ISBN 0 86037 021 6
This offers an excellent introduction and the themes it covers include the Book, ideas of God, creation, prophethood, creed, aspects of morality and society and the state.

Brown, K. (ed.), *The Essential Teachings of Islam*, Rider, 1987. ISBN 0 7126 1669 1 (also available as an Arrow paperback, 1992).
From a series of books designed for the followers of a faith and for those 'outside' who want to discover more. A passage for reading for each day of the year is offered – in this case drawn from Qur'an and Hadith – followed by a commentary drawing the reader's attention to important points.

Cragg, K. (ed.), *Readings in the Qur'an*, Collins, 1988. ISBN 0 00 599087 4
Selected teaching translated by an editor, well known for his sympathetic studies of Islam, though he writes out of a Christian tradition. Carefully indexed so that one can always trace the full context of a passage in the Qur'an.

Maulana, Muhammad Ali, *A Manual of Hadith*, Curzon Press, 1979. ISBN 0 7007 0110 9
A manual of Hadith drawn from Bukhari's collection and covering key aspects of Muslim life. Brief introductory notes and commentary on each aspect. Arabic and English text.

Robinson, N., *The Sayings of Muhammad*, Duckworth, 1991. ISBN 0 7156 2365 6
This collection of Hadith is selected and translated by Robinson, drawing mainly on Bukhari's collection but supplemented by sayings from other canonical collections. The sayings are presented under 24 headings including: The Qur'an, the Unity of God; Prayer and the Mosque; the Fast of Ramadan; Women,

Marriage and Divorce, abstracted from Bukhari's original 97. An accessible and readable collection.

Muhammad

Because of the (commonly) divergent perspectives here between Muslim and non-Muslim authors, books are listed separately.

Muslim authors

Bashier, Z., *The Makkan Crucible*, Islamic Foundation, 1991. ISBN 0 86037 204 9

Bashier, Z., *Sunshine at Madinah*, Islamic Foundation, 1990. ISBN 0 86037 196 4
Two volumes which draw on original Arabic sources and modern writings on the Sirah (biography of the Prophet) to present Muhammad in a way which expresses a Muslim point of view. *Sunshine at Madinah* also pays attention to the nature and characteristics of the society and state established under Muhammad which, it is suggested, offer a model for the present.

Lings, M., *Muhammad*, Allen & Unwin, 1983. ISBN 0 04 297042 3 (Hbk) (Also available in pbk)
A biography of the Prophet based on the earliest sources.

Zakaria, R., *Muhammad and the Qur'an*, Penguin, 1991. ISBN 0 14 014423 4
The author was prompted to write this as old prejudices about the Prophet and the Qur'an emerged in the wake of the publication of Rushdie's *The Satanic Verses*. This is not strictly a biography, nor a translation of the whole text of the Qur'an, but an attempt to 'bring out the essentials of what Allah has pronounced and what his messenger preached and practised'. Particular attention is given to dealing with those aspects of the Prophet's life which are attacked by non-Muslims. This book also contains a selection of Qur'anic verses freely translated in a contemporary spoken style.

Non-Muslim authors

Armstrong, K., *Muhammad*, Gollancz, 1991. ISBN 0 575 05012 8
Subtitled 'A Western Attempt to understand Islam', Karen Armstrong's book distinguishes her approach to a biography of the Prophet by taking as her starting point the reality of Muhammad's religious experience, and recognizing the inheritance of the representation of Muhammad in the West.

Cragg, K., *Muhammad and the Christian*, Darton, Longman & Todd, 1984. ISBN 0 232 51599 9
How non-Muslims might/should see and understand Muhammad may be seen as an underlying tension in their encounter with the Muslim tradition. Cragg addresses the issue from within a Christian tradition, but comes to it only after a careful description of the multiple significance of Muhammad within Islam.

Rodinson, M., *Muhammad*, Penguin, 1971. ISBN 0 14 021271 X
These are probably the two most frequently cited treatments of Muhammad – though both are unacceptable to Muslims in their approach and estimation of the Prophet. Most recent books present similar problems for the Muslim, though Armstrong's book has received some favourable comment.

Watt, M., *Muhammad: prophet and statesman*, OUP, 1961. ISBN 0 19 881078 4

Belief and practice

Al-Ghazali, *Inner Dimensions of Islamic Worship*, Islamic Foundation, 1983. ISBN 0 86037 125 5
Selections from the author's major work *Ihya*, exploring prayer, almsgiving, fasting, pilgrimage etc., with regard to their inner qualities, their spiritual, moral and social dimensions. There are many memorable quotations from the Prophet and earlier Muslim writers, all seeking to integrate action, thoughtfulness, and meditation in perfect balance.

Amin, M., *Pilgrimage to Mecca*, Macdonald & Jane's, 1978. ISBN 0 354 04347 1
A photographic record of the Hajj which beautifully captures the spirit and devotion of the worshippers. Many of the pictures are excellent discussion starters. The multi-faceted approach, including the making of the Kiswah, makes the journey a living experience for all who read, look and meditate.

Hamid, A. W., *Islam: the natural way*, MELS (61 Alexandra Road, Hendon, London NW4 2RK),

1989. ISBN 0 948196 09 2
Written by a Muslim, this book is intended for anyone, Muslim or non-Muslim, who wishes to understand the main concerns of Islam and the foundations on which it is built. The reader is addressed in a personal way and invited to engage with existential issues. It is an accessible and readable book with a clear layout, and covers areas not always readily available elsewhere, e.g. on family, livelihood, and on Muslim attitudes to other religions.

Lemu, B. A. and Heeren, F., *Women In Islam*, Islamic Council of Europe/Islamic Foundation, 1978. ISBN 0 86037 004 6
Short booklet based on papers given by two women converts to Islam, where they set out to address this 'misunderstood' area. They focus on women in Islam, family life in Islam and discuss related issues such as dress and inheritance.

Nasr, S. H. (ed.), *Islamic Spirituality: foundations*, SCM, 1985/1989 (Pbk). ISBN 0 334 02429 3
In the series World Spirituality: An Encyclopaedic History of the Religious Quest. A full and detailed collection of papers. Sections on the inner dimensions of prayer, pilgrimage, fasting and jihad and on the Qur'an as foundation of Islamic spirituality are particularly helpful. Useful – used selectively – for 'A' level.

Rahman, A., *Islam: ideology and the way of life*, Muslim Schools Trust, 1980 (78 Gillespie Road, London N5 1LN). ISBN 0 907052 04 5
A book of basic information about Islam. The first part looks at Muslim understanding of God and the nature of human response, whilst the second looks at faith and practice, offering chapters, e.g. on education, economics, the legal system and the social system.

Ullah, M. Z., *Islamic Concept of God*, Kegan Paul International, 1984. ISBN 0 7103 0076 X
A very clear exposition in short chapters of the relationship between God and humankind in everyday life. Many helpful references and quotations speak of good and evil, happiness and sorrow as well as all aspects of faith. An unusual and thought-provoking introduction.

Islamic culture

Brend, B., *Islamic Art*, British Museum, 1991. ISBN 0 7141 1443 X
Documentation of Islamic art over 1,200 years, from the 7th to 19th centuries CE. Looks at architecture, manuscripts, ceramics and glass, metalwork, textiles and carpets from a wide range of locations, exploring both a shared heritage and the diversity of styles. A concluding section addresses the question of the specific nature of Islamic art, its influence beyond Islam and its 'activity' in the present.

Burckhardt, T., *The Art of Islam*, World of Islam Festival Publishing Co, 1976. ISBN 0 905035 00 3 (Hbk)

Lings, M. and Safadi, Y. H., *The Qur'an*, World of Islam Festival Publishing Co, 1976. ISBN 0 905035 21 6

Nasr, S. H., *Islamic Science*, World of Islam Festival Publishing Co, 1976. ISBN 0 905035 02 X (Hbk)
Two unique books giving insight into the meaning and significance of art for Muslims (rather than just the art historian's perspective), whilst the third maps out a distinctive Muslim perspective on the world as well as recognizing the insights and achievements of Islamic science.

Islam in Europe

Barton, S., *The Bengali Muslims of Bradford*, University of Leeds, Community Religions Project, 1986.
A small study of one group of Muslims in the UK; offers particular insight into the part played by the Imam in the community.

Nielsen, J., *Muslims in Western Europe*, Edinburgh University Press, 1992. ISBN 0 7486 0309 3
This volume has much to offer: a brief history of the presence of Muslim communities in Europe; a country by country examination of their specific situation in the different countries; a section devoted to the comparative consideration of issues common to Muslims in all Eastern European countries, e.g. role of the family, questions of worship, organization, education and religious thought. Useful bibliographical essay for those who want to take these concerns further.

Raza, M. S., *Islam in Britain: past, present and future*, Volcano Press (PO Box 139 Leicester LE2 2YH), 1991. ISBN 1 870127 35 8
Looks at Islam in its secular British context and is based on interviews, questionnaires, research reports and other sources examined by the author. Addresses questions to the Muslim community in Britain about where they stand in the present. Considers topics such as leadership, Muslim political participation, youth and Westernization.

Note: for those wanting to gain a picture of Islam in countries outside Europe *The World's Religions* (1988) (see p. 158) offers useful surveys of Islam across the world under its section on Islam: the section is also available as a separate book: P. Clark (ed.), Routledge, *Islam*, 1990. ISBN 0 415 05814 7

Teacher handbooks

Ashraf, S. A., *Islam: Teacher's Manual*, (The Westhill Project RE 6–16), Stanley Thornes, 1988. ISBN 0 7487 1040 X
Intended as an introduction to Islam for teachers, the book deals with key ideas, beliefs, spirituality and practices. A teaching scheme is provided incorporating sample units of work.

Lynch, M., *Islam*, CEM, 1990. ISBN 1 85100 X
This book contains 11 headings, each of which deals with basic aspects of Islam. The text is straightforward information, broken up by simple line drawings which may be photocopied (though some may want better quality drawings to present to children).

Sarwar, G., *Islam*, Muslim Educational Trust, 1984. ISBN 0 907261 03
A detailed book with sections on basic beliefs, duties and on the life of the Prophet. There are a large number of Qur'anic references and a section giving examples of Hadith. Intended as a text for Muslim children of secondary school age; interesting for the teacher to use as a source and for insight into a 'confessional' approach.

Tames, R., *Approaches to Islam*, John Murray, 1982. ISBN 0 7195 3914 5
This is still a useful starting point for teachers, with its succinct introductory essays and bibliographies;

the latter contain many 'classics', but need updating now – as do the teaching schemes in Part Two.

Islam

Books for the classroom

Aggarwal, M. and Nazir, A., *I am a Muslim*, Franklin Watts, 1985. ISBN 0 86313 138 7
Written for the lower end of the age-group, the volume explores the life of an 11-year-old boy living with his family in Birmingham. Each brief section is introduced by a bold informative sentence by the boy and the colour pictures are an excellent resource. KS 2.

Ardavan, J., *Growing up in Islam*, Longman, 1990. ISBN 0 582 00287 7
A lively presentation of what it means to grow up in a Muslim family. Written for the middle years. A comprehensive survey illustrated by excellent personal comments and memories. Again, a useful book for older students also. KS 2–3.

Ashraf, S. A., *Islam*, Stanley Thornes, 1991. ISBN 1 871402 10 7
A text designed for GCSE classes, but probably one to which teachers will turn for reference. The text is quite difficult for GCSE candidates. Provides a historical perspective, a study of 'the foundations of Islam and the Islamic way of life'. It concludes with reflections on Islam in the world today. KS 4 and above.

Azzam, L. and Gouverneur, A., *The Life of the Prophet Muhammad*, Islamic Texts Society, 1985. ISBN 0 946621 02 0
Written for young people of 10–12 years of age. The clarity and attractive style make this a readable and enjoyable biography for all ages. The text is based on traditional Muslim biographical literature and Hadith; an authentic introduction to the life of the Prophet. KS 2–3–4.

Brine, A., *Religions through Festivals: Islam*, Longman, 1989. ISBN 0 582 31786 X
Based on the beliefs and practices of one community of British Muslims, this volume explores Ramadan, and fasting, the Night of Power which 'celebrates' the Qur'an, Eid ul-Fitr, the Hajj and Eid ul-Adha and New Year's Day. Well illustrated, the text is matched by interesting and lively comments and quotations. KS 3.

Brine, A., *Islam, (Themes in Religion)*, Longman, 1991. ISBN 0 582 02967 8
A lively and thoughtful presentation with challenging quotations and diverse tasks, frequently encouraging research and discussion. The material is made relevant and interesting for children of all faiths and none. A strong active learning approach with many good sized, coloured illustrations which destroy any danger of stereotyping. KS 4–GCSE.

Bennett, O., *Festival! Ramadan and Eid ul-Fitr*, Macmillan Education, 1986. ISBN 0 333 37898 9

Kerren, R., *Festival! Ramadan and Eid ul-Fitr* (Teachers' Notes), Macmillan Education, 1986. ISBN 0 333 37902 0
A joint publication of Macmillan and the Commonwealth Institute. The topic book attempts to look at the festival within its religious, cultural and historical context, and also at its customs and traditions. The Teachers' Notes include photocopy master worksheets. KS 2–3.

Davies, M., *The Life of Muhammad*, Wayland, 1987. ISBN 0 85078 904 4
Six stories highlighting key moments in the life of the Prophet. The book (written by a practising Muslim) provides brief but helpful notes for teachers and uses interesting geometric and calligraphic illustration. KS 2.

Kendrick, R., *Islam (Examining Religions)*, Heinemann Educational, 1989. ISBN 0 435 30314 7
The scheme follows the pattern of others in the series written to be used with GCSE syllabuses. It is organized in self-contained double page spreads explaining 76 aspects of Islam – the life of Muhammad, beliefs, rituals, history and modern issues etc. The text is accompanied by thinking points, things to do, a quick quiz and work for individual folders. KS 4 – GCSE.

Khattab, H., *Stories from the Muslim World*, Macdonald, 1987. ISBN 0 356 11563 1
Thirteen stories relating to the beginning of Islam, Muslims in history and including folk tales from the Muslim world. KS 2.

Mayled, J., *Muslim Festivals* (Teachers' Book), RMEP, 1990.
A book which accompanies earlier classroom material (1982) on Ramadan and Eid ul-Fitr, offering a basic overview of aspects of Islam and 30 worksheets which extend beyond the theme of festivals. KS 3.

Morris, A. and Larson, H., *Uzma's Photo Album*, A & C Black, 1989. ISBN 0 7136 3099 X
Picture book with simple text tells of Uzma's visit to Pakistan and her experiences there; these are shared with her class with the help of her mother. Offers a glimpse into one Muslim child's life and experience. KS 1–2.

Read, G. & Rudge, J., *Muslims 1*, Mary Glasgow, 1988. ISBN 1 85234 073 8
Muslims 2, Mary Glasgow, 1988. ISBN 1 85234 074 6
Muslims 3, Mary Glasgow, 1988. ISBN 1 85234 075 4

Hunt, D., *Muslims 4*, Stanley Thornes, 1989. ISBN 1 871401 17 4

Ashraf, S. A., *Islam* (Teacher's Manual), Mary Glasgow, 1988. ISBN 1 85234 071 1
Materials from the Westhill Project RE 5–16 developed across the age phases to foster understanding of the tradition as expressed in personal, family, community and public life. Twenty colour photographs in A3 format, with background information (*Muslims Photopak*, ISBN 1 85234 072 X) complement the books. The teacher's handbook provides a detailed introduction to Islam, in five parts: Islam: a world religion, Muslim beliefs, Muslim spirituality, Muslim practices, and Islam past and present. Suggestions for approaching Islam and sample teaching units for junior and secondary age phases comprise the remainder of the book. A useful glossary and list of terms is provided. All these resources are now published by Stanley Thornes Ltd. KS 2–3–4.

Stone, S., *Eid ul-Fitr*, A & C Black, 1988. ISBN 0 7136 3054 X
Picture book with clear text which approaches this festival from the perspective of two Muslim children and their class discovering Islam through a range of experiences, including the celebration of Eid ul-Fitr.

Sugich, S., *Living in Makkah*, Macdonald, 1987. ISBN 0 356 10327 7
Well illustrated and clearly written, in consultation

with Muslims. Focuses on Hajj, but also provides a picture of daily life in Makkah throughout the year. KS 2–3.

Tames, R., *The Muslim World*, Macdonald, 1984. ISBN 0 356 07520 6; (Pbk) Simon and Schuster, 1989. ISBN 0 7500 1194 7
The brief but explicit text is matched by some excellent illustrations, e.g. the Muslim boys reading the Qur'an. A reference book rather than a text book, it explores the rise and spread of Islam, beliefs and rituals, art and science. A useful book for older students also. KS 2–3.

Wood, A., *Being a Muslim*, Batsford, 1987. ISBN 0 7134 4667 6
From the series 'Looking into World Religions', which sets out to give insight into world religions by introducing them through a range of literature and other sources. Black and white photographs, but not of a very good quality. KS 3–4.

Wood, J., *Muslim, (Our Culture)*, Franklin Watts, 1988. ISBN 0 86313 673 7
A very attractive introduction to the faith, using enlarged illustrations from *I am a Muslim* on each page with full lines of bold text. The illustrations are excellent for discussion. KS 1.

Judaism

Books for teachers

A selection of books which is drawn largely from within the Jewish tradition.

Alexander, Philip (ed.), *Textual Sources for the Study of Judaism*, Manchester University Press, 1984. ISBN 0 71901 700 9
Alexander has gathered together an impressive collection of extracts from original texts which, taken together, give an invigorating insight into the literary activity of the Jewish people, as well as the impact of historical circumstances on Jewish cultural and religious life.

Authorised Daily Prayer Book, Singers Prayer Book Publication Committee, 1990. ISBN 0 521 50762 6
The centenary edition of this comprehensive prayer book has the added advantage of a number of essays

(as well as explanatory notes) giving insight into a range of features of Jewish liturgy throughout the year. Also, an invaluable bonus is the Ethics of the Fathers, that section of the Talmud always reprinted in the Prayerbook, which gives access to the thinking of the rabbis as well as reminding the student of the forms of Jewish study/worship.

Engle, Fanny and Blair, Gertrude, *The Jewish Festival Cookbook*, Dover, 1987. ISBN 0 486 25573 5
While the text is a little too rooted in Eastern Europe (its form is that of the authors reminiscing about what the festivals were like when they were girls), there are a large number of excellent recipes, all placed in the context of the celebration of key festivals. The truly thorough teacher will seek a book that gives Oriental Jewish recipes to maintain a balanced palate!

Gilbert, Martin, *Holocaust, The Jewish Tragedy*, Fontana, 1986. ISBN 0 006 37194 9
One of the great and definitive texts on the subject. Gilbert's marshalling of the facts replicates the inexorable process of the 'Final Solution'.

Gilbert, Martin, *Jewish History Atlas*, Weidenfeld, 1992. ISBN 0 297 2112 1
Like Gilbert's other atlases, this provides graphic, memorable and comprehensive insights into the history of the Jewish people. The technique is simple but brilliant. The straightforward maps help comprehension and support a coherent sense of Jewish history and the interrelationship between one episode and another.

Heschel, Susannah, *On Being a Jewish Feminist*, Schocken Books, 1988. ISBN 0 805 20745 7
Heschel's book is a valuable reminder that it is important to Jews to keep interpreting the tradition in the light of new pressures and ideas. There is a widespread misconception that there is something intrinsic to Judaism which is inimical to feminism. This book challenges those ideas and will ensure a more balanced presentation of the issues in class discussions.

Hertz, J. H., (ed.), *Pentateuch and Haftorahs*, Soncino, 1988. ISBN 0 900689 21 8
The best way in to Jewish perspectives on the Torah. Hertz's commentary is a model of enlightened

scholarship. Almost every verse of Torah receives treatment drawing on rabbinic interpretations through the ages, as well as the findings of the secular scholarship current in his day.

The Jewish Chronicle
The national Jewish newspaper. A regular subscription and a weekly skim of its columns will give one of the best insights into the preoccupations and priorities of the Jewish community at any given time.

Levi, Shonie and Kaplan, Sylvia, *Guide for the Jewish Homemaker*, Schocken Books, 1978. ISBN 0 8052 0087 8
Feminism has not come to Levi and Kaplan! This book gives an unselfconscious and spirited exposition of the Jewish woman as homemaker. Nowhere is it suggested that that must be all she does, but throughout the book every line suggests that, whatever else she does, it will not be as good as making a Jewish home. An important counterbalance to Heschel's book (see above).

Newman, Louis I. (ed.), *The Talmudic Anthology*, Behrman, 1945. ISBN 0 87441 303 6
A lovely anthology of rabbinic sayings on almost every topic under the sun. A lazy browse through its pages will give a deeper understanding of the attitudes of the rabbis than a considerable amount of more methodical study.

Rose, Aubrey (ed.), *Judaism and Ecology*, Cassell, 1992. ISBN 0 304 32378 0
A collection of essays which reveals that Judaism has a long and valued tradition of respect for the environment. The book offers a timely reminder, since most people's experience of Jews is as city-dwellers, that the Jews are in origin an agricultural people and the aspirations to the land demand the re-assessing of the Laws and traditions relating to agricultural and ecological behaviour.

Rosenbaum, Irving J., *The Holocaust and Halakhah*, Ktav, 1976. ISBN 0 87068 296 2
A fascinating and remarkable book. Rosenbaum discusses moral and religious dilemmas that arose during the Holocaust and presents the solutions offered at the time by Jewish religious law (halakhah). The vitality of Jewish thought, even in its darkest hour, is testimony to the indomitability of the Jewish spirit.

Schauss, Hayyim, *The Jewish Festivals*, JC Publications, 1986. ISBN 0 900498 96 X
Reprinted in 1986, this was first written in 1938. As a result, the Hebrew names of festivals are written in an archaic form of Hebrew that most students of Judaism will not recognize and there is no reference to the modern festivals that have emerged following the establishment of the State of Israel, like Yom Ha'atzma'ut – Israel Independence Day. For all that, it is almost certainly still the definitive text and well worth having.

Strassfeld, M., *The Jewish Holidays: a guide and commentary*, Colophon Books, Harper and Row, 1985. ISBN 0 06 091225 1
In the same vein as the Jewish Catalogues, this book weaves the traditional and the contemporary, the communal and the individual, the letter and the spirit. Full and detailed text, with margin commentary from five colleagues of Strassfeld.

Steinsaltz, Adin, *The Essential Talmud*, Basic Books, 1976. ISBN 0 465 02063 1
Without doubt, the best way in to the Talmud. The book contains separate sections on the history, format and content of the Talmud.

Unterman, Alan, *Jews, Their Religious Beliefs and Practices*, Routledge, 1981. ISBN 0 415 04026 4
An excellent summary of the beliefs and practices of Judaism. The book's only weakness is one to which Unterman himself alludes. He does not deal with those moral and religious principles and teachings which he believes to be broadly normative in Western society. The failing of this approach is, first, to assume that there is any agreement on what represents those principles and, secondly, by not including them, Judaism appears to be a rather obscure tribal religion, obsessed with ritual and out of touch with the pressing moral and religious issues of the day.

Wouk, Herman, *This is My God – The Jewish Way of Life*, Souvenir Press, 1988. ISBN 0 285 63067 9
One of the most readable and fluent introductions to what it is to be a Jew. It can virtually be read as a novel, the fiction being that Wouk imagines himself

writing to explain to his child what being Jewish means to him.

Judaism

Books for the classroom

Eban, Abba, *My People – History of the Jews*, two vols., Behrman, 1976/1979. ISBNs 0 87441 263 3 and 0 87441 280 3
Volume One covers the period up to the 19th century; Volume Two starts from 1776. Attractively illustrated, fluently written, these two history books make the full span of Jewish history accessible to children. KS 3 and KS 4.

Forta, Arye, *Examining Religions: Judaism*, Heinemann Educational, 1989. ISBN 0 435 30513 9
One of the best books of its kind. Forta ranges over the full span of Jewish practice, taking the pupil beyond GCSE level, but always in accessible language. The only weaknesses are a lack of imagination on activity suggestions, poor illustrations and a certain imbalance between Orthodox and Progressive practice. He tends to present 'ultra-orthodox' practice as normative. KS 4 and beyond.

Frank, Anne, *The Diary of Anne Frank*, Pan, 1953. ISBN 0 330 10737 2
Generations of children have gained an understanding of what it is to be a normal Jewish girl in abnormal circumstances through this beautiful and poignant book. No fiction writer has done better. KS 3–4.

Gersh, Harry, *When A Jew Celebrates*, Behrman, 1986. ISBN 0 87441 091 6
Gersh examines the various different occasions that Jews celebrate by reviewing a Jew's progress through time. There are illuminating sections on the various stages of the life cycle, the different festivals and even a little section at the end about the end of days and the Messianic Age. Suitable for top end KS 3 and KS 4, but at its best when judiciously used by the teacher.

Gilbert, Martin, *Atlas of the Holocaust*, Pergamon, 1988. ISBN 0 08 036761 5

Martin Gilbert has perfected the techniques of using maps to reveal the processes of history. Pupils will explore the subject by themselves through working out the implications of the maps before them. A particularly effective way of accessing the subject of the holocaust, which is all too often overlaid with the kind of emotionalism or moral demand that leads pupils to withdraw from or reject the subject. KS 3–4.

Jacobs, Louis, *The Book of Jewish Practice*, Behrman, 1987. ISBN 0 87441 460 1
Louis Jacobs is one of the great communicators of Jewish teaching and practice and almost anything by him is worth reading. This is one of his few works designed directly for the pupil and, except for occasional overestimates as to the correct level of language, this would give the interested pupil much food for thought and resources for further study. KS 4.

Lawton, Clive A., *I Am A Jew*, Franklin Watts, 1984. ISBN 0 86313 139 5
Good full colour photographs, and a two-level text which has a Jewish girl talking about her own life and Lawton expanding the details make this one of the best introductory primary books on the subject. KS 1–2.

Lawton, Clive A., *Religions Through Festivals – Judaism*, Longman, 1989. ISBN 0 582 31790 8
A ready-made series of lessons, taking the pupil through all the festivals of Judaism and connecting them up with the central themes and teachings that they convey. A wide-ranging and imaginative collection of activities are suggested, facilitating course work. KS 3.

Lawton, Clive and Erricker, Clive, *Themes in Religion – Judaism*, Longman, 1992. ISBN 0 582 02969 4
Similar in format to *Religions Through Festivals*, this text explores key themes in Judaism taking the pupil into KS 4 and to GCSE.

Lawton, Clive, *The Seder Handbook*, Board of Deputies of British Jews, 1984.
This little handbook gives the teacher and pupil all they need to know to organize and enact their own model passover Seder in the classroom or school hall. It includes instructions, recipes, and abridged text and songs. KS 2–3–4 and beyond.

Mitchener, James A., *The Source*, Corgi, 1965.
ISBN 0 552 08790 4
Just one, but possibly the best, of the blockbuster novels that give an effective insight into aspects of Jewish life. Other authors like Maisie Moscoe, Leon Uris and Chaim Potok produce novels that reveal information about Jews and Judaism as part of their fabric, but *The Source* takes the reader right through the span of Jewish history. KS 4.

Parfitt, Tudor, *Operation Moses*, Weidenfeld, 1985.
ISBN 0 297 78672 5
A telling of the remarkable operation by the Israeli authorities to airlift the Jews of Ethiopia out of their famine- and war-torn country. As inspiring for the stoic determination of the Ethiopian Jews as for the inescapable theme of Jewish solidarity across racial boundaries. KS 4.

Patterson, Jose, *Mazaltov – A Jewish Wedding*, Hamish Hamilton, 1988. ISBN 0 241 12269 4
An attractive, well illustrated account of a Jewish wedding which took place in Britain recently. The book reveals, through its pictures and text, just how similar Jewish weddings and the aspirations of the participants are to most weddings in Britain. Along the way it also shows the distinctive features of Jewish weddings without allowing Jews to appear as if they are from another planet! KS 2.

Ray, E., *Sofer: The Story of a Torah Scroll*, Torah Aura Productions, 1986. ISBN 0 933873 04 2
A slim large format book with good black and white photographs, a beautifully written Hebrew alphabet and an interesting and informative commentary on each character. If you want to know how a scroll is written, how tephillin are made, or mezuzot prepared – this is all here. And there is more: the qualities of the person who is a scribe come through, too. KS 2–3–4 and adult.

Siegel, Strassfeld and Strassfeld (eds.), *The First Jewish Catalogue*, Jewish Publication Society of America, 1973. ISBN 0 8276 0042 9

Strassfeld and Strassfeld (eds.), *The Second Jewish Catalogue*, Jewish Publication Society of America, 1976. ISBN 0 8276 0084 4
Both catalogues are taken together because they are similar in format. Although perhaps a little dated now, they still represent one of the most refreshing, amusing and informative explorations of Jewish practice and belief. They give practical guides to practice, philosophical explanations and ideas for exploring traditions more deeply. Lovely books for pupils (and teachers) to research in and explore. KS 4.

Wood, Angela, *Judaism – Dictionaries of World Religions*, Batsford, 1984. ISBN 0 7134 3656 5
A comprehensive and invaluable glossary of terms used in (the study of) Judaism. A voyage through its pages is almost as good as an organized course on the subject. Unfortunately the pictures are mostly poor. KS 2–3–4.

Wood, Jenny, *Our Culture – Jewish*, Franklin Watts, 1988. ISBN 0 86313 671 0
This is a simplified version of Lawton's *I Am a Jew* (see above). As such, it is almost the only well designed book to give children a good visual access to the subject at their own level of interest. KS 1.

Sikhism

Books for teachers

General

Three brief introductions for teachers with no previous knowledge of the Sikh religion:

Nesbitt, E., in the *Hutchinson Encyclopaedia of Living Faiths*, Hutchinson, 1988. ISBN 0 091735769

Shackle, C., *The Sikhs*, Minority Rights Group (29 Craven Street, London WC2N 5NT), 1986.
ISBN 0 94669041 2

Cole, W. O. and Piara Singh Sambhi in the Introduction to *A Popular Dictionary of Sikhism*, Curzon Press, 1990. ISBN 0 7007 0204 4
This dictionary is an essential aid for teachers and students at GCSE and beyond.

More detailed studies are found in:

Cole, W. O. and Piara Singh Sambhi, *The Sikhs: Their Religious Beliefs & Practices*, Routledge, 1989 (reprint). ISBN 0 7100 8843 4
This is widely used internationally in colleges and universities; covers all aspects of Sikh religion.

Macauliffe, M. A., *The Sikh Religion*, six vols., OUP, 1963. Now published in three books by S. Chand & Co Ltd, New Delhi and available from Books from India, 45 Museum Street, London WC1A 1LR.
This overview of Sikhism is now 30 years old but is unsurpassed as a comprehensive presentation of the Sikh story from 1469 to 1708. The quality of translation of extensive sections of the Sikh scriptures is still highly regarded by many scholars.

Sikh history and Sikhs in the present

This is well covered in the following books:

Barrier, N. G. and Dusenbery, V. A., *The Sikh Diaspora*, Manohar, 1991. ISBN 81 7001 047 0
Examines and surveys the presence of Sikhs worldwide.

Kapur, R. A., *Sikh Separatism*, Vikas, 1987.
ISBN 0 7069 3788 0
This is a 'must for anyone who wants to know about the Sikhs and the problems they face today' according to Khushwant Singh. Essential reading for anyone trying to understand the tragic events of 1984 and their aftermath.

McLeod, W. H., *The Evolution of the Sikh Community*, OUP, 1976. ISBN 0 19 826529 8; *The Sikhs*, Columbia University Press, 1989. ISBN 0 213 06814 X; and *Who is a Sikh?*, OUP, 1989. ISBN 0 19 826548 4
McLeod's method of historical analysis and its findings have been severely criticized by some Sikhs who consider his aim, quite wrongly, that of under-mining the Panth. He is applying Western approaches to a religion which is not familiar with them.

O'Connell, J. T., Israel, M. and Oxtoby, W. G., *Sikh History & Religion in the Twentieth Century*, University of Toronto, 1988. ISBN 0 9692907 4 8 (Hbk); 0 9692907 5 6 (Pbk)
A collection of papers on issues relating to the modern period of Sikh history, society and religion.

Singh, D., *Western Perspective on the Sikh Religion*, Sehgal, New Delhi, 1991. ISBN 81 85477 02 7
A critical and perceptive examination of western studies of Sikhism from the 18th century until 1989.

Singh, Harbans, *Heritage of the Sikhs*, Manohar, 1985.

This is a survey of the period to 1969. A revision to cover the next 20 years is planned.

Singh, Khushwant, *A History of the Sikhs*, two vols., Princeton, 1966/OUP (India Edition), 1977.
ISBN 0 19 560600 0 and 0 19 560601 9 (available from Books from India).
This is the standard history and is essential to anyone studying the historical context of this religion.

Theology

McLeod, W. H., *The B 40 Janam Sakhi*, Guru Nanak Dev University, Amritsar, 1980.
The most accessible translation of a Janam Sakhi for English readers. It contains excellent notes; a Sikh Glossary in its own right.

McLeod, W. H., *Guru Nanak and the Sikh Religion*, OUP, 1968. ISBN 0 19 560806 2
Contains an excellent introduction to the teachings of Guru Nanak. The first section of the book, a quest for the historical Nanak of the kind which Westerners have embarked upon with regard to Jesus, was not well received by most Sikhs.

Singh, Dharam, *Sikh Theology of Liberation*, Harman Publishing House, New Delhi, 1991.
ISBN 81 85151 59 0
A detailed study of this particularly important area of Sikh beliefs.

Singh, Sher, *Philosophy of Sikhism*, Lahore, 1944 Amritsar, 1986.
A classic which has not been ousted by subsequent publications.

Textual sources

The Rehat Maryada Shromani Gurdwara Parbandhak Committee, Amristsar.
This authoritative Sikh Code of Discipline is the guide which should determine Sikh conduct, corporate and individual. (Copies may be available from gurdwaras.)

Manmohan Singh, *Guru Granth Sahib*, eight vols., Shromani Gurdwara Parbandhak Committee, Amritsar, 1969.

Gopal Singh, *Guru Granth Sahib*, four vols., World Sikh University Press, New Delhi, 1978.

Gurbachan Singh Tulib, *Guru Granth Sahib*, four vols., Punjabi University, Patiala, 1989.
There are no fully satisfactory translations of the complete scriptures, the *Guru Granth Sahib*. These are the three which are available. Selections are contained in Macauliffe (see above) and McLeod, W. H., *Textual Sources for the Study of Sikhism*, Manchester University, 1984, which contains extracts from many other Sikh writings and is, in effect, a survey of Sikhism through its most important texts.

Visual sources

McLeod, W. H., *Popular Sikh Art*, OUP, Delhi, 1991. ISBN 0 19 562791 1

Singh, Khushwant and Rai, Raghu, *The Sikhs*, Lustre Press Pvt Ltd, Varanasi, 1984.
Both the above, apart from being useful texts, are rich sources of visual material.

Sikhism in Britain

Kalsi, S. G., *The Evolution of a Sikh Community in Britain*, Leeds University Community Religions Project, 1992. ISBN 1 871363 03 9
A study of religious and social change among the Sikhs of Leeds and Bradford which pays particular attention to caste groups.

Darshan Singh Tatla, and Nesbitt, Eleanor M., *Sikhism in Britain: an annotated bibliography*, Centre for Research in Ethnic Relations, University of Warwick, 1987. ISBN 0 948303 06 9
Invaluable for its list of articles and books covering all aspects of Sikhs in the UK.

Fiction

Sharma, Partap, *Days of the Turban*, Futura, 1986. ISBN 0 7088 3640 2
Informed, gripping fiction set in turbulent Punjab of the 1980s.

Sikhism

Books for the classroom

Aggarwal, M. and Lal, H. S., *I am a Sikh*, Franklin Watts, 1984. ISBN 0 86313 147 6
The large print and excellent coloured photographs make this an attractive book to use with younger pupils. KS 1–2.

Arora, R., *Guru Nanak and the Sikh Gurus*, Wayland, 1987. ISBN 0 85078 906 0
Three stories about Guru Nanak, one concerning Guru Angad Dev, plus that of Guru Gobind Singh and the creation of the Khalsa. KS 2.

Babraa, D. K., *Religions Through Festivals: Sikhism*, Longman, 1989. ISBN 0 582 31787 8
The stories of the major festivals and the ways in which they are celebrated are well covered in this excellently illustrated book. KS 2–3–4.

Bennett, O., *A Sikh Wedding*, Hamish Hamilton, 1985. ISBN 0 241 11572 8
Attractive colour photographs. Covers both well known and less public features of a Sikh wedding. KS 1–2.

Bennett, O., *Listening to Sikhs*, Unwin Hyman, 1990. ISBN 0 04 448119 5
Well illustrated, interestingly written. A particular feature is the comments of Sikhs about their beliefs and practices. KS 3–4.

Bennett, O., *Our New Home*, Hamish Hamilton, 1990. ISBN 0 241 12569 3
Well illustrated text focusing on the blessing of a new home by temporarily installing the Guru Granth Sahib. KS 2.

Clutterbuck, A., *Growing up in Sikhism*, Longman, 1990. ISBN 0 582 00286 9
A straightforward, well written introduction viewed through the insights of children growing up in Sikhism. Its themes include rites of passage, festivals, scriptures, and worship. KS 2–3.

Cole, W. O., *A Sikh Family in Britain*, RMEP, 1985. ISBN 0 08 031780 4
A survey of those things which are important to young Sikhs living in Britain, offering background material on why Sikhs came to Britain and the beginnings of Sikhism, as well as information on many aspects of Sikh life. KS 2–3–4.

Cole, W. O., *Thinking about Sikhism*, Lutterworth/Clark, 1981. ISBN 0 7188 2421 0
Concentrates on beliefs and their significance.

Cole, W. O., and Sambhi, P. S., *A Popular Dictionary of Sikhism*, Curzon Press, 1990. ISBN 0 7007 0202 4
Essential reference book for GCSE and 'A' level work as well as KS 4.

Cole, W. O., and Sambhi, P. S., *Baisakhi*, RMEP, 1982. ISBN 0 08 031790 1
A detailed study of the stories, beliefs and practices relating to this important festival.

Dhanjal, B., *Sikhism*, Batsford, 1987. ISBN 0 7134 5202 1
A clearly written, well illustrated dictionary. A valuable library resource. KS 3–4–GCSE.

Harrison, S., *At Home and Abroad with Amardip and Rema*, Macmillan, 1986. ISBN 0 333 38610 8
The story of a Coventry family returning to the grandparental home in India. This series helps British children make the journey to other countries. The short hair of the family may upset some Sikhs, but it is authentic! KS 2–3.

Mansukhani, Gobind Singh; Kaur, Kanwaljit; Dua, Harcharan Singh; Grewal, Balwant Singh and Singh, Yadwinder, *Learning the Sikh Way*, British Sikh Education Council (10 Featherstone Road, Southall, Middlesex), 1990. ISBN 0 900 69215 4
Lavishly illustrated with photographs and paintings, this book, compiled by distinguished Sikh writers, should be in every school and will particularly boost the self-esteem of Sikh pupils. It covers the main areas of Sikh beliefs and practices.

Sambhi, P. S., *Sikhism*, Stanley Thornes, 1989. ISBN 1 871402 12 3
One of a series of GCSE text books written by practising members of particular faiths. Teachers in primary schools have found it a useful information book for their own use. It covers many aspects of Sikh belief and has useful sections, e.g. on the family, prayer and meditation, the status of women, equality and justice and Sikhism today. KS 4–GCSE.

Singh, D. and Smith, A., *The Sikh World*, Macdonald, 1985. ISBN 0 356 07525 7
Comprehensive, clearly written and beautifully presented, this is an essential book in any school where the Sikh religion is taught. KS 2–4–GCSE.

Singh, Rami and Jugnu, *Stories from the Sikh World*, Macdonald, 1987. ISBN 0 356 13165 3
Nine well told stories attractively illustrated by Jeroo Roy. Suitable for most ages of primary school children.

Souza, A., *The Sikhs in Britain*, Batsford, 1986. ISBN 0 7134 5100 9
A story of Sikh settlement, and the role of the gurdwara especially, seen through the lives of three families. Plenty of illustrations, not always of good quality. KS 4–GCSE.

Thorley, Sarah, *Sikhism in Words and Pictures*, REMP, 1989. ISBN 0 08 035102 6
Attractively designed book consisting of self-contained chapters on major aspects of Sikhism. KS 2–3.

Wood, J., *Our Culture: Sikh*, Franklin Watts, 1988. ISBN 0 86313 670 2
Colour picture book, derived largely from *I am a Sikh* (see above) with simple text. KS 1.

Fiction

Ashley, Bernard, *Running Scared*, Franklin Watts, 1986. ISBN 0 74511 099 1

Griffiths, Helen, *Hari's Pigeon*, Hutchinson, 1982. ISBN 0 091 494 10 9

Webster, Len, *The Turban-wallah, a Tale of Little India*, DVP, 1984. ISBN 0 1 927150 5
Three works of fiction, all giving engaging stories with accurate Sikh background detail. The generous use of colour photographs in these books in particular make them accessible to children at KS 1 in discussions with the teacher. KS 3–4.

III Further perspectives

The following titles are suggested by the authors of the articles in Section Three.

Bahá'í

(Books are arranged in ascending order of difficulty. *The Bahá'í Glossary*, by Marzich Gail, is very useful for meanings and pronunciation of Arabic and Persian words in the Bahá'í Writings.)

Esselmont, J. E., *Bahá'u'lláh and the New Era*, Bahá'í Publishing Trust, London, 1923/1974.

Ferraby, John, *All Things Made New*, Bahá'í Publishing Trust, London 1975.

Hatcher, William S. and Martin, Douglas J., *The Bahá'í Faith: the emerging global religion*, Harper and Row, San Fransisco, 1984.
An introduction to the history, teachings, administrative structure and community life of the Bahá'í Faith.

Huddleston, John, *The Earth is but One Country*, Bahá'í Publishing Trust, London, 1976.
The purpose of this book is to show how the Bahá'í Faith meets the needs of mankind today. The emphasis is on the practical means to the end.

Humanism

Blackham, H. J., *Humanism*, Penguin, 1968.
This classic account looks at history, philosophy and social aspects of humanism in some depth. Only available in libraries.

Herrick, Jim, *Against the Faith: some Deists, Sceptics and Atheists*, Glover and Blair, 1984.*
An attempt to give an account of the historical development of humanist ideas concentrating on individuals. Suitable for sixth-formers and the general reader.

Knight, Margaret, *Humanist Anthology: from Confucius to Bertrand Russell*, Pemberton Books, 1961.*
An anthology with extracts from a very diverse range of writers, including Epicurus, Voltaire, Hume and Einstein. Can be dipped into with profit by all readers from about 15 up.

Kurtz, Paul, *The Transcendental Temptation: a critique of religion and the paranormal*, Prometheus Press, USA, 1986.*
A very wide-ranging and thorough book by an American Professor of Philosophy. Covers scepticism and the paranormal as well as humanism.

Russell, Bertrand, *Why I am not a Christian and The Faith of a Rationalist*, Rationalist Press Association, 1983.*

Two short essays by a great 20th-century philosopher and humanist. Extremely lucid and suitable for a wide range of readers.

Smoker, Barbara, *Humanism*, Ward Locke, Educational, then National Secular Society, 1973.*
An introduction to humanism suitable for teenagers and for adults looking for a basic beginning.

Educational material relating to humanism can be acquired from the British Humanist Association, 14 Lamb's Conduit Passage, London WC1R 4RH

Items marked * can be obtained from the Rationalist Press Association, 15 Lamb's Conduit Passage, London WC1R 4RH

Inter-faith dialogue

Abhishktananda, *Hindu-Christian Meeting Point*, Christian Institute for the Study of Religion and Society, Bangalore, 1969.
A Christian monk turned sannyasin. Explores the meeting point in terms of spirituality and religious experience and is the forerunner of the more celebrated Bede Griffiths.

Cohn-Sherbok, D., *The Salman Rushdie Controversy in Interreligious Perspective*, Edwin Mellen Press, Lampeter, 1990.
A superb collection of essays dealing with the complex and explosive issues surrounding *The Satanic Verses*. Two Muslim contributions, a Jewish and a Hindu contribution and the other essays by Christians. Useful as the basis of class debates.

Coward, H., *Pluralism: Challenge to World Religions*, Orbis, New York, 1985.
An excellent introduction to sources and varieties of approach from within each of the five major religions and their attitudes to each other.

D'Costa, G., *Theology and Religious Pluralism*, Blackwell, Oxford, 1986.
Deals with the last 100 years of Christian attitudes to other religions and three detailed studies of selected Christian theologians, followed by a discussion of dialogue on a personal and institutional level.

D'Costa, G. (ed.), *Faith meets Faith*, BFSS (National RE Centre, West London Institute of Higher Education,

TW7 5DU), 1987.
A collection of essays from the five major religions, Sikhism and Humanism addressing the question of religious pluralism.

Doumlin, H., *Christianity meets Buddhism*, Open Courst, La Salle, Illinois, 1974.
A classic work on the very different issues raised by this particular East-West encounter in comparison with the encounter of the three Semitic faiths.

Griffiths, P. J. (ed.), *Christianity through non-Christian Eyes*, Orbis, New York, 1991.
A collection of source documents portraying the differing attitudes towards Christianity of other religious traditions. A fine collection, obtainable through Fowler Wright Books, UK.

Hick, J. and Askari, H. (eds.), *The Experience of Religious Diversity*, Gower, Aldershot, 1985.
Practitioners from different religious traditions write on their attitude towards other religions. Exemplifies the plurality within religious pluralism.

Lamb, C., *Belief in a Mixed Society*, Lion, London, 1985.
Written by an Anglican clergyman long involved in inter-faith matters, this deals with dilemmas primarily posed to Christians in a mixed society.

Lothain Community Relations Council, *Religions and Cultures: a guide to patients' beliefs and customs for health service staff*. Lothian CRC, Edinburgh, 1988.
An interesting booklet which deals with the differing religious groups' needs when in hospital. One could use this in many differing ways for student exercises.

Metzer, J. and Hick, J., *Three Faiths: One God*, Macmillan, London, 1989.
An interesting and uneven set of papers resulting from a trialogue between Jews, Christians and Muslims meeting in California. This is evidence of the fragmentary and sometimes discordant results of dialogue.

O'Neill, M., *Women Speaking, Women Listening: women in interreligious dialogue*, Orbis, New York, 1990.
A good guide to issues concerning women and inter-faith dialogue and the complexities and ambiguities involved in this whole area.

Watt, W. M., *Muslim–Christian Encounters, Perceptions and Misperceptions*, Routledge, London, 1991.
Specifically deals with the history of Muslim–Christian encounter. Full of fascinating details and insights, it places dialogue within its proper social, political and religious context. The final chapter shows how Watt, as a Christian, suggests a way forward into the future.

Jainism

Kalghatgi, *Study of Jainism*, Prakrit Bharati Academy, Jaipur, 1988.
An introductory text suitable for GCSE students.

Marrett, P., *Jainism Explained*, Jain Samaj Europe, Leicester, 1985.
A simple, concise, introductory book.

Oldfield, K., *Jainism: the path of purity and peace*, Christian Education Movement, UK, 1989.
A short introductory text with illustrations produced for teachers and useful for secondary students.

Shah, A. K., *Experiments with Jainism*, 1991. Available from 199 Kenton Lane, Harrow, Middlesex HA3 8TL.
This book covers practical aspects of ethics and religion focusing on Jainism. Useful at secondary level and above.

Tobias, M., *Life Force: the world of Jainism*, Asian Humanities Press, Berkeley, California, 1991.
This book is concerned with ecology and Jainism. Useful for teachers and students in higher education.

The Kogi of Northern Colombia

Ereira, A., *The Heart of the World*, Jonathan Cape, 1992.
This is the only work specific to the Kogi which has been published in the UK. A small number of interesting publications are available in the USA by G. Reichel-Dolmatoff.

'The loom of life: a Kogi principle of integration', *Journal of Latin American Lore*, vol. 4. no. 5, Los Angeles, 1978. 'The Great Mother and the Kogi Universe: a concise overview', *Journal of Latin American Lore*, vol. 13, no. 1, Los Angeles, 1987.

New Age
Non-fiction

Bloom, William (ed.), *The New Age*, Century, 1991.

A selection of writings from ecological, spiritual and psychological viewpoints. Some wonderful extracts!

Bloom, William, and Button, John, *The Seeker's Guide*, Harper Collins, 1992.
A how-to-get it, where-to-find it guide for every possible sphere of New Ageism.

Bly, Robert, *Iron John*, Element, 1991.
The best guide to the elusive 'New Man'.

Dass, Ram, and Gorman, Paul, *How can I help?* Rider, 1985.
Wonderful, moving guide of possibilities for carers in the broadest sense. Some stories to touch the heart.

Houston, Jean, *The Possible Human*, Tarcher, 1982.
An intellectual and spiritual feast with self-explanatory exercises.

Kubler-Ross, Elizabeth, *On Death and Dying*, Macmillan, 1981.
Facing something which will happen to all of us. Beautifully told.

Levine, Steven, *A Gradual Awakening*, Century, 1980.
A how-to guide for would-be meditators.

Peck, M. Scott, *The Road Less Travelled*, Rider, 1983.
Easy to read description of the personal journey. A best-seller.

Spangler, David, *Revelation – The Birth of a New Age*, Findhorn, 1976.
Excellent analysis from a visionary's perspective.

Starhawk, *The Spiral Dance*, Harper-Collins, 1979.
A rebirth of the ancient religion of the Great Goddess. Feminism at its best.

Trevelyan, Sir George, *Operation Redemption*, Turnstone, 1985.
A brilliant summation of the possibilities for humanity.

Verney, Bishop Stephen, *Into the New Age*, Fontana, 1976.
A Christian bishop's perspective – fairly scholarly.

There are many 'alternative' bookshops. One of the best is:
Watkins Books Ltd
19–21 Cecil Court
London WC2N 4HB
(071 836 2182)
They have a mail order service.

Rastafarianism

Augier, Roy, Nettleford, Rex and Smith, M. G., *The Rastafari Movement in Kingston, Jamaica*, Institute of Social and Economic Research, University of the West Indies, 1960.

Barrett, Leonard, *The Rastafarians – The Dreadlocks of Jamaica*, Heinemann.

Blyden, E., *Christianity, Islam and the Negro Race*, OUP, London.

Campbell, Horace, 'Rastafari: Culture of Resistance', in *Race and Class*, vol. XXII, no. 1.

Catholic Commission for Racial Justice, *Rastafarians in Jamaica and Britain*, 1982.

Cashmore, E., *Rastaman: the Rastafarian movement in England*, Allen and Unwin.

Clapham, Christopher, *Haile Selassie I Government*, Longman, 1969.

Cruse, Harold, *The Crisis of the Negro Intellectual: from its origins to the present*, W. H. Allen, London.

Darkwah, R. H. Kofi, *Shewa, Menelik and the Ethiopian Empire*, Heinemann, London.

Diop, Cheikh Anta, *The African Origin of Civilization: myth or reality*, Lawrence Hill, New York.

Drake, St Clair, *The Redemption of Africa and Black Religion*, Third World Press.

Garvey, Amy Jacques, *The Philosophy and Opinions of Marcus Garvey*, vols. I, II and III, Cass, London.

Hurwitz, S. J. and E. F., *Jamaica: a historical portrait*, Pall Mall, 1971.

James, G. G. M., *Stolen Legacy*, Julian Richardson Association Publishers, San Francisco.

Allen, C. and Johnson, R. W. (eds.), *African Perspectives*, CUP.

Means, Rev. Sterling M., *Ethiopia and the Missing Link in African History*, Atlantis Publishing, Pennsylvania.

Moseley, L., *Haile Selassie I: the conquering lion*, Weidenfeld, London.

Nettleford, Rex, *Mirror, Mirror: identity, race and protest in Jamaica*, Collins and Sangster, 1970.

Owens, Joseph, *Dread: the Rastafarians of Jamaica*, Sangster.

Pankhurst, Richard, *Ethiopia*, Lalibela House, 1961.

Perham, Margery, *The Government of Ethiopia*, Faber.

Sandford, Christine, *The Lion of Judah Hath Prevailed*, Greenwood Press, 1972.

Selassie, Haile, *The Autobiography of Emperor Haile Selassie I*, OUP.

Simpson, G. E., *Political Cultism in West Kingston, Jamaica*, vol. 2, Institute of Social and Economic Research, University of West Indies.

Udom, Essien, *Black Nationalism: the rise of the Black Muslims in the USA*, Penguin, 1962.

Ullendorff, Edward, *The Ethiopians: an introduction to country and people*, OUP.

Watson, G. Llewellyn, 'Social Structure and Social Movements: The Black muslims in the U.S.A. and the Rastafarians in Jamaica', *The British Journal of Sociology*, vol. XXIV, no. 2, June 1973.

Williams, Eric, *From Columbus to Castro: the history of the Caribbean, 1492–1969*, Andre Deutsch.

Zoroastrianism

Boyce, Mary, *Zoroastrians: their religious beliefs and practices*, Routledge, 1979.

Sources for the Study of Zoroastrianism, Manchester/Chicago, 1984.
Two general studies of Zoroastrianism (the latter is a compendium of new translations from all phases of the religion).

Specifically on the theme of the Zoroastrian diaspora there are no books yet published but three are imminent:

Hinnells, J. R. and Writer, R., *The Living Flame: Zoroastrians in Britain*, Manchester.

Hinnells, J., *The Contemporary Global Zoroastrian Diaspora*, OUP.

Writer, R.,. *Contemporary Zotoastrians: an unstructured nation?*, University Press of America.

Hinnells, John, *Persian Mythology*, London, 1985; *Zoroastrianism and the Parsis*, London, 1981.

Mehta, A., *The Story of our Religion: Zoroastrianism*, Bombay, 1988.
A book produced by a Zoroastrian school teacher, in cartoon form, for young Zoroastrians.

Non-book resources

I General suppliers/producers

Academy Television, 104 Kirkstall Road, Leeds LS3 1JS (0532 461528).
Video Catalogue available: draws on Channel Four, HTV, Scottish TV, Thames TV, Tyne Tees, Worldwide Television News and Yorkshire TV, but religious programmes available to date are disappointing.

Ann & Bury Peerless, 22 King's Avenue, Minnis Bay, Birchington, Kent CT7 9QL (0843 41428).
Excellent slide sets of a very high quality. Most relate to India and Sri Lanka and primarily to Hinduism, Sikhism and Buddhism. (Send s.a.e. for list.)

Articles of Faith, Christine & Leslie Howard, Bury Business Centre, Kay Street, Bury BL9 6BU (061 705 1878).
Mail order for a wide range of artefacts and visuals, relating to six world religions and to Chinese culture. Offers courses related to use of artefacts. List of services and catalogue available.

BBC Education Information, White City, 201 Wood Lane, London W12 7TS (081 746 1111).
Information about support material available for RE programmes; some videos available for purchase.
Note: orders are usually to be sent to other addresses.

Central Independent Television, Video Resource Unit, Broad Street, Birmingham B1 2JP (021 643 9898).

The Religious Catalogue is worth obtaining and provides some excellent programmes, many recently produced and broadcast.

Chansitor Publications Ltd, St Mary's Works, St Mary's Plain, Norwich, Norfolk NR3 3BH (0603 612914).
Distributor of CEM Videos and most of those formerly in the PEP/RMEP catalogue, including the Videotext series produced by Exmouth College.

Christian Education Movement, Royal Buildings, Victoria Street, Derby DE1 1GW (0332 296655).
Professional organization for RE teachers supporting all aspects of RE. Produces some poster material and picture packs; sells many PCET pictures; has produced a number of videos. Catalogue and membership details from Derby address; videos from Chansitor Publications, Norwich (see above).

Commonwealth Institute, Kensington High Street, London W8 6NQ (071 603 4535)
The shop here carries books, cards, pictures and artefacts relating to many countries and cultures. The Institute offers a loan service to schools.

Educational Media International, 235 Imperial Drive, Harrow, Middlesex HA2 7HE (081 868 1908/1915).
Catalogue and useful RE Video Bulletin available. List includes many former ILEA titles (includes video lecture and discussions on Auschwitz which was out of circulation for some time and is helpful in approaching the Holocaust).

Edward Patterson Associates, Treetops, Cannongate Road, Hythe, Kent CT21 5PT (0303 264195).
Film and Video Catalogue available. Religion list is short and not dated. 'Preview to purchase' service offered. Hire also available.
Focal point Audio Visual Ltd, 251 Copnor Road, Portsmouth, Hants PO3 5EE (0705 665249).
Slide sets and some video material available. Catalogue.

Jackson Contra-Banned, Wood Lea, 47 Storths Road, Birkby, Huddersfield, W Yorkshire HD2 2XW (0484 530855).
Sells a wide range of materials from many places around the world, but produces no catalogue.

Contact by phone or letter saying what you require.

Minority Group Support Service, Southfields Old School, South Street, Coventry CV1 5EJ (0203 26888).
Picture books, packs, relating to Hindu, Sikh, Muslim traditions. Also Afro-Caribbean resources.

Philip Green Educational Ltd, 112a Alcester Road, Studley, Warwickshire B80 7NR (0527 854711).
Noted here because of their high quality picture packs and slides. Only one pack (Festivals and Celebrations) has an RE focus: other packs may serve (in primary school) as discussion starters, e.g. Senses, Families.

Pictorial Charts Educational Trust, 27 Kirchen Road, London W13 0UD (081 567 9206).
Well known supplier of educational wallcharts. Many good items in their RE list. Catalogue available.

Shooting Stars, Film and Video Distribution, 225a Brecknock Road, London N19 5AA (071 284 1695 or 071 434 9869).
A company which aims to make available films about minority faiths and cultures. Video programmes available to date look at aspects of Jewish life, religion, identity and history. Leaflet available.

The Slide Centre Ltd, Ilton, Ilminster, Somerset TA19 9HS (04605 5151).
Carries a selection of material: biblical, Christian and some relating to Islam; generally rather old material. Catalogue available.

Soma Books Ltd, 38 Kennington Lane, London SE11 4LS (071 735 2101).
Books, craft, posters, cards on world religions. Free catalogue available.

Sussex Video and Sussex Tapes, Microworld House, 2–6 Foscote Mews, London W9 2HH (071 266 2314).
Catalogue available. Video and audio tapes relating to music and dance of interest in RE. Otherwise 'light' on religion.

TVS Education, TVS, Television Centre, Southampton SO9 5H2 (0703 834297).
Documentary-style video programmes, some relating to religions in society. List available for Religious Studies.

II A selection of addresses by religion

Buddhism

The Buddhist Society, 58 Eccleston Square, London SW1V 1PH (071 834 5858).
A wide selection of audio tapes for purchase. Catalogue available.

The Meridian Trust, 330 Harrow Road, London W9 2HP (071 289 5443).
The Buddhist Film and Video Archive. Catalogue and regular updates available; materials are graded according to quality. Materials relate mainly to Tibetan Buddhism.

Tharpa Publications, 15 Bendemeer Road, London SW15 1JX (081 788 7792).
Catalogue of quality 'Visual Dharma' reproductions available. Mahayana tradition.

Windhorse Imports, PO Box 7, Hay on Wye, Hereford HR3 5TU (0497 821116).
Artefacts relating to Tibetan Buddhism – of good quality, and expensive. Artefacts produced in India; some profits fed back there.

Wisdom Publications, 402 Hoe Street, London E17 9AA (081 530 5588).
Books, Tibetan Buddhist cards, posters, prints, calendars, colouring books. Catalogues available.

Note that artefacts and audio-visual materials are also frequently available from the many Buddhist centres/monasteries in the UK. (See *The Buddhist Directory*, available from the Buddhist Society.)

Christianity

Asian Christian Art Association, Kansai, 23 Takenouchi-cho, Ichijoji, Skayo-Kukyoto, 606 Japan.
Listed here because of two publications, *Christian Art in Asia* (1975) and *The Bible through Asian Eyes* (1991), both with full-colour plates and providing an introduction to non-Western Christian perspectives. Second book available in UK via CCBI, Inter-Church House, 35 Lower Marsh, London SE1 7RL.

CTVC, Hillside Studios, Merry Hill Road, Bushey, Watford WD2 1DR (081 950 4426).
Christian video material, some appropriate for school use. Catalogue available and regular updates.

The Fig Tree, Celia and Tony Holden, 11 New Road Dafen, Llanelli, Dyfed (0554 755690).
Supply workpacks, books and booklets, mounted and unmounted icons relating to Orthodox Christianity. Also offer courses/exhibitions.

St Paul Book and Media centre, 199 Kensington High Street, London W8 6BA (071 937 9591). (Branches also in Birmingham, Liverpool and Glasgow.)
Well stocked (Roman Catholic) centre, offering a very wide variety of materials for RE.

In addition, SPCK bookshops in 25 cities stock a range of visual resources and artefacts as well as books. Specific Christian traditions, e.g. Salvation Army, Methodist, also produce their own lists of resources, some of which are non-book material.

Hinduism

Books from India, 45 Museum Street, London WC1A 1LR (071 405 7226/5784).
Produces a number of catalogues, e.g. on dance, music, food and cookery. Stocks some poster material, Amar Chitra Katha and Chitra Bharati comics, and music.

ISKON Educational Services, Bhaktivedanta Manor, Letchmore Heath, Watford, Herts WD2A 8EP (0923 859578 or 0923 249144).
Picture and colouring books, posters; audio and video tapes; artefacts. Educational services leaflet and catalogue available.

Gohil Emporium, 381 Stratford Road, Sparkhill, Birmingham B11 4J2 (021 771 3048).
Wide range of religious artefacts from India. Will respond to requests, provide price lists and supply by post.

Islam

Islamic Book Centre, 120 Drummond Street, London NW1 2HL (071 388 0710).
Sells a wide range of Islamic books and artefacts.

Islamic Cultural Centre and London Central Mosque (Regent's park Mosque), Park Road, London NW8 2HL (071 388 0710).
The mosque sells some posters and cards, as well as a selection of books.

The Islamic Foundation, Publications Unit, Unit 9, The Old Dunlop Factory, 62 Evington Valley Road, Leicester LE5 5LJ (0530 244944).
Audio-visual resources catalogue available on request – posters, maps, audio cassettes, audio-visuals etc.

Muslim Educational Trust, 130 Stroud Green Road, London N4 (071 272 8502).
Publishes booklets; also a limited range of poster material.

Judaism

Centre for Jewish Education, The Sternberg Centre for Judaism, 80 East End Road, Finchley, London N3 2SY (081 246 2288).
Educational consultancy to progressive Judaism in Great Britain. Produces video catalogue.

Jewish Education Bureau, 8 Westcombe Avenue, Leeds LS8 2BS. (0532 663613).
Pioneer in providing schools and colleges with materials for teaching about Judaism. List includes good book selection, visuals, audio and video material and artefacts. (Send s.a.e. for list.)

Jewish Memorial Council Bookshop, Woburn House, Upper Woburn Place, London WC1H 0EP (071 387 3081).
Provides artefacts for sale (as well as books of Jewish and Israeli interest). Has mail order department and offers discounts to schools.

Jewish Music Distribution, The London Jewish Music Centre, PO Box 2268 London NW4 3UW (081 203 8046).
Extensive collection of cassettes and CDs available. Catalogue.

Sikhism

DTF (Degh Tegh Fateh), 41 Dudley Street, Luton, Beds LU2 0NP (0582 450950/27725).
For all kinds of Sikh religious artefacts, books, audio and visual cassettes. Catalogue available.

Religious education centres

BFSS National RE Centre,
West London Institute of Higher Education, Lancaster House, Borough Road, Isleworth, Middlesex TW7 5DU (081 568 8741 Ext. 2656).

The National Society's RE Centre, 23 Kensington Square, London W8 5HN (071 937 4241).

The Regional RE Centre (Midlands), Westhill College, Weoley Park Road, Selly Oak, Birmingham B29 6LL (021 472 7245 Ext. 258).

The Welsh National Centre for RE, School of Education, University College of North Wales, Deiniol Road, Bangor, Gwynedd LL57 2UW (0248 382956).

York RE Centre, University College of Ripon and York, St John, Lord Mayor's Walk, York YO3 7EX (0904 656771 Ext. 209).
Also office address for the Federation of National and Regional RE Centres (see page 155).